CREEPSHOWS

'My view is: here it is. Here's this story. If somebody wants
to make it into a movie – I *love* movies.'

Stephen King
Cinefantastique vol 25 no 3, June 1994

CREEPSHOWS

THE ILLUSTRATED STEPHEN KING MOVIE GUIDE

First published in the United States in 2002 by Billboard Books,
an imprint of Watson-Guptill Publications,
a division of VNU Business Media, Inc.
770 Broadway, New York, NY 10003
www.watsonguptill.com

First published in 2001 by Titan Books,
a division of Titan Publishing Group Ltd.
144 Southwark Street, London, England SE1 OUP

Creepshows: The Illustrated Stephen King Movie Guide © Stephen Jones 2001.
All rights reserved.
Introduction © Mick Garris 2001.
All artwork by Bernie Wrightson copyright © Bernie Wrightson and reproduced
by permission of the artist.
All photographs by Seamus A. Ryan copyright © Seamus A. Ryan.
All rights reserved.
Stephen Jones has asserted his right to be identified as Author of this Work, in
accordance with the Copyright, Designs and Patents Act, 1988.

Designed by Caroline Grimshaw.

Front cover image © Bernie Wrightson.
Back cover images:
Carrie © United Artists Corporation.
The Shining © Warner Bros Inc.
Misery © Castle Rock Entertainment.
The Shawshank Redemption © Castle Rock Entertainment.
The Green Mile © CR Films, LLC.
Stephen King image © Seamus A. Ryan.

Library of Congress Cataloging-in-Publication Data for this title can be obtained
from the Library of Congress.

ISBN: 0-8230-7884-1

Printed and bound in China

First US printing 2002

1 2 3 4 5 6 7 8 9 / 10 09 08 07 06 05 04 03 02

Page 4: Stephen King.
Page 5 above: Stephen King as his hometown namesake, Dr Bangor, in *Thinner*.
Page 5 below: Stephen King as an impatient bus driver in the TV series *Golden Years*.

CREEPSHOWS

The Illustrated
STEPHEN KING
Movie Guide

EX LIBRIS, KIDDIES!! HEH·HEH·HEH

STEPHEN JONES

Introduction by
MICK GARRIS

BILLBOARD BOOKS
An imprint of Watson-Guptill Publications/New York

Introduction

by Mick Garris

When asked how he feels about all the movies that have ruined his books, Stephen King has a simple reply along the lines of, 'They may not be good movies, but they haven't ruined the books. Look, here they are, lined up on the bookshelf.' He has often had good cause to be defensive, for the big and little screens have not always done well by his work. There are many reasons. Some of them have to do with respect for the material, some with the distribution of talent before and behind the camera (or a distinct lack thereof), and some just come down to a simple, obvious cause: books ain't movies.

Above: *Stephen King, Mick Garris and Clive Barker, behind-the-scenes on Sleepwalkers.*
Opposite page: *Mick Garris, behind-the-scenes on Steve Martini's The Judge.*
Below: *Mick Garris (right) and Brian Krause, behind-the-scenes on Sleepwalkers.*

Yes, they can become movies, sometimes deliriously successfully. I think few would quibble with the excellence of David Cronenberg's *The Dead Zone* or Rob Reiner's adaptations of *Misery* and 'The Body' (*Stand by Me*), or Frank Darabont's of 'Rita Hayworth and Shawshank Redemption' (*The Shawshank Redemption*) or *The Green Mile*. Movies don't get much better, and Stephen King movies never do.

Those adaptations succeed artistically because they succeed in channeling King's distinctive voice. They respect that, despite the huge commercial success of Steve's novels and stories, they are told by a master storyteller, a man with a voice we love to listen to. They succeed because they recognize that King's stories are not just about the monster in the closet but, rather, about the people who own the house in which the Closet Monster resides. The worst of the Stephen King books-into-movies adaptations — and they are legion

— think that King is about what I like to call the 'boinks': that is, the seat-lifters, the jumps, the bed-wetting jolts that pepper the films. But the fact is, if you don't get caught up in the lives of the characters, the propulsion of the story and dramaturgy, the rubber monsters and dripping goo don't mean diddley, Bo.

I have had the incredible good fortune of making several movies with Stephen King. I leave it to you to consider their merits and demerits; I know that the author of this volume in your hands holds one feature film that King and I made together in very low regard, though he has said kind things about the mini-series. The first and foremost thought in my mind when taking on one of these epics is: 'Please, God, don't let me make another shitty Stephen King movie!' I do my best. I respect the material and try my best to treat it like Shakespeare. I don't look down my nose at — dare I say it? — *Horror Movies* and don't consider it slumming. On the contrary, the best script I've ever had in my hands was Steve's own adaptation of *The Shining* for the television mini-series we concocted. It's the drama, the human moments that matter. Sometimes the mechanics of horror and making an audience jump can become more craft than art. But getting you there is the hard part...and the part that nobody notices if you're doing the job well.

I first met Steve (it's hard to call him Stephen once you get to know him) at a book signing at a store in Santa Monica, California. I was a reader with a book I wanted signed, despite the long, long, long line. But the second time I met the man, I was, dear God, *directing* him on the set of *Sleepwalkers*. Now, *Sleepwalkers* was the first original screenplay (that is to say, the first script not based on one of his published works) ever to be produced. It had a very low budget, and the producers were tough cookies and hammered on me every day about getting everything done on time and on budget. That morning was to be a big day. Playing cameo roles in the same scene were Clive Barker and Tobe Hooper. King, Barker and Hooper were not only all going to be in the same scene, they were all going to be in the same *shot*.

and the weight of screaming producers and a fast-passing sun roiling my guts, I headed over to the hot outdoor set we had turned into a cemetery. And there was King, all six foot five of him, with a big grin on his face, and everything relaxed. He hadn't met Clive before (though I think he'd met Tobe) and this one-shot scene was quite the little party. He had fun with his part, we all had fun with his part, and then, when crew members started to swarm around him after he'd given one an autograph, he disappeared like graveyard mist. That was the last I saw of him until I took the work print of my cut to show him in New York. That was even more nerve-wracking. He and Tabby and I watched the film alone, raw and lacking most of the effects, temporary music trying to plug the holes. All I saw was everything I wished I could do over. But — roiling guts and clammy palms to the contrary — he, well, he seemed to *like* it.

There is no laugh quite like the genuine, uninhibited, delighted laugh of Steve King. It wakes you up, it makes you happy, it makes *you* laugh. I've heard it a lot and it's a bracing, wonderful thing to participate in. Steve is a serious, thoughtful man — don't get me wrong — but he loves the things that make him laugh. And he loves the film-making process. That's one of the reasons I so like to cast him in the films we do together (and why I assume other film-makers do likewise): there's nothing like having King on the set. It lifts the whole crew right up into the stratosphere.

When we were shooting *The Stand* in Utah — outside for months on end in the least co-operative weather possible — King and Gary Sinise and I would join in on guitar with Adam Storke as his character, Larry Underwood, singing 'Eve of Destruction'. Any excuse to pick up the guitar would make for an impromptu hootenanny...until I had to call for quiet to get the next shot. Even if King was ultimately the boss. I think *The Stand* was the first King movie where he really *was* Executive Producer in more than just title. He was on location for over half of the shoot and the movie was the better for it. He had written the script himself (several versions, actually; he and the producers had tried for years to make it as a feature film at Warner Bros with George Romero), it was his biggest-sell-

So, when I bit into my morning bowl of craft service granola and my bicuspid busted in half, and I had to rush off to receive emergency dental surgery and a temporary brass cap, all I could think about was being back in time to shoot in the two-hour window King had given us. We had been talking regularly on the phone during the course of pre-production, and had had wonderful telephone times, but we hadn't really *met*. I would discuss ideas that I thought might make things better and the next day, by golly, there would be pages in the fax machine, and they'd be *good*. We would laugh on the phone and understand each other's movie, music and TV references, and it was great. But that was on the phone. We hadn't really had any face time. I was to meet him about five minutes before we were rehearsing the shot.

So with a throbbing brass-capped molar

Above top: Ruby Dee and Molly Ringwald in a publicity shot from The Stand.
Above: Mick Garris, behind-the-scenes on The Stand.

ing book of all time and it meant a lot to him. That said, Steve never told me how he thought I should shoot a scene. He might have had some ideas — and you're a fool not to listen to his ideas — but the directing was my job, the writing and producing his. He's the best producer I've ever had.

A while back I said that books ain't movies. Books are much more internal than external and movies have to be the opposite. They have to show you, not tell you. Though King's books and stories are very cinematic and might read like movies — just think of all the wonderful internal dialogue that goes through his characters' minds: Johnny Smith in *The Dead Zone*, Jack Torrance in *The Shining* — it takes respecting the source material to begin to make a good movie. I think even Steve's respect for the film-making form has increased since we first met. I think he reached much further creatively with his script for *The Stand* and the others that followed than he did in *Sleepwalkers*. I have seen him take film-making as seriously as he takes his books, and I'm sure that's not always been the case.

I have been fortunate enough to jump onto the King ferry into the waters of cinema a handful of times and, with luck, we'll do it again. As of this writing, the question I'm most asked is, 'When is *Desperation* going to become a movie?' It's been on and off so many times that I don't know which it is by now. King has written a wonderful screenplay but, since it doesn't revolve around teenagers and isn't jokey or a parody, it is not exactly what the studios want to make. To many a film executive 'horror' means *Scream*. And *Desperation* ain't *Scream*. But if and when it finally falls into place, we've all got reason to rejoice.

The films of Stephen King are a wild and varied collection, ranging from the cheapest, tawdriest schlock thrillers (some of those loveable in their eager scruffiness) to the biggest-of-budget tuxedoed Oscar fodder. It's a wide canon that is finally receiving its due in this book. But, if history is our teacher, it won't be long before a second volume is required.

In June of 1999, we came dreadfully close to losing the man who inspired everything in this book, but a year and a half later, as of this writing, he has mended much quicker and more successfully than anyone had guessed at the time. What he went through is far more horrifying than any of the movies contained within. Real life can come crashing down with far more terror than anything on a movie screen. That accident alongside a Maine highway ultimately had a happy ending, even if not all of these movies do.

I think I'll stay and watch the credits.

Mick Garris

Mick Garris
Toronto, Ontario, Canada
3 December 2000

Below: Mick Garris, behind-the-scenes on Stephen King's The Shining.
Below bottom: Melvin van Peebles and Courtland Mead in a publicity shot from Stephen King's The Shining.

CARRIE

If Only They Knew She Had the Power.

USA, 1976. Director: **Brian De Palma**. Producer: **Paul Monash**. Screenplay: **Lawrence D. Cohen**. Based on the Novel by **Stephen King**. Editor: **Paul Hirsch**. Associate Producer: **Louis A. Stroller**. Director of Photography: **Mario Tosi**. Music: **Pino Donaggio**. Art Directors: **William Kenny** and **Jack Fisk**. United Artists Corporation. Colour. 98 minutes.

Sissy Spacek (Carrie [White]), **Piper Laurie** (Margaret White), **Amy Irving** (Sue Snell), **William Katt** (Tommy Ross), **Nancy Allen** (Chris Hargenson), **John Travolta** (Billy Nolan), **Betty Buckley** (Miss Collins), **P.J. Soles** (Norma [Watson]), **Sydney Lassick** (Mr Fromm), **Stefan Gierasch** (Mr Morton), **Priscilla Pointer** (Mrs Snell), **Michael Talbot** (Freddy), **Doug Cox** (The Beak), **Harry Gold** (George), **Noelle North** (Frieda), **Cindy Daly** (Cora), **Dierdre Berthrong** (Rhonda), **Anson Downes** (Ernest), **Rory Stevens** (Kenny), **Edie McClurg** (Helen), **Cameron De Palma** (Boy on Bicycle).

Teenager Carrie White is a shy, repressed school-girl who is the object of derision by many of her fellow classmates at Bates High School. Kept in a state of sexual ignorance by her religious fanatic mother, Margaret, one day in the shower Carrie discovers she is menstruating and becomes hysterical, much to the delight of her tormentors, who include Sue Snell, Chris Hargenson and Norma Watson. As the school prepares for the forthcoming prom, Sue is troubled over her treatment of Carrie and asks her boyfriend, Tommy Ross, to take Carrie to the prom. He reluctantly agrees. But when Chris is banned from the dance because she is unrepentant about her behaviour towards Carrie, she plots a vicious revenge with the help of her boyfriend, Billy Nolan. When Margaret forbids her daughter to attend the prom, Carrie's latent telekinetic powers are finally revealed. Carrie and Tommy are elected King and Queen of the prom, but Chris and Billy release a bucket of pig's blood they have rigged above the throne, drenching Carrie. When the other students once again begin to laugh at Carrie, she uses her paranormal powers to shut the doors of the gym, which erupts into a blazing inferno.

FACT FILE

The final scene of Margaret White's crucifixion is underscored by Bernard Herrmann's violin music from *Psycho*.

Carrie is based on Stephen King's 1974 début novel, which bears an uncanny resemblance to Robert Silverberg's story 'A Slob Can Hate!', in the September 1959 *Web Detective Stories*. However, the author does admit that 'in some way I've never been able to figure out,' the book was also inspired by B-movie favourite *The Brain from Planet Arous* (1957). 'You have to remember that the genesis of *Carrie* was no more than a short story idea,' he recalled.

Stephen Edwin King was born in 1947 on 21 September (the same date as Carrie White's birthday). His father Donald, a philandering vacuum cleaner salesman, went out to buy a packet of cigarettes when King was aged two and never came back. He left behind boxes and boxes of stories which he had submitted to such pulp magazines as *Argosy* and *Blue Book*. His mother Nellie Ruth raised the boy and his four year-old brother David alone, dragging him to church three times a week. She died of cancer in February 1974 at the age of fifty-nine, without ever seeing her son's first novel, *Carrie*, in print. Perhaps this was where he found the inspiration for Carrie's fanatical mother Margaret White, or even the deranged Annie Wilkes in *Misery*? 'She had a bit of Annie Wilkes in her,' King admitted. 'Anybody does. She could get mad.'

From 1962-66 King attended Lisbon Falls High School, Maine, and from there went on to the University of Maine in Orono. His first published story, 'I Was a Teenage Grave Robber', appeared in 1966 in Marv Wolfman's fanzine *Comics Review* and two years later, at the age of twenty, he made his first professional short story sale to *Startling Mystery Stories* with 'The Glass Floor'.

After graduating in 1970, King was earning $1.60 an hour in an industrial laundry when he met twenty-one year-old Tabitha Jane Spruce in the university library. Barely able to meet the bills, they married in January the following year, and King became a teacher of English at

Previous page: Carrie (Sissy Spacek) uses her paranormal powers.
Below: Margaret White (Piper Laurie) comforts her daughter.

Hampden Academy, Maine.

With the sale of several more stories and four unpublished novels under his belt, the author began writing a short story entitled 'Carrie' in the laundry room of his rented trailer home. However, King felt that the finished manuscript was 'a certified loser' and tossed it into the wastebasket, from where it was rescued by Tabitha. Desperate for ideas for another book, he revised and expanded the short story into a novel. In the spring of 1973, King's manuscript found its way out of the slush pile and on to the desk of editor William Thompson at Doubleday, who purchased it for an advance of $2,500 against royalties (Thompson actually upped the approved advance by $1,000). But it was the sale of paperback rights to New American Library, for a then-phenomenal $400,000, that allowed the author to quit teaching and write full time.

'When *Carrie* came out in hardcover, the total sale of that book in the first edition hardcover was about 11,000 copies,' King told Adam Pirani and Alan McKenzie in *Starburst*. 'And that's in the United States. In England that would be a very respectable sale, but in America it's not worth much. It did well in paperback, but it didn't get on the [bestseller] list. What happened is the De Palma film came out, and the De Palma film was great. Usually, a movie tie-in doesn't mean very much, *if the* movie stinks, because it doesn't go anywhere. But if the movie's great, a lot of times, it'll take off. That's really what made it happen for me, I think.'

Fledgling director Brian De Palma had previously made the comedy *Get to Know Your Rabbit* (1972) and the low budget horror film *Sisters* (aka *Blood Sisters*, 1972) before a writer friend suggested he read King's novel. After contacting his agent, De Palma discovered that a number of studios were interested but none had optioned the project yet. 'So I called around to some of the people I knew and said it was a terrific book and I'm very interested in doing it,' he told Mike Childs and Alan Jones in *Cinefantastique* magazine. However, it was only after he had made *Phantom of the Paradise* (1974) and *Obsession* (1975), that United Artists — who now owned the rights — contacted him.

As a first time novelist, King let Doubleday have all film rights to *Carrie*. Producer Paul Monash purchased them, but was turned down by Paramount, Twentieth Century-Fox and other studios, before finally getting a deal with United Artists, who was looking for its own supernatural property after the success of *Rosemary's Baby* (1968) and *The Exorcist* (1973).

While still an assistant to Monash, Lawrence D. Cohen had rewritten an initial script by another writer. Cohen's first screenplay successfully added some humour to the horrors in its view of the teenager as an outsider.

Texas-born Sissy Spacek was not De Palma's first choice for the lead role. The wife of the film's art director Jack Fisk (she had previously assisted him as a set decorator on *Phantom of the Paradise*), the actress initially tried out for all the major parts until her screen test confirmed her as the definitive Carrie. 'I was very surprised when Brian did the screen tests that I was asked to test for Carrie and not Chris, as I had assumed' the actress explained to Childs and Jones. 'Only three of us tested for Carrie.'

A scene with Spacek playing Carrie at the age of six years old against an oversized set was perhaps wisely cut from the final print.

Piper Laurie was a leading actress in the 1950s, whose career hit a peak with an Academy Award nomination for her role in *The Hustler* in 1961. The following year she had married film critic Joseph Morgernstern and they moved to Woodstock, outside New York City, to raise a daughter. *Carrie* marked her

first film appearance in fifteen years. 'I liked the idea of making Margaret White very beautiful and sexual,' De Palma told Childs and Jones, 'instead of the usual dried-up old crone at the top of the hill.'

However, that was not exactly how the actress saw the role: 'I got the script and read it; I thought it was terrible,' she told Allan Hunter in *Films and Filming*. 'I thought they had to be kidding, even if I never made another film I wasn't going to do this.' Laurie's answer was to play the character of religious zealot Margaret White as comedic! It was an approach which director De Palma did not approve of. 'I never really changed my concept of the character as a comedy figure,' Laurie confided, 'but I just knew that if I went too far he would stop me.' She also found some of the sequences absurd. 'It seemed ridiculous for a grown-up person to be doing something like that. When we were filming scenes where all the knives go into me it was done slowly and then speeded up on film. Several times when they said cut I'd just roar with laughter.'

After being spotted by De Palma at his friend George Lucas' audition for Princess Leia in *Star Wars*, Amy Irving made her feature début as the 'nice girl', Sue Snell. After she suggested it to De Palma, Irving's real-life mother, actress Priscilla Pointer, played Sue's mother in the film. Nancy Allen, who portrayed the scheming Chris Hargenson, was the director's girlfriend and later married him.

Relative newcomer John Travolta had appeared in *The Devil's Rain* (1975) and was the star of the popular television sitcom *Welcome Back Kotter* (1975-78) when he was cast as 'bad boy' Billy Nolan. 'Sissy Spacek was excellent,' King told Peter S. Perakos in *Cinefantastique*, 'but right behind her — in a smaller part than it should have been — was John Travolta. He played the part of Billy Nolan the way I wish I'd written it, half-funny and half-crazy.'

Carrie was filmed over a fifty day schedule and went $200,000 over its $1.6 million

Above top: Piper Laurie decides to play Margaret White as a comedy figure.
Above: Unwitting catalysts Billy Nolan (John Travolta) and Chris Hargenson (Nancy Allen).

elling backwards!) is still guaranteed to have audiences jumping out of their seats more than a quarter of a century later.

'I never in a million years thought *Carrie* would have such an impact,' Irving subsequently revealed. It's funny how that ending has stayed with people. I remember being at a sneak preview — I think it was Halloween Eve — and the audience scared me because all of a sudden they jumped three feet out of their seats when Sissy's hand came out of the grave.'

Released in November 1976, radio commercials at the time described the film as a cross between *American Graffiti* (1973) and *Psycho* (1960), and homages to the latter abound, from the opening slow-motion shower scene to the name of the high school Carrie attends.

'De Palma was at the peak of his talents,' screenwriter Lawrence Cohen revealed to Gary L. Wood in *Cinefantastique*. 'I think the difference between the King movies that are successful and the movies that are not successful, both commercially and artistically, is that the director adds the other quotient.'

Carrie grossed more than $15 million and, despite her initial misgivings about her comeback project, Piper Laurie was more than a little surprised when both she and Sissy Spacek received Best Actress Academy Award nominations for their performances. Both women lost out to Faye Dunaway for *Network* (1976).

This first film adaptation of a Stephen King book (the author's name is mis-spelled 'Steven' on the trailer) has since become a modern classic and the iconographic image of Carrie covered in pig's blood at the prom is immediately recognisable to any horror fan. All the more surprising then that a sequel, *The Rage Carrie 2*, again featuring Amy Irving and produced by Paul Monash, did not appear until 1999. A disastrous musical stage adaptation was performed by the Royal Shakespeare Company on both sides of the Atlantic in 1988.

'*Carrie* started Steve off on the right foot with films,' Cohen told Wood, 'and *that* fed his publishing career.'

The Special 25th Anniversary Edition DVD included two forty-five minute documentaries, *Acting Carrie* and *Visualizing Carrie*, plus a featurette on *Carrie the Musical.* ✝

Above top: *Carrie makes her own way home from the prom.*

budget. The climactic prom sequence — designed by De Palma to be shown in split-screen — was filmed at the abandoned Pier Avenue School in Hermosa Beach, about forty miles outside Los Angeles. A sticky mixture of karo syrup and food colouring was used to represent the pig's blood poured over Carrie, and Spacek reputedly slept in the concoction for two nights so that it would appear the same in every scene.

Unlike King's source novel, the director also decided to play down Carrie's telekinesis, only using her powers when he thought it was dramatically valid. 'It's basically about adolescent trauma,' De Palma explained to Harry Wasserman and Charlie Frick in *Oui* magazine. 'Her telekinesis is an extension of her anger.'

'In the book, Carrie destroyed the entire town on the way home,' King explained in *Cinefantastique*. 'That didn't happen in the movie, mostly because the budget was too small. I wish they could have done that.'

Even if Carrie's ultimate revenge on the senior class went slightly over-the-top with its display of murderous pyrotechnics, then the final, surprising shock scene (in which Irving is filmed in reverse — note the car trav-

SALEM'S LOT
(AKA SALEM'S LOT THE MOVIE/BLOOD THIRST)

The Ultimate in Terror!

USA, 1979. Director: **Tobe Hooper**. Producer: **Richard Kobritz**. Teleplay: **Paul Monash**. Based on the Novel by **Stephen King**. Executive Producer: **Stirling Silliphant**. Director of Photography: **Jules Brenner**. Warner Bros/CBS-TV. Colour. 200 minutes. 150 minutes [TV movie]. 112 minutes [overseas theatrical].

David Soul (Ben Mears), **James Mason** (Richard K. Straker), **Lance Kerwin** (Mark Petrie), **Bonnie Bedelia** (Susan Norton), **Lew Ayres** (Jason Burke), **Julie Cobb** (Bonnie Sawyer), **Elisha Cook** (Weasel), **George Dzundza** (Cullie Sawyer), **Ed Flanders** (Dr Bill Norton), **Clarissa Kaye** (Marjorie Glick), **Geoffrey Lewis** (Mike Ryerson), **Barney McFadden** (Ned Tebbetts), **Kenneth McMillan** (Parkins Gillespie), **Fred Willard** (Larry Crockett), **Reggie Nalder** (Kurt Barlow), **Marie Windsor** (Eva Miller), **Barbara Babcock** (June Petrie), **Bonnie Bartlett** (Ann Norton), **Joshua Bryant** (Ted Petrie), **James Gallery** (Father Callahan), **Robert Lussier** (Nolly Gardner), **Brad Savage** (Danny Glick), **Ronnie Scribner** (Ralphie Glick), **Ned Wilson** (Henry Glick).

Two years earlier, novelist Ben Mears returned to his home town, Salem's Lot, Maine, drawn by forces he cannot comprehend. One by one the inhabitants are disappearing and the community is dying. Ben fears that the answer lies in the old Marsten house, a traditionally spooky structure recently purchased by the mysterious antique dealer Mr Straker and his elusive business partner Mr Barlow. Soon the writer and local teenager Mark Petrie find themselves caught up in a battle between good and evil as the bodies of the local townsfolk begin returning from the dead as hypnotic, blood-drinking vampires.

'**S**alem's Lot itself was the ball and *Dracula* was the wall I kept hitting it against, watching to see how and where it would bounce, so I could hit it again,' Stephen King explained in *Danse Macabre*, adding: 'At the same time, because the vampire story was so much a staple of the EC comics I grew up with, I decided that I would also try to bring in that aspect of the horror story.'

King's sprawling 1975 vampire novel (written under the title *Second Coming*) was in turn inspired by the early college story 'Jerusalem's Lot', written in 1967 as a course requirement and first published in the 1978 collection *Night Shift*. In a twist on Don Siegel's classic 1956 movie *Invasion of the Body Snatchers* (which King has described as having

Left: Reggie Nalder does his best Nosferatu impression.

an 'odd, almost dream-like beauty'), the inhabitants of a small town are gradually overwhelmed, not by alien pods, but by a plague of vampires.

Purchased the year it was published with the understanding that King would not write the screenplay, Warner Bros initially developed five or six scripts by Stirling Silliphant, Robert Getchell, Mike Nichols, Larry Cohen and others at an estimated cost of $1.8 million. 'It was a mess,' King admitted to Bill Kelley in *Cinefantastique*. 'Every director in Hollywood who's ever been involved with horror wanted to do it, but nobody could

Above: Lance Kerwin finds himself in the grip of the mysterious Mr Barlow.
Right: Ed Flanders meets a more bloody death in the overseas theatrical print.

come up with a script.'

According to Tobe Hooper, at one time he was in early negotiations with Warner Bros to direct Silliphant's script, with William Friedkin (*The Exorcist* [1973], etc) set to produce.

The studio then contacted George A. Romero. 'George Romero and I had made *Martin* (1976), which is about a vampire in a small town,' Richard P. Rubinstein explained in *Fear* magazine, 'and *Salem's Lot* is about a vampire in a small town. Warners asked us if we'd be interested in doing it, we said yes, they introduced us to Steve who said, "Great".' This was when the project was originally being considered for theatrical release, 'Then Warners

decided to do it for television,' continued Rubinstein, 'and we decided we didn't want to do that.'

'When I first learned that *Salem's Lot* was being done for television rather than as a theatrical release, I was disappointed.' admitted King, who had wanted genre veteran Richard Matheson to write the script.

When he could not get Romero, the vice-president for production at Warner Bros Television, thirty-eight year-old Richard Kobritz, hired Emmy Award-winning scriptwriter and producer Paul Monash to adapt the book as a mini-series. As the creator of the popular television serial *Peyton Place* (1964-69) and the producer of Brian De Palma's *Carrie* (1976), Monash was a perfect choice to knock King's multi-character novel into shape. 'His screenplay I like quite a lot,' King told Kelley. 'Monash has succeeded in combining the characters a lot, and it works.'

The new script remained fairly faithful to the book while condensing the story and characters into three and a half hours. However, among several major alterations to the source novel, Monash's teleplay replaced King's cultured undead villain Barlow with a monstrous, silent creature of the night, and moved the climatic confrontation to his lair, now in the cellar of the Marsten House.

After screening *The Texas Chain Saw Massacre* (1974) for the first time, Kobritz chose thirty-six year-old Hooper to direct. The Texas-born Hooper's only other horror film had been the troubled low budget Southern Gothic, *Eaten Alive* (aka *Death Trap* [1976]).

For Hooper, the offer to direct *Salem's Lot*

could not have come at a better time. His career was at an all-time low after he had wasted eighteen months in a fruitless development deal with Universal and was replaced after four days shooting on *The Dark* (1978) by first assistant director John 'Bud' Cardos. 'I knew Tobe was our man from the day I met him,' said the producer. 'And he's come through like a champ.'

Kobritz sent James Mason the script, and the respected British actor loved the part of the European antiques dealer Straker, who buys the old, deserted Marsten House. Television actor David Soul was cast two months before the start of filming and made a surprisingly solid hero as writer-turned-vampire hunter Ben Mears, while Oscar nominee (for *They Shoot Horses, Don't They?* [1969]) Bonnie Bedelia was chosen to play insipid heroine Susan Norton, who turned into a great bloodsucker in the show's Guatemalan coda.

Having first seen him in Alfred Hitchcock's 1956 remake of *The Man Who Knew Too Much*, genre fan Kobritz always had Austrian-born character actor Reggie Nalder (real name Alfred Reginald Natzick) in mind to play Barlow as a blue-skinned recreation of Max Schreck's vampire from F.W. Murnau's silent 1922 film *Nosferatu* (an idea left over from Larry Cohen's draft script). 'I wanted nothing suave or sexual,' explained Kobritz about his concept of Barlow as the essence of evil,

'because I just didn't think it'd work; we've seen too much of it.' King himself was not happy with the Nosferatu-looking Nalder: 'It was just a dreadful steal on the make-up. That *was* bad.'

However, as a result, the film's major

Above: Reggie Nalder as 'the essence of evil'.
Below: Mr Barlow is finally dispatched in the customary manner.

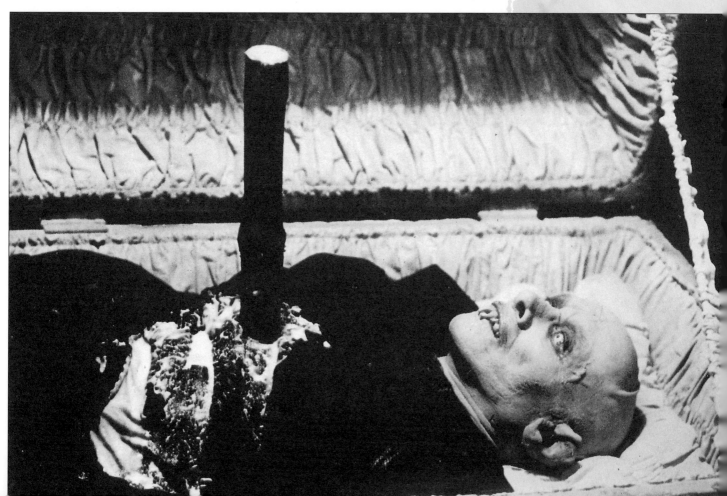

Above: David Soul's novelist meets James Mason's menacing antiques dealer.

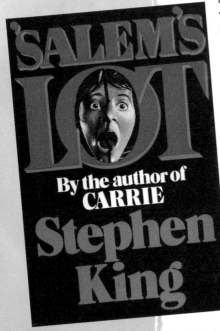

seven days of principal photography. Hooper estimated that he was doing between thirty-five and forty camera set-ups a day while he worked for two months on three hours sleep a night.

The two-part mini-series was telecast over four hours on CBS-TV on 17 and 24 November 1979, during the ratings 'sweeps' period. 'I like it much better that *The Shining*,' declared King. 'It's got this sick, feverish energy that is running through it... It certainly wasn't typical of horror movies made for television.' However, King also told Paul R. Gagne in *Cinefantastique* that he 'Objected to the fact that the network showed the two parts of the film a week apart, rather than on consecutive nights. I think that did a lot of damage to the continuity of the thing.'

The film was subsequently shortened into a single three hour movie of the week, while the more violent (but even shorter) European theatrical release and domestic video version suffered from a jumpy storyline and the appearances by veteran guest stars Lew Ayres, Elisha Cook Jr and Marie Windsor being reduced to just a few scenes. However, the death of Dr Bill Norton (Emmy Award nominee Ed Flanders) — who is impaled by Straker on a wall of mounted antlers (which ends with a close-up on the character's face in some television versions) — is shown in all its graphic detail in the shorter, overseas release, along with some bloodier vampire stakings. 'I like the movie version better,' King revealed to Tony Crawley. 'It seems tighter.'

In 1979, NAL/Signet Books published a paperback tie-in which included '8 pages of blood-chilling photos'.

Talk of a subsequent *Salem's Lot* network television series came to nothing. However, Larry Cohen, whose early script Kobritz described as 'really *lousy*', and who lost his challenge to Monash's sole screenplay credit in a Writer's Guild arbitration, wrote and directed a belated sequel, *A Return to Salem's Lot*, released in 1987.

In 2001, producer Denise DiNovi was reportedly developing a theatrical remake of *Salem's Lot* through Warner Bros/Village Roadshow, to be scripted by Joe Gangemi and directed by P.J. Hogan. At the same time, producer Mark Wolper hired Peter Filardi (*The Craft* [1996], etc) to write a new four-hour *Salem's Lot* mini-series for TNT. †

change/flaw now had Straker's character expanded to become the prime villain, with the undead Barlow relegated to a distinctly minor role. 'The biggest problem I had with it,' revealed George Romero, 'was that the vampire wasn't the lord. The vampire was an attack dog for James Mason.'

Budgeted at $4 million, with financing split between CBS and Warner Bros, filming began on location for two weeks on 10 July 1979. Production designer Mort Rabinowitz built a full-scale mock-up of the creepy Marsten House on location in the northern California town of Ferndale, just outside Eureka, which stood in for rural Connecticut. The exterior of the mansion cost an estimated $100,000 to create from scratch. Another $70,000 was spent constructing the interior rooms back at Warner's Burbank studios, where the final six weeks of the shoot was based. The decaying inside of the old house was designed to reflect Straker's hidden, festering soul.

Shooting wrapped on 29 August after thirty-

THE SHINING

A Masterpiece of Modern Horror.

UK/USA, 1980. Producer and Director: **Stanley Kubrick**. Screenplay: **Stanley Kubrick** and **Diane Johnson**. Based Upon the Novel by **Stephen King**. Executive Producer: **Jan Harlan**. Warner Bros Inc/The Producer Circle Company/Peregrine. Colour. 146 minutes [subsequently cut to 144 minutes]. 119 minutes [in the UK].

Jack Nicholson (Jack Torrance), **Shelley Duvall** (Wendy Torrance), **Danny Lloyd** (Danny [Torrance]), **Scatman Crothers** ([Dick] Hallorann), **Barry Nelson** ([Stuart] Ullman), **Philip Stone** ([Delbert/Charles] Grady), **Joe Turkel** (Lloyd), **Anne Jackson*** (Doctor), **Tony Burton*** ([Larry] Durkin), **Lia Beldam** (Young Woman in Bath), **Billie Gibson** (Old Woman in Bath), **Barry Dennen** ([Bill] Watson), **David Baxt** (Forest Ranger 1), **Manning Redwood** (Forest Ranger 2), **Lisa Burns** and **Louise Burns** (Grady Daughters), **Robin Pappas*** (Nurse), **Alison Coleridge** (Secretary [Susie]), **Burnell Tucker*** (Policeman), **Jana Sheldon*** (Stewardess), **Kate Phelps** (Receptionist), **Norman Gay** (Injured Guest). [* Does not appear in the final UK print.]

Struggling writer Jack Torrance accepts a job as winter caretaker at the luxurious Overlook Hotel, a resort in the Colorado mountains which is closed for the season. Torrance is told by the manager, Stuart Ullman, that a previous caretaker, Grady, possibly driven insane by the isolation and the loneliness of the job, had shot his wife and brutally murdered his twin daughters with an axe before committing suicide in 1970. Unperturbed, former schoolteacher Jack takes up residence at the huge, snow-bound hotel with his wife Wendy and their seven year-old son Danny. However, Danny has an imaginary friend, Tony, who speaks to him and shows him visions of the two little dead girls. The hotel's head chef Dick Hallorann warns the boy not to enter Room 237 and reveals that he has the same psychic gift, which he tells Danny his grandmother called 'shining'. Meanwhile, the long, lonely days begin to have an effect on Jack. When Wendy decides to check on the progress of the novel he claims to be writing, she discovers that the Overlook has finally taken possession of her husband. Now it is time for his family to pay the price...

Stephen King's third novel was influenced by Shirley Jackson's 1959 book *The Haunting of Hill House* (which in *Danse Macabre* the author ranked as one of the only two 'great novels of the supernatural in the last hundred years'). Written just after his twenty-seventh birthday and originally called *Darkshine*, the book's title was changed to *The Shine* before finally ending up as *The Shining*. The first draft was turned out in less than four months and, although originally published in a hardcover edition of only 50,000 copies in 1977, it subsequently became a huge success in paperback and established King's phenomenal grip on the bestseller lists.

During the latter half of the 1970s, at his estate in Hertfordshire, England, reclusive American writer, producer and director Stanley Kubrick had been reading voraciously, looking for a new project ever since the release of his version of Thackeray's 18th century costume drama *Barry Lyndon* in 1975. When the manuscript of *The Shining* was sent to him by a Warner Bros executive, Kubrick quickly acquired the rights to King's novel from filmmaker Robert Fryer at The Producer Circle Company. In October 1978 he announced that it would be his next film. 'I thought it was one of the most ingenious and exciting stories of the genre I had read,' the maverick director told Michel Ciment in the book *Kubrick*. 'The novel is by no means a serious literary work, but the plot is for the most part extremely well worked out, and for a film that is often all that really matters.'

Declining to work with King's own screenplay because he did not want to be influenced by someone else's view of the book (not even the author's!), Kubrick co-scripted his version with 'serious' American novelist Diane Johnson, who was then teaching a course on the Gothic novel at the University of California in Berkeley.

Together, Kubrick and Johnson attempted to craft a script that would avoid any comparisons with the then-current glut of supernatural films flooding

A MASTERPIECE OF MODERN HORROR

A STANLEY KUBRICK FILM
JACK NICHOLSON SHELLEY DUVALL "THE SHINING"
SCATMAN CROTHERS, DANNY LLOYD STEPHEN KING
STANLEY KUBRICK & DIANE JOHNSON STANLEY KUBRICK
JAN HARLAN THE PRODUCER CIRCLE CO.

> **FACT FILE**
>
> Philip Stone's character, the hotel's previous caretaker, is first referred to as 'Charles' by Ullman, but he later introduces himself to Jack as Delbert Grady.

Above: The Torrance family set out on the road to hell.

FACT FILE

Footage from the helicopter shots used behind the opening titles of *The Shining* were subsequently edited into Ridley Scott's *Blade Runner* (1982).

the boxoffice. 'The problem was to extract the essential plot and to re-invent the sections of the story that were weak,' Kubrick told Ciment. The director believed that the virtues of the book lay 'almost entirely in the plot', and the two collaborators made a list of the scenes they thought should be included, which they then shuffled around until Kubrick approved of the order.

Amongst the more significant changes made by the writing team was moving the novel's Room 217 to 237 (apparently after a request by the management of the hotel where exteriors were filmed so that their guests would not be put off after seeing the film!), deleting the wasp attack, and replacing the scene in the book where the hotel's topiary sculptures come to life. 'The maze ending may have suggested itself from the animal topiary scenes in the novel,' continued Kubrick. 'I don't actually remember how the idea first came about.'

'It's very funny to me that he chose a hedge maze,' King told Peter S. Perakos in *Cinefantastique*, 'because my original concept *was* to create a hedge maze. And the reason that I rejected the idea in favour of the topiary animals was because of an old Richard Carlson film, *The Maze*.'

For the role of Jack Torrance, the caretaker whose life begins to spin out of control, Kubrick controversially chose former Roger Corman leading man Jack Nicholson (*The Raven* [1963], etc). During the 1970s, Nicholson's wild man image had softened somewhat, and he was now considered a serious boxoffice star. 'I believe that Jack is one of

the best actors in Hollywood,' Kubrick told Ciment. 'In *The Shining*, you believe he's a writer, failed or otherwise.'

King, who admitted that he would rather someone like Don Siegel had directed *The Shining*, revealed in an interview with Adam Pirani and Alan McKenzie in *Starburst* magazine that he had originally wanted Michael Moriarty, Martin Sheen or even Jon Voight to play the role of Jack Torrance: 'To me, he would have been much more convincing as an ordinary man going crazy.

'But when Nicholson smiles...it's the smile of a man who's insane. Then you realise that he's just being very pleasant, that's just the way Jack Nicholson smiles.'

A former *Look* photographer, Kubrick was famous for his obsessive attention to detail and insisted on having control over every aspect of his later films. He was known to shoot up to 100 takes of a scene until he was finally satisfied with the result. 'Stanley's demanding,' Nicholson told *Newsweek*'s Janet Huck in a 1980 interview. 'He'll do a scene fifty times and you have to be good to do that. There are so many ways to walk into a room, order breakfast or be frightened to death in a closet. Stanley's approach is, how can we do it better than it's ever been done before? It's a big challenge.'

During the long shoot, there was some tension between Kubrick and his star, as Nicholson recalled: 'I complained that he was the only director to light the sets with no stand-ins. We had to be there even to be lit. Just because you're a perfectionist doesn't mean you're perfect.' The actor candidly admitted that if a performer didn't give the director what he wanted, he'd beat it out of them, 'With a velvet glove, of course.'

Actress Shelley Duvall was someone who felt Kubrick's 'velvet glove' when her role meant that she had to remain hysterical for nearly four months on the set. The director would reportedly tell her, 'Shelley, that's not it. How long do we have to wait for you to get it right?'

'I think she brought an instantly believable characterisation to her part,' Kubrick said, and the actress later admitted: 'Stanley makes you do things you never thought you could do.' However, King thought that Duvall's whining heroine was 'an example of absolutely grotesque casting,' while critic Douglas E. Winter has described her performance as 'astonishingly inept', claiming that she 'nearly sabotages the entire affair'.

After the local Warner Bros office placed advertisements in newspapers for parents to send in photographs, around 5,000 young boys were interviewed in Chicago, Denver and Cincinnati for the role of the gifted Danny Torrance, before Kubrick cast the then-five and a half year-old Danny Lloyd, who came from a small town in Illinois.

Black American character actor Scatman Crothers was cast just three weeks before shooting began, after Kubrick failed to get the white actor he wanted for the role as the psychic Hallorann. The former song-and-dance man had never heard of Kubrick until he was called upon to play the sympathetic cook.

Budgeted at $13 million, principle photography began at EMI Elstree Studios in Borehamwood, just outside London, on 1 May 1978, although pre-production had actually started nearly two and a half years earlier.

Kubrick and production designer Roy Walker created the entire interior of the Overlook Hotel on sound stages at Elstree. The hotel's full-scale exterior and a quarter-scale version of the 100 yard-long hedge maze were constructed on the studio's backlot, which was equipped with artificial snow machines. Exterior location filming of the hotel took place at the Timberline Lodge, near Mount Hood National Forest in Oregon, and towards the end of principal photography two second unit camera crews were sent to Glacier National Park, Montana, to shoot establishing shots and the scenes of Hallorann returning to the Overlook.

According to director of photography John Alcott, Kubrick used no more than ten principal crew members except when filming the special effects sequences. 'He inspired me,' said Alcott, who had worked on the director's three previous projects. 'It was necessary to

have moving camera shots without cuts,' Kubrick revealed to Ciment, 'and of course the Steadicam made that much easier to do.'

Kubrick used Alcott's camera to turn the Overlook into the film's true focus. Conceived by Roy Walker as a synthesis of different hotel designs from all over America, it serves as a labyrinthine trap which has snared the dysfunctional Torrance family. Whether it is Danny's headlong peddling through the deserted corridors on his tricycle, the then-innovative Steadicam following directly behind him and giving us a child's-height view of the looming rows of closed and ominous doors, or the camera moving restlessly through the snow-covered maze as an axe-wielding Jack pursues his terrified son, Kubrick is less concerned with the characters or the story, and instead seems to be trying to create the ultimate haunted house movie.

Kubrick would call King from England at odd hours of the day and night, and he once abruptly asked the writer, 'Do you believe in God?'

'Kubrick builds this two-hour-and-twenty-minute crescendo of terror with a mastery that is itself more than a bit demonic. He not only gets the horror, he gets the perverse beauty of horror — a major achievement.'
Newsweek, 26 May 1980

Above: As usual, Stanley Kubrick's direction was hands-on.
Left: Cinematographer John Alcott and Stanley Kubrick (right), behind-the-scenes.

Above: Publicity montage: 'Heeereee's Johnny!'

'The impression I got from our conversation is that Kubrick *does not* believe in life after death,' King revealed in *Cinefantastique*. 'Yet, he thought that any vein of the supernatural story (whether it is horrifying, or whether it is pleasant) is inherently *optimistic* because it points towards the possible survival of the spirit.'

This was perhaps best illustrated by Kubrick's 'surprise' ending, where he has the camera move into a close-up of a 1921 photograph showing Jack as a guest at a 4 July ball in the hotel. As King explained in an interview with Peter S. Perakos in *Cinefantastique*: 'From the beginning, when I first talked to Kubrick some months ago, he wanted to change the ending. He asked me for my opinion on Hallorann becoming possessed, and then finishing the job that Torrance started, by killing Danny, Wendy, and lastly himself. Then, the scene would shift to the spring, with a new care-taker and his family arriving. However, the audience would see Jack, Wendy and Danny in an idyllic family scene — as ghosts — sitting together, laughing and talking.'

'Ghost stories appeal to our craving for immortality.' Kubrick told Jack Kroll in *Newsweek*. 'If you can be afraid of a ghost, then you have to believe that a ghost may exist. And if a ghost exists, then oblivion might not be the end.'

Although Kubrick wanted his final scene to suggest the reincarnation of Jack's character, it comes across as simply a hoary horror cliché which King himself wisely ignored in the novel.

'I kept telling Kubrick that it's his movie and, I mean, Christ Almighty, he bought it and supposedly he knew what he was doing. It doesn't make sense, in either a literal fashion or a metaphysical fashion!' said the author. 'The production is beautifully mounted — and Kubrick produces all sorts of interesting effects...I simply do not agree with his apparent sensibility that that can be a pay-off for the hollowness at the centre of the story.'

Although originally scheduled for a seventeen-week shoot, *The Shining* did not wrap principal photography until April 1979, eleven months after filming had started.

The film, which was estimated to have gone $5 million over budget, was released in May 1980 in America and was an instant success, grossing nearly $40 million in its first few weeks. 'I hope the audience has had a good fright, has believed the film while they were watching it, and retains some sense of it,' was how Kubrick summed up the movie to Ciment.

Kubrick's sprawling adaptation of King's novel was a significant disappointment to many fans of the book. Instead of the major horror film everybody expected, the unpredictable director insisted that he had simply been making an 'objective' ghost story about The House That Jack Built. 'I just remember being really disappointed because it wasn't Steve,' said George R. Romero. 'It was something else.'

'Kubrick knew exactly where all the scares should go and where all the payoffs should come,' King told Paul R. Gagne in *Cinefantastique*. 'It seems as though he simply said, "This is too easy. I'm not going to do it that way." So he didn't, and what he got was very little.'

Just days after *The Shining* was released in the United States, Kubrick decided to cut the final two-minute coda, in which hotel manager Ullman (played by Barry Nelson) visits Wendy Torrance in hospital and compliments her on having survived her ordeal. After generally negative reviews in America, the film was preview-tested before its opening in the United Kingdom and Kubrick decided to remove several further scenes. These involved Danny being examined by a doctor (Anne Jackson) after his first vision of the Grady twins, much of the lead-up to the introduction to Dick Hallorann, and Hallorann's conversation with garage owner Larry Durkin (Tony Burton) upon his return flight from Florida. After also tightening up several other sequences, the film's

original running time was reduced by a further twenty-five minutes to just 119 minutes.

Vivian Kubrick's thirty-five minute behind-the-scenes documentary *Making 'The Shining'* featured interviews with major cast and crew members (and included a visit to the set by actor James Mason).

'Could it have been done better?' King asked in a 1982 *TV Guide* article. 'Over the years I've come to believe that it probably could not. The film is cold and disappointingly loveless — but chilling.' However, after his disillusionment with Kubrick's adaptation, King himself scripted a television mini-series remake in 1997. He also revealed during a promotional chat on the Internet that he was interested in writing a sequel to *The Shining* featuring Danny Torrance, but 'just never got around to it'. †

'Kubrick piles it all on, but the effect is strangely unconvincing…Even Nicholson, that most consummate of actors, descends to the level of an old-time B-movie, the mad axe-man snarling his hatred and — yes, *limping* through corridors like a take-off of Vincent Price in *House of Wax*. Alas, Kubrick's carefully-nurtured mystique disappears in an amorphous cloud of mediocrity. Sorry Stanley. This time you blew it.'

The Standard, 2 October 1980

CREEPSHOW

A Very Scary Movie.

USA, 1982. Director: **George A. Romero**. Producer: **Richard P. Rubinstein**. Original Screenplay: **Stephen King**. Executive Producer: **Salah M. Hassanein**. Director of Photography: **Michael Gornick**. Associate Producer: **David E. Vogel**. Make-up Special Effects: **Tom Savini**. Production Designer/ Scenic Special Effects: **Cletus Anderson**. Editors: **Pasquale Buba**, **Paul Hirsch**, **George A. Romero** and **Michael Spolan**. Costume Design: **Barbara Anderson**. Original Music: **John Harrison**. Laurel Show, Inc/United Film Distribution Company/Warner Bros. Colour. 120 minutes.

Hal Holbrook (Henry Northrup), **Adrienne Barbeau** (Wilma Northrup), **Fritz Weaver** (Dexter Stanley), **Leslie Nielsen** (Richard Vickers), **Carrie Nye** (Sylvia Grantham), **E.G. Marshall** (Upson Pratt), **Viveca Lindfors** (Aunt Bedelia), **Ed Harris** (Hank Blaine), **Ted Danson** (Harry Wentworth), **Stephen King** (Jordy Verrill), **Warner Shook** (Richard Grantham), **Robert Harper** (Charlie Gereson), **Elizabeth Regan** (Cass Blaine), **Gaylen Ross** (Becky Vickers), **Jon Lormer** (Nathan Grantham), **Don Keefer** (Mike the Janitor), **Bingo O'Malley** (Jordy's Dad & Cameos), **John Amplas** (Nathan's Corpse), **David Early** (White), **Nann Mogg** (Mrs Danvers), **Tommy Atkins*** (Billy's Father), **Iva Jean Saraceni** (Billy's Mother), **Joe King** (Billy), **Christine Forrest** (Tabitha Raymond), **Chuck Aber** (Richard Raymond), **Cletus Anderson** (Host), **Katie Karlowitz** (Maid), **Peter Messer** (Yarbro), **Marty Schiff** (Garbage Man #1), **Tom Savini** (Garbage Man #2), **Darryl Ferrucci*** (Transformed Jordy Verrill). [* Uncredited in the final print.]

Right: Harry Wentworth (Ted Danson, left) hears some bad tidings from the jealous Richard Vickers (Leslie Nielsen).

An irate father throws his young son Billy's première edition of the horror comic Creepshow in the trash. At which point, a spectral 'host' materializes and begins flipping through the pages of the magazine as each story comes to life. In 'Father's Day', the fractious Grantham family are celebrating the death of the patriarch, Nathan. However, this year their departed dad has planned a surprise Father's Day party of his own. 'The Lonesome Death of Jordy Verrill' reveals what happens when the eponymous backwoods farmer discovers a meteor that has fallen from the sky onto his land. Taking the space rock back to his shack, Jordy soon discovers that there's more to this meteor than meets the eye as he begins to undergo a strange and bizarre transformation. In 'Something to Tide You Over', jealous husband Richard Vickers buries his cheating wife Rebecca and her lover Harry Wentworth up to their necks on the beach to await the high tide. After watching their slow deaths on video equipment, Vickers is interrupted by something the sea has washed back up. College English professor Henry Northrup decides to get rid of his shrewish, nagging wife Wilma after he learns that an ape-like creature captured during an 1834 Arctic expedition is still living inside 'The Crate'. Upson Pratt is a cranky, reclusive millionaire whose self-obsessed inner sanctum is invaded during a power black-out by the giant cockroaches he fears in 'They're Creeping Up on You'. The film ends with the young boy's voodoo revenge on his father for throwing out his precious comic book.

'As a kid, I cut my teeth on William B. Gaines' horror comics,' Stephen King revealed in *Danse Macabre*. 'These horror comics of the fifties still sum up for me the epitome of horror, that emotion of fear that underlies terror, an emotion which is slightly less fine, because it is not entirely of the mind.'

Having first been introduced during the development of *Salem's Lot* (1979), King was sitting in his Maine home with George A. Romero and Richard P. Rubinstein in the summer of 1979 when the trio came up with a concept which the author described as, 'Scaring an audience so badly and so continuously that they will have to almost literally crawl out of the theatre.'

Conceived around the same time, the creative team also announced a planned version of King's novel *The Stand* and an original Romero-King 70mm 3-D project, to be made before the middle of the decade.

Inspired by Gaines' infamous EC comic books, King agreed to write an original screenplay for an $8 million horror anthology. 'We liked the idea and Steve said, "Okay, I'll write a screenplay in two months,"' producer Richard P. Rubinstein told Tony Crawley in *Starburst*. 'And in two months to the day, a screenplay was there. Six stories. Steve sees them as telegrams of terror.'

Except for a little tidying up, the 142-page script King wrote was what Romero shot. The director did a shot-by-shot breakdown of each story, fleshing out sequences which the screenplay had left up to the film-maker's experience and imagination. 'Even though it contains different stories, we are treating *Creepshow* as a single film,' Rubinstein was at pains to point out to *Fangoria*'s Bob Martin during a set visit.

Production began in late July of 1981, just three weeks after Romero had finished work on the troubled *Knightriders* (1981), in which King and his family made a cameo appearance. Filming took place with a mostly non-union crew on a sound stage situated in the former gymnasium of Penn Hall Academy, an abandoned high school in a wooded suburb of Pittsburgh. Half the picture was shot on sets, with 'Father's Day' based at a Gothic mansion in the suburb of Fox Chapel and a sequence for 'Something to Tide You Over' filmed on the Maine coast. Some scenes for 'The Crate' (based on a story in the July 1979 issue of *Gallery*) were shot at Romero's *alma mater*, Carnegie Mellon University, while the remainder of the production utilised locations in and around Pittsburgh.

'We're going as far as we can to make this movie a comic book,' said director and co-editor Romero. Cinematographer Michael Gornick used saturated colour and a mostly stationary camera to create the suggestion of comic book panels, while the comic book-patterned background effects were created 'live' on the set, using screens and lighting scrims designed by production designer Cletus Anderson. 'We could see the results straight away,' explained Romero. 'You can see whether or not it works.'

'I thought they looked great,' agreed King.

Rather than rely on their usual repertoire of Pittsburgh actors, the film-makers made a conscious decision to go for a more recognisable 'name' cast.

Swedish-born actress Viveca Lindfors initially had reservations about agreeing to appear in a horror movie. In the end, however, the veteran performer admitted that, 'If I had ignored *Creepshow* because it was a

horror movie, I would have missed out on one of the most creative working experiences in my career.'

King himself played the avaricious dumb redneck who is transformed into a green alien fungus in the comedic 'The Lonesome Death of Jordy Verrill' (based on his story 'Weeds' from the May 1976 issue of *Cavalier*). To create the plant effect, King wore latex make-up appliances created by Savini for the early stages of the growth and dyed yak and horse hair was glued directly onto his face and hands. 'I just wanted to cover him in moss. Make him itch!' joked Romero.

For 'The Crate' episode (based on a King story in the July 1979 issue of the American men's magazine *Gallery*) special make-up effects designer Tom Savini created an upper-body creature costume of latex and yak hair worn by his nineteen year-old assistant Darryl

Above: *From left to right: producer Richard P. Rubinstein, director George Romero and Stephen King, behind-the-scenes.*
Below: *Wilma Northrup (Adrienne Barbeau) meets the inhabitant of 'The Crate'.*

'A lively and good-natured tribute to the spirit of the EC horror comics of the 1950s…King has a fondness for a pulpy approach to horror, but his usual knack for dialect and sardonic humor seems a bit halfhearted at times.'
Cinefantastique vol 13 no 4, April-May 1983

Ferrucci, with various hydraulic and puppet movements controlled off-screen by up to eight technicians. However, although everybody agreed that the result was extremely effective, Romero made the decision to cut most of the footage of the monster (nicknamed 'Fluffy' by the crew) from the final print, with Savini's agreement.

Max von Sydow was originally approached to play miserly multi-millionaire Upson Pratt in 'They're Creeping Up on You' (originally titled simply 'Bugs') before the role went to E.G. Marshall. The then-seventy-two year-old stage and screen actor refused to use a stand-in for most of the scenes involving 22,000 cockroaches, despite a clause in his contract. 'God I was impressed,' recalled King.

Principal photography wrapped in late November after seventeen weeks (a relative luxury for Romero, who was used to working on smaller budgets). 'We only have three or four weeks for each story,' the director told Paul R. Gagne, 'and we *have* to get it within that time.'

After the first cut came in at nearly three hours, *Creepshow* eventually had its world première in a 129-minute version at the Cannes Film Festival in May 1992. The film received a very positive review in *Variety*, which helped sales to foreign markets. 'It's like the proverbial rollercoaster ride,' King said in *Cinefantastique*, 'where you laugh and you scream, and it doesn't leave a bad taste in your mouth. You just feel like, "Wow, that was great! Let's go do it again!"'

After convincing Romero to trim the film down to two hours, Warner Bros opened it domestically on 29 October for the Halloween weekend, when it grossed around $10 million. 'Warners had a chance to push *Creepshow* through the roof,' King later claimed, 'and they chose not to do it. They chose to put it in their pockets and

get out.'

New American Library/Plume released a paperback graphic novel of the film, featuring interior illustrations by acclaimed comic book artist Bernie Wrightson (who initially dropped the final 'e' from his first name to avoid confusion with another Bernie Wrightson, who won the Gold Medal in the 1968 Olympics for high diving). The artist would go on to work on other King-related projects.

A belated sequel, unimaginatively titled *Creepshow 2*, finally followed five years later. ✝

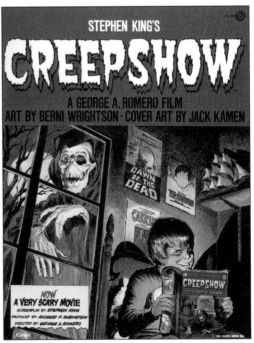

CUJO

Please God. Get Me Out of Here.

USA, 1983. Director: **Lewis Teague**. Producers: **Daniel H. Blatt** and **Robert Singer**. Screenplay: **Don Carlos Dunaway** and **Lauren Currier** [**Barbara Turner**]. Based on the Novel by **Stephen King**. Associate Producer: **Neil A. Machlis**. Director of Photography: **Jan de Bont**. Production Designer: **Guy Comtois**. Editor: **Neil Travis**. Casting: **Judith Holstra** and **Marcia S. Ross**. Music by **Charles Bernstein**. Sunn Classic Pictures, Inc/The Taft Entertainment Company/Warner Bros/Republic Pictures. Colour. 91 minutes.

Dee Wallace (Donna Trenton), **Daniel Hugh-Kelly** (Vic Trenton), **Christopher Stone** (Steve Kemp), **Ed Lauter** (Joe Camber), **Kaiulani Lee** (Charity Camber), **Mills Watson** (Gary Pervier), **Danny Pintauro** (Tad Trenton), **Billy Jacoby** (Brett Camber), **Sandy Ward** (Bannerman), **Jerry Hardin** (Masen), **Merritt Olsen** (Professor), **Arthur Rosenberg** (Roger Breakstone), **Terry Donovan-Smith** (Harry), **Robert Elross** (Meara), **Robert Behling** (Fournier), **Claire Nono** (Lady Reporter), **Daniel H. Blatt** (Dr Merkatz).

Castle Rock is a sleepy Maine, New England, town. A place where people can live in peace and security. But today Cujo, a usually friendly, full-grown Saint Bernard belonging to auto repair worker Joe Camber, is not feeling peaceful. The bat bite on his nose is infected and he has developed a violent fear of water and a vicious temper. While Vic Trenton is out of town for ten days on a business trip, his unfaithful wife Donna — who has recently ended her adulterous affair with local furniture stripper Steve Kemp — has car trouble. Stopping at the now-deserted Camber home, Donna and her anxious twelve year-old son Tad soon have something more than a broken-down Pinto to worry about — a 200 pound rabid dog whose one purpose in life is to tear them apart.

Above: Donna Trenton (Dee Wallace) protects her son against the rabid Saint Bernard.

B ased on Stephen King's 1981 novel, the first draft of which was written during the author's three-month stay in the United Kingdom in 1977. The book was inspired by King's actual encounter earlier the same year with an ill-tempered Saint Bernard dog at a remote garage.

'I'd always wondered whether or not it would be possible to write a novel restricted to a very small space,' he told Adam Pirani and Alan McKenzie in *Starburst*, 'and my first idea was whether or not it would be possible to write a 400-page novel that was entirely set in a stalled elevator. And then it sort of expanded to the idea of the automobile, and I couldn't keep it all in the automobile — I felt that I had to lead up to it.

'But I began to think of it as a low-budget novel. It *was* like a movie, it's more visual than any of the others, because the setting is so restricted.'

Low budget production company Taft Entertainment purchased the film rights the year the book was published and approached King to adapt his work to the screen. King, who had been impressed by the company's earlier production *The Boogens* (1981), agreed. 'I thought my script was pretty good,' said the author. 'It was not as faithful to the book as the final result was.'

King's original screenplay was twice revised by Barbara Turner (credited under the name 'Lauren Currier') and later rewritten by Don Carlos Dunaway, and although the rewrites stayed fairly close to

FACT FILE

Sheriff Bannerman (played by Sandy Ward), who is killed by Cujo while investigating Donna's missing car, returned to life in the guise of Tom Skerritt the same year for David Cronenberg's adaptation of King's *The Dead Zone*, also set in Castle Rock.

Above right: Donna is attacked by the 200 pound Cujo.

Below right: Donna is trapped in her car by the vicious Saint Bernard.

the author's original concept, King himself was denied a credit by The Writer's Guild of America when Turner lodged a protest. 'I was in England at the time,' he told Paul R. Gagne in *Cinefantastique*, 'and I just didn't have time to mess with it.'

At the time, Hungarian-born Peter Medak (*The Changeling* [1980], etc) was set to direct. When Medak dropped out of the production after one day's shooting, he was replaced by former Roger Corman film editor Lewis Teague. Teague brought in Dunaway to change the script's downbeat ending.

The major difference between the novel and the film version was that in the latter the injured Tad was allowed to survive. Although King had made it clear to his publisher that a 'happy ending' was 'non-negotiable', when Taft brought up the idea again, he told them: '"Fine, let the kid live and see how that works." I was never really against the idea.'

Cujo was filmed over eight weeks in Mendocino County in Northern California on a budget of just $5 million. Kansas-born Dee Wallace was cast as the adulterous Donna Trenton. She was not the first choice for the role, but agreed to do it after being asked by producers Daniel H. Blatt and Robert Singer, for whom she'd worked on *The Howling* (1980).

Wallace admitted to Tony Crawley in *Starburst* that both she and newcomer Danny Pintauro were 'scared to death' on set and that the boy was really screaming. 'Working conditions were…very difficult!' revealed Wallace, who was treated for exhaustion for two months after filming was completed.

The five Saint Bernard dogs used were trained by Karl Lewis Miller (who also worked on Teague's subsequent King adaptation, *Cat's Eye* [1985], which included a brief cameo appearance by Cujo). One of the most difficult scenes to shoot was during the climax, when the crazed canine had to crash through the car window. After all attempts to get the trained dogs to do the stunt had failed, the production even tried to use a German Shepherd in a Saint Bernard suit.

The filming inside the car took five weeks to complete. Two different vehicles were actually used, one of which was a breakaway prop, with removable sections to allow access for cinematographer Jan de Bont (later the director of such blockbusters as *Speed* [1994], *Twister* [1996] and the remake of *The Haunting* [1999]).

Cujo was released by Warner Bros in August 1983 and boxoffice earnings quickly passed $10 million. '*Cujo* is rooted in reality,' the director explained to Tim Hewitt in *Cinefantastique*. 'It's really a film about ordinary fears, the threads of fear that twine through our lives.'

Prior to release, there was apparently some discussion amongst the producers about whether or not Dee Wallace's character should even kill the rabid Saint Bernard at the end, in case the scene upset dog-lovers in the audience. 'I could not believe it,' co-writer Don Carlos Dunaway told Gary L. Wood. 'I thought it was *insane*!'

For King, *Cujo* remains one of his favourite adaptations of his own work. ✝

THE DEAD ZONE

In His Mind, He Has the Power to See the Future. In His Hands, He Has the Power to Change It.

Canada, 1983. Director: **David Cronenberg**. Producer: **Debra Hill**. Screenplay: **Jeffrey Boam**. Based on the Novel by **Stephen King**. Director of Photography: **Mark Irwin**, CSC. Production Designer: **Carol Spier**. Film Editor: **Ronald Sanders**. Associate Producer: **Jeffrey Chernov**. Costume Designer: **Olga Dimitrov**, RCA. Music Composer and Arranger: **Michael Kamen**. Dino De Laurentiis Corporation/Paramount. Colour. 103 minutes.

Christopher Walken (Johnny Smith), **Brooke Adams** (Sarah Bracknell), **Tom Skerritt** (Sheriff [George] Bannerman), **Herbert Lom** (Dr Sam Weizak), **Anthony Zerbe** (Roger Stuart), **Colleen Dewhurst** (Henrietta Dodd), **Nicholas Campbell** (Frank Dodd), **Martin Sheen** (Greg Stillson), **Sean Sullivan** (Herb Smith), **Jackie Burroughs** (Vera Smith), **Geza Kovacs** (Sonny Elliman), **Roberta Weiss** (Alma Frechette), **Simon Craig** (Chris Stuart), **Peter Dvorsky** (Dardis), **Julie-Ann Heathwood** (Amy), **Barry Flatman** (Walt), **Raffi Tchalikian** (Denny #1), **Ken Pogue** (Vice President), **Gordon Jocelyn** (Five-Star General), **Bill Copeland** (Secretary of State), **Jack Messinger** (Therapist), **Chapelle Jaffe** (Nurse), **Cindy Hines** (Natalie), **Helene Udy** (Weizak's Mother), **Ramon Estevez** (Teenage Boy with Camera), **Joseph Domenchini** (Young Weizak), **Roger Dunn**, **Wally Bendarenko** and **Claude Rae** (Reporters), **John Koensgen** (TV Anchorman), **Les Carlson** (Brenner), **Jim Bearden** (Deputy #1), **Hardee Lineham** (Deputy #2), **William Davis** (Ambulance Driver), **Sierge LeBlanc** (Denny #2), **Vera Winiauski** and **Joe Kapnaiko** (Polish Peasants), **Dave Rigby** (Truck Driver), **Stephen Flynn*** (Young Johnny), **Dick Warlock*** (Chuck Spier). [* Does not appear in the final print.]

Awakening from a five-year coma following a terrible road accident, small town school teacher Johnny Smith discovers that he has lost his job and his fiancée. However, even more traumatic than these revelations is the realisation that he has gained a strange power. By touching a person, he shares a psychic bond with them and can see visions of their past, present and, most frightening of all, their future. As he recovers, aided by the sympathetic Dr Sam Weizak, knowledge of his bizarre ability spreads. The police of Castle Rock enlist his talents to help solve a series of particularly gruesome rape-murders. After preventing a young boy from drowning, Smith realises that he can not only see the future, he can also change it. When he encounters ruthless, amoral politician Greg Stillson, Smith has an apocalyptic revelation which reveals what Stillson is capable of should he become President of the United States.

In his memoir *On Writing*, Stephen King revealed that his 1979 novel *The Dead Zone* arose from two questions he asked himself: 'Can a political assassin ever be right? And if he is, could you make him the protagonist of a novel? The good guy?'

It was the author's first number one hardcover bestseller and, after turning down an offer for the book from producer John Peters because he reportedly did not like what the former hairdresser had done with *Eyes of Laura Mars* (1978), King eventually sold the rights to Lorimar Productions in 1980. *The Dead Zone* was originally set to be produced by Sydney Pollack and directed by Hollywood veteran Stanley Donen (*Singin' in the Rain* [1952], etc). Paul Monash, who had previously produced *Carrie* (1976) and adapted *Salem's Lot* (1979) as a mini-series for television, wrote two drafts of the screenplay. 'Neither of the drafts was particularly successful,' King told Paul R. Gagne in *Cinefantastique*.

Monash was replaced by New Yorker Jeffrey Boam, who completed his first draft

Above: Johnny (Christopher Walken) gets his gun as he prepares to take fate into his own hands.

Below right: Martin Sheen as fanatical
politician Greg Stillson.
Below bottom: Dr Sam Weizak (Herbert
Lom) monitors Johnny's progress.

the day Ronald Reagan was elected President of the United States. 'King's book is longer than it needed to be,' Boam explained to *Cinefantastique*'s Tim Lucas. 'The theme of *The Dead Zone* is basically that moral, decent people have human responsibilities thrust upon them, and they can either ignore them or do something about them.'

After seeing Cronenberg's *The Brood* (1979), Carol Baum of Lorimar had asked the maverick Canadian director about his possible interest in the project before learning that Donen had been signed. Michael Cimino was also on board as director at one time.

When Lorimar decided to close its feature film division after a series of boxoffice disasters, rights in the property lapsed until Dino De Laurentiis bought them in early 1982. Around the same time, Cronenberg happened to meet independent producer Debra Hill (*Halloween* [1979], etc) while he was visiting John Landis' office at Universal Studios. Hill explained that she was now producing the film on behalf of De Laurentiis and she thought that Cronenberg would be perfect as the director. 'It seemed very fateful that the offer would come full circle,' Cronenberg told Lucas.

However, De Laurentiis decided that there were still problems with the script. Several more drafts had been completed — including one by the author himself (which focused on the Castle Rock killer but was rejected by De Laurentiis for being 'too complex') and, remarkably, another by acclaimed Russian film-maker Andrei Konchalovsky — but Cronenberg was not happy with any of them.

In the end, the director decided that the screenplay Jeffrey Boam had already written for Stanley Donen had the best creative potential. So, together with Debra Hill, he and Boam locked themselves away in a Toronto hotel room for three days to restructure and re-adapt the book. Not least was the problem that King's novel comprised three parallel narratives. 'Stephen tried to do it that way, but I didn't think it worked,' Cronenberg told Phil Edwards and Randy Lofficier in *Starburst* magazine. 'I also thought that his

script gave more emphasis to the Frank Dodd murders than I wanted to in the film I wanted to make. His script was very different from the book — very different in tone. I think that, ironically I suppose, our version of the film is closer in tone to the book than Stephen's script was.'

'I think he missed the point of his own book,' said Boam.

At one point, Cronenberg and Boam planned to change the 'dead zone' itself: in

King's book it is depicted as a recurring blank spot in Johnny's psychic visions. The movie did dispense with Johnny's causative brain tumour, and the concept of having him age prematurely every time he used his powers was also eventually dropped. Boam's 'trick' ending, in which the Castle Rock killer escaped from a mental institution and almost murdered Johnny's former fiancée, Sarah Bracknell, in a hospital parking garage, was also rejected by the director. 'We had to 'reinvent' the book,' continued Cronenberg, 'condense it without worrying about being faithful to it in any literary, bookish way. Still, I think we have been faithful to the book in terms of sustaining its tone.'

Filming on the estimated $7 million production began on 10 January 1983, with various wintry locations in the Ontario town of Niagara-on-the-Lake standing in for New England. Interiors were shot at Toronto's Lakeshore Studios. King himself was not actively involved with the production. 'I just hope I can fuse my strengths and Stephen's

'Not only the finest work to date by director David Cronenberg and the best adaptation of a Stephen King novel, but a splendid film by any standard…In almost every way and on many levels, *The Dead Zone* is a glowing success.'

Cinefantastique vol 14 no 2, December 1983-January 1984

FACT FILE

Castle Rock is also the setting for Lewis Teague's adaptation of *Cujo*, made the same year.

FACT FILE

The scissors suicide of the Castle Rock killer, Deputy Frank Dodd (Nicholas Campbell), has been cut from some TV prints.

strengths and come up with a terrific movie,' Cronenberg told Tim Lucas. 'I'd hate to have him say it's as bad as *The Shining*!'

The author had apparently suggested Bill Murray for the role of Johnny but the actor was not available. It was De Laurentiis who recommended Christopher Walken, despite the fact that Cronenberg wanted Nicholas Campbell and was worried that Walken was too old for the part. After working with the actor, the director admitted: 'I think Chris Walken is fantastically good in this role.'

Cronenberg also wanted Hal Holbrook (*Creepshow* [1982], etc) for the role of Sheriff George Bannerman, but De Laurentiis (who had casting control) rejected the suggestion because he had never heard of the actor!

For flashback sequences to World War II Poland, the former Yugoslavia was originally considered. However, to keep down production costs, the invasion scenes were eventually shot at night in an abandoned brickworks in Cheltenham, just outside Toronto. During the filming of these scenes, an extra was badly burned in an accident involving an explosive 'squib'.

With shooting completed in late March, Cronenberg had a long discussion with King which resulted in some additional editing to the scenes in which presidential candidate Greg Stillson hides behind a small child. A three-minute pre-credits sequence, involving a childhood hockey accident that first triggered Johnny's psychic powers, was also removed during the editing process.

When Michel Legrand pulled out after only being given eight weeks to compose the score and Cronenberg's choice of composer, Howard Shore, was ruled out by De Laurentiis, Michael Kamen had just three weeks to deliver his music for the film.

The Dead Zone was released on 21 October by Paramount. Based on the reaction of preview audiences, the publicity campaign had been changed a month earlier from promoting the film as a horror thriller to a more mainstream drama. Grossing more than $8 million in the United States and Canada, it was Cronenberg's biggest hit — both critically and commercially — up to that date. 'Cronenberg did one of the great jobs of his life,' King later said. 'He got tremendous performances out of people, but the movie was not able to break through.'

In a bizarre postscript, years later the widow of 'renowned' psychic Peter Hurkos claimed that her long-dead husband was responsible for Stephen King being hit by a minivan in 1999, because he had 'stolen' Hurkos' life story for his novel *The Dead Zone*.

Television network UPN announced it was developing a one-hour television series entitled *Stephen King's The Dead Zone* by Michael Piller (*Star Trek Voyager* [1995-2001], etc) for the 2001-2002 season. Anthony Michael Hall was set to play psychic Johnny Smith and Nicole deBoer his character's love interest in the pilot. †

Above top: Johnny has a psychic vision of a child's burning bedroom.

'The moviemakers — producer Debra Hill, director David Cronenberg — are as trapped as this misfortune teller in his inconvenient talent. They can only repeat the same trick with variations, one of which (you should be warned) involves scissors being stuck down someone's gizzard.'

The Standard, 3 May 1984

CHRISTINE
(AKA JOHN CARPENTER'S CHRISTINE)

She's a Killer.

USA, 1983. Director: **John Carpenter**. Producer: **Richard Kobritz**. Screenplay: **Bill Phillips**. Based Upon the Novel by **Stephen King**. Director of Photography: **Donald M. Mogan**, ASC. Production Designer: **Daniel Lomino**. Editor: **Marion Rothman**. Executive Producers: **Kirby McCauley** and **Mark Tarlov**. Co-Producer: **Larry Franco**. Music: **John Carpenter** and **Alan Howarth**. Associate Producer: **Barry Bernardi**. Casting: **Karen Rea**. Columbia Pictures/Polar Film/Columbia-Delphi Productions. Colour. 110 minutes.

Keith Gordon (Arnie [Cunningham]), **John Stockwell** (Dennis [Guilder]), **Alexandra Paul** (Leigh [Cabot]), **Robert Prosky** ([Will] Darnell), **Harry Dean Stanton** ([Rudolph] Junkins), **Christine Belford** (Regina Cunningham), **Roberts Blossom** ([George] LeBay), **William Ostrander** (Buddy), **David Spielberg** (Mr Casey), **Malcolm Danare** (Moochie), **Steven Tash** (Rich), **Stuart Charno** (Vandenberg), **Kelly Preston** (Roseanne), **Marc Poppel** (Chuck), **Robert Darnell** (Michael Cunningham), **Douglas Warhit** (Bemis), **Richard Collier** (Pepper Boyd), **Bruce French** (Mr Smith), **Keri Montgomery** (Ellie), **Jan Burrell** (Librarian), **Charles Steak** (Shoppie).

Christine is the name of a red and white 1958 Plymouth Fury. 'She' is only a car but, unlike other vehicles of chrome and steel, she is possessed of evil and has the power to choose her owner and destroy anybody who stands in her way. It is 1978 in Rockbridge, California, and seventeen year-old Arnie Cunningham is becoming inexplicably obsessed with the old car he bought from the strange Mr LeBay. The rusty wreck seduces the teenager, until he is consumed by an irrational passion for her sleek, rounded body. Arnie's friends Dennis and Leigh can only watch helplessly as his personality begins to change dramatically under the influence of his beloved Christine. She demands his complete and unquestioning devotion, and when Arnie's enemies begin to interfere, they quickly become the objects of the car's horrifying, supernatural wrath.

I n his 1980 essay entitled 'On Becoming a Brand Name', Stephen King explained, 'The writer's job is to write. There are no brand names in the little room where the typewriter or the pen and notebook sit waiting. There are no stars in that place.'

Despite his protestations, by the early 1980s King had himself become a literary and movie 'brand name'. *Christine* is based on King's 1983 novel (which is dedicated to George Romero). He sold the book to Viking and New American Library for an advance of $1 each as a reaction to critics who accused

the best-selling author of being more interested in the money than the work.

Although the novel was based on an old idea King had about a car in which the speedometer ran backwards through time, it may also have been inspired by another film about a demonically possessed automobile, *The Car* (1977). 'There is a marvellous opening sequence where the car chases two bicyclists through Utah's Zion State Park,' King recalled in *Danse Macabre*, 'it's horn blaring arrhythmically as it gains on them and finally runs them down.' (A similar scene appears in *Christine* when the blazing car pursues a school bully.)

'It's a horror story about a romantic triangle,' revealed Richard Kobritz, who had previously worked with John Carpenter on the NBC-TV movie *Someone's Watching Me!* (1978) and had also produced the 1979 CBS mini-series of King's *'Salem's Lot*. Kobritz quit his job as vice-president for production at Warner Bros Television in early 1983 and formed Polar Film to purchase King's novel for $500,000 after he had read it in galley form.

Scriptwriter Bill Phillips, who had previously worked on the final rewrite of Carpenter's aborted version of *Firestarter*, wrote several drafts of *Christine* before delivering the completed script. Much of the dialogue was taken directly from King's original text.

When Randy Lofficier and Phil Edwards asked him why he had chosen a 1958 Plymouth Fury for his novel, King explained: 'Because they are almost totally forgotten cars. It was the most mundane 1950s car that I could remember and it's not a car that already had a legend attached to it — like the

'50s Thunderbird or Ford Galaxies.'

As the author explained: 'An audience can relate, to a certain degree, to something like a haunted house — *The Amityville Horror* — traditional horrors like ghosts, vampires and things like that. You give them a car, or any inanimate object, and you're suggesting something that is either along the pulpy lines of EC comics, or else obviously symbolic. The car is a symbol for the technological age or for the end of innocence, when it plays such a part in adolescence and growing up. When you do that, you're really starting to take a risk — but that's where the excitement is. If you can make somebody go along with that concept, that's really wonderful.'

The story's locale was moved from suburban Pittsburgh (King's homage to Romero) to sunny Southern California. Another major change from the novel was that, in the film, it is the car itself which is evil, while in the book it is suggested that it is Christine's previous owner, the dead Roland LeBay, who is exerting his malign influence over Arnie. King told *Starburst*: 'When the film people came to me, I said, "Look, this is your decision. You decide what you're going to do with the story." But, later, I was told that in the opening sequence, when the car rolls off the assembly line, one of the workmen is dead behind the wheel. This would give you the idea that the car is bad from the beginning.'

The $10 million independent production was rushed into production in late April 1983, just days *before* King's novel made the hardcover bestseller lists. According to Kobritz, the time between the date he first read the galleys in 1982 and the film's release was just seventeen months, making it one of the fastest King adaptations from book to movie.

Arnie's garage, where he restores the classic car, was shot in an abandoned building in the industrial California town of Irwindale. Twenty-three identical Plymouth Furies were used during the filming. Many of them were acquired from vintage car collectors at a total cost to the production of $500,000.

Filming lasted until early July and Columbia Pictures, anticipating a boxoffice hit, decided to move the release date up from the following summer to December. The movie grossed less than $10 million domestically. King later revealed in *Cinefantastique* that, 'looking at *Christine* at the Zeigfeld in New York was like trying to check the electricity in a dead circuit.'

Years later, Carpenter admitted in *Fear* magazine: 'The film didn't turn out very good. I was the one who screwed it up. I simply left out stuff from the novel that I should have used in the film — like the rotting corpse that's haunting the teenager who buys the car.' In fact, screenwriter Bill Phillips later appropriated King's image of Roland LeBay's rotting ghost for a series of drinking and driving advertisements. 'It's effective,' he explained.

King's original novel quotes the lyrics from a number of rock 'n' roll songs, which the author added to his second draft while in Pittsburgh filming *Creepshow* (1982). Likewise, the film's soundtrack features many classic rock songs and was available on Motown records. ✝

Above top: *Arnie's enemies attempt to wreck Christine.*
Above: *From left to right: Keith Gordon, Alexandra Paul and John Stockwell.*

CHILDREN OF THE CORN

(AKA STEPHEN KING'S CHILDREN OF THE CORN)

And a Child Shall Lead Them...

USA, 1984. Director: **Fritz Kiersch**. Producers: **Donald P. Borchers** and **Terrence Kirby**. Screenplay: **George Goldsmith**. Based on the Short Story by **Stephen King**. Executive Producers: **Earl Glick** and **Charles J. Weber**. Special Visual Effects: **Max W. Anderson**. Director of Photography: **Raoul Lomas**. Film Editor: **Harry Keramidas**. Art Director: **Craig Stearns**. Music: **Jonathan Elias**. Casting: **Linda Francis**. New World Pictures/Angeles Entertainment Group, Inc/Cinema Group Venture/Inverness Productions, Inc/Hal Roach Studios/Gatlin Productions. Colour. 93 minutes.

Peter Horton (Burt [Stanton]), **Linda Hamilton** (Vicky [Baxter]), **R.G. Armstrong** ([Chester] Diehl), **John Franklin** (Isaac), **Courtney Gains** (Malachai), **Robby Kiger** (Job), **Anne Marie McEvoy** (Sarah), **Julie Maddalena** (Rachel), **Jonas Marlowe** (Joseph), **John Philbin** (Amos), **Dan Snook** (Boy), **David Cowen** (Dad), **Suzy Southam** (Mom), **D.G. Johnson** (Mr Hansen), **Patrick Boylan**, **Elmer Soderstrom** and **Teresa Toigo** (Hansen's Customers), **Mitch Carter** (Radio Preacher).

Under the sun in the rural mid-west, the cornfields are dying of thirst. Only human blood will feed them. In the small, sleepy community of Gatlin — the 'nicest little town in Nebraska' — a gaunt twelve year-old preacher named Isaac commands the children to kill everyone over the age of eighteen. Three years later, one youngster tries to escape Isaac's rule and has his throat cut by Malachai, Isaac's most evil disciple. Dr Burt Stanton and his girlfriend Vicky Baxter are driving west to Seattle, where Stanton is to start his first hospital internship, when they hit the dying boy as he staggers out onto the main highway. Stanton puts the child's corpse in the trunk and the couple head toward Gatlin. Chester Diehl, the grizzled old proprietor of a roadside gas station, attempts to detour them but is unsuccessful, and for failing he is murdered by Malachai. Arriving in the deserted town, Stanton and Vicky discover a frightened little girl, Sarah, who lapses into psychic trances. But while Stanton is off exploring the town, Malachai and the other children capture Vicky and prepare to crucify her on a cross made of cornstalks to their evil deity, 'He Who Walks Behind the Rows'.

'**K**ids can be mean and unlovely,' Stephen King wrote in *Danse Macabre*, 'and when you see them at their worst, they can make you think black thoughts about the future of the human race.'

Children of the Corn was based on King's short story, originally published in the March 1977 issue of *Penthouse* and reprinted the fol-

lowing year in the *Night Shift* collection.

The author's own first draft screenplay had been unsuccessfully touted around the studios in the late 1970s, but was rejected because it was felt that there were too many King projects then in development.

In the early 1980s, the project was picked up by then-thirty-five year-old Harry Wiland, a documentary film-maker from Maine. King did a re-write of his script, and the relatively low budget film was set to star young actor Lance Kerwin (who had appeared in the 1979 television mini-series of 'Salem's Lot). 'We are on the same wavelength,' said Wiland, explaining his relationship with King to Paul R. Gagne in *Cinefantastique*, 'and we both see the potential of this movie. We both see things that need to be fleshed out or polished, and we're doing it.'

Although filming was set to take place in the small Kansas towns of Butler and Lawrence in the summer of 1981, the production was put into turnaround at the last minute when Twentieth Century Fox pulled out, leaving Wiland and producer Joe Masefield $2 million short of the anticipated budget after Home Box Office had already contributed $750,000.

The project finally ended up at Hal Roach Studios, who asked writer George Goldsmith to rewrite King's script before it came to the attention of New World Pictures. 'It's the idea of dogma being an evil thing,' Goldsmith explained to Gagne. And King confided to the same writer that, 'The story is not exactly calculated to send you out of the theatre with sunshine in your heart.'

New World's senior vice president in charge of production, Donald P. Borchers, came on board in 1983 and took the project to producer Terrence Kirby and thirty-two year-old direc-

'King's short story is better suited to the screen than his sprawling novels, but this low budget movie throws out too many of his unconventional ideas and does its best to convert the intriguing notion into a very familiar horror film…The finale features the appearance of He Who Walks as a disappointing red cloud and some particularly banal monster-fighting and plot-resolving business.'

City Limits, 27 July-2 August 1984

tor Fritz Kiersch, who were partners in their own television commercial production company in Los Angeles. Borchers had worked with the team some years earlier when he had been an assistant director.

Kirby and Kiersch accepted the assignment and went into pre-production the following day, originally scouting locations in Kansas. 'But the drought and heatwave of the summer had withered the corn too much,' recalled co-producer Kirby. Nebraska was also ruled out when the towns they saw didn't have the visual sense the pair were looking for.

Six weeks after the search began, filming commenced on the relatively low budget — $3 million — adaptation. It was shot over twenty-seven days during September and October 1983 in Siouxland, Iowa.

Both Peter Horton and Linda Hamilton got their first starring roles as the hapless couple plunged into a rural nightmare. Eighteen year-old John Franklin was cast as the androgynous-

looking preacher, Isaac, while Courtney Gains (who was the same age) portrayed Malachai, his sociopathic executioner. The other children of the corn were played by thirty young people from Sioux City. 'They had to come off as terrifying,' said Kiersch, 'and they did.'

As the close-mouthed gas station operator whose mechanical skill is needed by the youth cult who have spared his life, all the scenes featuring veteran character actor R.G. Armstrong were shot in a single day when the production looked as if it might go over schedule and over budget.

Used to the fast pace and many different camera set-ups often required for television

'The corn is as high as a crucifixion victim's eye as a young couple stumble on this situation and remain unsuspecting for longer than their apparent intelligence would warrant.'
The Standard, 26 July 1984

'Even in his heyday, [Roger] Corman would have been hard-pressed to serve up a genre programmer more silly and unintentionally hilarious. King's mass-market fiction has inspired some momentous cinematic dreck, but *Children of the Corn* is a new low even by schlock standards.'
Cinefantastique vol 14 no 4/5, September 1984

commercials, Kiersch was able to generate more footage than would normally be expected in a four week schedule. Often forced to think on his feet, the director would usually do no more than three takes of any scene.

However, filming did not always go smoothly. When art director Craig Stearns complained to Kirby that the corn was not green enough, the producer told him, 'Then spray it green', which he did.

The children's mythic deity was depicted as both a burrowing creature and a glowing cloud. 'As He Who Walks Behind the Rows had to personify the elements and take different shapes and forms, I think we achieved that nebulous quality,' Kiersch told Alan Jones in *Starburst* magazine. 'I came up with the mole effect while we were on location mainly because up until that point nothing much had happened apart from a plant wrapping itself around a man.' The cheap-looking effect was created simply by placing an upturned wheelbarrow in a trench, covering it over with earth and then pulling it along with an off-camera tractor.

The director admitted that he was disappointed with the film's special effects support: 'The effects at the ending really do suck,' he told Jones. 'We had a lot of problems there mainly because we had to shoot all those scenes first, before the corn changed from green to gold.'

Except for the brief prologue and a few flashbacks, the film's action all takes place during a twelve-hour period from early morning into night. The editing took ten weeks to complete, with the script making several major changes to King's original story, including a new 'upbeat' ending. 'It's okay sometimes if the protagonist dies at the end,' scriptwriter George Goldsmith explained to Paul Gagne, 'but it's not often that the film succeeds commercially.'

In a repeat of his experience on *Cujo* (1983), The Writer's Guild of America rejected King's script recognition when Goldsmith petitioned for sole credit. However, King subsequently discovered that the script which New World Pictures had represented to him as the final screenplay had, in fact, little in common with the finished film. 'I didn't need the screen credit,' the author explained in *Cinefantastique*. 'What happens if the picture's a dog and your name is on it and it's not supposed to be?...in other words, I'm willing to take the credit if the reaction's good, and I won't if everybody says that this is a real piece of shit.'

Released in March 1984, *Children of the Corn* grossed almost $7 million domestically and has inexplicably become one of the most successful of the many King adaptations to film, spawning no less than six direct-to-video sequels to date.

'King actually wrote a nice letter to New World about the movie,' Kiersch informed Alan Jones in *Starburst*, 'and I was pleased because, as it is a short story stretched out to feature length, lots of people are quick to find fault with it.

'But we did very well for the amount of money this film cost as it does come across as a more expensive production knowing the size and scope of it. It works well on certain levels.'

'*Children of the Corn* is extraordinarily successful,' Donald P. Borchers told Thomas Crow in *Fangoria*, 'but I do *not* think that it's true to King's original.'

King summed up his feelings in *Cinefantastique*, saying, 'The picture was a dog.' †

Firestarter

Will She Have the Power...to Survive?

USA, 1984. Director: **Mark L. Lester**. Producer: **Frank Capra Jr**. Screenplay: **Stanley Mann**. Based on the Novel *Firestarter* by **Stephen King**. Associate Producer: **Martha Schumacher**. Director of Photography: **Giuseppe Ruzzolini**. Art Director: **Giorgio Postiglione**. Editor: **David Rawlins**. Music Composers and Performers: **Tangerine Dream**. Universal City Studios/Dino De Laurentiis. Colour. 115 minutes.

David Keith (Andrew McGee), **Drew Barrymore** (Charlie [Charlene] McGee), **Freddie Jones** (Dr Joseph Wanless), **Heather Locklear** (Vicky McGee), **Martin Sheen** (Captain Hollister), **George C. Scott** (John Rainbird), **Art Carney** (Irv Manders), **Louise Fletcher** (Norma Manders), **Moses Gunn** (Dr Pynchot), **Antonio Fargas** (Taxi Driver), **Drew Snyder** (Orville Jamieson), **Curtis Credel** (Bates), **Keith Colbert** (Mayo), **Richard Warlock** (Knowles), **Jeff Ramsey** (Steinowitz), **Jack Magner** (Young Serviceman), **Lisa Anne Barnes** (Serviceman's Girlfriend), **Larry Sprinkle** (Security Guard), **Cassandra Ward-Freeman** (Woman in Stall), **Scott R. Davis** (Bearded Student), **Nina Jones** (Grad Assistant), **William Alspaugh** (Proprietor), **Laurens Moore** (Old Man), **Anne Fitzgibbon** (Old Lady), **Steve Boles** (Mailman), **Stanley Mann** (Motel Owner), **Robert Miano** and **Leon Rippy** (Blinded Agents), **Carole Francisco** (Joan Dugan), **Wendy Womble** (Josie), **Etan Boritzer** and **Joan Foley** (DSI Technicians), **John Sanderford** (Albright), **Orwin Harvey** and **George Wilbur** (DSI Orderlies), **Carey Fox** (Agent Hunt).

Apparently the result of Andy and Vickie McGee participating in a government-sponsored hallucinogenic experiment while college students, their eight year-old daughter 'Charlie' has an unusual gift. Forced to flee after the murder of his wife, Andy and Charlie are pursued by the Department of Scientific Intelligence, a covert government information service nicknamed 'The Shop', which will stop at nothing to learn the secret of the girl's pyrokinetic abilities and use her as a living weapon. Andy has waning paranormal powers of his own, most notably the ability to 'push' people into acting upon his telepathic suggestion. He manages to protect his daughter and himself from capture by finding temporary shelter with an elderly farm couple, Irv and Norma Manders. However, ruthless DSI administrator Captain 'Cap' Hollister will not allow his department to be outwitted and he dispatches The Shop's most experienced assassin, the death-obsessed John Rainbird, to hunt them down.

Left: *Andrew McGee (David Keith) and his daughter Charlie (Drew Barrymore) are caught in a trap.*

'I love movies,' King said at the time, 'and when I go to see a movie that's been made from one of my books, I know that it isn't going to be exactly like my novel because a lot of people have interpreted it. But I also know it has an idea that I'll like because that idea occurred to me, and I spent a year or a year and a half of my life working on it.

'From the very beginning, I thought that *Firestarter* was a more 'movie-able' book than some of my others. But, at the same time, I worried a lot about somebody getting hurt, even burned up while they were trying to pull off some of these things.'

Inspired by actual recorded cases of pyrokinesis or 'spontaneous combustion', King's novel was written over the period 1976-77 and published in 1980. Although it bears some basic similarities to John Farris' 1976 novel *The Fury*, it was actually half-completed before Farris' book was published. 'This field is so damned narrow that you're

'Conceived not as a human drama but as a simple-minded special effects exhibition…The strength of this film is in the strength of the novel: the spark of a unique idea about a girl who can start fires with her mind. But neither bears out the promise.'

Cinefantastique vol 15 no 1, January 1985

STEPHEN KING

FIRE-STARTER

A Novel by the Author of THE DEAD ZONE

Below: Charlie flexes her pyrokinetic abilities.

always on somebody's feet,' King explained to Paul R. Gagne in *Cinefantastique*.

The movie rights were purchased in 1980 for $1 million by Egyptian film producer Dodi Fayed (who was subsequently killed in the car crash which also took Princess Diana's life in Paris in August 1997). It was planned to make the film through a British-based company called Allied Stars.

At one time, director John Carpenter and scriptwriter Bill Lancaster (who had collaborated on *The Thing* [1982]) were set to be reunited on the project, then budgeted at $20 million. Bill Phillips (Carpenter's *Christine* [1983], etc) also worked on a rewrite. 'The problem with King's novels are that sometimes they're a bit funky,' Carpenter explained to Thomas Nilsson in *Fear* magazine, 'the plot doesn't translate to the movies that well. *Firestarter* was one project that I was involved with for a while. I thought that one could have been good because there you have a very clear understanding of what's happening. Unfortunately,

it didn't work out in the end.'

King was also reportedly approached about directing the film himself.

Fayed eventually passed the rights on to Dino De Laurentiis, who in turn sold them to Universal. Canadian-born screenwriter Stanley Mann was hired to write a new script, which King described to Gagne as having 'some things that are almost bril-

liant in terms of the genre.'

'It's always difficult to condense a literary work,' admitted the experienced Mann, who also makes a cameo appearance. 'But I always try to be as faithful to it as possible while making compensations to keep a dramatic line. I was very pleased to have received a letter from Stephen after he had read my script, saying, most graciously, that he thought it was the best adaptation of one of his novels that he's seen.'

The $15 million production began filming on 12 September 1983, in western North Carolina, in the Blue Ridge Mountain towns of Chimney Rock and Lake Lure. Early in the sixty-seven day schedule a five-ton generator had to be replaced when it toppled off a narrow road and down an embankment on its way to the location.

The majority of the filming was completed in and around Wilmington, NC, where De Laurentiis built a sound stage out of a warehouse near the airport which had once been used to manufacture containers for nuclear waste. The lot that served as the *Firestarter* headquarters was subsequently expanded into De Laurentiis' North Carolina Film Corporation Film Studios, which included three sound stages, property and wardrobe departments, offices and a commissary, all under the supervision of Martha J. Schumacher.

De Laurentiis, King later recalled, saw the then-eight year-old Drew Barrymore as the Shirley Temple of her generation. The young actress had first encountered King's novel a year and a half earlier: 'My mom had seen this book at the grocery store with a picture of a little girl on it and she said, "Gee, this looks kinda like you,"' Barrymore recalled. 'She said it was okay if I bought it and so I did. When I read it, I came into the kitchen where my mom was making dinner and said, "I'm the Firestarter. I'm Charlie McGee!"'

According to thirty-seven year-old director Mark L. Lester, David Keith (*An Officer and a Gentleman* [1982], etc) was the fifteenth choice to play Andrew McGee, the father trying to keep his daughter out of the hands of a clandestine government agency. Former photographic model and television star Heather Locklear (*T.J. Hooker* [1982-86], etc) made her movie début as Charlie's ill-fated mother.

As John Rainbird, the shrewd Native American operative who has a special interest in his assignment, King described George C. Scott's involvement as '*brilliant* casting'. However, Martin Sheen, who replaced an ailing Burt Lancaster, was too young for the role of Hollister.

Filmed simultaneously by ten cameras, the impressive destruction of the DSI headquarters, a three sided wood and plaster façade

ments that he makes about people, attacking these movies.' King responded in the same issue of the magazine: 'Mark's assertion that I saw the movie and loved it is erroneous. I saw *part* of an early rough cut. When I saw the final cut, months later (at a première in Bangor, Maine), I was extremely depressed. The parts were all there, but the total was somehow much less than the sum of those parts...'

King, De Laurentiis and Barrymore were reunited later the same year for *Cat's Eye*, while the subversive operations of The Shop again resurfaced in the 1991 television mini-series *Golden Years* and *The Lawnmower Man* (1992).

A *Firestarter* television series was proposed but never made in the late 1990s. In December 2001 the Sci-Fi Channel broadcast a four-hour mini-series sequel, *Firestarter: Rekindled* (filmed under the title *Firestarter The Next Chapter*), scripted by Philip Eisner and directed by Robert Iscove. Set twenty years after the original, 'Charlie' McGee (Marguerite Moreau) uncovered the university experiment responsible for her psychic powers while a sociopathic agent (Malcolm McDowell) used an army of gifted children to hunt her down. Other cast members included Danny Nucci and Dennis Hopper. †

'*Firestarter* suffers, like most adaptations of Stephen King's occult thrillers, from monotony of effect... Charlie can launch a nice line in fireballs and detonate bullets in flight, but why everyone stands around when she turns the heat on them is a puzzle that makes wholesale incineration into just a major irritation.'
The Standard, 5 July 1984

constructed at the privately-owned Orton Plantation at a cost of more than $200,000, took just two days to rig with a mixture of diesel fuel and propane gas before being reduced to rubble for the film's explosive climax. With a script involving nearly $1 million worth of potentially dangerous pyrotechnic special effects, representatives from two local fire departments were on set at all times to act as advisors. As a result of the production's concern about safety, there was not a single injury during filming.

Shooting wrapped in November, and King, De Laurentiis and Drew Barrymore attended the film's world première on 9 May 1984 in Bangor, held as a fundraiser to benefit the Maine-based consumer protection organisation COMBAT. Two days later, Universal released *Firestarter* to disappointing boxoffice results. The film eventually grossed around $7.5 million. King later admitted that the project was 'one of my most visual novels and a resounding failure as a film,' but claimed that it had somehow missed the chance 'to be a truly awful picture, like *Myra Breckinridge*.'

Director Mark Lester told Gary L. Wood in *Cinefantastique*: 'After the movie came out, I was appalled at some of the things he said... I'm just appalled that a man of his wealth would actually stoop to these slanderous com-

CAT'S EYE

I'll Be Watching You!

USA, 1984. Director: **Lewis Teague**. Producer: **Martha Schumacher**. Screenplay: **Stephen King**. Music: **Alan Silvestri**. Creatures Creator: **Carlo Rambaldi**. Director of Photography: **Jack Cardiff**. Film Editor: **Scott Conrad**, ACE. Production Designer: **Giorgio Postiglione**. Costume Designer: **Clifford Capone**. Famous Films Productions NV/Dino De Laurentiis/MGM-UA Entertainment Co. Colour. 94 minutes.

Drew Barrymore (Our Girl [Alicia Morrison/Girl on TV/Amanda]), **James Woods** ([Richard] Morrison), **Alan King** (Dr Donatti), **Kenneth McMillan** (Cressner), **Robert Hays** ([Johnny] Norris), **Candy Clark** (Sally Ann), **James Naughton** (Hugh), **Tony Munafo** (Junk), **Court Miller** (Mr McCann), **Russell Horton** (Mr Milquetoast), **Patricia Benson** (Mrs Milquetoast), **Mary D'Arcy** (Cindy Morrison), **James Rebhorn** (Drunk Businessman), **Jack Dillon** (Janitor), **Susan Hawes** (Mrs McCann), **Shelly Burch** (Jerrilyn), **Sal Richards** (Westlake), **Jesse Doran** (Albert), **Patricia Kalember** (Marcia), **Mike Starr** (Ducky), **Charles Dutton** (Dom), **Frank Welker** (Special Vocal Effects).

On a crowded New York City sidewalk, a stray cat has a vision of a young girl who pleads to the feline for help. In 'Quitters, Inc.' the eponymous organisation guarantees that it's clients will give up smoking forever. But smoker Richard Morrison gets more than he bargained for. After observing the fate of Morrison's wife, the cat escapes from Dr Donatti's office and reaches Atlantic City, New Jersey, where it once again witnesses the image of the pleading girl. In 'The Ledge', tennis coach Johnny Norris is having an affair with the wife of professional gambler Cressner. Out of revenge, the jealous husband forces Norris to walk around the narrow ledge outside his high-rise penthouse apartment. After helping Norris turn the tables on Cressner, the cat continues its journey until it finally arrives in Wilmington, North Carolina, at the home of Amanda, the little girl in the visions. Only the faithful feline, now called 'The General', knows that a hideous troll monster is living within the walls of Amanda's room and attempting to steal the breath from the girl while she is sleeping.

Follow the newest cat-and-creature game as played through

> 'Cat's Eye is a relative rarity: a trio of stories directed by Lewis Teague, all linked by Stephen King's script and a peripatetic pussy-cat that pads photo-genically through each, stealing scenes from pedigree Equity members.'
> *The London Standard,*
> 7 November 1985

> 'A brisk black comedy shrewdly seeking the macabre humor inherent in all King fiction.'
> *Cinefantastique* vol 15 no 3, July 1985

Cat's Eye was conceived in mid-1983, during the shooting of *Firestarter* (1984). Dino De Laurentiis was so pleased with the work of that film's young star, Drew Barrymore, that he asked Stephen King to create a project especially for her. The following day, the author returned with a fifteen-page treatment of a story idea entitled 'The Cat', about a little girl menaced by a malevolent force, and the mysterious feline who turns up to protect her. Delighted with the idea, De Laurentiis asked King to combine the new idea with two other stories.

In the 1970s, British-based Milton Subotsky acquired the film rights to several Stephen King stories from the author's *Night Shift* (1978) collection, which proved to be an annuity for the American-born producer. 'Quitters, Inc.' (first published in *Night Shift*) and 'The Ledge' (from the July 1976 *Penthouse*) were two of these stories, which he subsequently sold to Dino De Laurentiis.

'My co-production credit at the end of *Cat's Eye* was a joke,' Subotsky later told Alan Jones. 'It really was the last credit you saw before the fade-out.' Despite having an agreement with De Laurentiis that he was also to be consulted about scripting, casting and editing on the film, Subotsky was never contacted. 'They violated that contract,' he revealed, 'and when I rang them, they threatened to sue me unless I withdrew the allegation.'

Budgeted at around $6 million, principal filming started on 4 June 1984, and *Cat's Eye* became the first feature to be shot entirely at De Laurentiis' newly-built North Carolina Film Corporation Film Studios in Wilmington. The start of production was held up for six hours when the Italian-born producer insisted on a priest blessing his studio before any footage could be shot.

As screenwriter, it was the first film that King decided to become actively involved with since he had teamed up with George R. Romero on *Creepshow* (1982). 'I loved what I had,' King told Tim Hewitt in *Cinefantastique*, 'and frankly, I didn't want anyone else to screw around with it.'

However, it was De Laurentiis who came up with the idea of using the vagabond cat as the connection between the three disparate stories. As King explained to Hewitt, his initial reaction was: 'The guy's got to be crazy. It's impossible.'

'Quitters, Inc.' had an ending that borrowed from Roald Dahl's classic 1953 short story 'Man from the South', while 'The Ledge' was possibly inspired by Jack Finney's tale 'Contents of the Dead Man's Pocket'.

The original final story 'The General' featured a troll monster created by Carlo Rambaldi in two months from foam latex and polyurethane over a metal framework. 'This creature has personality,' explained Rambaldi. 'He's terrible, but at the same time he is also sympathetic. What I tried to do was to contrast these ideas.' The life-size troll had a cable-activated head and twenty-seven different points of movement, controlled by six people operating twelve different levers. Other scenes were filmed utilising a little person in a costume and even a hand-puppet.

Because the troll is supposed to appear only six inches tall, two identical sets of Amanda's bedroom had to be built: a life-size version complete with normal furniture, and another eight times larger to dwarf the actor playing the hideous creature. The oversized bedroom took twenty people more than five weeks to construct, at a cost that exceeded $150,000.

Sixteen cats were trained for the film by Karl Lewis Miller, who also worked on Lewis Teague's previous King adaptation, *Cujo* (1983). 'It's a chance to go back and do things right,' the director explained to Tim Hewitt. 'The main difference is that I've had a chance to work on the material with Stephen King this time. That's been really satisfying.'

Shooting wrapped on 4 August 1984 after

nine weeks and the film was released in April 1985, grossing a miserable $8 million domestically. A prologue sequence, which explained the connection between the cat and Drew Barrymore's character, was cut without Teague's knowledge prior to release at the insistence of MGM/UA's Frank Yablans, the distributor. 'The difference between the critic cards of screenings with and without that section was that the people who saw the prologue said they understood the movie,' King explained to Gary L. Wood in *Cinefantastique*.

Although the author's proposed cameo as an animal control officer never made it to the screen, the film does feature an appearance by Cujo, the rabid Saint Bernard, plus various other King in-jokes, including the car from *Christine* (1983), James Woods watching *The Dead Zone* (1983) on television and Candy Clark reading *Pet Sematary* in bed.

Later, after his relationship with De Laurentiis had soured, King revealed to Wood that while '*Cat's Eye* was the worst, in terms of boxoffice, of the films I did with Dino. It was the best, overall, in terms of what I got out of it, other than *Dead Zone*...I felt like I was involved with the picture.' †

Above: In 'Quitters, Inc.', the intimidating Dr Donatti (Alan King, left) ensures that Richard Morrison (James Woods, centre) will give up smoking — or else!
Below: Our Girl (Drew Barrymore) and the feline protagonist.

Stephen King's Silver Bullet

He Makes Evil an Event.

USA, 1985. Director: **Daniel Attias**. Producer: **Martha Schumacher**. Screenplay: **Stephen King**. Based on the Novelette *Cycle of the Werewolf* by **Stephen King**. Associate Producer: **John M. Eckert**. Film Editor: **Daniel Loewenthal**. Music: **Jay Chattaway**. Director of Photography: **Armando Nannuzzi**. Costume Designer: **Clifford Capone**. Production Designer: **Giorgio Postiglione**. Creatures Creator: **Carlo Rambaldi**. Famous Films BV/Dino De Laurentiis/Paramount Pictures. Colour. 95 minutes. 94 minutes [in the UK].

Gary Busey (Uncle Red), **Everett McGill** (Reverend [Lester] Lowe/Werewolf), **Corey Haim** (Marty Coslaw), **Megan Follows** (Jane Coslaw), **Terry O'Quinn** (Sheriff Joe Haller), **Bill Smitrovich** (Andy Fairton), **Robin Groves** (Nan Coslaw), **Lawrence Tierney** (Owen Knopfler), **Kent Broadhurst** (Herb Kincaid), **Leon Russom** (Bob Coslaw), **Joe Wright** (Brady Kincaid), **Heather Simmons** (Tanny Sturmfuller), **James A. Baffico** (Milt Sturmfuller), **Rebecca Fleming** (Mrs Sturmfuller), **William Newman** (Virgil Cuts), **Sam Stoneburner** (Mayor O'Banion), **Lonnie Moore** (Billy McLaren), **Rick Pasotto** (Aspinall), **Cassidy Eckert** (Girl), **Wendy Walker** (Stella Randolph), **Michael Lague** (Stella's Boyfriend), **Myra Mailloux** (Stella's Mother), **William Brown** (Bobby Robertson), **Herb Harton** (Elmer Zinneman), **David Hart** (Pete Sylvester), **Graham Smith** (Porter Zinneman), **Paul Butler** (Edgar Rounds), **Crystal Field** (Maggie Andrews), **Julius LeFlore** (Smokey), **Roxanne Aalam** (Uncle Red's Girl), **Pearl Jones** (Mrs Thayer), **Ish Jones Jr** (Mr Thayer), **Steven White** (Outfielder), **Conrad McLaren** (Mac), **Tovah Feldshuh** (Voice of Older Jane), **James Gammon** (Arnie Westrum).

Every month when the moon was full, It came back - Its only fear was the ... Silver Bullet

STEPHEN KING'S *Silver Bullet*

DINO DE LAURENTIIS PRESENTS STEPHEN KING'S SILVER BULLET GARY BUSEY EVERETT McGILL COREY HAIM MUSIC BY JAY CHATTAWAY BASED ON THE NOVELETTE 'CYCLE OF THE WEREWOLF' BY STEPHEN KING SCREENPLAY BY STEPHEN KING PRODUCED BY MARTHA SCHUMACHER DIRECTED BY DANIEL ATTIAS Released by COLUMBIA-EMI-WARNER Distributors

> 'When King gets down to what he knows best — fleshcreeping suspense with a black comic edge — the results are enjoyable enough.'
> *Films and Filming*, August 1986

Each month during 1976 when the moon is full, the town of Tarker's Mills is plagued by a series of savage murders. After his friend Brady Kincaid be-comes another victim of the monstrous killer, disabled thirteen year-old Marty Coslaw investigates from the eponymous motorised wheelchair built for him by his disreputable Uncle Red. When Marty is attacked by a werewolf, he escapes the creature by firing a Fourth of July rocket into its eye. His older sister Jane searches the town for someone with a recent injury and discovers that the Reverend Lester Lowe is now wearing an eye patch. When the two siblings attempt to convince

Uncle Red that the town minister is a powerful lycanthrope preying on the locals, they put all their lives in jeopardy...

'**M**ore traditional werewolf stories almost always — knowingly or unknowingly — mimic the classic story of Narcissus,' Stephen King explained in his 1981 non-fiction study *Danse Macabre*, referring to the Greek myth about the youth who fell in love with his own reflection in a pool of water. 'In the Lon Chaney Jr version, we observe Chaney observing himself in the Ever-Popular Pool of Water as he undergoes the transformation back from monster to Larry Talbot. We see the exact same scene occur in the original TV film of *The Incredible Hulk* as the Hulk returns to his David Banner form. In Hammer's *Curse of the Werewolf*, the scene is repeated yet again, only this time it's Oliver Reed who's watching himself undergo the change.'

Following *Firestarter* (1984) and *Cat's Eye* (1985), *Silver Bullet* became the third King film in two years to be based at Dino De Laurentiis' North Carolina Film Corporation Film Studios in Wilmington, Delaware.

It was scripted by the author and based on his 1983 novella *Cycle of the Werewolf*, originally published in a limited edition and illustrated by acclaimed comic book artist Bernie Wrightson (who had previously worked on the graphic adaptation of King's *Creepshow*). The story had been conceived as a calendar project in 1979 — the book is broken into twelve sections, each devoted to a month of the year — before it grew into something more substantial.

King sent an early copy of the book to De Laurentiis and, as he later admitted to Gary L. Wood in *Cinefantastique*: 'I can remember sitting in a room with Dino De Laurentiis and saying, "Does America need another werewolf story?"' The Italian-born producer thought so, and commissioned King to write the script.

The author admitted that the screenplay allowed him to expand the story and 'to do what should have been done with it.' One of the major changes King made to his original novella was to make the wheelchair-bound Marty the plot's unifying character. Also, in an apparent homage to Harper Lee's *To Kill a Mockingbird*, the story was narrated by Marty's grown-up sister.

Chosen by De Laurentiis on the strength of his short UCLA film, *Leon's Case* (1982), the film marked the directorial début of Daniel Attias, a former assistant director on Steven Spielberg's *E.T. The Extra-Terrestrial* (1982) and *Firestarter*.

Although Attias was impressed with the script's emphasis on the characters, he had some concerns about the supernatural elements of the project which he talked with King about. 'When you're dealing with a writer as successful and as talented as King,' the director revealed to Tim Hewitt in *Cinefantastique*, 'it comes as something of a surprise to find such an open mind and a recognition that the film is necessarily a collaboration.'

Budgeted at $7 million, location shooting took place over an eight-week schedule in the small town of Burgaw, North Carolina, less than twenty miles from De Laurentiis' studio complex.

For his role as the monster, stage and screen actor Everett McGill attempted to convey the impression of a man trapped inside the body of an animal by perfecting a loping walk which combined the attributes of both human and beast.

The articulated werewolf suit worn by both McGill and stunt co-ordinator Julius LeFlore was created in just five weeks by Carlo Rambaldi, who had previously designed the deadly troll in *Cat's Eye* (1985). Operated by twelve levers, the head was capable of various human facial expressions — including the ability to smile and talk.

It took Rambaldi and his crew three attempts to come up with an acceptable design for the creature. De Laurentiis originally decided he wanted something that was part werewolf and part something else, so Rambaldi produced a pointy-eared werewolf-ape hybrid but it was rejected after De Laurentiis changed his mind. After a second design was also turned down, the production finally settled on Rambaldi's disappointing full-body suit topped with a mechanical mask constructed of flexible polyurethane over a metal framework. 'My creation is directed toward a real wolf,' Rambaldi explained to Hewitt.

The film also reputedly contained the largest gathering of werewolves ever seen on film when, during a hallucination sequence, an entire funeral congregation transforms into leaping lycanthropes. Forty gymnasts and dancers were made up as more humanoid-looking werewolves by Michael McCracken Jr, who was also responsible for the different techniques used to transform the compassionate Reverend Lowe into Rambaldi's snarling creature.

Despite Attias' claim that 'it's quite a simple matter to create the emotion of fear,' a number of sequences were re-shot when it was decided to increase the film's horror content. One of these involved a scene where the werewolf pulled a victim down through the floor by his ankles. The effect was created with the actor being lowered on a hydraulic platform through a hole in a breakaway balsawood floor. More blood was added for the reshoot.

Along with problems with the early werewolf design, the production also ran into protests from a North Carolina religious group, The Faith Christian Fellowship, who objected to the film being shot on public property. However, despite the opposition, a local church allowed its chapel to be used as a location.

Released in North America in October 1985, the film grossed a measly $5.4 million domestically. Two months later, NAL/Signet Books published an oversized paperback tie-in which included '8 pages of dramatic movie photos', the original novella and film script, plus an introduction and afterword by King written especially for that edition. †

Above: Everett McGill as the suspicious Reverend Lowe.
Below: One of Bernie Wrightson's superb full-page paintings for Cycle of the Werewolf.

'"Glory be to God, let it end", is a line screenwriters should avoid, lest it be echoed with an "Amen" by critics.'
The London Standard, 19 June 1986

MAXIMUM OVERDRIVE

Who Made Who?

USA, 1986. Writer for the Screen and Director: **Stephen King**. Producer: **Martha Schumacher**. Executive Producers: **Mel Pearl** and **Don Levin**. Music: **AC/DC**. Director of Photography: **Armando Nannuzzi**. Film Editor: **Evan Lottman**, ACE. Costume Designer: **Clifford Capone**. Production Designer: **Giorgio Postiglione**. Dino De Laurentiis Productions Inc/De Laurentiis Entertainment Group. Colour. 97 minutes.

Emilio Estevez (Bill Robinson), **Pat Hingle** (Hendershot), **Laura Harrington** (Brett), **Christopher Murney** (Camp Loman), **Holter Graham** (Deke), **Yeardley Smith** (Connie), **John Short** (Curt), **Ellen McElduff** (Wanda June), **J.C. Quinn** (Duncan), **Frankie Faison** (Hardy), **Pat Miller** (Joe), **Jack Canon** (Max), **Barry Bell** (Steve), **John Brasington** (Frank), **J. Don Ferguson** (Andy), **Leon Rippy** (Brad), **Bob Gooden** (Barry), **R. Pickett Bugg** (Rolf), **Giancarlo Esposito** (Videoplayer), **Martin Tucker** (2nd Man), **Marla Maples** (2nd Woman), **Ned Austin** (Bridgemaster), **Richard Chapman Jr** (Helper), **Bob Gunter** (Coach), **Bill Huggins** (Umpire), **Stephen King*** (Man at Cashpoint). [* Uncredited in the final print.]

When the Earth passes through the tail of a rogue comet hiding a large UFO, trucks and other machines take on a life of their own and become sentient killers. Young honeymooners Connie and Curt, along with other travellers, escape the carnage on the highway and take sanctuary in the Dixie Boy truck stop in Wilmington, North Carolina. Soon short-order cook Bill Robinson, who is on parole from the local penitentiary for robbery, and the diner's staff and customers find themselves surrounded by vengeance-seeking vehicles, led by a Green Goblin-faced 'Happy Toyz' truck. The restaurant's owner, 'Bubba' Hendershot, breaks out his collection of stolen military weapons and Robinson reluctantly agrees to refill the killer convoy with gas while leading a small group of survivors against the rampaging machines...

'I'd like to direct once,' Stephen King told *Starburst* magazine in the early 1980s, 'because I have a feeling that I could probably make a movie that would scare a lot of people *very badly*. I *think* I have the capability, but I'm not sure. I might really screw it up.' The King of Horror didn't know how prophetic he was.

The author admitted that the inspiration for his story 'Trucks', originally published in the June 1973 issue of *Cavalier* and one of King's personal favourites, was Alfred Hitchcock's film *The Birds* (1963). It was one of six stories from King's *Night Shift* (1978) collection which British-based producer Milton Subotsky had acquired the film rights to in the 1970s (and offered the author a chance to direct).

After unsuccessfully attempting to develop the story as part of an anthology movie of

'machine' stories, Subotsky eventually sold it in the mid-1980s to Dino De Laurentiis with the proviso that he would be credited as co-producer. 'They violated all the agreements of the contract and threatened to sue me,' he revealed to Alan Jones in *Cinefantastique*. 'The trouble was that the original deal included them taking a look at my own Edward and Valerie Abraham script for *The Machines*, and what ended up in *Maximum Overdrive* are ideas from the other two stories that they didn't option.' However, after King telephoned him, Subotsky conceded that any similarities in the scripts were probably coincidental. An arbitration ruling by The Writers Guild of America agreed.

During the mid-1980s, De Laurentiis had produced a string of King adaptations — *The Dead Zone* (1983), *Firestarter* (1984), *Cat's Eye* (1984) and *Silver Bullet* (1985) — and with no less than seven major films based on his books and stories released over just a three year period, Stephen King looked like he was starting to saturate the boxoffice. 'It's a thing that will play itself out in time,' the author told Paul R. Gagne in *Cinefantastique*. 'It'll pass.'

The problem was that most of these films were not successful at the boxoffice. De Laurentiis decided that the next obvious step for the millionaire author was for King to direct one of his features himself. The producer gave him that opportunity with *Maximum Overdrive*.

When King originally scripted *Maximum Overdrive*, he had no intention of directing it himself. However, while scouting truck stop locations in Wilmington with Giorgio Postiglione, the production designer convinced him that nobody else could direct the film. De Laurentiis agreed to let him try, and paid him a reported $70,000, but even King would not get final cut of his own film. 'I agreed to do *Maximum Overdrive* for Dino because win, lose, or draw — and the man can have some pretty outlandish ideas at times — he has never told me a lie,' King revealed to Joseph Treadway.

After two month's pre-production, and despite having no film school experience, King finally stepped behind the camera in July 1985 and proved that he knew as much about adapting his own work to the screen as those previous directors who had tried, and usually failed, before him. 'There've been *so* many movies made from my stuff and there've been only about four of them that have been well-reviewed,' he explained to Tim Hewitt in *Cinefantastique*.

Once again based at the North Carolina Film Corporation Film Studios in Wilmington, the $10 million production (initially simply titled *Overdrive*) shot for seven weeks over the summer. 'Perhaps if it had worked out the way we originally planned things might have been a little different,' King explained to Jo Fletcher in *Knave*. 'We planned to film from the beginning of September through to the first couple of weeks of December, but we made the picture in the summer, which was sheer insanity.'

It did not help the fledgling director that he was working with a crew which mostly spoke no English, and he spoke no Italian. Discussions which should have taken only a few minutes invariably lasted for twenty or more.

'I was surprised by how little I actually knew,' King admitted to Hewitt. Learning as he went along, King used storyboards when he needed them or relied on improvisation to get him through a scene. 'I didn't know if I could work with actors,' King admitted to Hewitt, 'but I knew I could choreograph trucks and

electric knives and stuff like that.' However, after filming was completed, the author-turned-director revealed that, in his opinion, the exact opposite was true: 'I had a lot more trouble with machines,' he revealed.

To create the illusion of the trucks driving themselves, special effects co-ordinator Steven Galich welded a rod to the gear shifts and attached a chain to the steering columns so that black-clad drivers could control their vehicles from the sleeper cab set back behind the driver's seat, out of sight of the cameras.

During the production, King's relationship with the often eccentric De Laurentiis was frequently strained. So much so, that the director took to wearing a T-shirt for the Italian producer's benefit which read:

bution company, De Laurentiis Entertainment Group (formerly Embassy Pictures). The movie quickly died at the boxoffice, and it was eventually released directly to video in the United Kingdom in 1988.

For King, it had been a crash course in film school. 'I didn't do a very good job of directing it,' he later admitted to Gary L. Wood in

Right: The driverless trucks attack.
Below: Director Stephen King in that *T-shirt.*

Che cazzo stiamo facendo qui? (which translates as 'What the dick are we doing here?'). The author also revealed he had a sense of humour when he made an uncredited cameo appearance as a customer who is called an 'asshole' by a bank machine.

'There was a long period during post production when I thought I had made a worthy successor to *Plan 9 from Outer Space*,' he recalled in *Cinefantastique*. However, there was one positive aspect King discovered about directing: 'I got to blow up a milk truck on my birthday — that was really cool!'

Heavy metal music fan King chose Australian band AC/DC to create the film's pounding score (available on the soundtrack album *Who Made Who*). 'When I sit down to write, I crank up the music real loud,' the writer told Marc Shapiro in *Fangoria*.

Originally set for release in March 1986, the film was sneak previewed in February to judge audience reactions. However, when this version was given an 'X' rating for excessive violence by the Motion Picture Association of America (MPAA), an angered King cut two gore scenes created by special effects make-up artist Dean Gates for a hard 'R' rating. 'I don't think we lost anything at all,' said the director.

Maximum Overdrive was finally released on 18 July by De Laurentiis' newly acquired distri-

Cinefantastique, claiming that he did not receive a lot of support from the De Laurentiis organisation, which was already in financial trouble.

'It was the kind of picture I'd go and see, the kind I'd pay money for,' the author told Jo Fletcher in *Knave*. He also claimed that the film's critical lambasting was an indication of its success: 'In the cities, in New York, Los Angeles, Washington, the critics crucified it. But a measure of my success in achieving what I set out to do was that one New York newspaper gave it zero stars and said, furthermore, there was a bathroom scene that was vulgar beyond description. And I thought, "Hot damn, I've succeeded!"'

After a string of costly failures, including King's directorial début and *King Kong Lives* (1986), De Laurentiis Entertainment Group posted a quarterly loss of more than $15 million the following June. The company was set a five month deadline by the banks to increase its net worth from films or to begin selling off assets. The company finally collapsed in 1988 with the departure of its founder.

When asked when he next planned to direct, King replied: 'I can't see myself doing anything like this again, at least not until my family has all grown up. I want to be around to enjoy them while I can.'

The story was remade as a television movie eleven years later under its original title, *Trucks.* ✝

Stand by Me

A New Film by Rob Reiner.

USA, 1986. Director: **Rob Reiner**. Screenplay: **Raynold Gideon** and **Bruce A. Evans**. Based Upon the Novella 'The Body' by **Stephen King**. Producers: **Andrew Scheinman**, **Bruce A. Evans** and **Raynold Gideon**. Director of Photography: **Thomas Del Ruth**. Production Design: **Dennis Washington**. Film Editor: **Robert Leighton**. Music: **Jack Nitzsche**. Casting: **Jane Jenkins**, CSA, and **Janet Hirshenson**, CSA. Columbia Pictures Industries, Inc/Act III Productions. Colour. 88 minutes.

Wil Wheaton (Gordie Lachance), **River Phoenix** (Chris Chambers), **Corey Feldman** (Teddy Duchamp), **Jerry O'Connell** (Vern Tessio), **Kiefer Sutherland** (Alec ['Ace'] Merrill), **Casey Siemaszko** (Billy Tessio), **Gary Riley** (Charlie Hogan), **Bradley Gregg** (Eyeball Chambers), **Jason Oliver** (Vince Desjardins), **Marshall Bell** (Mr Lachance), **Francis Lee McCain** (Mrs Lachance), **Bruce Kirby** (Mr Quidaciolou), **William Bronder** (Milo Pressman), **Scott Beach** (Mayor Grundy), **Richard Dreyfuss** (The Writer), **John Cusack** (Denny Lachance), **Madeleine Swift** (Waitress), **Popeye** (Chopper), **Geanette Bobst** (Mayor's Wife), **Art Burke** (Principal Wiggins), **Matt Williams** (Bob Cormier), **Andy Lindberg** (Lardass Hogan), **Dick Durock** (Bill Travis), **O.B. Babbs** (Lardass Heckler #1), **Charlie Owens** (Lardass Heckler #2), **Kenneth** and **John Hodges** (Donelley Twins), **Susan Thorpe** (Fat Lady), **Korey Scott Pollard** (Moke), **Rick Elliott** (Jack Mudgett), **Kent Lutrell** (Ray Brower), **Chance Quinn** (Gordon's Son), **Jason Naylor** (His Friend).

*S*uccessful writer Gordie Lachance looks back to the summer of 1959, when he was twelve years old. Lying to his parents, he sets out with three friends from the town of Castle Rock, Oregon, to find the body of missing teenager Ray Brower, believed to have been hit by a train. Vern Tessio is enthusiastic but overweight, Teddy Duchamp is the comedian, but bears the scars of his father's physical abuse, and the leader of the group is Chris Chambers, who only pretends to be tough. Gordie is still trying to come to terms with the accidental death of his older brother, Denny, and it is Chris who convinces him of his capability as a storyteller. Following the railroad tracks through the woods, they are attacked by Milo Pressman's vicious junkyard guard-dog Chopper, nearly run down by a locomotive on a narrow single-track bridge, are covered in leeches after wading through a stagnant swamp and confront a teenage gang led by the thuggish Ace Merrill. Eventually they find the body of the boy in the undergrowth, and the experience forces them to re-examine their relationships and grow a little closer to adulthood.

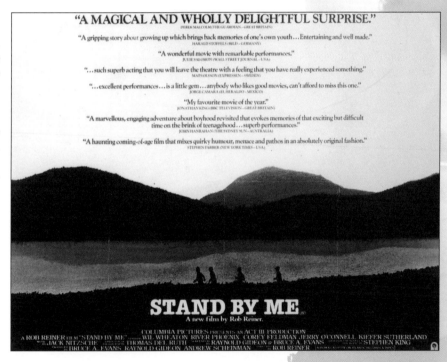

"A MAGICAL AND WHOLLY DELIGHTFUL SURPRISE."
DEREK MALCOLM (THE GUARDIAN - GREAT BRITAIN)

"A gripping story about growing up which brings back memories of one's own youth...Entertaining and well made."
HARALD STOFFELS (BILD - GERMANY)

"A wonderful movie with remarkable performances."
JULIE SALOMON (WALL STREET JOURNAL - USA)

"...such superb acting that you will leave the theatre with a feeling that you have really experienced something."
MATS OLSSON (EXPRESSEN - SWEDEN)

"...excellent performances...is a little gem...anybody who likes good movies, can't afford to miss this one."
JORGE CAMARA (EL HERALDO - MEXICO)

"My favourite movie of the year."
JONATHAN KING (BBC TELEVISION - GREAT BRITAIN)

"A marvellous, engaging adventure about boyhood revisited that evokes memories of that exciting but difficult time on the brink of teenagehood...superb performances."
JOHN HANRAHAN (THE SYDNEY SUN - AUSTRALIA)

"A haunting coming-of-age film that mixes quirky humour, menace and pathos in an absolutely original fashion."
STEPHEN FARBER (NEW YORK TIMES - USA)

STAND BY ME
A new film by Rob Reiner.

COLUMBIA PICTURES PRESENTS AN ACT III PRODUCTION
A ROB REINER FILM "STAND BY ME" STARRING WIL WHEATON RIVER PHOENIX COREY FELDMAN JERRY O'CONNELL KIEFER SUTHERLAND MUSIC JACK NITZSCHE DIRECTOR OF PHOTOGRAPHY THOMAS DEL RUTH WRITTEN BY RAYNOLD GIDEON & BRUCE A. EVANS BASED ON THE NOVELLA BY STEPHEN KING PRODUCED BY BRUCE A. EVANS RAYNOLD GIDEON ANDREW SCHEINMAN DIRECTED BY ROB REINER

*S*tephen King described *Stand by Me* to Tim Hewitt in *Cinefantastique* as: 'the finest thing that's ever been made from my work.'

Based on the author's atmospheric novella 'The Body', written directly after he completed *'Salem's Lot* (1975) and eventually published in the 1982 collection *Different Seasons*, this evocative tale of an idyllic late 1950s New England summer still managed to carry an undercurrent of simmering violence and the macabre.

The story may have had its roots in a traumatic childhood incident which the author no longer has any direct memory of, as he explained to London's *Evening Standard* newspaper. 'My mother said to me, "I think you may have seen this friend of yours run over by a train". This was a kid who was apparently a playmate who shared a backyard with me when I was about

FACT	FILE

'The Revenge of Lard Ass Hogan', the story told by Gordie Lachance to his friends in *Stand by Me*, was originally published by King in the July 1975 issue of *The Maine Review* before a revised version was incorporated into 'The Body'.

Right: *From left to right: Geordie, Chris, Vern and Teddy find the missing body in the woods.*

Below: *From left to right: Wil Wheaton, Jerry O'Connell, Corey Feldman and River Phoenix in a publicity shot.*

three. There were train tracks behind that backyard.

'One day I came back and I was white. I wouldn't talk and I went upstairs and closed my door. That boy, my mother said, was found run over on the tracks. And then she said, "They had to pick up the pieces in a basket." That is what I remembered.

'If there are things in those later stories that grew out of any childhood trauma it isn't anything I saw. I believe they grew out of my mother saying, "They had to pick him up in a basket."'

Screenwriters Raynold Gideon and Bruce A. Evans (*Starman* [1984], etc) wanted to option King's story, but could not meet the author's reported asking price of $100,000 up-front plus ten per cent of the gross profits. The duo spent the next year pitching the coming-of-age project to the major studios, who all rejected it.

'The Body' was finally optioned by Martin Shafer, who was president of production at

Embassy Communications. The film was originally going to be directed by British-born Adrian Lyne (*Fatal Attraction* [1987], etc), until he dropped out due to other commitments and was replaced by actor-turned-director Rob Reiner, who had already read the script. 'When Rob Reiner wanted to do

Stand by Me,' King revealed to *Cinefantastique*'s Michael Beeler, 'he had no money and I was advised against doing the deal, because it was a real question about whether he could ever finish production.'

Reiner, who is the son of director Carl Reiner, made his début behind the camera with the spoof rockumentary *This is Spinal Tap* (1984), which became a cult favourite. 'I'm not a big horror fan,' he told Gary L. Wood in *Cinefantastique*. 'That's what attracted me to 'The Body'. Because to me it wasn't really a horror piece. It was a character piece about four boys who go through a rite of passage.

'To me, *Stand by Me* was a very simple short story, a character study,' continued Reiner, who admitted that he had never read anything by the author. 'So I didn't have any feelings of, "Am I going to be able to make a successful Stephen King film?"'

The director worked closely with Gideon and Evans to adapt the novella. Then in June 1985, two days before filming was set to commence, Embassy Communications was sold to the Coca-Cola Company, who owned Columbia Pictures, and the project was immediately cancelled.

It was rescued by former Embassy co-owner Norman Lear, who had produced the hit television sit-com *All in the Family* (1971-78), in which Reiner played Meathead, Archie Bunker's son-in-law. Through his Act III Productions, Lear personally came up with the $8 million budget.

Principal photography began on 17 June 1985 in Oregon. The film was shot in sixty days, mostly on location in and around Eugene,

Cottage Grove and Brownsville, the latter doubling for King's Castle Rock, Maine. In August, the production moved to McCloud, California, for two weeks shooting which included the sequence on the railroad trestle.

Once filming was completed, Reiner still had problems finding a distributor. Despite showing it to every major studio, only Columbia Pictures was interested and purchased worldwide distribution rights. When preview audiences gave it the thumbs down, it was decided not to market it as a Stephen King film. 'We actually played down King's name because we didn't want people to have the idea that this was a bloody, gory horror movie,' Reiner explained to Gary Wood. 'When you say my name people think of monsters,' King told Wood, 'and it isn't a monster story.'

The title was changed from *The Body* at the last minute and Ben E. King's 1961 title song was added to the soundtrack. 'It sounded like either a sex film, a body-building film, or another Stephen King horror film,' recalled Raynold Gideon. 'Rob came up with *Stand by Me*, and it ended up being the least unpopular suggestion.'

Richard Dreyfuss' cameo as the King-like narrator (who apparently turns his word processor off without saving the story in the final scene) was added in May 1986, replacing the same scenes featuring another actor.

Initially released in just five cities on 8 August opposite King's own directorial début, *Maximum Overdrive, Stand by Me* went on to gross more than $50 million domestically, becoming a number one US boxoffice hit and the most commercially successful Stephen King adaptation since Stanley Kubrick's *The Shining* (1980).

Director Reiner captured the simplicity of the author's story perfectly, helped by a literate script and fine performances. His nostalgic recreation of a perfect childhood summer looked like a Norman Rockwell painting brought to life and was nominated for an Academy Award for Best Screenplay Adaptation.

It was a rare experience for King, who explained at the time to Jo Fletcher in *Knave*: 'Unless I play an active part in the creative development of a film, I don't feel that I have any responsibility for a book when it goes on screen. They can embarrass a writer, sort of like showing up at a party with your flies open, but these things pass, while the books remain.'

Michael Gillis' thirty-seven minute documentary, *Walking the Tracks: The Summer of Stand by Me* (2000), featured interviews with King, the director and key cast members.

In 1990, Reiner directed another superior Stephen King adaptation, *Misery.* †

Above: *'Ace' Merrill (Kiefer Sutherland, with knife) and his gang also lay claim to the body.*
Below: *Richard Dreyfuss as the adult Geordie Lachance.*

CREEPSHOW 2

The Terror Begins When the Curtain Goes Up.

USA, 1987. Director: **Michael Gornick**. Producer: **David Ball**. Screenplay: **George A. Romero**. Based on Stories by **Stephen King**. Executive Producer: **Richard P. Rubinstein**. Associate Producer: **Mitchell Galin**. Additional Music: **Rick Wakeman**. Music Composer: **Les Reed**. Film Editor: **Peter Weatherley**. Directors of Photography: **Richard Hart** and **Tom Hurwitz**. Animation Design & Supervision: **Rick Catizone**. Sound Editor: **Jim Shields**. Production Designer: **Bruce Miller**. Costume Designer: **Eileen Sieff**. Casting Director: **Leonard Finger**. Make-Up Effects Creators: **Howard Berger** and **Ed French**. New World Pictures/Laurel. Colour. 89 minutes.

Lois Chiles (Annie Lansing), **George Kennedy** (Ray Spruce), **Dorothy Lamour** (Martha Spruce), **Tom Wright** (The Hitchhiker), **Tom Savini** (The Creep), **Daniel Beer** (Randy), **Page Hannah** (Rachel), **Jeremy Green** (Laverne), **Don Harvey** (Andy Cavenaugh), **David Holbrook** (Fatso Gribbens), **Stephen King** (Truck Driver), **Holt McCallany** (Sam Whitemoon), **Frank S. Salsedo** (Ben Whitemoor), **Paul Satterfield** (Deke), **Domenick John** (Boy Billy), **Philip Doré** (Curly), **Maltby Napoleon** (Indian 1), **Tyrone Tonto** (Indian 2), **Dan Kamin** (Wood'nhead), **Deane Smith** (Mr Cavenaugh), **Shirley Sonderegger** (Mrs Cavenaugh), **David Beecroft** (Annie's Lover), **Richard Parks** (George Lansing), **Cheré Bryson** (Woman at Accident), **Joe Silver** (Voice of Creep), **Gordon Connell**, **Marc Stephan Delgatto**, **Jason Late**, **P.J. Morrison**, **Brian Noodt** and **Clark Utterback** (Animation Voices).

Right: Hollywood veterans George Kennedy and Dorothy Lamour in the 'Old Chief Wood'nhead' segment.

'Each of the episodes is ghoulish fun. But the script also displays a distinct lack of originality. The Stephen King stories are predictable and two of the three tales depend on an overworked revenge motif.'
Cinefantastique vol 17 no 5, September 1987

'*Creepshow 2* comes saddled with crude direction, a curiously moral tone and stories whose ideas do not easily cross over to a visual/literal medium...We must all be model kids and model wives, or else Stephen King's imagination will get us. Therein lies the film's hypocrisy, imparting a particularly unpleasant flavour to the whole proceeding.'
Films and Filming, November 1987

Elmville, Maine: a courier truck is delivering the latest edition of the Creepshow *horror comic to the news-stands. Thirteen year-old Billy is there to claim the first copy off the stacks, and so is his old friend The Creep. The rotting ghoul introduces his newest tales of terror...'Old Chief Wood'nhead' is a cigar-store Indian chief who comes to life to avenge the murders of kindly general store proprietors Ray and Martha Spruce by young Sam Whitemoon and his two accomplices. Back in Elmville, Billy collects a mail-order plant bulb from the post office...It is late October, and college kids Deke, Laverne, Randy and Rachel drive up to Cascade Lake for an out-of-season swimming party on 'The Raft'. One by one they are consumed by a floating black blob. In Elmville, Billy is set upon by a local gang of bullies...Cheating housewife Annie is driving home from her lover when, in her haste, she hits and kills 'The Hitch-hiker'. Leaving her victim behind, she is shocked when his crushed and bloody corpse suddenly reappears seeking revenge. Returning to Elmville, Billy is finally cornered by the bullies in his private patch of Giant Venus Flytraps...*

Stephen King's first sequel, *Creepshow 2*, is a cheap-looking follow-up, again based on three stories and a wraparound by the author, but this time scripted by the earlier film's director, George A. Romero.

Two of the stories were original, left over from the first *Creepshow* (1982), plus 'The Raft' (first written in 1968 as 'The Float' and possibly published in *Adam*), which a bored

King re-wrote from memory during the final editing of *Creepshow*. It was published in the November 1982 issue of the men's magazine *Gallery* and later reprinted in King's second collection, *Skeleton Crew* (1985).

As King explained to Adam Pirani and Alan McKenzie in *Starburst*: 'What happened with *Creepshow 2* was that Richard Rubinstein, who produced *Creepshow*, said: "Will you write the screenplay?" But George wasn't going to direct the picture, and so it made me very nervous about writing it. So we did *Creepshow 2* on the basis that we were a team, and that we were going to do it like that. What we finally decided on was that I would do a scenario, which I did, this time for three stories plus a much more complex wraparound story than the one that was on the first film, that George would do the screenplay, and then we would have a mutual consultation on directors.'

After Warner Bros, who released the first film, decided to pass on the project, two other stories Romero had scripted for the film were cut by producer Rubinstein, who recycled one of them, 'Cat from Hell', in his later anthology *Tales from the Darkside The Movie* (1990). 'Pinfall', the fifth tale about a zombie bowling team, still has yet to appear. 'I wrote it from a couple of pages that Steve had sketched out,' Romero told Gary L. Wood in *Cinefantastique*. 'It was my *total* favourite.

'It'll probably turn up in another movie somewhere,' added a rueful Romero, who left his partnership in Laurel in 1985.

Romero's former sound editor and cinematographer Michael Gornick was chosen to direct. 'I had developed as a director after having done some episodes of *Tales from the Darkside*,' Gornick explained to Edward Gross in *Fangoria*. 'They liked the idea because of my experience, and thought I would be a safe bet because I had done TV half-hours and this film would be segmented, in essence, as half-hour episodes.'

Budgeted at just $3.5 million, production on *Creepshow 2* began in September 1986 on locations in Prescott, Arizona, for the filming of 'The Raft' and exteriors on 'Old Chief Wood'nhead'. However, the shoot was beset by unseasonable weather, and the cast and crew had to brave the rain and bone-chilling water of Granite Basin Lake, near Prescott, where 'The Raft' was shot. The set for 'Old Chief Wood'nhead' was constructed at the abandoned Iron King Mine in Humboldt, Arizona. However, new owners revived the operation just after filming began, and scenes had to be filmed around the noise of the ancient machinery.

The production then moved to Bangor, Maine, for the interiors of 'Wood'nhead', the final episode of 'The Hitch-hiker' and the live-

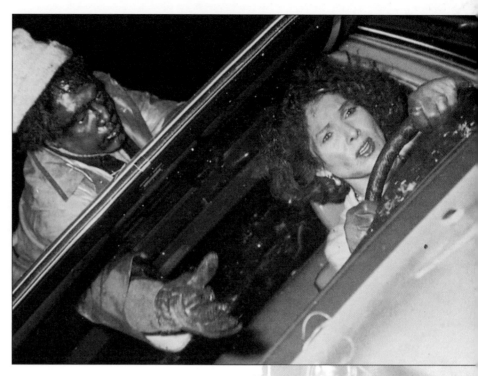

action sequences for the wraparound. It marked the first time that a King adaptation had been shot in the author's hometown and injected an estimated $750,000 into the local economy, as the unit braved icy temperatures of between 20°F and 30°F during the mostly outdoor night shoots.

Unlike *Creepshow*, King was not on set all the time, although he did often visit the location in his home state. The author also turned up briefly in the third episode as a truck driver who stops to see if he can assist at the scene of a gruesome accident.

With each section linked by childish cartoon sequences, *Creep-show 2* was released in May 1987 to a lacklustre boxoffice gross of just under $5 million. 'I think I've done very well,' said Gornick. 'A very credible job with the material at hand.'

'There wasn't enough money, there wasn't enough time,' King later admitted to Gary L. Wood, 'and still we came out with one piece that was good, 'The Hitch-hiker'. That turned out pretty well.'

In the early 1990s, there was talk of *Creepshow 3* being an animated feature by Ralph Bakshi, and later of it being a television production featuring all-new stories. It has yet to be made. †

Above: Annie Lansing (Lois Chiles) is menaced by the hitch-hiker (Tom Wright) who will not remain dead.

A Contemporary Suspense Melodrama.

USA, 1987. Director: **Alan Bridges**. Producers: **Richard Kobritz** and **William Frye**. Screenplay: **Ken Wheat** and **Jim Wheat**. Granat Entertainment/Granat Releasing Corporation. Colour.

Rick Schroder (Todd Bowden), **Nicol Williamson** (Kurt Dussander), **Richard Masur** (Edward French), **Ashley Laurence** (Becky Trask).

Californian teenager Todd Bowden discovers that former Nazi war criminal Kurt Dussander is living in secret in his home town. The sixteen year-old blackmails the elderly man into recalling the Holocaust and his role in the death camps. When the boy becomes fascinated by Dussander's descriptions of torture and degradation, the impressionable youngster is corrupted and turns to murder.

'The nature of evil is a natural preoccupation for any writer,' Stephen King revealed in *Playboy*, 'and Nazism is probably the most dramatic incarnation of that evil.' After the author had completed the first draft of his novel *The Shining* in late 1974, he spent two weeks writing the novella 'Apt Pupil' before taking a three-month hiatus.

In the summer of 1987, former vice president for production at Warner Bros Television, Richard Kobritz (who had previously produced the Stephen King adaptations *Salem's Lot* [1979] and *Christine* [1983]), teamed up with veteran Hollywood producer William Frye (Boris Karloff's television series *Thriller* [1960-62], etc) to shoot a $5.5 million independent production of King's tale of moral corruption. It was the second story to be taken from the author's 1982 collection of four novellas, *Different Seasons*.

Rejecting an earlier draft of the script written by B.J. Nelson (who later claimed that his version was 'a little too shocking to people, *too* disturbing'), Kobritz commissioned a new screenplay from Jim and Ken Wheat.

British film and television director Alan Bridges was chosen to direct and filming started on 13 July 1987. 'What attracted me

to *Apt Pupil* was that it was such a tense search through an odd relationship,' Bridges explained to Gary L. Wood in *Cinefantastique*. 'I don't really think the script measured up to the novella, to be honest.'

Although Kobritz had initially wanted James Mason (with whom he had worked on *Salem's Lot*) to play Dussander, the actor died just a week before the producer purchased the rights. After considering Alec Guinness, Paul Scofield and John Gielgud for the role, British stage and screen actor Nicol Williamson was eventually cast as the former Nazi.

Seventeen year-old Rick (formerly Ricky) Schroder, best known for his appearance as a child actor in Franco Zeffirelli's remake of *The Champ* (1979), was Kobritz's first and only choice to play the all-American teenager obsessed with the horrors of the Holocaust.

The movie had a production schedule of eleven weeks, with location filming set in and around Los Angeles. However, when the film's backers apparently ran into financial problems, and cheques to the cast and crew began to bounce, the plug was pulled with just a reported eleven days of principal photography remaining. Although an hour's worth of footage was assembled, the movie was never finished and it was eventually shelved. 'I got a rough assemblage of about three quarters of the film,' King later told Gary Wood. 'And *that* was good! That sucker was *real* good!'

Ashley Laurence, then fresh from playing the heroine in Clive Barker's *Hellraiser* (1987), revealed: 'I only got to work for about one and a half days before the plug was pulled. Obviously, I regret our version not happening. I think it would have been interesting, at least.'

Although there were attempts to revive the project in January 1988 and screening cassettes were available at that year's American Film Market in Los Angeles, they were unsuccessful. ✝

Above: Nicol Williamson as former Nazi Kurt Dussander.

FACT FILE

Apt Pupil was finally turned into a movie a decade later by director Bryan Singer.

It is the Year 2019. The Running Man is a Deadly Game No One Has Ever Survived. But...Schwarzenegger Has Yet to Play.

USA, 1987. Director: **Paul Michael Glaser**. Producers: **Tim Zinnemann** and **George Linder**. Screenplay: **Steven E. De Souza**. Based on the Novel *The Running Man* by **Richard Bachman**. Executive Producers: **Keith Barish** and **Rob Cohen**. Director of Photography: **Thomas Del Ruth**. Production Designer: **Jack T. Collis**. Editors: **Mark Roy Warner**, **Edward A. Warschilka** and **John Wright**. Music: **Harold Faltermeyer**. Costume Design: **Robert Blackman**. Casting: **Jackie Burch**. Taft Entertainment Pictures/Keith Barish Productions/Home Box Office/TriStar Pictures. Colour. 101 minutes.

Arnold Schwarzenegger (Ben Richards), **Maria Conchita Alonso** (Amber Mendez), **Yaphet Kotto** (Laughlin), **Jim Brown** (Fireball), **Jesse Ventura** (Captain Freedom), **Erland Van Lidth** (Dynamo), **Richard Dawson** (Damon Killian), **Marvin J. McIntyre** (Weiss), **Bernard Gus Rethwisch** (Buzzsaw), **Professor Toru Tanaka** ([Professor] Subzero), **Mick Fleetwood** (Mic), **Dweezil Zappa** (Stevie), **Karen Leigh Hopkins** (Brenda), **Sven Thorsen** (Sven), **Eddie Bunker** (Lenny), **Bryan Kestner** (Med Tech), **Anthony Penya** (Valdez), **Kurt Fuller** (Tony), **Kenneth Lerner** (Agent), **Dey Young** (Amy), **Roger Bumpass** (Phil Hilton), **Dona Hardy** (Mrs McArdle), **Lynne Stewart** (Edith Wiggins), **Bill Margolin** (Leon), **Joe Leahy*** (Narrator), **Anthony Brubaker** (Soldier #1), **Joel Kramer** (Soldier #2), **Billy Lucas** (Soldier #3), **George P. Wilbur** (Lieutenant Saunders), **Tom Rosales Jr** (Chico), **Sandra Holt** (Suzie Checkpoint), **Daniel Celario** (Barrio Foreman #1), **Mario Celario** (Barrio Foreman #2), **Sidney Chankin** (Custodian), **Kim Pawlik** (Newscaster), **Roger Kern** (Travel Pass Guard), **Barbara Lux** (Elderly Lady), **Franco Columbu** (911 Security Officer #2), **Lin Shaye** (Propaganda Officer), **Boyd R. Kestner** (Yuppie Yeller), **Wayne Grace** (911 Security Officer #1), **Charlie Phillips** (Teen-Age Punk), **Greg Lewis** (Manager Locker Room), **John William James** (Barrio Bettor), **Jon Cutler** (Underground Tech). [* Uncredited in the final print.]

The year is 2019, twenty-two years after a massive earthquake devastated the city of Los Angeles. Ben Richards is a former police officer in a United States ruled by a totalitarian government and the media. Framed for and wrongly convicted of the mass slaughter of sixty innocent civilians, Richards escapes with fellow convicts Laughlin and Weiss. After refusing to join the underground resistance movement, Richards is recaptured along with unwilling accessory Amber Mendez and forced to participate in the eponymous television game show. Hunted by 'the Stalkers', a select group of 21st century athletic superstars who are highly-skilled assassins, Richards and Mendez must race against time through a gladiatorial death course, with survival as the only prize.

'No, that's not me,' Stephen King emphatically told Pat Cadigan, Marty Ketchum and Arnie Fenner in *Shayol* magazine in 1982. 'I know who Dick Bachman is though...there are a *lot* of people who think I'm Dick Bachman. I went to school with Dicky Bachman and that isn't his real name. He lives in New Hampshire and *that* boy is crazy! That boy is absolutely crazy.'

Of course, the author was lying. Eventually a Washington bookseller checked in the Library of Congress and discovered that the first 'Richard Bachman' book had been inadvertently copyrighted under King's name.

'Stephen King's novel was much different and far better science fiction and has largely been thrown out.'
Cinefantastique vol 18 no 2/3, March 1988

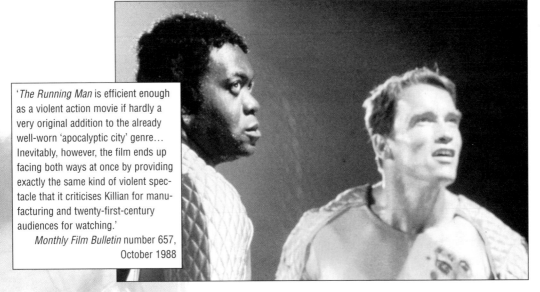

Above: *Laughlin (Yaphet Kotto) and Ben Richards (Arnold Schwarzenegger, right) run to survive.*

Between 1977 and 1984 King published five novels under the 'Bachman' alias: *Rage* (1977), *The Long Walk* (1979), *Roadwork* (1981), *The Running Man* (1982) and *Thinner* (1984). 'I think I did it to turn the heat down a little bit,' explained the author, 'to do something as someone other than Stephen King. I think that all novelists are inveterate role players and it was fun to be someone else for a while — in this case, Richard Bachman.'

George Linder was the owner of Quadra Medical Corporation, the largest supplier of lightweight wheelchairs in the United States, when he found a copy of *The Running Man* in a bookstore: 'I contacted the author's agent and was a bit taken aback to learn that he was asking a comparatively great deal of money for the option on a book which had less than 100,000 copies in print. I mean, who had ever heard of Richard Bachman?' Eventually Linder secured the non-negotiable option for $20,000, only to discover a couple of years later that Bachman was actually King. 'I felt like I'd found a Rembrandt in K-mart!' he later told Gary L. Wood in *Cinefantastique*.

Linder took the project to Rob Cohen and Keith Barish, who were then setting up a slate of ten big-budget genre pictures through Taft/Barish. 'I bought it with the understanding that we would use King's name on the advertising,' Cohen explained to Alan Jones.

Basically a reworking of such other post-holocaust movies as *Rollerball* (1975), *Logan's Run* (1976) and *The Prize of Peril* (1982), *The Running Man* began filming in 1985 in Canada, with John Veitch and George Linder producing and Christopher Reeve playing Ben Richards. Greek-born George Pan Cosmatos (*Rambo First Blood II* [1984], etc) was the director. 'It was the worst experience I've ever had in the busi-

ness,' Cohen revealed to Jones. 'Cosmatos was the least talented, least co-operative, and the most horrible person I've ever had dealings with. We fired him after spending $700,000 on the picture.' When the budget mushroomed from $11 million to $18.6 million, Cohen and Barish terminated the production and took a chance on starting it all over again.

After considering Ferdinand Fairfax as director, the producers eventually decided on former cinematographer Andrew Davis. For their new star, they chose body-building champion-turned-action man Arnold Schwarzenegger.

Cohen and Barish had rejected a script which Linder had already written with some friends in the movie business, and instead they hired Steven E. De Souza, whose credits already included the action films *48 Hours* (1982) and *Commando* (1985).

Filming began in September 1986 at the Kaiser Steel Mill in Fontana, California, with the first three days shooting devoted to the film's opening prison sequence. However, the new production soon ran into its own problems when the producers replaced Davis after just two weeks with actor-turned-director Paul Michael Glaser (*Starsky & Hutch* [1975-79], etc).

Glaser, who only had two days of pre-production before he started shooting, managed to make a number of changes to the production and modify the script's action scenes into the available schedule and budget. Despite maintaining the troubled production's sixty-one day schedule, Glaser still brought the film in $17 million over the original $10 million budget due to technical difficulties.

'Directing is basically problem solving,' the director revealed to Dan Scapperotti in *Cinefantastique*. 'When you come into something in the middle like I did, your problem solving goes up about 300%.'

Distributer TriStar reluctantly pushed back the planned summer opening to November 1987 when Schwarzenegger contractually prevented the film from competing against his other sci-fi blockbuster of the year, *Predator*. The film grossed a disappointing $16 million in the North American market.

'It was totally out of my hands,' King later told Gary Wood in *Cinefantastique*. 'I didn't have anything to do with making it...It doesn't have much in common with the novel at all, except the title.' †

A Return to Salem's Lot

A Film by Larry Cohen.

USA, 1987. Director: **Larry Cohen**. Producer: **Paul Kurta**. Screenplay: **Larry Cohen** and **James Dixon**. Story: **Larry Cohen**. Based on Characters Created by **Stephen King**. Executive Producer: **Larry Cohen**. Director of Photography: **Daniel Pearl**. Music: **Michael Minard**. Editor: **Armond Lebowitz**. Associate Producers: **Barry Shils** and **Janelle Cohen**. Warner Bros/Larco. Colour. 96 minutes.

Michael Moriarty (Joe Weber), **Samuel Fuller** (Van Meer), **Andrew Duggan** (Judge Axel), **Ricky Addison Reed** (Jeremy [Weber]), **June Havoc** (Aunt Clara [Hooper]), **Evelyn Keyes** (Mrs Axel), **Tara Reid** (Amanda), **James Dixon** (Rains), **Jill Gatsby** (Sherry), **Ronee Blakley** (Sally [Weber]), **David Holbrook** (Deputy), **Katya Crosby** (Cathy), **Brad Rijn** (Clarence), **Georgia Janelle Webb** (Sarah), **Robert Burr** (Doctor Fenton), **Jacqueline Britton** (Mrs Fenton), **Gordon Ramsey** (Allen), **David Ardao** (Car Salesman), **Kathleen Kichta** (Vampire Woman), **Edward Shils** and **Richard Duggan** (Farmer Vampires), **Stewart G. Day** (Jeremiah), **Lynda A. Clark** (Townsperson), **Nancy Duggan** (Farm Girl), **Ron Milkie** (Townsperson), **Ted Noose** and **Jim Gillis** (Hobos), **Rick Garia** (Cameraman), **Bobby Ramsen** (Jungle Guide), **Peter Hock** (Farmer Drone).

While *filming a ritual human sacrifice in South America, anthropologist Joe Weber is called back to New York, where his ex-wife Sally insists that he take their estranged son, Jeremy, off her hands because of the boy's persistent dysfunctional behaviour. Desperate to form a new bond with his son, Weber takes Jeremy to the quiet Maine town of Salem's (formerly Jerusalem's) Lot, where they move into an old house he has inherited from his late 'Aunt' Clara. Although the town looks picture postcard perfect, the few people they meet on the streets are distant and unfriendly. After witnessing an attack on a young girl and discovering that Aunt Clara is not dead, Weber learns from the town patriarch, Judge Axel, that Salem's Lot is home to a community of vampires who fled persecution in Europe more than 300 years earlier. When the Judge offers Weber the opportunity to chronicle the vampires' gore-drenched history in a Bible, and with Jeremy gradually slipping under the influence of the undead inhabitants, the scientist finally realises that he and his son have been chosen to join the bloodsucking sect. Only with the help of aged Nazi-hunter Dr Van Meer can Weber hope to lift the terrifying curse on the town forever and save Jeremy from the powers of darkness before it is too late...*

The title gives it away: this is *a* return, not *the* return to Salem's Lot. About the only thing that Larry Cohen's low-budget sequel has in common with Stephen King's novel and the superior 1979 television mini-series is the name of the vampire-haunted New England town. 'Creating sequels to hit pictures for the video market is a good idea,' Cohen explained to Steve Swires in *Fangoria*.

Born in New York in 1938, Cohen's idiosyn-cratic film career as a writer and director has encompassed such titles as the *It's Alive* trilogy (1973, 1978 and 1986), *God Told Me To* (aka *Demon*, 1977), *The Stuff* (1985), *Q — The Winged Serpent* (1982) and *Wicked Stepmother* (1989), and he was also the creator of *The Invaders* (1966-67) television series.

He had been one of several writers initially brought in to develop a script for the original mini-series, and even though producer Richard Kobritz had described his work as 'really *lousy*' and Cohen had lost his challenge to Paul Monash's sole screenplay credit in a Writer's Guild arbitration, he was given the title for this name-only

Left: Pregnant vampire Cathy (Katya Crosby) is splashed with holy water

'While the depiction of a vampire life style is effective and interesting, Cohen still has trouble with plot and pacing. Too many transitions give the impression that scenes have been missed out, and the characters' viewpoints change to suit the plot.'
Monthly Film Bulletin number 668, September 1989

FACT FILE

Currently hot in Hollywood with films like *Josie and the Pussycats* (2001), *American Pie* (1999) and *Urban Legend* (1998), actress Tara Reid made her movie début as a twelve year-old in *A Return to Salem's Lot*, in which she played an undead seductress.

Above right: *Judge Axel (Andrew Duggan) is impaled on the Stars and Stripes.*

Right: *Veteran director Samuel Fuller as fearless vampire killer Van Meer.*

sequel in a two picture deal with Warner Bros after plans for a weekly *Salem's Lot* television series were dropped by the studio.

'I wasn't a particular fan of the first picture, but I liked the book,' Cohen explained in *Psychotronic* magazine. 'They said they'd give me the property if I'd make a sequel...no particular restrictions or guidelines. I wrote an original screenplay using the idea of vampires in New England.'

According to an interview with Paul Taylor in *Monthly Film Bulletin*, Cohen revealed that King was paid '$100,000 for the use of the title, but no input.'

Instead of basing his script on the old legends, Cohen decided to create his own. He came up with the idea of a community of vampires which had emigrated to America to escape persecution. 'They came to a new world looking for religious freedom, in their own way' he revealed.

Filmed in Vermont and New York over five weeks during the summer of 1986, Cohen cast his regular leading man Michael Moriarty as the anthropologist hero who defeats the Norman Rockwell-like community of the undead. 'Michael Moriarty is a man you can toss things to,' Cohen told Kim Newman in *Shock Xpress* magazine. 'You can throw him a watermelon and he'll work it into the act. Then you throw him a meatcleaver. He creates a whole eccentric piece out of it.'

Another Cohen favourite, character actor Andrew Duggan, appeared in one of his final roles as the vampires' creepy leader, and veteran Hollywood leading ladies June Havoc and Evelyn Keyes turned up as members of the bloodsucking community.

'I like to work with old actors that I saw when I was a kid,' Cohen explained to Newman. 'I get a kick out of having them work with me.'

Samuel Fuller, the maverick director of such films as *Underworld U.S.A.* (1961), *Shock Corridor* (1963) and *The Naked Kiss* (1964), played the testy Nazi-hunter. 'I think he thought I was going to write a cameo for him,' explained Cohen, who owned the house once lived in by Fuller and used it as a location while making *A Return to Salem's Lot.* 'Little did he know he was going to be on screen for forty-five minutes.'

Released directly to video in the United States in July 1988, the film was all but ignored by critics. It was eventually given a belated video release in the United Kingdom in 1989, but

Cohen's uneven narrative, the cheap-looking special effects and the variable performances effectively doomed this quickie follow-up.

'Hooper's film was humourless,' Cohen told *Fangoria*'s Steve Swires. 'My movie has loads of laughs. If anything, it's an original, rather than a sequel.' †

Pet Sematary

Sometimes Dead is Better.

USA, 1989. Director: **Mary Lambert**. Producer: **Richard P. Rubinstein**. Screenplay: **Stephen King**. Based Upon the Novel by **Stephen King**.
Executive Producer: **Tim Zinnemann**. Co-Producer: **Mitchell Galin**. Director of Photography: **Peter Stein**. Production Designer: **Michael Z. Hanan**.
Editors: **Michael Hill** and **Daniel Hanley**. Costume Designer: **M. Stewart**. Music: **Elliot Goldenthal**. Associate Producer: **Ralph S. Singleton**.
Casting: **Fern Champion** and **Pamela Basker**, CSA. Paramount Pictures Corporation. Colour. 102 minutes.

Dale Midkiff (Louis Creed), **Fred Gwynne** (Jud Crandall), **Denise Crosby** (Rachel Creed), **Brad Greenquist** (Victor Pascow), **Michael Lombard** (Irwin Goldman), **Miko Hughes** (Gage Creed), **Blaze Berdahl** (Ellie Creed), **Susan Blommaert** (Missy Dandridge), **Mara Clark** (Marcy Charlton), **Kavi Raz** (Steve Masterton), **Mary Louise Wilson** (Dory Goldman), **Andrew Hubatsek** (Zelda), **Liz Davies** (Girl at Infirmary), **Kara Dalke** (Candystriper), **Matthew August Ferrell** (Jud as a Child), **Lisa Stathoplos** (Jud's Mother), **Stephen King** (Minister), **Elizabeth Ureneck** (Rachel as a Child), **Chuck Courtney** (Bill Baterman), **Peter Stader** (Timmy Baterman), **Richard Collier** (Young Jud), **Chuck Shaw** (Cop), **Dorothy McCabe** (Seatmate #1), **Mary R. Hughes** (Seatmate #2), **Eleanor Grace Courtemanche** (Logan Gate Agent), **Donnie Greene** (Orinco Driver), **Lila Duffy** (Budget Clerk), **John David Moore** (Hitchhike Driver), **Beau Berdahl** (Ellie Creed II).

Dr Louis Creed and his family move from Chicago to a new home in rural Ludlow, Maine, situated next to a dangerously busy main road. They are soon befriended by their nearest neighbour, Jud Crandall, who warns them to keep away from the highway. He confides to Creed that many local pets have been killed on the road and are buried in a cemetery created by the local youngsters in the backwoods. While the doctor is getting used to his new job at the local college, student Victor Pascow is knocked down by a truck and killed. But he returns from the dead to warn Louis about what lies beyond the children's Pet Sematary. When the family's beloved pet cat Church is killed by a passing truck, Crandall leads Creed to a Native American Micmac burial ground deeper in the woods, where he buries the flattened feline in the stony soil. The following day, the cat returns home — magically restored to life but somehow...different. Later, when Creed's infant son Gage is killed on the same stretch of road, the distraught father exhumes the boy's crushed corpse and insists on re-burying the body in the ancient graveyard, despite Crandall and Pascow's dire warnings. Although what returns looks like Gage, the malevolent soul inhabiting the body is no longer that of an innocent little child...

I n 1980, describing *Pet Sematary* to Abe Peck in *Rolling Stone*, Stephen King said: 'It's put away. I have no plans to publish it in the near future. It's too horrible. It's worse than *The Shining* or any of the other things. It's too horrible.'

Set in the town of Ludlow, also the location for much of King's 1989 novel *The Dark Half*, the author revealed that '*Pet Sematary* arose from my daughter's grief when her beloved cat, Smucky, was run over on the highway near our house.' The first draft was completed in May 1979, while King was writer-in-residence at his *alma mater*, the University of Maine. His rented house in nearby Orrington bordered the local truck route.

'This is the first screenplay that Stephen King has adapted from one of his own novels, and while it is a generally competent effort, there are some absolute howlers in the dialogue...There is also a taut *Halloween*-style ending that almost justifies the preceding hour-and-a-half. But ultimately there are still too many unanswered questions.'
Films and Filming, November 1989

Above: Jud Crandall (Fred Gwynne) warns the Creed family about the supernatural cemetery.
Previous page: Miko Hughes as the homicidal Gage Creed.

'Thanks to the excellent script penned by Stephen King himself, this long-awaited film rendition of his scariest novel to date also proves to be the most faithful adaptation yet.'
Cinefantastique vol 19 no 5, July 1989

'In *Pet Sematary* there is a little boy who runs into a road and a truck runs him over,' King told London's *Evening Standard* newspaper. 'At that time my little boy had run into a road and a truck was coming. I caught him by one leg and yanked him down and saved his life — which is what God made parents for, to save their kids' lives. When I wrote about that, I did have the feeling of being on a psychiatrist's couch articulating some traumatic possibility.'

However, the author considered the book too bleak for him to continue working on it and put it away until 1982, when he rewrote the manuscript and allowed Doubleday & Co to publish it the following November to resolve a dispute over royalties. Doubleday backed a first hardcover printing of 350,000 copies with a $200,000 advertising and promotional campaign.

Laurel's Richard P. Rubinstein acquired the film rights to the novel two years after it had sold an incredible 750,000 copies in hardcover (double the sales King had managed before). After turning down a $1 million offer, King sold the film rights to Rubinstein for just $1,000 up front. However, the deal was done only after the author

received certain commitments from the producer. 'I promised Steve that I would make the picture in Maine,' Rubinstein explained to John Gilbert in *Fear* magazine. 'I also promised Steve that I would look for the financing for the movie and try to find someone who agreed with me that his screenplay ought to be shot with no changes.'

A variation on W.W. Jacobs' classic 1902 short story 'The Monkey's Paw' (which is mentioned in the book), *Pet Sematary* was King's first produced screenplay based on one of his own books.

George A. Romero was originally announced to direct in 1986, and he had already prepared effects storyboards and was ready to begin shooting when a deal structured by Laurel fell through at the last minute.

Unwilling to give up creative control, Rubinstein talked with various distributors, including Universal and United Artists, for four years before coming to an agreement with Paramount (who had previously turned the project down twice). Most of the companies he had spoken to were concerned about the movie's content, particularly the role of young Gage Creed. 'There were a lot of people over the history of this project that wanted me and Steve to make the child older,' explained Rubinstein. 'For us, the fact that this child was meant to be so young was, in fact, what increased the terror and the impact.'

'I was just finishing *Monkey Shines* (1988) when Richard [Rubinstein] got the deal to produce it,' Romero explained to David Kuehls in *Fangoria* magazine. 'He had a fixed time schedule in which to shoot, and I just couldn't make it in time. That was a big disappointment...I really wanted to do that.'

With Romero now not available and the start of shooting unable to be postponed, Rubinstein promised King that he would find a director who would be enthusiastic about the project.

Arkansas-born Mary Lambert was best known as the director of several Madonna music videos, stretching back to the singer's first, 'Like a Virgin'. Her experimental thriller *Siesta* (1987), starring Ellen Barkin, Isabella Rossellini and Jodie Foster, had hardly been noticed upon release, but had impressed Rubinstein and King. 'I thought that Mary's sensibilities were offbeat enough and perverse enough,' explained Rubinstein. 'We looked at Mary's music videos and took an educated guess that Steve and Mary would get along.'

'When I originally was approached about directing this movie,' Lambert explained to Frederick C. Szebin in *Cinefantastique*, 'they told me they wanted someone who could bring a little more to it than just beautiful babysitters getting killed with regularity.'

The $10 million production, Laurel's largest budget up to that time, was filmed on location in Ellsworth, Maine, over a sixty-day period from August to October 1986. King had insisted that it be shot in his home state to help boost the local economy, which benefited from an estimated $1.5 million of the film's budget. It also meant that he could be around to give any advice that might be needed and, with filming taking place less than an hour from his Bangor home, King made one of his cameo appearances as the town minister at Missy's funeral. 'He did not spend every day on the set,' Rubinstein told John Gilbert in *Fear*, 'he did not spend every minute talking to Mary, but once or twice a week he would come round and certainly give everybody an emotional boost.'

For the scenes involving the murderous scalpel-wielding Gage, special make-up effects artist David Anderson designed and created a fully-articulated puppet (dubbed the 'Gage-thing' by the crew) which required seven operators. Lambert's concept of the revived little boy was as a broken doll that had come back from the dead. However, her decision to refrain from showing most of the blood and gore until the very end of the film did not impress the Motion Picture Association of America (MPAA), who insisted on cutting most of the footage of the puppet Gage during the climatic sequence before it would grant the film an 'R' rating.

The film was originally scheduled for release by Paramount on 10 February, but that date was pushed back to 21 April when the stu-

dio ordered extra post-production work. When test screenings of two alternative endings were not well received by preview audiences, Lambert was told to make the film's final scene more graphic. After shots of a three inch pincered bug emerging from Rachel Creed's ear were deemed too extreme for audiences to handle, the film now ends with a slimy kiss between Louis and his ravaged, reanimated wife.

'*Pet Sematary* is about a love of a father for his child that is obsessive to the point of breaking certain taboos, passing certain boundaries that shouldn't be passed,' Lambert explained to Frederick Szebin. 'I think I brought a sense of mystery and mysticism to the story that they were looking for,' continued the director. 'There are certain aspects of this story that take it beyond just another horror movie.'

'I thought it was really good,' said King.

Actress Denise Crosby credited the author for the film's success: 'I think the fact that he wrote the script made a big difference,' she told Gary Wood. 'He can really tell a story. That's his genius.' Audiences agreed, and the film took more than $16 million in its first week at the North American boxoffice, eventually achieving a domestic gross of $57 million. An unnecessary sequel, again directed by Lambert, followed three years later.

When George Romero was asked some years later by *Cinefantastique*'s Gary L. Wood what he would have done differently, he replied: 'I would have done it *better*.' †

Above: Louis Creed (Dale Midkiff, left) receives advice from dead student Victor Pascow (Brad Greenquist).

> 'The viewer is made to feel personal grief with some realism, and that's something which most horror film-makers have never handled or ever been willing to handle.'
> *Fear* no 11, November 1989

Tales from the Darkside
The Movie

Four Ghoulish Fables in One Horrific Masterpiece.

USA, 1990. Director: **John Harrison**. Producers: **Richard P. Rubinstein** and **Mitchell Galin**. 'Lot 249' Screenplay: **Michael McDowell**, 'Cat from Hell' Screenplay: **George A. Romero**, 'Lover's Vow' Writer: **Michael McDowell**. 'Lot 249' Inspired by the Story by **Sir Arthur Conan Doyle**, 'Cat from Hell' Based on a Story by **Stephen King**. Co-Producer: **David R. Kappes**. Director of Photography: **Rob Draper**. Production Designer: **Ruth Ammon**. Editor: **Harry B. Miller III**. Special Make-Up Effects: **KNB EFX Group**. Make-Up Effects Consultant: **Dick Smith**. Casting: **Julie Mossberg** and **Brian Chavanne**. Laurel Darkside Movie, Inc/Paramount Pictures. Colour. 93 minutes.

Deborah Harry (Betty), **Christian Slater** (Andy Smith), **David Johansen** (Halston), **William Hickey** (Drogan), **James Remar** (Preston), **Rae Dawn Chong** (Carola), **Robert Klein** (Wyatt), **Matthew Lawrence** (Timmy), **Robert Sedgwick** (Lee), **Steve Buscemi** ([Edward] Bellingham), **Julianne Moore** (Susan [Smith]), **David Forrester** (Priest), **Donald Van Horn** (Moving Man), **Michael Deak** (Mummy), **George Guidall** (Museum Director), **Kathleen Chalfant** (Dean), **Ralph Marrero** (Cabbie ['Lot 249']), **Paul Greeno** (Cabbie ['Cat from Hell']), **Alice Drummond** (Carolyn), **Delores Sutton** (Amanda), **Mark Margolis** ([Dick] Gage), **Ashton Wise** (Jer), **Philip Lenkowsky** (Maddox), **Joe Dabenigno** (Cop #1), **Larry Silvestri** (Cop #2), **Donna Davidge** (Gallery Patron), **Nicole Leach** (Margaret), **Daniel Harrison** (John), **Joel Valentine** (Special Gargoyle Voice).

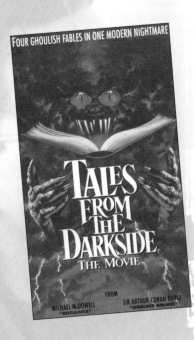

In 'The Wraparound Story', a young boy, Timmy, is captured by suburban witch Betty and tells her three scary stories from the eponymous book to delay her from cooking him. In 'Lot 249', impoverished college student Edward Bellingham uses a 3,000 year-old mummy to gain revenge for being framed for stealing. Crippled pharmaceuticals tycoon Drogan hires professional hitman Halston to kill a black cat which is seeking revenge for medical experiments carried out on its fellow felines in 'Cat from Hell'. And a winged gargoyle allows struggling artist Preston to survive if he can keep a secret in 'Lover's Vow'. In the end, Betty runs out of patience, but it is she who ends up in the oven...

'The film brings moviegoers the stories that, frankly, we couldn't make for television,' producer Richard P. Rubinstein told Philip Nutman in *Fear* magazine.

It took four years for Laurel to develop its low budget television series *Tales from the Darkside* (1983-88) into a spin-off movie. Following the boxoffice success of *Pet Sematary* (1989), Paramount gave the producer $3 million to shoot the anthology movie over a forty-day schedule in a former school house in Yonkers, New York, in August 1989.

Continued Rubinstein: 'In the course of exploring a great deal of exciting material over a period of many years, we came across stories that, for various reasons — relating to the scope, subject matter, or the intricate effects required — were better suited to the big screen.'

However, that was not exactly true. As George A. Romero revealed to David Kuehls in *Fangoria*, his script based on Stephen King's story 'The Cat from Hell' (originally published in the June 1977 issue of *Cavalier*) was initially written for *Creepshow 2* (1987): 'That screenplay contained five segments, like the original *Creepshow* (1982),' Romero explained. 'They were all based on stories written by Steve, two of which were already published; the others were sketches, ideas...When Richard [Rubinstein] made *Creepshow 2*, he only used three of the stories. Then he took one of the two that were left and put it in *Darkside*, and was able to use both Steve's and my name.'

Although he was no longer actively involved with Laurel, Romero was initially unaware that his script was being used and claimed he didn't see any profit from the film because the company already owned the rights to his work.

Screenwriter and novelist Michael McDowell, who had previously adapted King's story 'The Word Processor of the Gods' for a 1985 episode of *Tales from the Darkside*, scripted the classic short story 'Lot 249' by Sir Arthur Conan Doyle (which replaced a previously-announced tale by Manly Wade Wellman). McDowell also added the original story 'Lover's Vow' (an uncredited reworking of Lafcadio Hearn's story 'Snow Woman' from *Kwaidan* [1963]), while his linking wraparound tale was a modern retelling of the 'Hansel and Gretel' fairy tale.

Romero's Pittsburgh friend John Harrison

FACT FILE

Julianne Moore, who was paid a reported $3 million to co-star in *Hannibal* (2001), made her screen début in *Tales from the Darkside The Movie* as Christian Slater's unscrupulous sister, who returns from the grave as a zombie.

had already written and directed eight episodes from the first four seasons of *Tales from the Darkside* when he was chosen to make his feature début at the helm of the movie version. 'I wanted to make a rollercoaster ride of a film,' he told Nutman in *Fear*, 'but one that doesn't sacrifice character to plot.'

Singer-turned-actress Deborah Harry of New Wave band Blondie was cast as the Bronxville witch intent on roasting her young prisoner. 'Debbie came through like a champ and gave much more to her role than I ever anticipated,' Harrison revealed to Alan Jones in *Cinefantastique*.

David Johansen, the former lead singer with 1970s glam rock band The New York Dolls, starred with creepy character actor William Hickey in the King story, for which Harrison eliminated as many cat shots as possible by utilising a prism for a cat's-eye view of the action which he dubbed 'Cat Cam'.

Rae Dawn Chong and James Remar portrayed the stone-crossed lovers in the original gargoyle episode, and the principal cast was rounded out by then-twenty year-old Christian Slater as the student whose friends are killed by a mummified Ancient Egyptian prince. The young actor had been directed six years earlier by Harrison in an episode of *Darkside*. 'I've always wanted to make a special effects movie,' Slater told Alan Jones, 'and the Mummy is the best co-star I've ever had. He doesn't talk back!'

'We aren't banging out this show or just giving an audience a rollercoaster ride with gore,'

Harrison explained to Jones. 'We are trying to get them in the mood and tell involving stories.'

As with the television series, veteran make-up artist Dick Smith (*The Exorcist* [1974], etc) was a consultant for all the episodes.

'I don't think the movie will appeal just to people who are into effects kinds of things,' Harrison told David Everitt in *Fangoria*. 'I think it'll have a broader audience.'

'The special visual effects and make-up effects are meant to embellish the story,' explained Rubinstein. 'Too many movies concentrate on that angle and lose the audience because the characters are weak.

'*Pet Sematary* was a success because we didn't dwell on the effects side at the expense of the performances, and I think *Tales from the Darkside The Movie* will succeed for that reason.'

The film opened in May 1990 and grossed more than $16 million domestically, but its release was delayed for a couple of years in the United Kingdom. 'It's a great showcase for my feature début,' Harrison explained to Jones in *Cinefantastique*, 'as each story has been done in a different style.' However, despite the film's success, talk of a *Tales from the Darkside 2* came to nothing. ✝

Above: KNB EFX's gargoyle from 'Lover's Vow'.
Below: Deborah Harry's witch listens to a scary story told by her dinner (Matthew Lawrence).

'Nothing about *Tales from the Darkside* is likely to give anyone much of a scare. But thanks to casting that is savvier than the horror norm, and to direction by John Harrison that is workmanlike and sometimes even witty, at least it's fun.'
The New York Times, June 1990

GRAVEYARD SHIFT
(AKA STEPHEN KING'S GRAVEYARD SHIFT)

It's a Living. But Not for Long.

USA, 1990. Producer and Director: **Ralph S. Singleton**. Producer: **William J. Dunn**. Screenplay: **John Esposito**. Based on the Short Story 'Graveyard Shift' by **Stephen King**. Executive Producers: **Bonnie Sugar** and **Larry Sugar**. Director of Photography: **Peter Stein**. Production Designer: **Gary Wissner**. Editors: **Jim Gross** and **Randy Jon Morgan**. Costume Designer: **Sarah Lemire**. Music: **Anthony Marinelli** and **Brian Banks**. Associate Producers: **Joan V. Singleton** and **Anthony Labonte**. Casting: **Richard Pagano**, **Sharon Bialy**, CSA, and **Mary Margiotta**. Graveyard, Inc/JVC/Sugar Entertainment/Paramount Pictures. 86 minutes.

David Andrews (John Hall), **Kelly Wolf** (Jane Wisconsky), **Stephen Macht** (Warwick), **Andrew Divoff** (Danson), **Vic Polizos** (Brogan), **Brad Dourif** (The Exterminator [Tucker Cleveland]), **Robert Alan Beuth** (Ippeston), **Ilona Margolis** (Nordello), **Jimmy Woodard** (Carmichael), **Jonathan Emerson** (Jason Reed), **Minor Rootes** (Stevenson), **Kelly L. Goodman** (Warwick's Secretary), **Susan Lowden** (Daisy May), **Joe Perham** (Mill Inspector), **Dana Packard**, **Skip Wheeler**, **Richard France**, **Anne Rooney** and **Raissa Danilova** (Millworkers), **Emmet Kane** (Exterminator's Assistant).

'R ats are nasty little buggers' opined Stephen King in *Danse Macabre*.

After leaving High School and while applying for scholarships, King got a job at Worumbo Mills and Weaving in Lisbon Falls, Maine. It was there that he heard from a fellow employee, who worked on a Fourth of July weekend clean-up crew, about huge rats living down in the mill's basement. Years later, during his final semester at college, King recalled the story — 'big as cats, goddamn, some as big as *dogs*'. The young author was also possibly inspired by Henry Kuttner's 1936 *Weird Tales* story 'The Graveyard Rats' and even Bram Stoker's classic tale 'The Burial of the Rats'.

'Graveyard Shift' originally appeared in the October 1970 issue of *Cavalier* and was reprinted in the 1978 collection *Night Shift*. 'Cavalier magazine bought the story for $200,' King recalled in *On Writing*. 'I had sold two other stories previous to this, but they had brought in a total of just $25. This was three times that, and at a single stroke. It took my breath away...I was rich.'

While making *Maximum Overdrive* (1986) in North Carolina, King was introduced to then-twenty-two year-old George Demick of Pittsburgh-based Brimstone Productions, who visited the set. King was so impressed with Demick, a friend of George R. Romero's and a film-maker who had worked as an apprentice on *Knightriders* (1981), that he sold him the rights for '$75 or something' to develop 'Graveyard Shift',

At the time, Demick already had the support of Tom Savini and John Harrison to handle the special make-up effects and music respectively, and he hired New York writer

When The Bachman Mill is reopened on the outskirts of Gates Falls, Maine, a crew of misfit night workers — including college-educated drifter John Hall and Castle Rock tomboy Jane Wisconsky — are hand-picked by bullying foreman Warwick to clean out the basement of the long-abandoned textile factory over the Fourth of July holiday. Despite the efforts of obsessed Vietnam vet exterminator Tucker Cleveland, the clean-up crew find themselves in a series of sub-basement tunnels battling a horde of deadly omnivorous rats from an adjoining cemetery. That's when the workers discover that the ravenous vermin are led by a giant mutant bat-rat monster.

'Made as an unabashed B-movie, *Graveyard Shift* has an offbeat, well-chosen cast of unfamiliar-looking actors, and they help give the film its gritty edge.'
The New York Times, October 1986

Left: Stephen Macht as Warwick, the bullying foreman of The Bachman Mill.

FACT FILE

Special vocal effects for *Graveyard Shift* were created by Frank Welker.

John Esposito to expand King's fifteen-page story into his first feature-length script.

The project was originally optioned by New World Pictures in 1986. Esposito admitted in *Fear* magazine that the short story gave him little to work with: 'I looked for a theme I wanted to comment on. It was a real American horror story, which is what King does best. I grabbed that angle and ran with it as fast as I could, because I only had a week.'

When Demick's free option expired, King subsequently sold the property for just $2,500 to fellow Maine resident William J. Dunn, a former school teacher who had done location work on *Creepshow 2* (1987) and *Pet Sematary* (1989).

Dunn, who had been instrumental in forming The Maine Film Commission with King's help, based the production in and around the author's home town of Bangor, which contributed an estimated $3 million to the local economy. Working with Esposito's already-completed script, Dunn hired Ralph S. Singleton to co-produce and make his directorial début. Singleton had received an Emmy award as producer on the popular TV series *Cagney & Lacey* (1982-88) and had also been associate producer on *Pet Sematary*.

With financial backing from Sugar Entertainment (who had successfully released the edited feature version of *Salem's Lot* [1979] into foreign markets), filming on the $10.5 million production began in June 1990 and lasted seven weeks.

Locations included the abandoned Bangor Waterworks, a local rock quarry, an old-fashioned diner and an ancient barn reputed to be one of the oldest in the state. For the central locale of The Bachman Textile Mill, location manager Laurie Dee Whitman found the Bartlett Yarns Mill in the nearby town of Harmony. Some sequences were also filmed in Hermon, Maine, where King actually wrote

'Graveyard Shift' back in the 1970s while living in a trailer and working as a high school teacher for $6,400 a year.

The author approved the script and even visited the set a number of times and looked at some footage. 'He was incredibly supportive,' recalled Esposito. 'We had breakfast before we started shooting. I met him and was star-struck, there he was — the master. He was very friendly and put me at ease. Before he left, he leaned over and said: "Wait until you see what they do to your script".'

Paramount opened the film on 26 October, in time for Halloween. After grossing just over $11 million at the domestic boxoffice, it had a brief theatrical release in the United Kingdom before going to video on 5 October 1992.

'In the course of selling things that I've written to various people, some of the things have turned out to be real coleslaw. You know?' King candidly revealed to Michael Beeler in *Cinefantastique*. '*Graveyard Shift* is not going to stand in film history.'

Singleton subsequently admitted that it had been difficult to develop King's short story into a movie: 'We had a hard time, story-wise,' he told Gregory Nicoll in *Fangoria*. 'It didn't have the fear and the scare. I had a big rubberised creature that we could never get to make the moves with an actor to make it terrifying. That hurt the film a lot.'

However, despite his disappointment, it did not stop Singleton from producing another King-inspired project, *Pet Sematary II*, just a couple of years later. ✝

'First-time director Singleton fails to exploit the potential menace afforded by the basement's darker recesses or the creature's subterranean hideout.'
Fear no 30, June 1991

The Master of Horror Unleashes Everything You Were Ever Afraid of.

USA/Canada, 1990. Director: **Tommy Lee Wallace**. Teleplay: **Lawrence D. Cohen** and **Tommy Lee Wallace**. Supervising Producer: **Matthew O'Connor**. Editors: **Robert F. Shugrue** and **David Blangsted**, ACE. Production Designer: **Douglas Higgins**. Director of Photography: **Richard Leiterman**. Music: **Richard Bellis**. Lorimar Television/The Konigsberg-Sanitsky Company/Green-Epstein Productions/Warner Bros/ABC-TV. Colour. 192 minutes.

Harry Anderson (Richie Tozier), **Dennis Christopher** (Eddie Kaspbrak), **Richard Masur** (Stanley Uris), **Annette O'Toole** (Beverly Marsh), **Tim Reid** (Mike Hanlon), **John Ritter** (Ben Hanscom), **Richard Thomas** (Bill Denbrough), **Tim Curry** (Pennywise), **Jonathan Brandis** (Young Bill), **Brandon Crane** (Young Ben), **Adam Faraizl** (Young Eddie), **Seth Green** (Young Richie), **Ben Heller** (Young Stanley), **Emily Perkins** (Young Beverly), **Marlon Taylor** (Young Mike), **Olivia Hussey** (Audra), **Michael Cole** (Henry Bowers), **Sheila Moore** (Mrs Kaspbrak), **Jarred Blancard** (Henry Bowers), **Florence Patterson** (Mrs Kersh), **Jay Brazeau** (Derry Cab Driver), **Nicola Cavendish** (Desk Clerk), **Drum Garrett** (Belch [Huggins]), **Gabe Khouth** (Patrick [Hockstetter]), **Ryan Michael** (Tom Rogan), **Charles Siegel** (Nat), **Venus Terzo** (Cyndi), **Tom Heaton** (Mr Keene), **Paul Batten** (Pharmacist), **Russell Roberts** (Greco), **Frank C. Turner** (Al Marsh), **Caitlin Hicks** (Patti Uris), **Bill Croft** (Koontz), **Tony Dakota** (Georgie Denbrough), **Steven Hilton** (Mr Denbrough), **Kim Kondrashoff** (Joey), **Noel Geer** (Bradley), **Chelan Simmons** (Laurie Anne), **Merrilyn Gann** (Mrs Winterbarger), **William B. Davis** (Mr Gedreau), **Susan Astley** (Aunt Jean), **Claire Brown** (Arlene Hanscomb), **Garry Chalk** (Coach), **Terence Kelly** (Officer Nell), **Amos Hertzman** (Chubby Kid), **Boyd Norman** (Gas Station Attendant), **Helena Yee** (Rose), **Suzie Payne** (Female Cabbie), **Donna Peerless** (Miss Douglas), **Stephen Makaj** (Ben's Father), **Scott Swanson** (Rademacher), **Megan Leitch** (Library Aide), **Deva Neil DePodesta** (Bum), **Katherine Banwell** (TV Announcer), **Douglas Newell** (Doctor).

The Master of Horror unleashes everything you were ever afraid of.

'Like King's most successful books, this is palatable, mass-market horror, skilfully done but hardly likely to extend the boundaries of the genre overmuch.'

Fear no 33, September 1991

In the small town of Derry, Maine, a series of child killings prompt local librarian Mike Hanlon to contact six old schoolfriends. Almost thirty years earlier, the seven, who were social outsiders, ostracised by other youngsters, had formed their own Loser's Club and survived a similar childhood nightmare that took the guise of a malevolent clown named Pennywise. All have done remarkably well over the years — the stuttering Bill Denbrough, who had been traumatised by the killing of his younger brother Georgie, is now a successful horror novelist married to Hollywood actress Audra; the once-overweight Ben Hanscom is an award-winning architect with an alcohol problem; poor girl Beverly Marsh is now a famous but insecure fashion designer; asthmatic Eddie Kaspbrak owns his own limousine service and is still dominated by his mother; class clown Richie Tozier has become a star television comedian who suffers from panic attacks, and the cowardly Stan Uris is a wealthy businessman who is unable to face the past. Honouring an oath, they return to Derry to confront an ancient evil that they presumed was dead. An unspeakable shape-shifting creature that feeds on the darkness lurking within them all.

'Everything that I know is in that book,' King revealed about his 1986 novel, one of his longest works at more than a thousand pages. The author admitted that his original idea for *It* came when he was, 'crossing a wooden bridge, listening to the hollow thump of my boot-heels, and thinking of 'The Three Billy Goats Gruff'.'

Initially developed as a television mini-series by ABC and Lorimar Productions, George A. Romero was set to direct. However, in an echo of his frustrating experience on *Pet Sematary* (1989), after working very closely on the script and creating numerous storyboards and notes, a scheduling conflict forced Romero to bow out. 'When I was involved it was seven hours long and Lawrence D. Cohen had done a fabulous script for that length,' Romero explained to David Kuehls in *Fangoria*. 'But then it was cut down to four, and it just didn't have the same impact then.'

Cohen, who had successfully translated *Carrie* (1976) to the screen for Brian De Palma, had never written for television before. He did a fine job paring King's blockbuster down to a coherent four-hour time-slot, during the course of which he dispensed with the book's convoluted flashbacks in favour of a more linear structure. 'He's a genius at being able to take elements that are good in a book and combine and compress them,' praised King. 'I

am a big fan of the potential of the mini-series,' Cohen explained to Gary L. Wood in *Cinefantastique*. 'It is akin to reading a novel. They allow that luxury of settling into a big chair, and watching that experience.'

However, even the author was initially sceptical that the show would ever be made. 'ABC is one of the networks that still has a fairly strong censorship code,' King explained to Wood. 'I think the first rule is that you can't put children in mortal jeopardy. And that's what *It* is about, children in mortal jeopardy.'

'Steve has an uncanny gift for writing about kids,' continued Cohen. 'He has a gift for creating what childhood and adolescence are like.'

John Carpenter protégé Tommy Lee Wallace was hired to direct, and he described Cohen's script as 'a brilliant piece of craftsmanship.'

About an ancient evil that returns every thirty years to plague a small town and kill the children, in the script this evil shape-shifting force takes on the form of Pennywise the clown (a gleefully evil performance by Tim Curry), various rotting corpses and even the shaggy lycanthrope from *I Was a Teenage Werewolf* (1957). However, it is in reality a twelve feet tall giant spider-monster (created as a full-size mechanical prop designed by Joey Orosco and Aaron Sims, and as a stop-motion miniature animated by Pete Kleinow and Gene Warren Jr

of Fantasy II).

King later described the creature as looking like 'a Delco battery'.

Filmed in Vancouver, Canada, *It* was originally screened by ABC-TV on Sunday 18 and Tuesday 20 November 1990, before being released on video the following year in the United Kingdom.

The first half of the story works best, with the children fighting the elemental evil. Using the traditional seven-act structure for a two hour TV movie, Cohen's script neatly showcased each of the seven main protagonists. However, director Wallace reportedly rewrote Cohen's second part because he thought it strayed too far from King's source novel.

'One of the things I believe I contributed in my rewrite was just packing in as much of what was memorable about the book,' Wallace told Gary Wood. However, as a result of his restructuring and the addition of extra flashback sequences, the second act was too fragmented.

'The expectations have to be tailored, to some degree, to the medium,' Wallace explained in *Cinefantastique*. 'On the other hand, I think it's a very successful telling of the story.'

'I liked *It* very much,' King told Michael Beeler in the same magazine. 'I thought they did a great job.' †

Above top: Tim Curry as the malevolent clown, Pennywise.

'The good moments, though, are choice, helped considerably by Tim Curry's lip-smacking portrayal of the horrifying Pennywise. Equally impressive are the youngsters used for the extensive childhood sequences…They perhaps best capture that special King sense of dread when threatened with everything you were ever afraid of.'
The New York Times, November 1990

MISERY

Paul Sheldon Used to Write for a Living. Now, He's Writing to Stay Alive.

USA, 1990. Director: **Rob Reiner**. Producers: **Andrew Scheinman** and **Rob Reiner**. Screenplay: **William Goldman**. Based on the Novel *Misery* by **Stephen King**. Director of Photography: **Barry Sonnenfeld**. Film Editor: **Robert Leighton**. Production Designer: **Norman Garwood**. Co-producers: **Jeffrey Stott** and **Steve Nicolaides**. Casting: **Jane Jenkins**, CSA, and **Janet Hirshenson**, CSA. Costumes: **Gloria Gresham**. Music: **Marc Shaiman**. Castle Rock Entertainment/Nelson Entertainment/Columbia Pictures. Colour. 107 minutes.

James Caan (Paul Sheldon), **Kathy Bates** (Annie Wilkes), **Frances Sternhagen** (Virginia), **Richard Farnsworth** (Buster), **Lauren Bacall** (Marcia Sindell), **Graham Jarvis** (Libby), **J.T. Walsh*** (Chief Sherman Douglas), **Jerry Potter** (Pete), **Tom Brunelle** (Anchorman), **June Christopher** (Anchorwoman), **Julie Payne** (Reporter #1), **Archie Hahn III** (Reporter #2), **Gregory Snegoff** (Reporter #3), **Wendy Bowers** (Waitress), **Misery the Pig** (Herself).
[* Uncredited in the final print.]

Following a freak auto accident during a fierce blizzard in the Colorado mountains, best-selling romantic novelist Paul Sheldon regains consciousness in the remote home of former nurse Annie Wilkes. She informs him that he has suffered serious injuries to his legs and upper body, adding that the storm has knocked down the telephone lines, but she has enough medical supplies to ease his pain until the weather clears and the road is open again. Even better, Annie turns out to be Sheldon's 'number one fan', with a complete collection of his novels about nineteenth century romantic heroine Misery Chastain and a virtual shrine dedicated to the author and his creation in her living room. However, when Annie discovers that Paul has killed off his immensely popular character in the soon-to-be-published final volume in the series, her adoration is revealed to be an insane obsession with the fantasy world of Misery. When his deranged captor forces him to burn the only manuscript of the new book because she does not approve of the profanity, and insists that he must bring Misery back to life, the physically incapacitated writer realises that his very survival depends on complying with her twisted demands until he can find a way to escape.

'This is an odd thing to say about the most successful writer in the world,' William Goldman told Nigel Floyd in *Fear* magazine, 'but I don't think King knows how good he is yet.'

Stephen King has described his 1987

novel (which was originally going to be published under the author's 'Richard Bachman' alias) as illustrating 'the powerful hold fiction can achieve over the reader.'

'What *Misery* turned out to be about was the life-saving quality of writing stories,' King revealed to Charles Leayman in *Cinefantastique*, 'how it takes you away and how it heals: both the people who do it and the people who consume it.'

Although the story has echoes of John Fowles' 1963 psychological novel *The Collector* and Don Siegel's 1971 film *The Beguiled* (based on the book by Thomas Cullinan, in which Clint Eastwood's Union soldier is preyed upon by a pair of sexually repressed Southern women who amputate his leg to prevent him from escaping), King's book was allegedly inspired by a meeting the author had with an intense young fan who asked to have his photograph taken with King and described himself as the writer's number one fan. His admirer turned out to be Mark Chapman, who subsequently shot Beatle John Lennon to death in New York City on 8 December 1980.

The author was reportedly initially reluctant to sell the novel to Hollywood because he was not particularly pleased with what had happened with many previous adaptations of his work. It was only because of actor-turned-director Rob Reiner's compassionate treatment of *Stand by Me* (1986) that the author agreed to sell the rights to Reiner's production company, Castle Rock Entertainment, with the stipulation that Reiner was on board as either producer or director. 'It was in the contract,' confirmed King.

FACT FILE

Future director Barry Sonnenfeld (*Men in Black* [1997], etc), who was mis-credited as 'Stonnenfeld' on early publicity material, not only photographed *Misery* but was also second unit director.

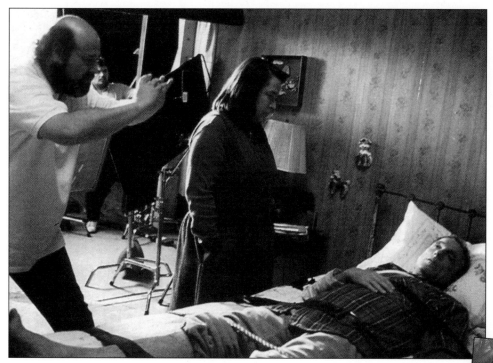

Left: Rob Reiner (left) directs Kathy Bates and James Caan, behind-the-scenes.
Below: Stephen King as Fabio in the fun frontispiece for the first American paperback printing of Misery in June 1988.

After eight other writers had worked on the script, producer Reiner asked William Goldman to consider writing the screenplay by first reading King's bestseller. 'I thought *Misery* was a terrific book, and I think Annie Wilkes is a fabulous character,' Goldman enthused. 'I was immediately transfixed with wanting to do it.' Goldman and Reiner worked together closely on the new script to make the character of Annie Wilkes more sympathetic, instead of the overbearing monster in King's novel.

Once Goldman had a version of the script everybody liked, Castle Rock approached George Roy Hill, who agreed to direct. However, the veteran director of *Butch Cassidy and the Sundance Kid* (1969) and *Slaughterhouse Five* (1972) pulled out when he read the scene where (as in King's novel) Annie graphically cuts off Sheldon's foot with a propane torch and axe. 'Of course, since it was the most important scene and the best scene, it had to stay,' Goldman recalled in his book *Which Lie Did I Tell?*

With the project about to be offered to Barry Levinson, it was Goldman's script, which found its focus in author Paul Sheldon's artistic predicament rather than his physical difficulties, that finally convinced Reiner to direct as well. 'I'm not particularly interested in horror films,' Reiner told Mark Salisbury in *Fear* magazine. 'I'm more interested in character, so I just used the elements of terror that were absolutely necessary.'

Reiner's first choices to play the role of the captive romance author (an obvious alter-ego for King himself) included such Hollywood A-list actors as William Hurt, Kevin Kline, Michael Douglas, Harrison Ford, Dustin Hoffman, Robert DeNiro, Al Pacino, Richard Dreyfuss, Gene Hackman and Robert Redford, all of whom turned it down. Then Warren Beatty expressed interest in the part. Despite having meetings with the producers, Beatty failed to commit to the project and Castle Rock eventually approached James Caan. After the producers considered Bette Midler, Tony Award-winning stage and screen actress Kathy Bates (who Goldman admitted he wrote the role for) was cast as Sheldon's psychotic fan, Annie Wilkes.

Filming took place on the $21 million thriller at the Hollywood Center Studios and on locations in northern California and Genoa, Nevada. Principal photography was completed in July 1990.

Goldman expanded the character of Buster, the wily sheriff of Silver Creek portrayed by former stunt man Richard Farnsworth, to open out the novel's housebound narrative. 'Goldman was able to take that script, which is this very inward, static situation where a woman is keeping this writer hostage, and he was able to create one new character, just one new character who's on the outside, who can move around,' King explained to Gary L. Wood in *Cinefantastique*. 'And the character is the synthesis of some of the minor characters in the book.'

The re-written, but still genuinely horrific foot 'hobbling' sequence — where Annie smashes both of Sheldon's ankles with a sledgehammer — was achieved with a pair of

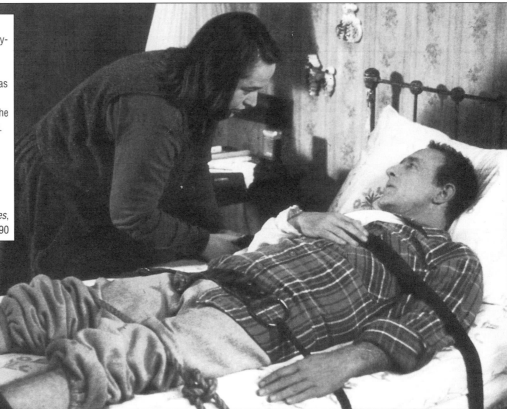

Above right: Annie Wilkes (Kathy Bates) makes sure that Paul Sheldon (James Caan) is comfortable.
Below: A Misery the Pig wordsearch competition from the promotional material.

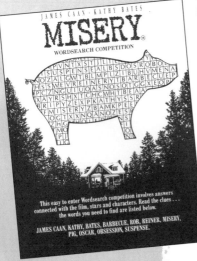

gelatin and Styrofoam legs courtesy of KNB EFX Group. 'I wasn't interested in showing bone,' explained the director. 'You see the twist and we're off it after a split second...It does become very terrifying and horrific, not so much from the graphicness but because it's happening to someone that we care about, that we've made an investment in — a real person.' The 'cheat' ending (obviously inspired by *Carrie*'s coda) reportedly had to be re-shot when preview audiences could not believe that Caan's character would be back on his feet again without a limp after the abuse he had endured eighteen months earlier.

Six months before the movie's release, Columbia Pictures bought full-page advertisements in such magazines as Rolling Stone and Premiere. Released in November 1990, the film was a critical success and grossed nearly $12 million during its first month of release, defying the predictions of those who said that horror films cannot make money during the holiday season. It went on to take more than $61 million in North America alone.

'It was a cat and mouse, psychological chess match between these two people,' said Reiner. 'That was what I was interested in.'

Bates won an Academy Award and a Golden Globe for her menacing portrayal of Annie, much to the surprise of scriptwriter Goldman, who predicted that 'She has no chance whatsoever to win' because *Misery* is a horror film.

In a bizarre case of fact echoing fiction, forty-four year-old Anne Hiltner of Trenton, New Jersey, brought a $25 million lawsuit against King in 1991, claiming that she was the model for Annie Wilkes. She also maintained that *Misery* was based on an unpublished manuscript King had stolen from her brother, James, who committed suicide in 1970. However, the author successfully contested the action, and his New York-based lawyer Arthur Greene revealed that 'Miss Hiltner is not a well woman' and had been writing to King and other authors, including Joyce Carol Oates, for years.

In April of the same year, King's wife Tabitha was alone in their home when she was confronted by a man apparently wielding a bomb. She fled to a neighbour's house across the street and called the police. Twenty-six year-old Texan Eric Keene was arrested and charged with terrorism and burglary. He claimed he was seeking revenge because the author had stolen a manuscript from one of his relatives.

'These are people with very poor self-image who are very confused about who they are and whether or not they exist,' the author explained, admitting that his own stories could possibly even feed such delusions. 'Any creative work can serve as an accelerant in the same way an arsonist uses gasoline to start a fire.' †

Sometimes They Come Back
(aka Stephen King's Sometimes They Come Back)

With *Pet Sematary* and *Misery* Stephen King Scared You to Death. Now He's Going to Scare You Back to Life.

USA, 1991. Director: **Tom McLoughlin**. Producer: **Michael S. Murphey**. Screenplay: **Lawrence Konner** and **Mark Rosenthal**. Based on a Short Story by **Stephen King**. Director of Photography: **Bryan England**. Editor: **Charles Bornstein**. Production Designer: **Philip Dean Foreman**. Costume Design: **Karen Patch**. Music: **Terry Plumeri**. Casting: **David Cohen**, CSA. Paradise Films/Dino De Laurentiis/CBS-TV/Trimark Home Video. Colour. 97 minutes.

Tim Matheson (Jim Norman), **Brooke Adams** (Sally Norman), **Robert Rusler** ([Richard] Lawson), **Chris Demetral** (Wayne Norman), **Robert Hy Gorman** (Scott Norman), **William Sanderson** (Mueller), **Nicholas Sadler** (Vinnie), **Bentley Mitchum** ([David] North), **Matt Nolan** (Billy), **Tasia Valenza** (Kate), **Chadd Nyerges** (Chip), **T. Max Graham** (Chief Pappas), **William Kuhlke** (Principal Simmons), **Duncan McLeod** (Old Officer Nell), **Nancy McLoughlin** (Dr Bernardi), **Zachary Ball** (Jimmy Norman), **Dick Solowicz** (Desk Sergeant), **Rodney McKay** (Police Officer), **Don Ruffin** (Young Mueller), **Kimball Gimmings** (Young Officer Nell).

Following a nervous breakdown, school teacher Jim Norman returns from Chicago to his home town of Stratford, Connecticut, with his wife Sally and son Scott. When he was nine years old, Jim witnessed the murder of his eleven year-old brother Wayne by a trio of local thugs in a railway tunnel. Now teaching at Harold Davis High School, Jim's favourite students are dying mysteriously and their places being taken by the spirits of the three sadistic hoodlums who were killed by a train in 1963. The terrorising trio blame him for their fiery deaths when he fled the tunnel and have returned from the grave on the anniversary of the incident seeking revenge. Now under suspicion by the police and aided by his brother's ghost, Jim discovers that only by confronting the past can he hope to rescue his family and change his future.

Above: *Jim Norman (Tim Matheson) continues to be haunted by the past.*

In *On Writing*, Stephen King revealed how his daughter Naomi needed some medicine which the family could not afford, until he discovered a cheque in the mail for $500 — the most he had received for a story up to that time — for 'Sometimes They Come Back'. It was 'a long story I hadn't believed would sell anywhere,' he recalled.

Originally published in the March 1974 issue of the men's magazine *Cavalier* and later reprinted in the *Night Shift* (1978) collection, 'Sometimes They Come Back' was the third and final story from British-based producer Milton Subotsky's proposed anthology film. Dino De Laurentiis had purchased the rights to the story but had not used it in *Cat's Eye* (1985). As a consequence, Subotsky (who died in 1991)

received a posthumous co-producer credit at the end of the film.

De Laurentiis announced his intention to film the story as early as 1984, while he was still working on *Firestarter*. However, following a string of boxoffice flops based on King's fiction, including *Cat's Eye*, *Silver Bullet* (1985) and King's own directorial début, *Maximum Overdrive* (1986), De Laurentiis' film production company went into financial crisis and eventually collapsed.

The Italian-born producer retained the rights to a few of King's stories, among them

FACT FILE

Sometimes They Come Back also includes clips from Dino De Laurentiis' *King Kong* (1976) remake on TV.

'Sometimes They Come Back'. After having the project in development for a number of years, De Laurentiis finally struck a deal with CBS entertainment president Jeff Sagansky to make the movie for television in the United States and release it overseas as a feature film.

To direct, they chose Tom McLoughlin, whose credits included the inventive *One Dark Night* (1982) and *Friday the 13th Part VI Jason Lives* (1986). 'Stephen King is our modern-day Edgar Allan Poe,' McLoughlin told Mark Dawidziak in *Cinefantastique*. 'I hold him in awe.'

Tim Matheson, a likeable actor best known for his role in *National Lampoon's Animal House* (1978), was cast as the troubled teacher who cannot escape his past. Brooke Adams, who had previously appear-ed in De Laurentiis' King adaptation *The Dead Zone* (1983), initially turned the film down after reading the script by Mark Rosenthal and Lawrence Konner (*Superman IV The Quest for Peace* [1987], etc). McLoughlin convinced her to reconsider after working on an uncredited rewrite with Tim Cring.

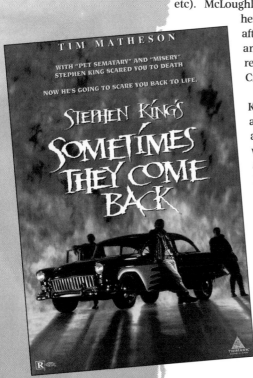

'Generally overlooked Stephen King adaptation isn't overtly bad, but it's too long and offers no real surprises…Bland rather than bad, the film shows its TV-movie origins.'
Cinefantastique vol 24 no 3/4, October 1993

Amongst the changes to King's story was the addition of a son to the Norman family, and a more upbeat ending in which Sally Norman was allowed to survive and Jim no longer had to sacrifice his fingers to raise a demon (this concept was saved for the almost unrelated sequel which followed four years later). 'There's more of a classic cathartic feel to the movie's ending,' McLoughlin explained to Dawidziak.

Filmed in the towns of Liberty and Rocheport, Missouri, Kansas City and Los Angeles over a five week schedule in November and December 1990, the make-up for the ghostly burned corpses of the bullies who return to haunt Jim Norman was created by Gabe Bartalos (*Frankenhooker* [1990], etc).

Although CBS had originally wanted the film for the February 'sweeps' period, McLoughlin was unable to deliver a rough cut in time and the production eventually aired on 7 May.

It turned out to be a surprisingly effective made-for-television horror movie, thanks to McLoughlin's atmospheric direction and a strong performance by Matheson.

'Hopefully, we've crafted a piece that will appeal to a wide audience and appease Stephen King fans,' said the director.

'You can't go that far on network television,' McLoughlin explained to Dawidziak, 'so this explores some of those fears and anxieties that take hold in your mind when you're a child.'

Extra scenes were apparently added to the April 1993 video release so that it could get an 'R' rating in the United States. †

Golden Years
(AKA Stephen King's Golden Years)

His Body Held the Secret of Time. Now Time...is Running Out!

USA, 1991. Directors: **Kenneth Fink** (Episode 1), **Allen Coulter** (Episodes 2, 4, 6), **Michael G. Gornick** (Episodes 3, 7), **Stephen Tolkin** (Episode 5). Supervising Producer: **Josef Anderson**. Producers: **Mitchell Galin** and **Peter R. McIntosh**. Created by **Stephen King**. Writers: **Stephen King** (Episodes 1-5) and **Josef Anderson** (Episodes 6-7). Story: **Stephen King** (Episodes 6-7). Executive Producers: **Richard P. Rubinstein** and **Stephen King**. Laurel-King Inc/CBS-TV/Republic Pictures. Colour. 104 minutes [pilot], 6 x 52 minutes [episodes]. 236 minutes [video].

Keith Szarabajka (Harlan [Ethan] Williams), **Felicity Huffman** (Terry Spann), **Ed Lauter** (General Louis Crewes), **R.D. Call** (Jude Andrews), **Bill Raymond** (Dr Richard Todhunter), **Frances Sternhagen** (Gina Williams), **Stephen Root** (Major Moreland), **John Rothman** (Dr Ackerman), **Tim Guinee** (Fredericks), **Mert Hatfield** (Sheriff Mayo), **Steve Ryan** (Trooper Jack), **Erik King** (Burton), **Paul Butler** (Captain Marsh), **Harriet Samson Harris** (Francie Williams), **Margo Martindale** (Waitress), **Anne Pitoniak** (Flo), **Kaiulani Lee** (Cybil), **Matt Malloy** (Redding), **Adam Redfield** (Jackson), **Jeff Williams** (Lt Vester), **Peter McRobbie** (Lt McGiver), **Sarah Melici** (Mrs Rogers), **Lili Bernard** (Harlan's Nurse), **Phil Lenkowsky** (Billy DeLois), **Graham Paul** (Rick Haverford), **J.R. Horne** (Dr Eakins), **Brad Greenquist** (Steven Dent), **Michael P. Moran** (Trucker), **Alberto Vazquez** (Janitor), **Susan King** (Dr Ackerman's Nurse), **Don Bland** (Technician), **Todd Brenner** (Man), **Tim Parati** (Attendant), **Randell Haynes** (Hawkins), **D. Garen Tolkin** (Technician No.1), **Stephen King** (Bus Driver), **Joe Inscoe** (Shop No.1), **Norman Craig Maxwell** (Shop Man), **J. Michael Hunter** (Pilot), **Richard Whiting** (Ernie), **Jonathan Teague Cook** (Cap'n Trips), **Josef Anderson** (Janitor), **Caroline Dollar** (Little Girl), **Peter R. McIntosh** (Shop Commander).

Seventy year-old Harlan Williams is a janitor at a secret government project at Falco Plains Agricultural Testing Facility, where the mad Dr Richard Todhunter is experimenting with a particle accelerator that speeds up the healing process in living tissue. When, after an explosion in a research laboratory, Harlan is exposed to a dusting of regenerative material and begins growing younger, he has to flee from sinister government agency The Shop. Aided by local head of security Terry Spann and her boss, General Louis Crewes, Harlan and his ageing wife Gina are pursued across the country by ruthless Shop assassin Jude Andrews...

'A s far as I'm concerned, I'm done with TV,' Stephen King told Paul R. Gagne in *Cinefantastique*, following the screening of the *Salem's Lot* (1979) mini-series on CBS-TV. 'My idea as a writer is that you go for broke every time. You really do try to scare people, you want to make them come up out of their seats. On TV that's not possible. There are all sorts of artificial restrictions on what you can and can't do...Most of what television touches within the horror genre turns to absolute drivel.'

Over the years, King continued to have little regard for the networks' approach to series television, as he explained to Joe Maurceri in *Shivers*: 'All they can see are adaptations of finished novels, preferably historicals, romances or horror stories, or they see this thing that is open-ended so you can do a series.

'I talked with ABC at one point about doing a one season series, one hour a week, the way *Rich Man, Poor Man* was done. At the end of the season it would finish, it would be over and that would be the end. They just looked at me.

'What they did say was, "What if it's successful?" They couldn't bear to let this child out of the labour camp if he could still turn out a few more things for them. I told them that if it's successful, you do the same thing next season with a different story, the way any novelist does it. They just didn't get it.'

However, in the early 1990s, Richard P. Rubinstein, the executive producer for Laurel Entertainment, convinced his old friend King to create and script a limited series on CBS.

With a storyline reminiscent of the James Gunn series *The Immortal* (1970-71), *Golden Years* aired as a mid-season replacement on Thursday nights. Harlan's old-age make-up was designed by Carl Fullerton and Neal Martz, while veteran Dick Smith (*The Exorcist* [1973], etc) was spe-

FACT FILE

Stephen King's covert government organisation 'The Shop' first appeared in *Firestarter* (1984), and *Golden Years* even includes a reference to John Rainbird.

'A potentially fascinating storyline is unsatisfyingly strung out over a hefty four hours of running time, which makes this a bit of an ordeal to get through in one sitting.'
The Dark Side no 20, May 1992

Right: *Gina Williams (Frances Sternhagen) and her husband Harlan (Keith Szarabajka) are forced to flee The Shop.*
Below: *Ed Lauter as the renegade General Louis Crewes.*

'Filled with eccentric stereotypes and dully paced by director Kenneth Fink, this "run for your health" mini-series suffers from tired blood.'
Cinefantastique vol 22 no 3, December 1991

cial make-up consultant. The eponymous theme song was sung by David Bowie.

Opening with a two-hour pilot on 16 July 1991, six further hour-long episodes followed before the network unceremoniously dropped the series on 22 August. Although the show was a ratings disappointment for CBS, *The Trials of Rosie O'Neill* (1990-92) starring Sharon Gless, which preceded *Golden Years* on the same channel and earned a lower viewing share, was renewed by the network. 'When they did the first two-hour episode, it rated extremely high,' King told W.C. Stroby in *Fangoria*, 'and the ratings subsided to a point which we thought was acceptable. We were never dead last in our time slot, unless we were up against *20/20*, which happened a couple of times.'

Along with making a cameo appearance as an impatient bus driver in the fifth episode and serving as co-executive producer, King wrote all but the final two shows and admitted that he 'was gearing up to write the rest of the episodes' when it was cancelled.

Richard Rubinstein went to CBS and asked about getting four hours in the winter season of 1991 to complete the narrative. Disappointingly, the network originally refused, but later relented and offered half the amount of time Laurel wanted. However, both Rubinstein and King agreed that two hours was not long enough.

'I knew how the story ended,' said King, 'and it could have been done in four hours.'

When the series was released for foreign distribution and on domestic video it was cut down to a muddled four hour version and included an alternate, upbeat ending written by Josef Anderson (who has a cameo) and not shown on television in the United States.

'When we got word that we weren't going to get an order for additional shows from CBS,' Rubinstein told Gary L. Wood, 'we decided that we could make that the original ending.'

'It's basically a condensed version of my concept of how the thing should have ended, with a lot of the intervening stuff taken out,' King explained in his interview with Stroby.

Despite his disappointment over network television's treatment of *Golden Years*, King teamed up with Laurel again just three years later to finally bring his long-cherished production of *The Stand* to the small screen. ✝

THE LAWNMOWER MAN

God Made Him Simple. Science Made Him a God.

USA/UK, 1992. Director: **Brett Leonard**. Producer: **Gimel Everett**. Screenplay: **Brett Leonard** and **Gimel Everett**. Based on a Short Story by **Stephen King**. Executive Producers: **Edward Simons**, **Steve Lane**, **Clive Turner** and **Robert Pringle**. Director of Photography: **Russell Carpenter**. Music: **Dan Wyman**. Editor: **Alan Baumgarten**. Production Designer: **Alex McDowell**. Costume Designer: **Mary Jane Fort**. Casting: **Sally Dennison** and **Patrick Rush**. Associate Producers: **Peter A. McRae** and **Masao Takiyama**. Allied Vision/Lane Pringle/Fuji Eight Co Ltd/New Line Cinema. Colour. 108 minutes.

Jeff Fahey (Jobe Smith), **Pierce Brosnan** (Lawrence Angelo), **Jenny Wright** (Marnie Burke), **Mark Bringleson** (Sebastian Timms), **Geoffrey Lewis** (Terry McKeen), **John Laughlin** (Jake Simpson), **Jeremy Slate** (Father McKeen), **Dean Norris** (Director), **Colleen Coffey** (Caroline Angelo), **Troy Evans** (Lieutenant Goodwin), **Rosalee Mayeux** (Carla Parkette), **Austin O'Brien** (Peter Parkette), **Michael Gregory** (Security Chief), **Joe Hart** (Patrolman Cooley), **Ray Lykins** (Harold Parkette), **Jim Landis** (Ed Walts), **Mike Valverde** (Day Gate Guard), **Dale Raoul** (Dolly), **Frank Collison** (Night Gate Guard), **Jonathan Smart** (Assistant), **Steffen Gregory Foster** (Letchworth), **Doug Hutchison** (Security Tech), **Denney Pierce** (Skinhead Guard), **Roger Cook** (Older Guard), **Craig Benton** (White Coat), **Randall Fontana** (Hotel Waiter), **Mara Duronslet** (Young Woman Clerk), **Duane Byrne** (Letchworth Buddy).

*A**t** a top secret scientific facility, the brilliant but obsessed Dr Lawrence Angelo has been experimenting on accelerating the intelligence of laboratory chimpanzees. Financed by covert government organisation 'The Shop', Angelo is forced to heighten the creatures' aggressive instincts as well, through his Virtual Reality Technology, which creates a realistic digital 3-D computer environment. Troubled by the moral implications of his work, Angelo resigns and continues his research privately. When the scientist uses a revolutionary drug he has developed on Jobe Smith, a full-grown man with the intelligence of a six year-old whose uncanny gardening skills have earned him the nickname of 'The Lawnmower Man', the results are rapid and amazing. But when the former handyman's mental powers of telepathy and telekinesis begin to develop far beyond normal, he is transformed by his uncontrollable hatred into a being of pure energy, powerful enough to create a new world order with himself as its mad Messiah.*

The *Lawnmower Man* is very loosely based on a Stephen King short story, originally published in the May 1975 issue of *Cavalier* and later reprinted in the *Night Shift* (1978) collection. British-based co-producer Milton Subotsky (to whose memory the film is dedicated) had owned the film rights to the story since the early 1980s. After Subotsky's death, the rights were eventually sold on to production partners Steve Lane and Bob Pringle.

'Steve Lane originally owned a Stephen King short story adaptation for TV and video,' Allied Vision chairman Edward Simons recalled. 'He called and asked if we wanted to be in on the property.' Allied liked the idea of buying into a 'franchise' that had a potential life of several years. After joining *The Howling* series with the third episode, *The Marsupials The Howling III* (1987), the company hoped that *The Lawnmower Man* could be exploited in the same way.

The husband and wife team of Brett Leonard and Gimel Everett had made their film début with the low budget zombie thriller *The Dead Pit* (1989). However, Leonard quickly discovered that there was a problem with adapting 'The Lawnmower Man'. 'The original seven page short story could not have been expanded into a feature film,' he explained, 'so when Allied Vision came to us, we realised we had to change it. We took the Lawnmower Man character and created a cautionary tale about this new technology of virtual reality. We did use King's whole story in one of the scenes, but in a completely different context.'

Leonard combined the tale with an existing script by Everett called *Cybergod*,

FACT FILE

The Shop previously turned up in the Stephen King adaptation *Firestarter* (1984) and the original TV mini-series *Golden Years* (1991).

Right: *The 'Liquid Lovers' sequence set in Virtual Reality.*
Below: *Jobe (Jeff Fahey) prepares to enter the virtual world.*

Below: *The transformed Jobe is pursued by Dr Lawrence Angelo through the computer environment.*

about a virtual reality experiment that went amiss, which was in turn inspired by Daniel Keyes' famed 1959 science fiction novel *Flowers for Algernon* (first filmed in 1965 as *Charly*). The title page on the screenplay apparently stated that the film was now only 'Suggested by a short story by Stephen King'.

'I read 'The Lawnmower Man' short story as preparation for the part,' Irish-born actor Pierce Brosnan revealed to Edward Murphy in *Starburst*, 'and I think it's great how they've advanced and fleshed-out King's basic idea.'

The $10 million futuristic thriller was shot on a tight thirty-six day schedule in a Los Angeles warehouse in the summer of 1991. To produce the film's much-hyped 'virtual reality' effects, the production used three California special effects houses to create the computer graphic animation.

Computer animator Jeff Hayes of San Francisco-based Angel Studios used a grid pattern drawn on Jeff Fahey's face to provide ref-

erence points so that he could digitize the actor's features into CyberJobe, lip-syncing Fahey's voice to the computer image. 'What sold me on the film was when they explained virtual reality,' the actor told Marc Shapiro in *Fangoria*, 'how they were going to take this emerging science and move it into the fantastic and the bizarre.' Co-executive producer Simons agreed: 'This film is unique in that it adds a new element, virtual reality, to the proven audience approval and appreciation for Stephen King's brand of suspense. We believe the high-tech visual concept of the film will dazzle audiences.'

The Lawnmower Man was given a 1,000 print release in North America in March 1992 through New Line Cinema. 'Liquid Lovers' and 'Cyber-Jobe' T-shirts were available for $15 and $16 each, respectively, and *The Lawnmower Man Graphic Novel* was an eighty-four page comic book based on the film.

With an impressive gross of more than $32 million domestically, Leonard told Gary L. Wood in *Cinefantastique* that his hope from directing the movie was that he would 'get to

Left: Dr Angelo (Pierce Brosnan) befriends slow-witted gardener Jobe Smith.

Below: In Britain, Stephen King's original story was reprinted in The 30th Pan Book of Horror Stories *(1989)*.

'This latest knock-off from the human word processor plays like an unholy coupling between Sissy Spacek in *Carrie* and Cliff Robertson in *Charly*… For a film whose hook is eye-catching mind games, its human protagonist is the heart of the matter.'

Cinefantastique vol 23 no 1, August 1992

meet Stephen King, and that he enjoys the film. I'm a tremendous fan of his.'

'I didn't even know about *The Lawnmower Man* movie until about three weeks before a poster for it turned up in my local theatre,' King told W.C. Stroby in *Fangoria*. In fact, not only did the author not enjoy the film, he thought that so little of his original story remained in the completed production that he sued to have his name removed from the credits, describing it in the *Los Angeles Times* as 'the biggest rip-off that you can imagine, because there's nothing of me in there. It just makes me furious...My name shouldn't be on it.'

'They've been faithful to one or two elements in the story,' Brosnan said in *Starburst*, 'and although the writer didn't have any involvement with the film, I think that his spirit was there in full.'

'There is one scene in the film which is the short story,' Leonard claimed to Gary Wood. 'Those coming to see the short story put on film will see it, but the entire context of it has been changed.' The director went on to claim that the original story could not translate into anything more than an episode of the television series *Tales from the Crypt*. 'Obviously Stephen King is a credible and marketable name,' the director continued. 'When he sells the rights to a short story, that's what he sells.' Bob Shayne, Chairman and CEO of New Line Cinema agreed: 'That's what we paid for...His name was the most important thing we were buying.'

Federal court Judge Constance Baker Motley ruled in favour of King, calling the billing 'false on its face' and misleading to the public. New Line was barred from further using King's name in conjunction with the film. A Second Circuit Court of Appeals ruled that King's name should be removed from the title, but allowed New Line to keep King's 'based on' credit after the studio paid $2.5 million in damages.

However, King was suspicious about New Line's willingness to comply with the court's ruling. He hired a team of private investigators in June 1993. As a result, New Line was found to be in contempt of court the following year for leaving King's name on the video release. The company would have had to pay King $10,000 a day plus any profits derived from home video sales since 17 May 1993, if his name had not been removed by the end of April.

A subsequent 140-minute 'Director's Cut' issued on video included thirty-two minutes of extra footage, while an unnecessary sequel followed in 1995. ✝

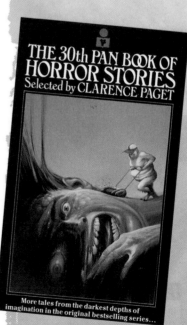

THE 30th PAN BOOK OF HORROR STORIES
Selected by CLARENCE PAGET

More tales from the darkest depths of imagination in the original bestselling series...

SLEEPWALKERS
(AKA STEPHEN KING'S SLEEPWALKERS)

They Feast on Your Fear – And It's Dinner Time.

USA, 1992. Director: **Mick Garris**. Producers: **Mark Victor**, **Michael Grais** and **Nabeel Zahid**. Writer: **Stephen King**. Co-producer: **Richard Stenta**. Director of Photography: **Rodney Charters**. Production Designer: **John DeCuir Jr.** Editor: **O. Nicholas Brown**. Executive Producers: **Dimitri Logothetis** and **Joseph Medawar**. Music: **Nicholas Pike**. Casting: **Wendy Kurtzman**, CSA, and **Lisa Mionie**, CSA. Columbia Pictures/Ion Pictures/Victor & Grais. Colour. 91 minutes.

Brian Krause (Charles Brady), **Mädchen Amick** (Tanya Robertson), **Alice Krige** (Mary Brady), **Jim Haynie** ([Sheriff] Ira), **Cindy Pickett** (Mrs Robertson), **Ron Perlman** (Captain Soames), **Lyman Ward** (Mr [Don] Robertson), **Dan Martin** (Andy Simpson), **Glenn Shadix** (Mr Fallows), **Cynthia Garris** (Laurie), **Monty Bane** (Horace), **John Landis** (Lab Technician), **Joe Dante** (Lab Assistant), **Stephen King** (Cemetery Caretaker), **Clive Barker** and **Tobe Hooper** (Forensic Techs), **Frank Novak** (Deputy Sheriff), **Rusty Schwimmer** (Housewife), **Nicholas Brown** (Officer Wilber), **Richard Penn** (State Policeman), **Ernie Lively** (Animal Control Officer), **Bojesse Christopher** (Crawford), **Lucy Boryer** (Jeanette), **Judette Warren** (Carrie), **Stuart Charno** (Police Photographer), **Karl Bakke** and **Diane Delano** (Police), **Roger Nolan** (Stenta), **Joey Aresco** (Victor), **Donald Petersen** (Boy with Ear Ache), **Hayden Victor** (Little Girl at School Bus), **Michael Reid MacKay** ('Charles' Sleepwalker), **Charles Croughwell** and **Karyn Sercelj** ('Mary' Sleepwalker), **Sparks** (Clovis), **Mark Hamill*** (Bodega Bay Sheriff). [* Uncredited in the final print.]

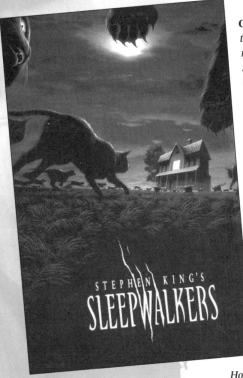

Charles Brady and his mother, Mary, are the last of a dying breed whose symbiotic needs are not of this world. They are Sleepwalkers, incestuous creatures that inspired mankind to create the legends of vampires and werewolves, and are able to stay alive only by feeding on the life-force of young female virgins. Outsiders capable of physically changing shape into reptilian-feline form, they are destined to roam the world hunting for fresh prey. Each time they settle into a new community, they must elude the net that immediately and inevitably begins to close around them. Their mortal enemies are cats, which are not fooled by the human disguises the creatures assume. Their search for victims takes Charles and Mary to the small town of Travis, Indiana, where high school student Tanya Robertson becomes the unsuspecting pawn in their desperate and lonely game of survival. However, the Deputy Sheriff's cat Clovis will not easily allow the innocent young girl to end up as the Brady's brunch...

FACT FILE

In Hong Kong, the film's English cable TV title is apparently *Sleepstalkers*.

'**B**y the early 1990s I'd written several films based on my own published works,' explained Stephen King in his introduction to former Universal Pictures publicist Mick Garris' first short story collection, *A Life in the Cinema* (2000). 'Some, like *Creepshow*, were pretty good; others, like *Silver Bullet*, were...well...not so good. I decided to take what I'd learned and write an original screenplay, and I had a bloody good time doing it.'

King described the result, *Sleepwalkers*, as being 'about a boy who loves his mother, what happens to that boy when he finally falls in love with a girl his own age.'

'Stephen was involved with the project from beginning to end,' director Garris told Simon Bacal in *Shivers*. 'He would always agree to changes which I thought would improve the script. Although I volunteered to make the changes, he'd say "Nah! Let me take a stab at it". So the next day there would be this wonderful scene sitting in the fax machine.'

Garris, who had previously met with Paramount executives to discuss doing *Pet Sematary* (1989), thought he was hired to direct *Sleepwalkers* on the basis of his handling of another oddball mother-son relationship in *Psycho IV The Beginning* (1990). 'There are some complicated relationships in addition to having jolts and the things you expect from a Stephen King horror story,' he explained to Gary L. Wood in *Cinefantastique*.

Filmed over fifty days in and around Los Angeles, the production shot on Sony's Columbia lot in Culver City, the Warner Bros backlot in Burbank and at various locations around town. 'The budget was extremely low for a feature shot on the lot,' revealed Garris.

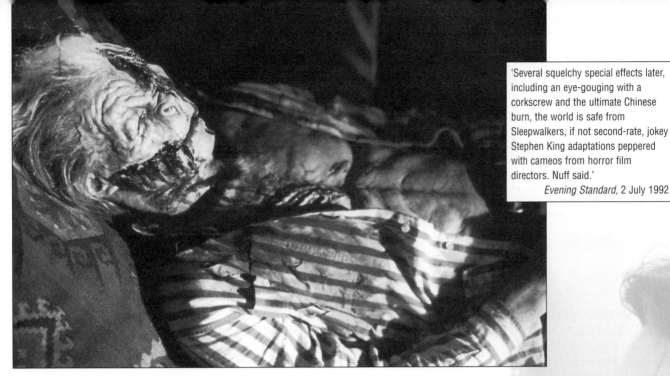

Although extra money was allocated for a few days of re-shooting after the production had wrapped, the director explained that the film's final budget 'came in well under $16 million.'

To portray the Sleepwalkers themselves, doubles for the actors were used in full body latex suits with animatronic heads, created by Alterian Studios, Inc. 'We couldn't put the actors in the suits,' explained project supervisor Tony Gardner. 'We did the suits on two actors who are very thin so we could build them up without making them look like Arnold Schwarzenegger. The whole idea is that they are supposed to be sleek, thin, elegant and very quick. So we had to get the two thinnest people we could find.'

For the sequences where mother and son transformed into their true forms, the special visual effects were created by Apogee Productions, Inc. 'When we saw tests of the morphing process, we were sold on it right away' explained Garris. 'Our aim was to use it in a subtle and organic manner.'

Although described by King in *The Dark Side* as 'one of the best movie versions of my work yet, and certainly one of the bloodiest!' *Sleepwalkers* was cut for an 'R' in the United States after receiving four consecutive 'NC-17' ratings for violence from the MPAA. Amongst the cuts were a bloody corkscrew being withdrawn from an eye socket and Mary Brady spitting out the fingers she has just chewed off Captain Soames' hand.

'This is horror played straight, without comedy,' confirmed the director.

Released on 10 April 1992, Mark Hamill made an uncredited appearance in the film's opening sequence set in Bodega Bay, California (a nod to Alfred Hitchcock's *The Birds* [1963]). There were also brief cameos by King (who described his role as a cemetery caretaker as 'just your basic country asshole') and horror directors Clive Barker, Tobe Hooper, John Landis and Joe Dante (the latter two sharing a scene that was originally meant to feature a single character played by George Romero, who had to pull out because of illness). These cameo appearances were originally intended to be played by people who had made previous King adaptations, but this idea was abandoned due to scheduling conflicts.

With a domestic gross of more than $29 million, King considered his first collaboration with Garris to be a success, despite the cuts that had been made to their film. 'He was very happy with the movie,' the director told Bill Warren in *Fangoria*, 'especially the cut you didn't see, and we work together really well...I know we'll work together again in the future.'

In fact, King and Garris became firm friends during the making of *Sleepwalkers*, and although talk of a sequel came to nothing, they subsequently re-teamed for two ambitious television projects, *The Stand* (1994) and *The Shining* (1997). †

Above: *The transformed Charles Brady (Brian Krause) is severely injured.*
Below: *In her true form, Mary Brady (Alice Krige) protects her son.*

The Town of Ludlow is in for Some New, Grave Surprises.

USA, 1992. Director: **Mary Lambert**. Producer: **Ralph S. Singleton**. Writer: **Richard Outten**. Director of Photography: **Russell Carpenter**. Production Designer: **Michelle Minch**. Film Editor: **Tom Finan**. Costume Designer: **Marlene Stewart**. Music: **Mark Governor**. Casting: **Richard Pagano**, **Sharon Bialy** and **Debi Manwiller**. Paramount Pictures/Columbus Circle Films. Colour. 100 minutes.

Edward Furlong (Jeff Matthews), **Anthony Edwards** (Chase Matthews), **Clancy Brown** (Gus Gilbert), **Jared Rushton** (Clyde Parker), **Darlanne Fluegel** (Renee Hallow), **Jason McGuire** (Drew Gilbert), **Sarah Trigger** (Marjorie Hargrove), **Lisa Waltz** (Amanda Gilbert), **Jim Peck** (Quentin Yolander), **Len Hunt** (Director), **Reid Binion** (Brad), **David Ratajczak** (Stevie), **Lucius Houghton** (Puppeteer), **Wilbur Fitzgerald** (First Assistant Director), **Elizabeth Ziegler** (Steadicam Operator), **Ken Fisher** (Assistant Steadicam), **Gil Roper** (Electrician), **Robert Easton** (Priest), **Judson Vaughn** (Reporter), **Bruce Evers** (Mover), **Janell McLeod** (School Teacher), **Christy Dennis** (Susan), **Rick Andosca** (Pathologist), **Joe Dorsey** (Caretaker), **Donna Lowery** (Newscaster), **Emily Woodward** (Twins' Mother), **Amanda Mitchell** (Screaming Twin), **J.L. Parker** (Potato Truck Driver).

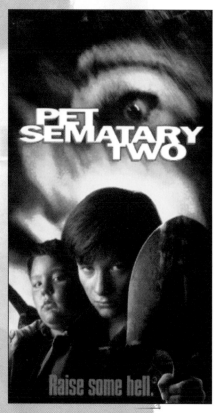

After his movie star mother Renee Hallow is accidentally electrocuted on a Hollywood horror movie set, inconsolable teenager Jeff Matthews and his veterinarian father Chase move into the summer house in rural Ludlow, Maine, built near a Native American Micmac burial ground that can bring the dead back to life. Local sheriff Gus Gilbert is an abusive bully who torments his overweight stepson Drew and kills the boy's beloved dog, Zowie. When Jeff and Drew bury Zowie in the Indian graveyard, the glowing-eyed dog returns from the dead and takes a bite out of Gus' throat on Halloween. Buried by the boys in the same ground, Gus returns as a homicidal zombie who enjoys skinning rabbits. Finally, the now-demented Jeff decides that it is time he used the Micmac magic to revive his dead mother...

FACT FILE

Former underage porn star Traci Lords sings 'Love Never Dies' over the end credits of *Pet Sematary II*.

When *Pet Sematary* (1989) grossed almost $60 million domestically, making it one of the most successful Stephen King adaptations to date, it was perhaps inevitable that Paramount, who owned the sequel rights, would eventually produce a follow-up.

However, King's name appears nowhere on this derivative, lower-budget sequel. 'I don't know if he's even been shown the script, to be honest,' *Fangoria*'s Gregory Nicoll was told by producer

Ralph S. Singleton, who was associate producer on the original and directed the 1990 adaptation of King's *Graveyard Shift*.

Singleton revealed that both Laurel, which produced the first film for Paramount, and King were paid off for the sequel. He also later admitted: 'What I've heard, too, is that Stephen King isn't crazy about the script. But I don't know, because I've never had a conversation with him about this film. It's never come up.'

'I read the script — or as much of it as I could stand,' King told W.C. Stroby in *Fangoria*, 'and I read enough to realise that it was exactly like the first *Pet Sematary* with different characters.' Besides the setting of Ludlow and the Native American burial ground, Richard Outten's original screenplay also tied in to the first film by bringing back the town's previous veterinarian, Quentin Yolander (Jim Peck), who was only mentioned in the original.

'This is a real *Stand by Me*-type of movie,' claimed Singleton. 'The other movie was about the parents; it was from their point of view. This film is told much more from the kids' point of view.'

The sequel was budgeted at $8 million ($2 million less than the original) and originally scheduled to shoot for forty days. Mary Lambert was brought back to resume her role as director, even though she was five months pregnant. 'I thought I could make a really good movie,' she told Gregory Nicoll. 'This one's a little more fun. It's just more lively. It's funnier and scarier.'

Although King had insisted that the first

film be shot in his home state of Maine to help boost the local economy, Singleton and Lambert scouted locations in Texas and North Carolina before deciding to base the sequel in and around Georgia's Riverwood Studios, near Atlanta. 'It's just too cold in Maine,' Singleton explained in *Fangoria*. 'In this part of Georgia it's country, not necessarily Southern. The idea was to sell rural Maine, and we've found that here.' However, despite the relocation, rain, snow and unseasonably below-freezing temperatures put the production behind schedule by around six days.

The creepy pet cemetery was filmed in an abandoned outdoor amphitheatre at Atlanta's Dunaway Gardens, while the Indian burial grounds were recreated on the granite dome of Georgia's Mount Arabia (an endangered plants reserve) and on the Riverwood soundstage.

Although the circular Micmac burial ground was redesigned by production designer Michelle Minch to look more authentic, the Native American tribe apparently objected to the association with bringing people back from the dead in King's novel and the first film, and they asked for their name to be removed from the script. 'I don't think King meant any harm to the Micmac Indians,' Singleton told Patricia Ross in *Cinefantastique*. 'I know we certainly didn't.'

Bart Mixon and David Barton of Steve Johnson's XFX, Inc supervised the on-set make-up effects, including the canine puppets which were built during pre-production in California. 'Basically, they're using the real dog wherever they can,' Mixon explained to Nicoll. 'If they want a weird look, like the first time you see the dog back from the dead, it's a puppet.'

The animal's glowing eyes were produced on set by using a beam-splitter, invented by second unit director Peter M. Chesney on *Pet Sematary*, to make the puppet appear more

demonic. Chesney also filmed some close-up work at high-speed of live dogs snarling and biting to make the creatures appear more vicious on screen. Various radio-controlled and cable-controlled heads were also utilised to simulate the dog's facial movements.

Two Alaskan Huskies were trained and handled by Animal Actors of Hollywood for the live-action scenes of the dogs. 'It's really hard to train them to do things that zombie dogs would do,' Lambert explained in *Cinefantastique*. 'They're so happy. They wag their tales.' The dogs also liked an edible makeup formulation of egg whites and gelatine so much that they licked it off their own bodies.

Local Georgia artist Bill 'Splat' Johnson was mostly responsible for creating the dead animal effects. Unfortunately, his mutilated creatures — constructed from scratch — were so realistic that someone reported the production to the Humane Society, claiming that animals were being killed on set.

Released on 28 August 1992, *Pet Sematary II* turned out to be an okay chiller up until the ludicrously over-the-top ending. However, it only managed to gross $17 million domestically — a particularly disappointing result given the original film's boxoffice success.

'I thank Stephen King for giving us the concept in the first place,' Singleton said to Patricia Ross. 'Without it, there wouldn't be a movie.' ✝

Left: Reanimated school bully Clyde Parker (Jared Rushton) has an axe to grind with Jeff.
Below: Jeff Matthews (Edward Furlong) and Drew Gilbert (Jason McGuire) do a little digging.
Below bottom: Director Mary Lambert, behind-the-scenes.

CHILDREN OF THE CORN II
THE FINAL SACRIFICE

These Children Are Home Alone, Too. But Their Parents Won't Be Coming Back.

USA, 1992. Director: **David F. Price**. Producer: **Scott A. Stone** and **David G. Stanley**. Screenplay: **A.L. Katz**, **Gilbert Adler** and **Bill Froehlich***. Based Upon the Short Story 'Children of the Corn' by **Stephen King**. Executive Producer: **Lawrence Mortorff**. Co-Producer: **Bill Froehlich**. Editor: **Barry Zetlin**. Director of Photography: **Levie Isaacks**. Music: **Daniel Licht**. Make-up Special Effects Coordinator: **Bob Keen**. Production Designer: **Greg Melton**. Casting: **Geno Havens**. Fifth Avenue Entertainment/Trans Atlantic Entertainment/Paramount Home Video. Colour. 93 minutes. [* Uncredited in the final print.]

Terence Knox ([John] Garrett), **Paul Scherrer** (Danny [Garrett]), **Ryan Bollman** (Micah), **Christie Clark** (Lacey), **Rosalind Allen** (Angela [Casual]), **Ned Romero** ([Frank] Red Bear), **Ed Grady** (Dr Appleby), **John Bennes** (Hollings), **Wallace Merck** (Sheriff Blaine), **Joe Inscoe** (Simpson), **Kelly Bennett** (Mary Simpson), **Rob Treveiler** (McKenzie), **Leon Pridgen** (Bobby), **Marty Terry** (Mrs Burke/Mrs West), **Ted Travelstead** (Mordechai), **Sean Bridgers** (Jebediah), **Aubrey Dollar** (Naomi), **Kristy Angell** (Ruth), **David Hains** (Fraser), **Bill Wagner** (Bingo Caller), **Bob Harvey** (Reporter), **Matt Hunter** (Dead Guy), **Erik Christenbury**, **Zack Clark**, **Michael Hall**, **Garrett LaCoss**, **Travis Langley**, **Michael Varner**, **Xeno Yuzna**, **Michelle Bowman**, **Amy Johnson**, **Aleasha Kivett**, **Mandy Newman**, **Christy Smith**, **Lelia Marlaine**, **Emily Mortorff**, **Morgan Mortorff**, **Jennifer Day**, **Holly Kidd**, **Talia Pierce**, **Mary Pollok**, **Tracie Stanley** (The Children of the Corn).

The small community of Gatlin, Nebraska, is alive with police and reporters as a result of the gruesome, ritualistic murder of the community's entire adult population by the children, led by a twelve year-old preacher named Isaac. Down on his luck tabloid reporter John Garrett arrives in town to try to get the story that will save his failing career. Reluctantly accompanied by his rebellious eighteen year-old son, Danny, Garrett stays at a bed and breakfast in a neighbouring town, where he attempts to question Micah, one of the orphans from Gatlin. Meanwhile, Danny falls for a young local girl, Lacey, and he gradually finds himself being pulled into the growing commune of those Gatlin children who survived the conflagration in the corn fields, now led by the fanatical Mordechai. When the killings begin again, Garrett is plunged into a dangerous web of town politics, ancient folklore and human sacrifice, as he teams up with Native American anthropologist Red Bear, whose knowledge and understanding of local legends could prove the key to discovering the deadly secret of the toxic corn and the supernatural entity known as 'He Who Walks Behind the Rows'.

Based on Stephen King's story in his 1978 *Night Shift* collection and filmed for just $3 million, the critically-panned *Children of the Corn* (1984) eventually grossed almost $12 million domestically and became, financially, one of the most successful Stephen King adaptations ever.

Seven years after New World Pictures had its surprise boxoffice hit and then sold on the sequel rights, Trans Atlantic Entertainment decided to make back-to-back sequels to two of its horror franchise properties. 'You can make a sequel to anything,' King told W.C. Stroby in *Fangoria*. 'It doesn't necessarily have to make sense, because sense isn't the point. The boxoffice is the point.'

Executive producer Lawrence Mortorff was the husband of actress Lindsay Wagner, and he was given the task of shooting *Children of the Corn II* and *Hellraiser III Hell on Earth* (1992) as cheaply as possible. He decided to base both productions in North Carolina, a 'right to work' state, and the films shared a number of key crew members, including British special effects make-up co-ordinator Bob Keen (*Hellraiser* [1987], etc.).

Besides creating a number of bloody corpses for *Children of the Corn II*, Keen and his small Image Animation crew also produced a flying corn stalk that impaled television reporter McKenzie through the throat and a fatal nosebleed, which Keen believed was the first time such a death had been shown on the screen. As well as co-ordinating the gory make-

'Director David F. Price fails to pick up the pacing and this horror film drags except for a few homicidal set-pieces.'
*Creature Features:
The Science Fiction, Fantasy,
and Horror Movie Guide*

'This is a (very slight) improvement on part I, with good photography and decent FX, but, as before, doesn't add up to much more than tasteless scenes of bratty kids offing dopey adults.'
Terror on Tape

Left: Angela (Rosalind Allen) is about to be sacrificed to the dark god of the corn.
Below: TV reporter McKenzie (Rob Treveiler) is impaled by a flying corn stalk.

up effects, Keen also directed the film's second unit work.

David F. Price, the son of former Columbia Pictures president Frank Price, was chosen to direct. Originally an actor, Price had been Richard Donner's assistant on *Ladyhawke* (1985) before making his directorial début with another sequel, the low budget vampire thriller *Son of Darkness To Die For II* (1991).

The script by A.L. Katz, Gilbert Adler and an uncredited Bill Froehlich followed on directly from the events in the first film.

Terence Knox, who was best known at the time for his starring role in the CBS-TV series *Tour of Duty* (1987-90), was cast as journalist John Garrett, who was drawn to Gatlin because of the bizarre murders and discovered more than he expected. His rebellious and resentful son was portrayed by Paul Scherrer. While veteran Native American actor Ned Romero played the spiritual mentor who guided Garrett on his quest for the truth.

Budgeted at around $1 million, *Children of the Corn II* (subtitled *Deadly Harvest* during shooting) was filmed over a four-week sched-ule in August 1991 in the towns of Liberty and Ramseur, North Carolina. However, a number of residents were not particularly impressed that their town was being used as a movie location: 'They've got cornstalks all across the street,' complained one of the disgruntled locals. 'I think the townspeople are getting tired of it. They can't drive where they want. Merchants say they're losing business.'

Originally set to open on Halloween by Dimension/Miramax, *Children of the Corn II The Final Sacrifice* eventually went directly to video in January 1993. Although it did not repeat the financial success of its predecessor, it still did well enough that *Children of the Corn III Urban Harvest* followed a year later. †

There Are Very Good Reasons to Be Afraid of the Dark.

USA, 1992. Writer for the Screen and Director: **George A. Romero**. Based on the Book by **Stephen King**. Producer: **Declan Baldwin**. Executive Producer: **George A. Romero**. Director of Photography: **Tony Pierce-Roberts**, BSC. Editor: **Pasquale Buba**, ACE. Music: **Christopher Young**. Production Designer: **Cletus Anderson**. Costume Designer: **Barbara Anderson**. Make-up Effects Creators: **John Vulich** and **Everett Burrell**. Casting: **Terry Liebling**, CSA. Orion Pictures Corporation. Colour. 121 minutes.

Timothy Hutton (Thad Beaumont/George Stark), **Amy Madigan** (Liz Beaumont), **Julie Harris** (Reggie DeLesseps), **Robert Joy** (Fred Clawson), **Chelsea Field** (Annie Pangborn), **Michael Rooker** (Alan Pangborn), **Royal Dano** (Digger Holt), **Rutanya Alda** (Miriam Cowley), **Beth Grant** (Shayla Beaumont), **Kent Broadhurst** (Mike Donaldson), **Tom Mardirosian** (Rick Cowley), **Glenn Colerider** (Homer Gamache), **Patrick Brannan** (Young Thad Beaumont), **Larry John Meyers** (Doc Pritchard), **Christina Romero** (Little Girl), **Rohn Thomas** (Dr Albertson), **Molly Renfroe** (Hilary), **Judy Grafe** (Head Nurse), **John Machione** (Male Nurse), **Erik Jensen** (Male Student), **Christine Forrest** (Trudy Wiggins), **Nardi Novak** (Pangborn's Receptionist), **Zachery (Bill) Mott** (Norris Ridgewick), **William Cameron** (Officer Hamilton), **David Butler** (Trooper #1), **Curt De Bor** (Trooper #2), **Drinda Lalumia** (Dodie), **Lamont Arnold** (NYC Cop #1), **Lee Hayes** (NYC Cop #2), **John Ponzio** (Todd Pangborn), **Jack Skelly** (Man in the Hallway), **Marc Field** (Donaldson Cop #1), **Rik Billock** (Donaldson Cop #2), **Bruce Kirkpatrick** (Officer #1), **David Early** (Officer #2), **Jeff Monahan** (Wes), **Jeffery Howell** (Dave), **Melissa Papp** (Rosalie), **J. Michael Hunter** (Garrison), **Therese Courtney** (Receptionist), **Marty Roppelt** (Young Officer), **Sarah** and **Elizabeth Parker** (Wendy and William Beaumont).

FACT FILE

The story young Thad Beaumont is writing before he collapses in 1968 is Stephen King's own tale 'Here There Be Tygers', first published that same year.

During an operation in 1968 on teenager Thad Beaumont, the surgeon discovers an eye and two teeth belonging to an undeveloped twin foetus embedded in the boy's brain. As the surgery is completed, the hospital is besieged by a flock of sparrows. Twenty-three years later, the grown-up Thad is a well-respected professor of creative writing in Castle Rock, Maine, who is also the author of several very successful novels written under the pseudonym 'George Stark'. Happily married to Liz and the father of young twins, Beaumont's life is almost idyllic, thanks to the popularity of Stark's books. When blackmailer Fred Clawson threatens to expose him as the writer of the Stark novels, Beaumont decides to go public with the information. However, nobody consults George Stark. When the decomposing doppelganger turns up and embarks on a murder spree, suspicion falls on Thad. Soon The Sparrows Are Flying Again...

'**O**bviously, I *am* Richard Bachman,' Stephen King told Joseph B. Mauceri in *Shivers* magazine, 'and when I write as Richard Bachman, it opens up that part of my mind. It's like a hypnotic suggestion where I become my idea of who Richard Bachman is. It frees me to be somebody who is a little bit different.' This was evidently the inspiration behind King's best-selling 1989 novel *The Dark Half*, in which the author attempted to finally exorcise his 'Richard Bachman' alias for good (the book even includes a dedication to his late fictional alter-ego).

Set in Ludlow (the rural town where the Creeds moved to in *Pet Sematary* [1989]), the author revealed that the book illustrated 'the powerful hold fiction can achieve over the writer'.

After the disappointment of being unavailable to direct both *Pet Sematary* and the ABC-TV miniseries *It* (1990), George A. Romero finally got the opportunity to bring one of his friend's books to the screen. 'I've always wanted to make a novel of Steve's into a film,' Romero told David Kuehls in *Fangoria*. 'So many people have tried but failed to either comprehend or retain his voice and intention. Maybe that will happen to me too. But I've always wanted a crack at it.'

The $15 million adaptation was the director's most expensive project to date. With principal photography commencing in October 1990, it was shot over fifteen weeks in and around Romero's home town of Pittsburgh, Pennsylvania.

After Ed Harris, Willem Dafoe and Gary Oldman were reportedly considered for the dual role, Timothy Hutton was eventually chosen to portray both author Thad Beaumont and his dark twin George Stark. To keep the dual identities totally separate, the method actor requested two different trailers and was even rumoured to have slept in two distinct hotel rooms depending on which character he was playing.

'*The Dark Half* is a Jekyll and Hyde story,' explained Romero, 'in the sense that it explores the dark side of all of us. It's a very thought-provoking story, because revealing our dark half not only affects our own lives but our families and relationships as well.'

After considering, amongst others, Michael Gough and John Hurt for the role, Julie Harris (*The Haunting* [1963], etc) was cast as the eccentric pipe-smoking authority on the occult, Reggie DeLesseps (male character 'Rawlie' DeLesseps in the novel). 'I talked to Steve about that one,' said Romero, 'and he said it was a great idea.'

Character actor Michael Rooker, who portrayed the eponymous psychopath in the controversial *Henry: Portrait of a Serial Killer* (1990), played local sheriff Alan Pangborn (the late Sheriff Bannerman's replacement, following his demise in *Cujo*). The character returned the following year in *Needful Things*, this time portrayed by Ed Harris.

Veteran character actor Royal Dano turned up as a gravedigger in his final role and John Amplas (the modern vampire in Romero's *Martin* [1976]) was Hutton's stand-in for the split-screen shots of Thad and Stark. King himself had hoped to appear in a cameo as a high-rise window cleaner who is revealed as one of Stark's disguises, but he was eventually unable to do so.

As the author's winged 'psychopomps', mythic creatures who conduct human souls between the lands of the living and the dead, the production utilised more than 4,500 cutthroat finches for the climactic sequence where the decaying Stark is literally torn apart by the beaks and claws of sparrows. The live-

action birds were eventually combined with around sixty-five of Optic Nerve's vacuformed mechanical creations, some of which were constructed from actual sparrow carcasses for close-up work, and computer-generated birds created by Video Image.

'I've tried to be as faithful as possible to the book,' said Romero, 'and it does hang on what Steve was working with.'

'I hope George will come out of this with his reputation enhanced,' King told Charles Leayman in *Cinefantastique*, and that he'll have a big hit.'

Following test previews, special effects re-shooting was completed in September 1991. However, the picture was caught up in the near-bankruptcy of Orion Pictures and only belatedly released in April 1993. ✝

'Romero's careful adaptation of an unwieldy tome tries hard to correct King's slapdash plotting, but is ultimately yoked to the novel's trite story and unable to articulate the more intriguing issues raised… The film's 'happy' ending is oddly unsatisfying.'
Sight and Sound
volume 3 issue 11 (NS),
November 1993

'*The Dark Half* is another nightmare vision by the best-selling author, who is fond of meditating in his own singular way, on the cost and dimensions of his success…Mr. Romero observes the conventions of the horror-film genre, but he observes them with inventive humor, and he holds off on the fancier special effects until virtually the last minute.'
The New York Times, 23 April 1993

Above: For George Stark, The Sparrows Are Flying Again…

PRESENTATION PROOF COPY
STEPHEN KING
THE DARK HALF

GEORGE STARK
NOT A VERY NICE GUY

THE TOMMYKNOCKERS

Something Wonderful is Happening in Haven. Pray It Doesn't Happen to You.

New Zealand/USA, 1993. Director: **John Power**. Teleplay: **Lawrence D. Cohen**. Based on the Novel by **Stephen King**. Executive Producers: **Frank Konigsberg** and **Larry Sanitsky**. Producers: **Jayne Bieber** and **Jane Scott**. Co-producer: **Lawrence D. Cohen**. Directors of Photography: **Danny Burstall** and **David Eggby**. Production Designer: **Bernard Hides**. Editor: **Tod Feuerman**. Music: **Christopher Franke**. Konigsberg-Sanitsky Productions/K&S II Partnership/ABC-TV/Vidmark. Colour. 200 minutes. 125 minutes [US video]. 170 minutes [UK video].

Jimmy Smits (James Gardner), **Marg Helgenberger** (Bobbi Anderson), **John Ashton** (Butch), **Allyce Beasley** (Becka Paulson), **Robert Carradine** (Bryant Brown), **Joanna Cassidy** (Ruth Merrill), **Annie Corley** (Marie Brown), **Cliff DeYoung** (Joe Paulson), **Traci Lords** (Nancy), **E.G. Marshall** (Gramps Ev Hillman), **Chuck Henry** (Chaz Stewart), **Leon Woods** (Hilly Brown), **Paul McIver** (Davey Brown), **Yvonne Lawley** (Mabel Noyes), **Bill Johnson** (Elt Barker), **John Steemson** (Barney Applegate), **Rick Leckinger** (Jingles), **Peter Rowley** (Benton Rhodes), **John Summer** (Mr Arberg), **Elizabeth Hawthorne** (Patricia McCardle), **Craig Parker** (Student Bartender), **Kay Helgenberger** (Pearl), **Larry Sanitsky** (Neurologist), **Helen Medlyn** (Neurologist #2), **Jim McLarty** (Dr Etheridge), **Daniel Bieber** (Boy at Vet), **Timothy Bartlett** (Mr Allison), **Karyn Malchus** (Tommyknocker).

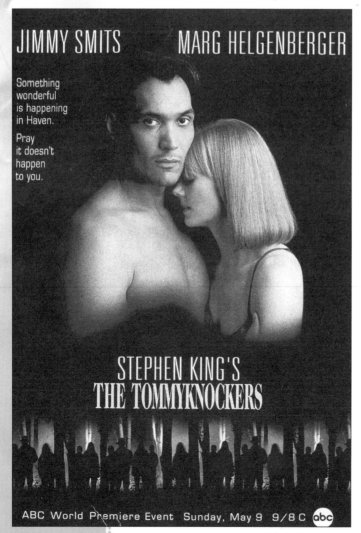

In the small New England town of Haven, Maine, novelist Bobbi Anderson is out walking with her dog in the woods when she stumbles over an odd, half-buried object behind her house. It turns out to be a spacecraft and, along with the other inhabitants of the town, she is taken over by aliens who want to repair their damaged ship. With most of the townsfolk transformed around the Fourth of July into glowing green-eyed zombie slaves, only a few people are immune, including Bobbi's boyfriend, alcoholic poet Jim Gardner, who is unaffected because of a steel plate he has in his head from a skiing accident. With the locals using their newly-acquired telepathic powers to invent bizarre new machinery, only Gardner and a few others have the power to prevent the 'Becoming'...

L*ate last night and the night before, Tommyknockers, Tommyknockers knocking at the door.*
I want to go out, don't know if I can, because I'm so afraid of the Tommyknocker man.

In his introduction to his 1987 novel, Stephen King pointed out that the above nursery rhyme is 'deceptively simple', explaining that, according to the dictionary definition, 'Tommyknockers' are either tunnelling ogres or a ghost which haunts deserted mines or caves. Taking this concept as his inspiration, the author combined his version of the myth with childhood fears, demonic dolls and evil-looking aliens.

'In the spring and summer of 1986 I wrote

Left: James Gardner (Jimmy Smits) encounters one of the spacecraft's alien inhabitants.

FACT FILE

In *The Tommyknockers*, police constable Ruth Merrill (Joanna Cassidy) accuses Bobbi's barking dog of 'acting like a regular Cujo'.

The Tommyknockers,' King revealed in his memoir *On Writing*, 'often working until midnight with my heart running at a hundred and thirty beats a minute and cotton swabs stuck up my nose to stem the coke-induced bleeding.'

Described by the author as 'a Forties-style science fiction tale', despite the big budget and an all-star cast, this four-hour mini-series is a virtual remake of the 1970 made-for-television movie *Night Slaves*, based on a novel by Jerry Sohl, which also featured a crashed spaceship, a small town taken over by aliens and a hero (played by James Franciscus) with a metal plate in his head. There are also probable nods to Ray Bradbury's *It Came From Outer Space* (1953), Jack Finney's *Invasion of the Body Snatchers* (1956) and Nigel Kneale's *Quatermass and the Pit* (aka *Five Million Years to Earth*, 1967) with their themes of buried spacecraft, possessed communities and reawakened evil. 'I've never considered myself a blazingly original writer in the sense of conceiving totally new and fresh plot ideas,' the author admitted to Eric Norden in *Playboy*. 'Most writers are essentially reworking a few basic themes.'

The script by Lawrence D. Cohen (whose previous King adaptations included *Carrie* [1976] and the ABC-TV mini-series *It* [1990]) was nothing more than an overlong pulp science fiction movie. However, Cohen told Gary L. Wood in *Cinefantastique* that he believed the project had 'the makings of something special,'

Aired over the 9 and 10 May 'sweeps' period in two parts of two hours each, the mini-series failed to repeat the network's rating success with *It*. 'I thought they did a pretty decent job with a book that wasn't top drawer to begin with,' King told Michael Beeler in *Cinefantastique*.

Jimmy Smits, then the star of the Emmy Award-winning NBC-TV series *L.A. Law* (1986-94), was cast as the alcoholic hero, while former underage porn star Traci Lords — who also sings over the end credits of *Pet Sematary II* (1992) — turned up as the sexy psycho postmistress.

Although John Power directed with an eye to the attractive New Zealand locations which ably represented King's rural northern Maine, when the reptilian aliens (designed and created by Alterian Studios Inc) were finally revealed, the wait hardly seemed worth it.

The video release was cut to 125 minutes in the United States and 170 minutes in the United Kingdom. ✝

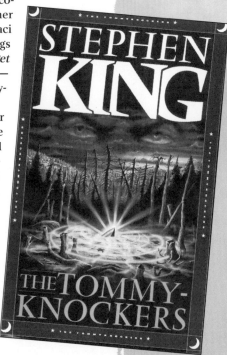

Stephen King's The Stand

The End of the World is Just the Beginning.

USA, 1994. Director: **Mick Garris**. Executive Producers: **Richard P. Rubinstein** and **Stephen King**. Teleplay: **Stephen King.** Based on His Book. Producer: **Mitchell Galin**. Supervising Producer: **Peter McIntosh**. Director of Photography: **Edward Pei**. Production Designer: **Nelson Coates**. Editor: **Pat McMahon**. Music: **W.G. Snuffy Walden**. Casting: **Lynn Kressel**. Greengrass Productions/Laurel/ABC-TV. Colour. 360 minutes.

Gary Sinise (Stu Redman), **Molly Ringwald** (Frannie Goldsmith), **Jamey Sheridan** (Randall Flagg), **Laura San Giacomo** (Nadine Cross), **Ruby Dee** (Mother Abagail), **Ossie Davis** (Judge Farris), **Miguel Ferrer** (Lloyd), **Corin Nemec** (Harold Lauder), **Matt Frewer** (Trashcan Man), **Adam Storke** (Larry Underwood), **Ray Walston** (Glen Bateman), **Rob Lowe** (Nick Andros), **Bill Faberbakke** (Tom Cullen), **Peter Van Norden** (Ralph), **Bridgit Ryan** (Lucy Swann), **Rick Aviles** (Rat Man), **Kellie Overbey** (Dayna Overbey), **Shawnee Smith** (Julie Lawry), **Max Wright** (Herbert Denninger), **Patrick Kilpatrick** (Ray Booth), **Ray McKinnon** (Charlie Campion), **John I. Bloom** (Joe Bob Brentwood), **Jordan Lund** (Bill Hapscomb), **Kellie Overbey** (Dayna Jurgens), **Bridgit Ryan** (Lucy Swann), **Kareem Abdul-Jabbar** (Monster Shouter), **Chuck Adamson** (Barry Dorgan), **Anthony Adler** (Dying Janitor), **Sam Anderson** (Whitney Horgan), **Steve Anderson** (Army Officer), **Kathy Bates*** (Rae Flowers), **Jesse Bennett** (Vic Palfrey), **Johnny Biscuit** (Norm Bruett), **Scott J. Bronson** (Man in Convoy), **Ervin Butler** (B-Ball Boy), **Hope Marie Carlton** (Sally Campion), **David Kirk Chambers** (Brad Kitchner), **Laura Conover** (Nurse), **Bill Corso** (Corpse in Lincoln Tunnel), **Kevin Doyle** (Sarge), **John Dunbar** (Dave Roberts), **Troy Evans** (Sheriff Baker), **Warren Frost** (George Richardson), **Cynthia Garris** (Susan Stern), **Leo Geter** (Chad Norris), **Sandra Gimpel** (Woman in Store), **Alan Gregory** (Al Bundell), **Mary Ethel Gregory** (Alice Underwood), **Thomasyn Harlow** (Cynthia), **Ed Harris*** (General William Starkey), **Jim Haynie** (Deputy Kingsolving), **Ryan Healy** (4th Teenager), **Thomas Holland** (Carl Hough), **Sherman Howard** (Dietz), **Ken Jenkins** (Peter Goldsmith), **David Jensen** (Major Jalbert), **Richard Jewkes** (Dick Ellis), **Kevin Kennedy** (Dave Zellman), **Michelle King** (Reporter), **Stephen King** (Teddy Weizak), **Robert Knott** (Len Carsleigh), **John Landis** (Russ Dorr), **Brittany Lewis** (Arlene), **Richard Lineback** (Poke), **Mike Lookinland** (Sentry No.1), **Elizabeth Lough** (Young Woman), **Bruce MacVittie** (Ace-High), **Dan Martin** (Rich Moffat), **Patrick McKinley** (Flu Buddy Man), **Frank Magner** (Vince Hogan), **William Newman** (Dr Soames), **Wendy Phillips** (Lisa Hull), **Sam Raimi** (Bob Terry), **Vince Rodriguez** (Lisa Driver), **Julie Simper** (Lila Bruett), **Sarah Schaub** (Gina McCone), **Tressa Sharbough** (Marcey Halloran), **David Sosna** (Some Man), **Barry L. Sullivan** (Joe), **George Sullivan** (Sargent), **Millie Teri** (Weeping Woman), **Rob Weller** (Game Show Host), **Michael D. Weatherred** (Mike Childress), **Mike Westenskow** (Paul Burlson), **Derryl Yeager** (Man in Street), **Brayton Yerkes** (Old Man in Store), **Jeff Gelb** (NY Radio Announcer), **Mick Garris*** (Applauding Man). [* Uncredited in the final print.]

A *deadly super-flu, nicknamed 'Captain Trips', escapes from a top-secret military installation in California, wiping out virtually the entire Earth's population within ten days. The few lonely and terrified survivors who have somehow managed to escape the terrible pestilence, set out on a desperate quest to find others who are immune to the virus. On the course of their journey and through their vivid dreams, they find themselves drawn by two powerful forces — the soothing and benevolent 106 year-old Mother Abagail, a prophet who represents the purity of spirit and seeks new beginnings for the Earth from her commune in Boulder, Colorado, or the Satanic Randall Flagg aka 'the Walkin Dude', the personification of corruption and darkness whose power base is in Las Vegas, Nevada. The ensuing confrontation is the age-old battle between Good and Evil, but this time with all that is left of humanity as the prize.*

FACT FILE

'Captain Trips', the nickname of the virulent super-flu virus in *The Stand,* also turned up in King's 1974 story 'Night Surf', and there was a character named 'Cap'n Trips' in the 1991 TV mini-series *Golden Years.*

'There were times when I actively hated *The Stand*,' Stephen King revealed about

his apocalyptic 1978 novel in *Danse Macabre*, 'but there was never a time when I did not feel compelled to go on with it.'

The author began the book four years earlier under the more prosaic title *The House on Value Street* (which was loosely based on the Patricia Hearst kidnapping), while living in Boulder, Colorado. It was inspired by a real-life chemical spill in Utah that killed a number of sheep and the doomsday proclamations of a Midwestern preacher on a religious radio station.

A film version was originally conceived when King, George A. Romero and co-executive producer Richard P. Rubinstein first met each other while discussing a possible version of *'Salem's Lot* for Warner Bros. 'Steve gave us the choice of any book or story of his that wasn't sold,' revealed Romero. 'We had the opportunity to buy the rights of *The Dead Zone* which we read in manuscript form, but when it came to a choice we chose *The Stand*.'

Around the same time as *Creepshow* was being made in the early 1980s, *The Stand* was already being considered as a $15 million project for Romero. Rubinstein told *Fangoria* at the time: '*The Stand* will require a major budget, which means a considerable amount of time spent arranging financing, and a tremendous amount of work to film. *The Stand* is an epic — in the David Lean sense of the word; a piece of tremendous scope, and yet also a people story.'

King apparently wrote 'about five drafts' of

the script before he gave up and told Rubinstein to find somebody else to encapsulate the epic story. 'I'm glad I'm out of it,' said the author.

Because of the problem with length, at one time Romero and King seriously considered shooting the film in two two-hour parts, entitled *The Stand* and *The Plague*, and then releasing them one after the other. 'It's a tough problem,' explained Romero. 'It really needs to be a long film — and that's expensive.' Other ideas discussed included renting the scale model of Las Vegas left over from Francis Ford Coppola's stylised musical *One from the Heart* (1982). Romero also talked about how much fun it would be to actually shoot in all the locations mentioned in the novel. 'We see *The Stand* as *The Godfather* of horror films,' the Pittsburgh director told *Cinefantastique* magazine, 'and that is Steve's quote, not ours.'

'The problem with *The Stand* has always been that we wanted to do it on a negative pick-up basis,' King explained to *Starburst* in the early 1980s. 'We've got to have final cut, that's the most important thing of all.'

However, when a number of adaptations of King's work flopped at the boxoffice in the late 1980s, funding became a problem. 'Had a couple of the movies based on Steve's books gone

Above: Nick Andros (Rob Lowe) arrives at the home of Mother Abagail (Ruby Dee).

Right: *Randall Flagg appears in a vision as a demon scarecrow to frighten Mother Abagail.*
Below: *Miguel Ferrer as Lloyd, the right hand of Evil.*

through the roof, I think we could have financed it in a minute,' Romero told Frederick C. Szebin in *Cinefantastique*. 'It's no fault of the material, even though I didn't think all the films were very good. It's just circumstance.'

After Romero severed most of his ties with Laurel Entertainment in 1985 to develop his own projects, John Boorman was at one time attached to direct.

During the early 1990s, and with Robert Duvall reportedly interested in playing Flagg, Warner Bros paid $30,000 for Rospo Pallenberg (*The Emerald Forest* [1985], etc) to write a feature script treatment, which King liked with reservations: 'I don't envy the work he had to do,' the author said in *Fangoria*. 'Adapting that sucker must have been tough.'

However, despite everyone apparently being happy with Pallenberg's adaptation, Warner Bros ultimately passed on the project, and a few years later King again found himself spending four months adapting his mega-novel into a 400-page screenplay when a television mini-series proved to be the answer to the problem of length.

The author initially expressed major reservations about *The Stand* being produced for televi-

sion. 'People have told me that *The Stand* would make a great TV miniseries,' King had earlier told Marc Shapiro in *Fangoria*, 'but I just can't see the end of the world being brought to you by mouthwash and toilet tissue.'

However, following its previous rating success with King's *It* (1990), ABC-TV could. Within days of the author turning in his first draft screenplay, the network greenlighted the project. 'The mini-series format grew up,' explained King.

Now on board as co-executive producer, the author rewrote his screenplay several more times before it was finally approved.

To tighten up the script, some character backstories were eliminated, a number of minor characters were dropped or combined with other roles, most of the sex and swearing were cut, and the time frame of the novel was moved up twenty years from the 1970s.

When ABC reputedly would not cover the entire $28 million budget, Laurel Entertainment (a subsidiary of Spelling Entertainment Group) stepped in to part-finance the project itself.

Although his name had been long connected with the project, George Romero was not offered the job of directing (apparently due to nebulous 'scheduling conflicts'), and instead it went to Mick Garris, who had previously worked with King on the disappointing *Sleepwalkers* (1992). 'The only reason I am here is because of Stephen King,' Garris told *Fangoria*'s Bill Warren. 'I don't think he's used to a director really wanting his input as much as I did — encouraging it, wanting to be faithful to the tone he set and really looking for his approval. If you have that offered to you, you'd be a fool not to take advantage of it.'

Shooting began in Utah in February 1993, and locations included the State Utah Prison, where the entire sex offender wing was physically re-located for a few days while the production was shooting in their cells. However, the production encountered an unusually long and cold winter as well as picket lines claiming that employees in the 'right-to-work' state were being exploited by the film-makers. Filmed over 104 days in and around Salt Lake City, New York City and Las Vegas, *The Stand* featured 125 speaking roles and more than 600 extras during the Las Vegas sequences alone.

After considering such names as James Woods, Lance Henriksen and even David Bowie, Jamey Sheridan was cast as Randall Flagg, who King has described as 'everything

Left: From left to right: Publicity shot of the forces of Good — Ossie Davis, Gary Sinise, Bill Faberbakke, Adam Storke, Molly Ringwald and Ruby Dee.
Below: One of Bernie Wrightson's striking illustrations from Stephen King's expanded 1990 edition of The Stand.

that I know of in the last twenty years that's really bad.' The evil 'Walkin' Dude' appears in various different disguises, including a rotted scarecrow, a grinning corpse and a horned demon all created by Steve Johnson's XFX, Inc.

Using a minimalistic-looking prosthetic make-up, Johnson's team aged Ruby Dee (who replaced Whoopi Goldberg when the latter had to bow out of the production) by more than forty years as Mother Abagail. The actress even had the whites of her eyes discoloured to enhance the illusion of old age.

Shown in four two-hour segments ('The Plague', 'The Dreams', 'The Betrayal' and 'The Stand') the eight hour mini-series was originally telecast over 8, 9, 11 and 12 May 1994 in the United States. It was a huge hit, and Steve Johnson's special effects won an Emmy Award for Best Achievement in Make-up. 'When I look at *The Stand* and I hear them say my words, at least I don't want to throw up,' King revealed to Michael Beeler in *Cinefantastique*. 'I look at it and on the whole I'm pretty proud of it.'

The author also turned up in an extended cameo as the driver who gives the scheming Nadine a lift to Boulder. In fact, Garris' predilection for guest appearances was given full reign in *The Stand*. 'I like to have cameos in my films,' Garris told Beeler. 'I think it's fun for the fans of a certain field to see people only *they* know.'

Besides featuring King, Kathy Bates has a two minute unbilled cameo as an outspoken radio talk-show host (a role originally scripted for a man) who is gunned down by American soldiers while on the air, and an uncredited Ed Harris plays the military General who thinks the answer to the plague might be found in Yeats and the barrel of a gun. Also amongst the cast were drive-in movie critic Joe Bob Briggs and directors Tom Holland, John Landis and Sam Raimi.

King's novel was reissued in 1990 in a rewritten and expanded edition illustrated by Bernie Wrightson. It not only contained a missing 150,000 words, 'arbitrarily cut' by publisher Doubleday because the accounting department thought it was too long to be commercially successful, but an additional 25,000 words of new material, adding up to more than 400 extra pages.

Although many people still regard *The Stand* as an analogy of the AIDS epidemic, the disease had not even been identified when the book was first published. 'When the AIDS thing started to happen, I couldn't believe how much it was like *The Stand*,' King admitted. 'It was almost as though I'd invented it myself.' In the unabridged version of the book, the disease is mentioned three times in passing. ✝

NEEDFUL THINGS

The Town of Castle Rock Just Made a Deal With the Devil...Now It's Time to Pay.

USA/Canada, 1993. Director: **Fraser C. Heston**. Producer: **Jack Cummins**. Screenplay: **W.D. Richter**. Executive Producer: **Peter Yates**. Director of Photography: **Tony Westman**. Production Designer: **Douglas Higgins**. Editor: **Rob Kobrin**. Music: **Patrick Doyle**. Associate Producer: **Gordon Mark**. Casting: **Mary Gail Artz** and **Barbara Cohen**. Based on the Book by **Stephen King**. Castle Rock Entertainment/New Line Cinema/Columbia Pictures. Colour. 120 minutes.

Ed Harris (Sheriff Alan Pangborn), **Max von Sydow** (Leland Gaunt), **Bonnie Bedelia** (Polly Chalmers), **J.T. Walsh** (Danforth Keeton III), **Amanda Plummer** (Nettie Cobb), **Valri Bromfield** (Wilma Jerzyk), **Ray McKinnon** (Deputy Norris Ridgewick), **Lisa Blount** (Cora Rusk), **Shane Meier** (Brian Rusk), **Duncan Fraser** (Hugh Priest), **W. Morgan Sheppard** (Father Meehan), **Don S. Davis** (Reverend Rose), **Campbell Lane** (Frank Jewett), **Eric Schneider** (Henry Beaufort), **Frank C. Turner** (Peter Jerzyk), **Gillian Barber** (Myrtle Keeton), **Deborah Wakeham** (Myra), **Tamsin Kelsey** (Sheila Ratcliff), **Lochlyn Munro** (John LaPointe), **Bill Croft** (Andy Clutterbuck), **Dee Jay Jackson** (Eddie Warburton), **Ann Warn Pegg** (Ruth Roberts), **Gary Paller** (George Cobb), **Sarah Sawatsky** (14 Year Old Girl), **Robert Easton** (Lester Pratt), **Mike Chute** (Young Hugh), **Mel Allen** (Baseball Announcer), **Trevor Denman** (Race Track Announcer), **K-Gin** (Raider).

When mysterious stranger Leland Gaunt opens his unusual antiques shop, Needful Things, in Castle Rock, Maine, almost overnight the townsfolk of the usually peaceful coastal community seem to go mad. Suddenly, for no discernible reason, close friends and neighbours begin turning against one another — inexplicably lashing out at each other in mindless acts of anger and violence. Sheriff Alan Pangborn is baffled and a little scared. Even his girlfriend Polly and their friend Nettie have been captivated by the seductive Gaunt, who promises that one of his shop's more unusual curios or collectibles will fulfil each and all of their deepest desires. Although Pangborn cannot prove anything, he begins to suspect that the sinister shop proprietor has provoked the local residents towards this hellish state in return for an apparently innocuous but ultimately depraved commitment from each of his bewitched customers. It is an obligation that the unsuspecting citizens of Castle Rock seem only too willing to pay.

'At some point I decided — first in my subconscious mind, I think, where all that Really Serious Work takes place — that the time had come to close the book on Castle Rock, Maine, where so many of my own favourite characters have lived and died...I wanted to *finish* things, and do it with a bang.' So explained Stephen King, who published his sprawling novel *Needful Things* in September 1991. Billed as 'The Last Castle Rock Story', the author's variation of Faustian bargains and mysterious antiques shops was possibly inspired by Richard Matheson's similar 1958 story 'The Distributor' in *Playboy* magazine.

The rights to King's novel were purchased by Rob Reiner's Castle Rock Entertainment for an impressive $1.75 million while the book was still in galley form.

Fraser C. Heston, the son of actor Charlton Heston, replaced Peter Yates (*Krull* [1983], etc) as director before production began. 'It's about good and evil,' Heston told *Fangoria* magazine, 'and it stars the Devil, played by Max von Sydow.'

After Castle Rock rejected an earlier first draft script by veteran King adapter Lawrence D. Cohen (*Carrie* [1976], etc) because of worries that he was being too faithful to the text, the unenviable task of adapting the author's 700-page novel into a workable screenplay fell to W.D. Richter, who admitted that he had never read any of King's other novels. 'I shudder thinking of how I had to go about it,' Richter told *Fangoria*'s Steve Newton. 'It's really daunting if you try to be too systematic about it, because you just start to think it can't be done and probably should be a mini-series. So I just started at the front and tried to economise as I went along. If a condensation occurred to me — a way to combine or skip over something — I'd take it as it came.'

Pre-production on the film began in August 1992 for a projected start date in mid-October. Heston flew to Sweden to meet with the actor he always envisioned for the principal role of Leland Gaunt: 'I loved Gaunt from the minute Fraser described him to me,' then-sixty-three year-old Max von Sydow recalled. 'I knew instantly that portraying him would be an actor's delight — wickedly full of possibilities, full of potential surprises.'

With interiors filmed at Canada's North Shore Studios, British Columbia, the production chose the coastal village of Gibsons Landing to transform into their ideal recreation of Castle Rock, Maine. 'We needed a single location where all the action would take place,' explained Heston, 'thereby creating a strong visual consistency.'

Some of the 2,500

residents of Gibsons Landing actively participated in the filming, as either supplementary crew members or extras, and the town's only bookstore apparently had trouble keeping King's novel in stock. However, as soon as the cameras started rolling, so did the thunder, as inclement bone-freezing rain poured down on the unit nearly every day.

Released in August 1994, the film barely managed to gross $13 million domestically. An extended 186-minute 'TV version' was released to American television station TBS on 22 May 1996. Amongst other scenes, it restored most of actress Lisa Blount's performance, which had originally ended up on the cutting room floor. As obsessed Elvis Presley fan Cora Rusk, she was another of Castle Rock's inhabitants who fell under Leland Gaunt's evil influence after buying a bust of The King along with his sunglasses.

As Heston recalled: 'Stephen wrote a big, complex book with a lot of peripheral information that works well in a novel, but which would be just too much for any film. Ultimately it boils down to hard choices. Any screenplay by its very nature must tell the larger story through a selection of highly-focused images. In my view, Rich Richter did a masterful job in making the choices he did. The structure is solid and the characters are interesting.' †

'Though this is by no means the grisliest or most witless film made from one of Mr King's horrific fantasies, it can lay claim to being the most unpleasant…Just when the film has begun to seem as tedious as it can be, it blossoms into last-minute speechiness, as the few remaining townsfolk renounce the devil and re-affirm humanity's fundamental goodness. Unfortunately for them, in this film the devil has all the good lines.'
The New York Times, 27 August 1993

Above: *The paranoid Danforth Keeton III (J.T. Walsh) begins to lose it.*
Left: *Max von Sydow as the devilish Leland Gaunt.*

FACT FILE

The character of Sheriff Alan Pangborn was previously portrayed by Michael Rooker in *The Dark Half* (1992), and although Stephen King recommended that the actor repeat his role, Castle Rock executives decided they wanted a bigger name in the part.

THE SHAWSHANK REDEMPTION

Fear Can Hold You Prisoner.
Hope Can Set You Free.

USA, 1994. Director: **Frank Darabont**. Producer: **Niki Marvin**. Screenplay: **Frank Darabont**. Based on the Short Novel 'Rita Hayworth and Shawshank Redemption' by **Stephen King**. Executive Producers: **Liz Glotzer** and **David Lester**. Director of Photography: **Roger Deakins**, BSC. Editor: **Richard Francis-Bruce**. Production Designer: **Terence Marsh**. Costume Design: **Elizabeth McBride**. Music: **Thomas Newman**. Casting: **Deborah Aquila**, CSA. Castle Rock Entertainment/Columbia Pictures. Colour. 142 minutes.

Tim Robbins (Andy Dufresne), **Morgan Freeman** (Ellis Boyd 'Red' Redding), **Bob Gunton** (Warden [Samuel] Norton), **William Sadler** (Heywood), **Clancy Brown** (Captain Hadley), **Gil Bellows** (Tommy), **Mark Rolston** (Bogs Diamond) **James Whitmore** (Brooks Hatlen), **Jeffrey DeMunn** (1946 D.A.), **Larry Brandenburg** (Skeet), **Brian Libby** (Floyd), **Neil Giuntoli** (Jigger), **David Proval** (Snooze), **Joseph Ragno** (Ernie), **Paul McCrane** (Guard Trout), **Jude Ciccolella** (Guard Mert), **Renee Blaine** (Andy Dufresne's Wife), **Scott Man** (Glenn Quentin), **John Horton** (1946 Judge), **Gordon C. Greene** (1947 Parole Hearings Man), **Alfonso Freeman** (Fresh Fish Con), **V.J. Foster** (Hungry Fish Con), **John E. Summers** (New Fish Guard), **Frank Medrano** (Fat Ass), **Mack Miles** (Tyrell), **Alan R. Kessler** (Laundry Bob), **Morgan Lund** (Laundry Truck Driver), **Cornell Wallace** (Laundry Leonard), **Gary Lee Davis** (Rooster), **Neil Summers** (Pete), **Ned Bellamy** (Guard Youngblood), **Joseph Pecoraro** (Projectionist), **Harold E. Cope Jr.** (Hole Guard), **Brian Delate** (Guard Dekins), **Don R. McManus** (Guard Wiley), **Donald E. Zinn** (Moresby Batter), **Dorothy Silver** (1954 Landlady), **Robert Haley** (1954 Food-Way Manager), **Dana Snyder** (1954 Food-Way Woman), **John D. Craig** (1957 Parole Hearings Man), **Ken Magee** (Ned Grimes), **Eugene C. De Pasquale** (Mail Caller), **Bill Bolender** (Elmo Blatch), **Ron Newell** (Elderly Hole Guard), **John R. Woodward** (Bullhorn Tower Guard), **Chuck Brauchler** (Man Missing Guard), **Dion Anderson** (Head Bull Haig), **Claire Slemmer** (Bank Teller), **James Kisicki** (Bank Manager), **Rohn Thomas** (Bugle Editor), **Charlie Kearns** (1966 D.A.), **Rob Reider** (Duty Guard), **Brian Brophy** (1967 Parole Hearings Man), **Paul Kennedy** (1967 Food-Way Manager), **Anthony Lucero***(Rory).
[* Does not appear in the final print.]

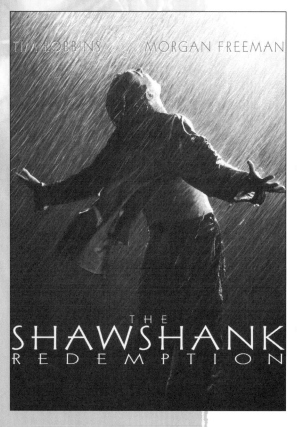

In 1946, soft-spoken, respected Maine banker Andy Dufresne is falsely accused and convicted of the murders of his unfaithful wife and her lover. Receiving a double life sentence, he is sent to brutal Shawshank State Prison, New England's toughest maximum security penitentiary. There he forges an unlikely friendship with seasoned lifer Red, who is a 'fixer' running a profitable sideline in procuring and smuggling anything in or out of the prison for a price. Dufresne also becomes popular with Shawshank's Warden Norton and some of the prison guards when he uses his financial talents to help several corrupt officials amass personal fortunes using prison labour. Over the next twenty years, against this backdrop of prison life, Dufresne finds a way to survive and teach others about the power of hope, friendship and redemption.

In 1976, following the completion of his epic novel *The Stand*, Stephen King discovered he had a case of writer's block. After starting and discarding two novels, he was only able to write the novella 'Rita Hayworth and Shawshank Redemption', which eventually appeared in his 1982 collection *Different Seasons*. The author admitted that his original tale about a prison-break was actually inspired by the home-spun narrators of novelist Max Brand, who had written the *Dr. Kildare* books. 'The result was a moody tale with more thinking than action in it,' explained the writer, 'not the sort of thing that usually makes a good movie.'

As if to prove him wrong, around 1987 twenty-four year-old screenwriter Frank Darabont wrote to King and asked if he could option the novella. Four years earlier, Darabont had made a short film out of King's story 'The Woman in the Room' which had greatly impressed the writer. While he agreed to grant an option, King admitted in his introduction to Darabont's 1995 book, *The Shawshank Redemption: The Shooting Script*: 'I never in a million years thought he would get the film made.'

'It was a story that captured my imagination

FACT FILE

The convincing 'mug shots' of Morgan Freeman used in the film are actually of the actor's son, Alfonso (who also has a cameo as the 'Fresh Fish' con), taken during pre-production by unit still photographer, Michael Weinstein.

Left: Andy Dufresne (Tim Robbins) and 'Red' Redding (Morgan Freeman) forge an unlikely friendship.
Below: Peter von Sholly's storyboards.

and sent my heart soaring,' revealed Darabont in his own introduction to the same book. 'It also instilled in me the hope that, someday, I might be lucky enough to put it on film.'

King moved on with other projects and Darabont directed the television movie *Buried Alive* (1989). Then in 1993, Darabont sent King a lengthy screenplay for *Rita Hayworth and Shawshank Redemption*. 'The story had a loose, amiable narrative; a first-person monologue, almost, by the narrator,' Darabont explained to Bill Warren in *Fangoria*. 'It didn't have what's generally perceived as a tight structure, and movies generally have those.'

However, King loved the script, and although initially dubious that the film would ever be made by Hollywood, he renewed Darabont's option. 'He did the screenplay pretty much on spec,' King recalled, 'sent it to me and I read it. It was just a mind-blowing piece of work.'

'It exposes people to a facet of King that isn't obvious, that isn't revealed quite enough,' Darabont told Warren. 'He's a great horror writer, but he's also written some amazing stories that aren't in the genre.'

The project was picked up by Castle Rock Entertainment, which had been founded on the success of another King movie adaptation from *Different Seasons*, Rob Reiner's critically acclaimed *Stand by Me* (1986). 'Castle Rock Pictures has more or less rescued my film-associated reputation from the scrap-heap,' King admitted in his introduction, 'and no picture had more to do with that than the one which eventually became known as *The Shawshank Redemption*.'

Having written the script on spec, Darabont had attached himself as director. However, according to Darabont himself, Castle Rock offered him 'shit loads of money' to allow Reiner to direct, which he refused.

Touted as a 'hot' script in Hollywood, among those actors who reportedly expressed interest in being cast in the film were Brad Pitt, Ray Liotta and Harvey Keitel (who just lost out playing Warden Norton to the taller Bob Gunton). Tom Cruise was actually set to portray Andy Dufresne, until he eventually pulled out and the role went to Tim Robbins.

Although in the late 1940s only one per cent of the Maine prison population was black, Castle Rock suggested Morgan Freeman for the pivotal role as the seasoned con 'Red' Redding — a red-haired Irishman in King's original story. 'We even kept Red's line in about his being Irish,' explained Darabont, 'which takes on an interesting and amusing new twist when spoken by Morgan.' Freeman was nominated for an Academy Award for Best Actor for his portrayal.

Taking his cue from music videos, Darabont recorded a temporary version of Freeman's voice-over — mostly taken verbatim from King's original novella — so that it could be replayed on the set during filming. Scenes could then be timed to exactly match the length of the narration. These sections were then replaced with a clean voice-over during post-production.

Pre-production began in January 1993 and lasted for five months. After two weeks of acting rehearsals, filming began during early summer at

Above: *Andy Dufresne rebels against the system.*

Below right: *Shawshank's 'fixer', 'Red' Redding.*

the abandoned 19th century Ohio State Reformatory in Mansfield, almost exactly halfway between Columbus and Cincinnati. Despite being primarily filmed in a real prison location, the giant cellblock was actually a set designed by Terence Marsh in a warehouse situated a mile from the prison.

Shooting in Ohio lasted three months and involved 2,000 extras. The sequence at the end of the movie, where Andy and Red are reunited on a beach in Mexico, was filmed on the final day of principal photography on Sain Croix in the US Virgin Islands. As Darabont pointed out in *The Shawshank Redemption: The Shooting Script*, although the scene is set in 1966, it features Tim Robbins driving a *1969* Pontiac GTO. Perhaps even more puzzling is how Andy Dufresne manages to stick back his poster of Raquel Welch in Hammer's *One Million Years B.C.* (1966) from the *inside* of his escape tunnel...?

During the nine months of post-production, King visited the editing room, while Darabont consulted with fellow director Rob Reiner and screened his almost-final cut to George Lucas — with whom he had worked on the television series *The Young Indiana Jones Chronicles* (1992-93).

During the sound editing, horror author and screenwriter David J. Schow contributed several uncredited pages of off-screen lines for the prison inmates to shout. 'The one I remember most distinctly is: "Who's the one with the curly hair and the Spanish good looks?",' recalled Darabont. 'That made everybody on the mixing stage laugh for days.'

The Shawshank Redemption was released in the United States on 10 September 1994. As with the earlier *Stand by Me*, Castle Rock Entertainment decided not to actively promote it as a Stephen King movie.

Unfortunately, despite the film receiving seven Academy Award nominations, including Best Adapted Screenplay and Best Picture, both the Academy and American audiences shunned the film, and it flopped at the US box-office, grossing only $28.3 million. 'It was crash and burn,' Darabont told *Empire*. 'As I discovered, there's a difference between the audience enjoying a movie and being convinced to show up in the first place...Thank God for video.' The film became the top video rental of 1995.

Darabont also received a Best Director nomination from the Directors Guild, plus Best Screenplay nominations from The Writers Guild and the Golden Globes. *The Shawshank Redemption* won the 1994 USC Scripter Award for best realisation of a book as a film, the Humanitas Prize for 1995, and the PEN Center West Literary Award for screenplay.

'It keeps winding up on these wonderful lists of all-time favourite movies voted for by the public,' added Darabont, who would next helm an adaptation of King's other 'prison' story, *The Green Mile* (1999). 'Any disappointment I might have felt at its initial failure has more than been compensated for. Ultimately you make a movie for people to see and enjoy. We seem to have succeeded.'

Russell Leven's hour long BBC-TV documentary *The Redeeming Feature* (2001) looked at the enduring appeal of *The Shawshank Redemption* and included interviews with King, Darabont and other key cast and crew members. ✝

THE MANGLER

There is a Little Piece of Everybody in...

USA/Israel/South Africa, 1994. Director: **Tobe Hooper**. Producer: **Anant Singh**. Screenplay: **Tobe Hooper**, **Stephen Brooks** and **Peter Welbeck**. Based on the Short Story by **Stephen King**. Director of Photography: **Amnon Salomon**. Production Designer: **Dave Barkham**. Editor: **David Heitner**. Music Composer and Conductor: **Barrington Pheloung**. Executive Producers: **Helena Spring**, **Harry Alan Towers**, **Sudhir Pragjee** and **Sanjeev Singh**. Visual Effects Supervisor: **Stephen Brooks**. Make-Up Effects: **Scott Wheeler**. The 'Mangler' Creator: **William Hooper**. Investec Bank Limited/Distant Horizon/Filmex/Allied Film Productions/New Line Cinema. Colour. 106 minutes.

Robert Englund (Bill Gartley), **Ted Levine** (John Hunton), **Daniel Matmor** (Mark Jackson), **Jeremy Crutchley** (Pictureman/Mortician), **Vanessa Pike** (Sherry Ouelette), **Demetre Phillips** (Stanner), **Lisa Morris** (Lin Sue), **Vera Blacker** (Mrs Frawley), **Ashley Hayden** (Annette Gillian), **Danny Keogh** (Herb Diment), **Ted Leplat** (Dr Ramos), **Todd Jensen** (Roger Martin), **Sean Taylor** (Derrick Gates), **Gerrit Schoonhoven** (Aaron Rodriguez), **Nan Hamilton** (Mrs Ellenshaw), **Adrian Waldron** (Mr Ellenshaw), **Norman Coombes** (Judge Bishop), **Larry Taylor** (Sheriff Hughes), **Irene Frangs** (Mrs Smith), **Megan Wilson** (Ginny Jason), **Odile Rault** (Alberta), **Ron Smerczak** (Officer Steele).

Police officer John Hunton investigates why a huge old Hadley Watson Model-6 Steam Ironer & Folder (also known as 'The Mangler') is grinding up the local workers at the Blue Ribbon Laundry in the sleepy Maine town of Rikers Valley. He discovers that the laundry's horribly crippled owner, Bill Gartley, is periodically sacrificing young virgins to the possessed machinery so that he and the other elders can maintain the town's unholy prosperity.

Stephen King's original story was published in the December 1972 issue of *Cavalier* and subsequently reprinted in his 1978 *Night Shift* collection. It was inspired by the time, in the early 1970s, when the struggling author earned just $60 per week working in an industrial laundry after he graduated from the University of Maine and was unable to find a job as a teacher.

The property was part of Milton Subotsky's original *Lawnmower Man* package bought by Allied Vision. Tobe Hooper reportedly contacted King and asked if he could get involved, providing he was faithful to the original story. Hooper then wrote several drafts of the screenplay with visual effects supervisor and second unit director Stephen Brooks. 'Stephen King got to see all the drafts,' Hooper told Joe Mauceri in *Shivers*. 'He gave his approval on many of the things we were trying to do even though he was busy working on *The Stand*.'

Hooper and Brooks expanded the character of Bill Gartley and added a haunted ice box, plus various background plot elements from King's story, into the main narrative. Legendary producer Harry Alan Towers also contributed to the script under his 'Peter

Welbeck' alias.

Filming took place in a converted warehouse, where all the major sets were built. Hooper's son William designed the old industrial laundry speed-pressing machine as well as the computer-generated image of the demonic mechanism.

'It took quite a few operators to make the thing work,' revealed the director. 'There were people actually in the machine and people hidden on the set working the speed so they could shut it off instantly.'

Released domestically in March 1995 and directly to video in the United Kingdom in September the same year, Hooper explained to Maurceri that 'Stephen is as happy with the film as we are. As it's turned out, *The Mangler* is more surreal. It's a dream-like piece, and the entire story takes place within a set twenty-four hour period.'

However, King apparently disagreed when he told Bill Warren in *Fangoria*: 'A lot of the movies based on my stuff have been done on a budget, like *The Mangler*, and have felt to me almost like studio crap by people who don't have big studio bucks.'

In 1999, Barnholtz Entertainment announced *The Mangler 2* starring Andrew McCarthy and Malcolm McDowell. The film was reportedly finally in pre-production in early 2001. ✝

THE DIRECTOR OF "POLTERGEIST" **TOBE HOOPER** STAR OF "A NIGHTMARE ON ELM STREET" **ROBERT ENGLUND** BASED ON A SHORT STORY BY **STEPHEN KING**

THERE IS A LITTLE PIECE OF EVERYBODY IN...

AN **ANANT SINGH** PRODUCTION

THE MANGLER

GUILD

'Add Towers to the fast-fading reputation of Tobe Hooper as a director with any vestige of talent left and *The Mangler* didn't have a hope in hell of succeeding.'
Starburst #202, June 1995

DOLORES CLAIBORNE

Sometimes an Accident Can Be an Unhappy Woman's Best Friend.

USA, 1995. Director: **Taylor Hackford**. Producers: **Taylor Hackford** and **Charles Mulvehill**. Screenplay: Tony Gilroy. Based on the Book by **Stephen King**. Director of Photography: **Gabriel Beristain**, BSC. Production Designer: **Bruno Rubeo**. Editor: **Mark Warner**. Costume Designer: **Shay Cunliffe**. Music: **Danny Elfman**. Casting: **Nancy Klopper**. Associate Producer: **Gina Blumenfeld**. Castle Rock Entertainment/Columbia Pictures. Colour. 131 minutes.

Kathy Bates (Dolores Claiborne), **Jennifer Jason Leigh** (Selena St. George), **Christopher Plummer** (Detective John Mackey), **David Strathairn** (Joe St. George), **Judy Parfitt** (Vera Donovan), **John C. Reilly** (Constable Frank Stamshaw), **Eric Bogosian** (Peter), **Ellen Muth** (Young Selena), **Bob Gunton** (Mr Pease), **Roy Cooper** (Magistrate), **Wayne Robson** (Sammy Marchant), **Ruth Marshall** (Secretary), **Weldon Allen** (Bartender), **Tom Gallant** (Searcher), **Kelly Burnett** (Jack Donovan), **Matt Appleby** and **Thomas Skinne**r (Kids on Street), **Vernon Steele** (Ferry Vendor), **Taffara Jessica Stella Murray** (Young Selena [Age 5]), **Susan Lane** (Crying Girl), **Frank Adamson** and **Ed Rubin** (Detective Supervisors), **Sandy MacDonald** (Sheriff), **Dean Eilertson** (Moving Man).

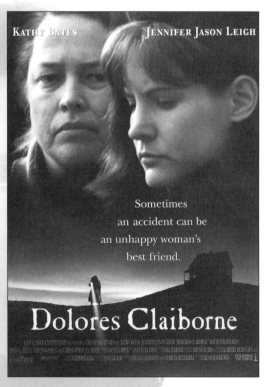

KATHY BATES   JENNIFER JASON LEIGH

Sometimes
an accident can be
an unhappy woman's
best friend.

Dolores Claiborne

Selena St. George, a successful if slightly neurotic New York magazine writer on the brink of a major story in Arizona, is suddenly forced to confront her troubled past when her mother Dolores Claiborne, who she has not seen for fifteen years, is accused of murdering her employer of twenty-two years — rich, crippled society matron Vera Donovan, for whom she worked as housekeeper and companion. Selena travels to Bangor, Maine, where Dolores admits that she and her former employer had not always got along. Eaten up with bitterness and old age despite her wealth, Vera Donovan had hovered on the brink of madness for many years. And when her demons became too strong, Dolores was there to take the abuse. Maybe one day Dolores had finally had enough. But what is the link with the suspicious death of her drunken and disparaging husband Joe during a total solar eclipse two decades earlier? Selena and shrewd local detective John Mackey both want to discover the truth, but for very different reasons. However, Dolores Claiborne's story turns out to be just a little bit darker, a little stranger and a lot more disturbing than anyone could have imagined...And sometimes being a bitch is all a woman has to hang on to.

Dolores Claiborne marked the end of Stephen King's $30 million plus multi-book contract with Viking/Penguin, the company that had published most of his novels since The Dead Zone back in 1979.

'What if a cleaning woman suspected of a murder she got away with (her husband) fell under suspicion for a murder she did not commit (her employer?)' was how King described his novel in his memoir On Writing.

After winning the Best Actress Academy Award in 1991 for her role in the King adaptation Misery (1990), Kathy Bates was perhaps an obvious choice to play the straight-talking murder suspect. 'Because he's such a wonderful writer,' Bates told Bruce Kirkland of the Toronto Sun newspaper, 'his characters have such opposites within themselves and express themselves so colourfully. There's just a lot to work on.'

Filmed on location in a number of fishing villages off the coast of Nova Scotia, Canada, an accidental fire on the set caused $1 million damage.

Director Taylor Hackford's reputation as a demanding and sometimes difficult director was confirmed by co-producer Charles Mulvehill, who recently worked with Hackford again on the Meg Ryan and Russell Crowe thriller Proof of Life (2000). He described the director's outbursts on set as 'Taylor's nut-outs', and went on to explain to William Prochnau in the Telegraph Magazine that he 'absolutely hated the man' by the end of Dolores Claiborne. 'Then time passed, it was a good movie, he called me, and...'

Much of the movie is told through flash-

Left: *Cathy Bates as murder suspect Dolores Claiborne.*
Below left: *Selena (Jennifer Jason Leigh) contemplates her future and her past.*

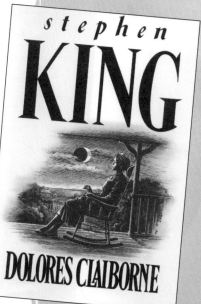

backs and the memories of the eponymous character over the previous two decades. 'It was a real challenge for an actor,' said the then-forty-six year-old Bates. 'She doesn't take any guff off anybody and she's become hard and crusty to do it.'

The film was released in March 1995 and grossed a disappointing $25 million domestically. However, when it came time to predict the Academy Awards, the film's consultant William Goldman maintained, 'No one gave a better performance than Kathy Bates in *Dolores Claiborne*.'

'I certainly had an affinity for this,' Bates told Bruce Kirkland. 'I went for the meat.' Despite that, she was beaten to the Oscar by Susan Sarandon in *Dead Man Walking*.

After being a secret substance abuser for many years, the now-recovering King admitted in a 1999 BBC documentary that 'In *Dolores Claiborne*, with the alcoholic father, some of the reactions there, some of the things I know about drinking, I know about drinking from having been a drunk. But a lot of the things that Joe St. George goes through in that book, are based on stories that I heard and people that I observed. Because, thank god, I was never a mean drunk.' ✝

Children of the Corn III
Urban Harvest

Based on the Story 'Children of the Corn' by Stephen King.

USA, 1994. Director: **James D.R. Hickox**. Producers: **Gary DePew** and **Brad Southwick**. Writer: **Dode B. Levenson**. Based on the Story 'Children of the Corn' by **Stephen King**. Supervising Producer: **Jim Begg**. Executive Producer: **Anthony L.V. Hickox**. Associate Producers: **Thomas C. Rainone** and **Donald Paul Pemrick**. Director of Photography: **Gerry Lively**. Editor: **Chris Peppe**. Music: **Daniel Licht**. Music Supervisor: **Robin Urdang**. Sound Design: **Jonathan Miller**. Creature Make-up Effects: **Screaming Mad George**. Production Design: **Blair A. Martin**. Wardrobe Supervisor: **Mark Bridges**. Casting: **Donald Paul Pemrick**, CSA. Park Avenue Productions/Force Majeure Productions/Illustra Films/Trans Atlantic Entertainment/Miramax Films/Dimension Home Video. Colour. 91 minutes.

Daniel Cerny (Eli), **Ron Melendez** (Joshua), **Michael Ensign** (Father Frank), **John Clair** (Malcolm), **Nancy Lee Grahn** (Alice [Porter]), **Jim Metzler** (William [Porter]), **Mari Morrow** (Maria), **Duke Stroud** (Earl), **Rance Howard** (Employer), **Brian Peck** (Jake), **Rif Hutton** (Arnold), **Garvin Funches** (T-LOC), **Johnny Legend** (Derelict Man), **Gina St John** (Diane), **Yvette Freeman** (Samantha), **Terrence Matthews** (Dwayne), **James O'Sullivan** (Charles), **Kelly Nelson** (Teacher), **Ed Grady** (Dr Appleby), **Nicholas Brendon** (Basketball Player One), **Anthony Hickox*** (Hans). [* Uncredited in the final print.]

After the younger brother kills their drunken father in the cornfields of Gatlin, orphans Eli and Joshua arrive in Chicago and are placed in the custody of a childless couple, William and Amanda Porter. While older brother Joshua attempts to adjust to their new urban lifestyle, his younger sibling plants a resistant strain of Gatlin corn in the courtyard of the abandoned warehouse next door. The satanic Eli uses his supernatural powers to kill anyone who discovers what he is doing, including his foster-mother Amanda, as he begins recruiting new converts from among his fellow students to the cult of 'He Who Walks Behind the Rows'. Only by destroying Eli's buried Bible can Josh and his friend Malcolm prevent a ritual massacre on the night of the Harvest Moon...

'**M**ick [Garris] and I were talking about this the other night,' King told Bill Warren in *Fangoria*. 'He asked if I've seen everything that's been based on my work. I realised I've never seen Larry Cohen's *Return to Salem's Lot*, and I've missed two of the *Children of the Corn* movies — and I like the genre, you know. There was one of those *Children of the Corn* movies, *Urban Harvest*, that I actually liked.'

Following *Children of the Corn II The Final Sacrifice* (1992), 'He Who Walks Behind the Rows' returned to the direct-to-video franchise in this second low budget sequel, which was filmed in December 1993 in and around Los Angeles.

This time the action moved from the Nebraska cornfields to urban Chicago. 'It's

basically one brother discovering the other is not what he seems to be,' co-producer Gary DePew explained to Anthony C. Ferrante in *Fangoria*. Ironically, DePew turned down a production assistant job on the original film back in 1984.

British-born film editor James Hickox made his directorial début on the sequel. The son of director Douglas Hickox (to whom the film is dedicated) and Academy Award-winning editor Anne V. Coates, he was helped by his older brother, director Anthony Hickox (*Hellraiser III Hell on Earth* [1992], etc), who served as executive producer and also worked uncredited as a second unit director on the production. 'I thought our styles would be more similar,' the younger Hickox told Ferrante, 'but we're pretty different.'

Two weeks before filming commenced, James Hickox was hit by a car and was on crutches for most of the shoot. However, the accident did not dampen his enthusiasm for the project: 'It's a movie that stands totally on its own, though it is a continuation of the previous story, only now set in the big city.'

Having rewritten Dode B. Levenson's script, Hickox was at pains to point out that, 'There's some blood in the film, but the effects are more part of the plot.'

Responsibility for creating the gigantic monstrosity that emerges from the cornfield during the climactic bloodbath fell to make-up effects designer Screaming Mad George and his crew. 'I wanted to put every disgusting element into the monster that I could,' he told Ferrante

Below: A derelict man (Johnny Legend) encounters the root of all evil.

in *Fangoria*. The finally-visualised creature, which was affectionately referred to on set as 'Jiffy the Corn Beast', looked more like a mutated venus flytrap, a combination human-plant-rattlesnake hybrid. Additional special make-up effects were designed and created by Kevin Yagher.

The film also included a flashback from the previous entry in the series depicting the death of Dr Appleby (played by Ed Grady), while director Ron Howard's father, character actor Rance Howard, turned up very briefly as William Porter's employee.

Dimension/Miramax considered releasing *Children of the Corn III Urban Harvest* theatrically in September 1994, but once again it finally went directly to video in 1995.

Although no longer having much to do with Stephen King's original *Penthouse* story, by now there was no stopping the franchise, and *Children of the Corn The Gathering* (1996) was next in the series. ✝

The Langoliers
(aka Stephen King's The Langoliers)

Prepare Yourself for the Flight of Your Life!

USA, 1995. Director: **Tom Holland**. Teleplay: **Tom Holland**. Based on the Novella 'The Langoliers' from *Four Past Midnight* by **Stephen King**. Producer: **David Kappes**. Editor: **Ned Bastille**. Director of Photography: **Paul Maibaum**. Production Designer: **Evelyn Sakash**. Casting: **Lynn Kressel**. Laurel-King Inc/ABC-TV/Republic Pictures. Colour. 180 minutes.

Patricia Wettig (Laurel Stevenson), **Dean Stockwell** (Bob Jenkins), **David Morse** (Brian Engle), **Mark Lindsay Chapman** (Nick Hopewell), **Frankie Faison** (Don Gaffney), **Baxter Harris** (Rudy Warwick), **Kimber Riddle** (Bethany Simms), **Christopher Collet** (Albert Kaussner), **Kate Maberly** (Dinah Bellman), **Bronson Pinchot** (Craig Toomy), **Tom Holland** (Harker), **Julie Arnold Lisnet** (Aunt Vicki), **Michael Louden** (Richard Logan), **Kimberly Dakin** (Doris Heartman), **David Forrester** (Danny Keene), **Chris Hendrie** (James Deegan), **Jennifer Nichole Porter** (Gate Agent), **John Griesemer** (Roger Toomy), **Christopher Cooke** (Craig [9 Years]), **Stephen King** (Tom Holby), **David Kelly** (Little Boy), **Stephanie Dunham** (Little Girl), **John Winthrop Philbrick** (Father).

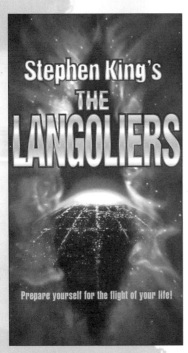

On 'red-eye' American Pride flight # 29 from Los Angeles to Boston, a group of ten airline passengers wake up to discover that everyone else on the plane, including the flight crew, has disappeared but left their belongings behind. The remaining passengers — who include a school teacher, a telepathic twelve year-old blind girl, a British government assassin, a mystery novelist, a music student and a pilot — realise that they are trapped in another dimension created by a rip in time. After landing the plane at a strangely deserted Bangor Airport, they are pursued by flying teeth monsters, dubbed 'The Langoliers', from the childhood nightmares of deranged businessman Craig Toomy.

Stephen King, who has admitted to a fear of flying, published this time-travel novella in his 1990 collection *Four Past Midnight*. It was inspired, the author revealed, by the mental image 'of a woman pressing her hand over a crack in the wall of a commercial jetliner...One night, while I was lying in bed, on the edge of sleep, I realised this woman was a ghost.'

Following their work together on the television mini-series *It* (1991), *The Tommyknockers* (1993) and *The Stand* (1994), King once again teamed up with co-executive producer Richard P. Rubinstein (who had optioned the story three years earlier) to make *The Langoliers* as a two-part, four-hour mini-series for ABC-TV. 'Basically, it's a popcorn movie,' Rubinstein explained to Dan Scapperotti in *Cinefantastique*. 'It's sort of light.' He went on to describe

the project as 'Steve King meets Irwin Allen' and called it 'Steve's version of *Ten Little Indians*'.

While developing a proposed film version of King's pseudonymous novel *Thinner* several years earlier with Warner Bros, Rubinstein had been introduced to Tom Holland, who the studio had brought in to direct. While still waiting for that project to happen, King and Rubinstein decided to hire Holland for *The Langoliers*.

The writer and director, whose genre credits included *Fright Night* (1985) and *Child's Play* (1988), revealed that he approached *The Langoliers* as if it was a theatrical release. 'Really, my sole intent in taking this assignment was to honour King's vision,' he told *Fangoria*. It took Holland, who also admitted to being 'absolutely terrified when I fly', fourteen months to write the script, which he described as 'the airplane ride from Hell'.

The production was filmed during the sweltering summer of 1994 in and around Bangor International Airport in Maine, followed by four months post-production. After rejecting all the available airline sets they saw, the production opted to buy its own. Most of the action was shot on an engineless L1011 airliner located by mechanical and engineering effects supervisor Vince Montefusco. 'The producers wanted authenticity, and that's what we're giving them,' he said.

The jet plane had its wings removed and was segmented into ten slices before being shipped from California's Mojave Desert up to Bangor on seven tractor trailers. There it was reassembled inside a hangar at Bangor Airport

'Despite its talky telescript (by director Tom Holland), it's still interesting how these oddball passengers figure out how to save themselves, and it's full of fascinating premises about the conduct of past, present and future.'

Creature Features: The Science Fiction, Fantasy, and Horror Movie Guide

and mounted on a hydraulic gimble to simulate the aircraft's movements.

With much of the budget being spent in other areas, Rubinstein decided against a star cast. 'We were looking for actors who could realise the roles effectively and not distract the audience,' explained the producer. Holland worked closely with his cast to ensure that the line between good and evil became blurred.

As manic business executive Craig Toomy, the man responsible for the passengers' predicament, mis-cast comedian Bronson Pinchot explained to Rodney A. Labbe in *Fangoria*: 'My character is a really venal kind of guy, so far removed from the usual physical comedy roles I'm offered.

'As Toomy, I've never felt so well-adjusted and behaved,' continued Pinchot. 'There's so much sick stuff coming out of me, it's cathartic — like a therapy session.'

Although King was not as involved in the production to the extent that he had been on previous projects based on his work, Holland revealed to Labbe that, 'Steve's been on the set, watching dailies, really taking a genuine interest...Basically, it's because of Steve's influence that we're up here.

'We gave him a good part too,' added the director about King's cameo as Toomy's chairman of the board.

Aware that the author had been unhappy with the eventual visualisation of his monster in *It*, Rubinstein and King discussed whether to use live-action or computer-generated images to create The Langoliers themselves. 'We felt that the computer-generated illusions texturally were very appropriate for this concept of pulling this out of your childhood fear of something both scary but a little bit cartoonish,' Rubinstein explained in *Cinefantastique*.

The creatures were created by Thomas A.B. Barham and a team of five CGI animators at New York-based Image Design from three 3-D models created by Vincent Guastini. 'The Langoliers can display an array of almost human emotions and facial movements,' Barham told *Fangoria*. 'Never once will you think of our monsters as fake or cartoonish — they're alive. They're real. They're *actors*.'

'We put a disproportional amount of money into the computer-generated effects for a television movie,' Rubinstein told Scapperotti.

However, despite the budget spent, when they finally turned up, King's Langoliers looked like flying Pac-Men with mouths full of oversized incisors.

This laughably cliché-ridden mini-series was shown during the May 'sweeps' period. Holland (who also appeared in a cameo) described it as 'A homage to *The Twilight Zone* and all those great, weird stories Rod Serling used to do so well.'

'I wasn't crazy about it,' King revealed in a *Fangoria* interview with Linda Marotta. 'That was more of a TV thing. But given what it was, it was fine. The best thing about it was that it gave Tom Holland and Richard Rubinstein the bona fides they needed to get Spelling Productions to go ahead with *Thinner*.'

Following *The Langoliers*, Laurel was quietly dissolved after eighteen years as a result of the merger of Viacom, Paramount and Blockbuster. ✝

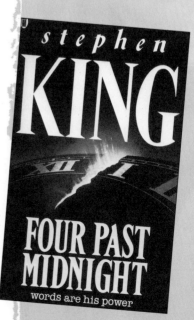

Above top: *The psychotic Craig Toomy (Bronson Pinchot) meets his worst childhood nightmare.*
Above: *Bethany (Kimber Riddle) and Albert (Christopher Collet) are confronted by flying teeth.*

stephen
KING
XII I
FOUR PAST MIDNIGHT
words are his power

Lawnmower Man 2
Beyond Cyberspace

God Made Him Simple, Science Made Him a God. Now, He Wants Revenge.

USA/UK, 1995. Director: **Farhad Mann**. Screenplay: **Farhad Mann**. Story: **Farhad Mann** and **Michael Miner**. Producers: **Keith Fox** and **Edward Simons**. Executive Producers: **Steve Lane**, **Robert Pringle**, **Peter McRae**, **Clive Turner** and **Avram Butch Kaplan**. Associate Producer: **Masao Takiyama**. Director of Photography: **Ward Russell**. Production Designer: **Ernest H. Roth**. Editors: **James D. Mitchell**, ACE, and **Joel Goodman**. Costume Designer: **Deborah Everton**. Music: **Robert Folk**. Casting: **Glenn Daniels**. Allied Film Productions/August Entertainment/Allied Entertainments/Fuji Eight Co, Ltd/New Line Cinema. Colour. 93 minutes.

Patrick Bergin (Dr Benjamin Trace), **Matt Frewer** (Jobe), **Austin O'Brien** (Peter [Parkette]), **Ely Pouget** (Cori [Platt]), **Camille Cooper** (Jennifer), **Kevin Conway** ([Jonathon] Walker), **Patrick La Brecque** (Shawn), **Crystal Celeste Grant** (Jade), **Sean Parhm** (Travis), **Mathew Valencia** (Homeless Kid), **Trever O'Brien** (Young Peter), **Richard Fancy** (Senator Greenspan), **Ellis Williams** (Chief of Security), **Castulo Guerra** (Guillermo), **Molly Shannon** (Homeless Lady), **Ralph Ahn** (Doctor), **David Byrd** (Judge), **Stephanie Menuez** (Female Lawyer), **Nancy Chen** (Cashier), **Amanda Hillwood** (News Anchor), **Patricia Belcher** (Impatient Customer), **Gregg Daniel** (Trace's Lawyer), **Arthur Mendoza** (Technician), **Dale E. House** (Helicopter Pilot), **John Benjamin Martin** (Henry the Guard), **Ayo Adejugbe** (Nigerian Businessman), **Yoshio Be** (Japanese Businessman), **Carl Carlsson-Wollbruck** (German Businessman), **David Gibbs** (Male Pilot), **Pamela West** (Female Co-Pilot), **Dan Lipe** (Security Guard), **Kenny Endoso** (Train Conductor).

Following the explosion at Virtual Space Industries, the transformed Jobe escapes from cyberspace and is rushed to hospital where Dr Cori Platt begins to rebuild his mind. Meanwhile, the patent to Dr Benjamin Trace's revolutionary new 'Chiron' microchip has fallen into the hands of Datatronic Systems Inc, owned by unscrupulous tycoon Jonathon Walker. In a dystopian near-future Los Angles, Walker needs the mind of the crippled Jobe to realise the chip's potential so that he can control the world's financial systems through his global network of computers. However, no one realises that Jobe has an agenda of his own. Now he can penetrate a realm of infinite possibility — the world of Virtual Reality — he can annihilate our reality. He can create a diabolical new world, a universe where he is the new Messiah. Only four teenage hackers and the reclusive Dr Trace possess the knowledge to stop him. The scientist and his young friends must enter the cyberscape environment of a huge VR city and prevent the megalomaniac Jobe from controlling the world through its technology.

Despite Stephen King having successfully sued to have his name removed from the credits of *The Lawnmower Man* (1992), that film's impressive boxoffice results and subsequent success on video convinced Allied Film Productions to go ahead with plans to create a potential 'franchise' from the character of simpleton turned supermind Jobe.

Allied chairman Edward Simons refused to rush into doing a sequel immediately. 'I was initially concerned because the technology hadn't moved ahead far enough,' he told David Bassom in *Starburst*. The lengthy pre-production schedule included storyboarding and timing every shot and testing the visual effects sequences on video. 'We all knew what we were getting into,' said Simons.

With original star Pierce Brosnan moving on to bigger and better things as the new James Bond in *Goldeneye* (1995), Patrick Bergin was cast as scientist Dr Benjamin Trace, 'the father of virtual reality', who must save the world. The role of the megalomaniac Jobe went to Canadian actor Matt Frewer, who portrayed the character in his usual over-the-top manner. The change was unconvincingly explained early in the film when Jobe is given facial reconstruction after being dragged from the rubble of the laboratory explosion. 'The cast changes were not easy to accommodate,' Simons admitted to Bassom. 'We were very concerned about the continuity, but we've overcome it, both with the script and the new actors.'

'The premise is that this one takes up where the first one left off,' Frewer explained to Todd French in *Cinefantastique*.

Original director Brett Leonard had also moved on, although he was still stuck in the world of virtual reality with *Virtuosity* (1995). In his place was commercials director Farhad Mann, who had previously worked with Frewer on the pilot episode of the American *Max Headroom* (1987) television series.

Filmed under the title *Lawnmower Man 2: Jobe's War*, the CGI effects used to visualise Jobe's Cybercity were created by Cinesite. However, although the sequel was apparently set in a *Bladerunner*-type future some decades after the first film, Austin O'Brien's returning character of Peter Parkette had only aged a few years between the two films.

'There is much more emotion in the second film than there was in the first one,' Simons told Bassom. 'If this does what we anticipate it is going to do at the boxoffice, then there will be another one.'

Shooting on the $15 million production wrapped in Los Angeles on Christmas Eve 1994 and post-production effects were completed in around a month. Not unexpectedly, King's name was nowhere to be found on the unnecessary sequel. Finally released directly to video on 12 January 1996, the producers made the decision to aim the film at a younger audience.

Frewer was rightly concerned that the complexity and ambiguity of the story would be toned down as a consequence. However, as the actor revealed to French: 'I think the movie Farhad's made is actually a far better film than the first *Lawnmower Man*. I also think that the VR effects are superior to the effects in the first movie.'

When the film flopped, plans for a third entry in the franchise, along with a *Lawnmower Man* television series, amusement park ride and series of computer games, quietly faded away. ✝

'This laughable miscalculation utterly fails to cash in on the sleeper success of its progenitor…By far, the worst failing is the attempt to turn this into a kids' movie, complete with PG-13 rating.'
Cinefantastique vol 28 no 1, August 1996

Above top: Jobe (Matt Frewer) rules a new Virtual Reality.
Above: The resurrected Jobe plans to control the world through its technology.

Sometimes They Come Back...Again
(aka Sometimes They Come Back 2)

True Evil Never Dies.

USA, 1995. Director: **Adam Grossman**. Screenplay: **Guy Riedel** and **Adam Grossman**. Story: **Guy Riedel**. Based on Characters Created by **Stephen King**. Producer: **Michael Meltzer**. Executive Producers: **Mark Amin** and **Barry Barnholtz**. Director of Photography: **Christopher Baffa**. Music Composer: **Peter Manning Robinson**. Editor: **Stephen Myers**. Supervising Editor: **Michael E. Polakow**, ACE. Line Producer: **Jo Ann May-Pavey**. Co-Producers: **Phillip B. Goldfine** and **Milton Subotsky**. Special Visual Effects: **Vision Crew Unlimited**. Production Designer: **Aaron Osborne**. Costume Designer: **Bonnie Ann Stauch**. Casting: **Ed Mitchell** and **Robyn Ray**, CSA. Trimark Pictures/Vidmark. Colour. 98 minutes.

Michael Gross (Jon Porter), **Alexis Arquette** (Tony Reno), **Hilary Swank** (Michelle Porter), **Jennifer Elise Cox** (Jules Martin), **W. Morgan Sheppard** (Father Archer Roberts), **Bojesse Christopher** (Vinnie Ritacco), **Patrick Renna** (Young Alan), **Gabriel Dell Jr** (Steve Pagel), **Jennifer Aspen** (Maria Moore), **Leslie Danon** (Lisa Porter), **Glen Beaudin** (Sean Patrick), **Molly Hagen** (Officer Violet Searcey), **Michael Stadvec** (Phil Thorn), **Michael Malota** (Young Jon), **Ingrid Sthare** (Jennifer Hadley), **Audree Gibbs** (Page Porter), **Matt Tracey** (Vinnie's Body Double).

Some things are better left... dead.

Psychologist Jon Porter and his daughter Michelle return to Porter's hometown of Grover Corner after the strange death of his mother. There they are menaced by a trio of demonic teenagers from the 1960s, led by Tony Reno, who sacrificed Jon's sister Lisa in a Satanic ritual before being electrocuted in a pool of blood. Now Reno and his fellow hoodlums have returned after thirty years and are looking to sacrifice Michelle at midnight on her eighteenth birthday.

'It's based more on the characters and tries to remain true to the theme and the morality of the original,' producer Michael Meltzer told Michael Beeler in *Cinefantastique*. 'I think there's a conscious effort to be respectful to Stephen King and what he's trying to say thematically.'

This direct-to-video sequel to the 1991 CBS-TV movie, which reportedly did extremely well in the international market, was basically a reworking of the first film.

USC film school graduate and former CAA mailroom clerk Adam Grossman, who rewrote the original first draft script by Guy Reidel, decided early on to take a more realistic approach to the material, citing *Carrie* (1976) as an example of what he and producer Michael Meltzer were trying to achieve.

'I love Stephen King,' the then-thirty year-old fledgling director told *Cinefantastique*. 'I think he's a wonderful storyteller. When I read the short story, I felt like this could be a really creepy movie.'

Actor Michael Gross, who played Steven Keaton on the hit NBC sitcom *Family Ties* (1982-89), had just completed *Tremors II Aftershocks* (1995) when he was cast as the single-parent psychologist still trying to come to terms with his sister's horrific death and trying to protect his daughter from her reincarnated murderers. 'I've never gone into this kind of demons and devils sort of stuff,' the actor explained to Beeler. 'And I thought it would be fun.'

Actor Alexis Arquette did not consider his character of Tony 'the bad guy', but he did admit to Beeler that 'He's less of a homicidal maniac and more of a really calculating Satanic observer.'

With a budget of just $3 million and a schedule that involved shooting fourteen hours a day, six days a week, principal photography wrapped in just under thirty days. Most of the picture was filmed in the Greater Los Angeles area, including location shooting in Griffith Park at the famous Bronson Cavern.

Grossman and his crew had to take the approach that smaller was better. 'If it's not going to look great, let's do something else' was the director's philosophy.

Despite the low budget, the shoot encountered few problems. However, while filming interiors for the Porter home in a reportedly haunted Victorian house in the Pasadena area of the city, a noisy neighbour demanded money from the production to remain quiet, and an entire day's worth of rushes were also lost when a white streak appeared down the middle of the developed film. The scenes had to be re-shot, much to the director's frustration.

To create the film's special effects, producer

Meltzer turned to Vision Crew Unlimited, a company which had recently been formed by effects co-ordinator Evan Jacobs and Jon Warren, both former employees of Richard Edlund's Boss Film Corporation. *Sometimes They Come Back...Again* was the first film they worked on as a team.

The special make-up effects were sub-contracted to Bart J. Mixon and Earl Ellis of ME*FX. 'We worked closely with both director Adam Grossman and producer Michael Meltzer to deliver the vision they sought,' explained Mixon, 'as well as interfacing with Vision Crew's physical effects on such sequences as the demon rising from the blood pool.'

Mixon and Ellis were also responsible for Alexis Arquette's climactic transformation into a pointy-eared demon with horns, a decapitation by lawnmower and the bloody demise of Michelle's psychic friend Jules (played by Jennifer Elise Cox), who is impaled by flying razor-sharp Tarot cards. 'It was done with prosthetics in gradual stages,' Cox explained to Thomas Crow in *Fangoria*. 'The most uncomfortable was my mouth, because I had to wear a mouthpiece with a card. It really looked weird.'

'We wanted to do fewer effects, but make them real sharp,' Jacob revealed to Crow.

In a stand-out performance, future Academy Award-winner Swank portrayed Porter's teenage daughter Michelle, who dreams of her father having sex with a snake-tailed demon. 'I'm cry-

ing about someone's ears being delivered to me in a box,' she revealed to Crow on set. 'It's not like I'm really moved. I have to open it up and freak out right away. It's very challenging in that regard. I didn't think it was going to be this difficult.'

The film was released directly to video in America in 1996. Following his successful law suit against the producers of *The Lawnmower Man* (1992), the decision was taken not to promote the movie as a Stephen King film. However, despite the 'Based on Characters Created by' credit, there was still only a very tenuous connection between the previous film and the follow-up (school teacher Jim Norman, the hero of the first movie, becomes one of Tony Reno's victims in this disjointed sequel).

The late Milton Subotsky, who optioned the original King story, once again received another posthumous co-producer credit.

'I think that any good horror movie is about disrupting what we think is safe,' explained Grossman, who co-scripted an even more nebulous sequel, *Sometimes They Come Back For More*, three years later. †

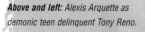
Above and left: *Alexis Arquette as demonic teen delinquent Tony Reno.*

'There isn't much coherence to the plot, but that never stops director Grossman from grossing out on electrocuted corpses, pools of blood six inches deep, and other visual delights designed to please empty-headed gore buffs.'

*Creature Features:
The Science Fiction, Fantasy,
and Horror Movie Guide*

Children of the Corn
The Gathering

In a Sleepy Midwestern Town...A Horrifying Evil is About to Rise Again!

USA, 1996. Director: **Greg Spence**. Writers: **Stephen Berger** and **Greg Spence**. Producer: **Gary DePew**. Based on the Short Story 'Children of the Corn' by **Stephen King**. Director of Photography: **Richard Clabaugh**. Associate Producer: **Jake Eberle**. Production Designer: **Adele Plauché**. Editor: **Chris** Cibelli. Music: **David Williams**. Casting: **Donald Paul Pemrick**, CSA. Miramax Film Corp/Dimension Films/Dimension Home Video. Colour. 85 minutes.

Naomi Watts (Grace Rhodes), **Brent Jennings** (Donald Atkins), **William Windom** (Doctor Rob Larson), **Karen Black** (June Rhodes), **Jamie Renee Smith** (Margaret Rhodes), **Mark Salling** (James Rhodes), **Toni Marsh** (Sandra Atkins), **Lewis Flanagan III** (Marcus Atkins), **Brandon Kleyla** (Josiah), **Salle Ellis** (Jane Nock), **Marietta Marich** (Rosa Nock), **Jonathan Patterson** (Charlie McLellan), **Joshua Patterson** (Scott McLellan), **Kay Bower** (Janet McLellan), **Samaria Graham** (Mary Anne), **Evan Greenwalt** (Convulsive Boy), **Adam Lidberg** (Michael), **Libby Villari** (Michael's Mom), **Bill Prael** (Concerned Father), **John Edson III** (Son of Concerned Father), **Stephen Earnhart** (Wilks), **Jim Krieg** (Mits), **Richard Gross** (Sheriff Biggs), **Harrison Young** (Drifter), **Chris Wheatley** (Josiah Double).

Medical student Grace Rhodes reluctantly returns home from college to Grand Island, Nebraska, to care for her disturbed mother June, younger brother James and sister Margaret. While working at the local clinic, she discovers that the town's children are being struck down by a mysterious virus which leaves them feverish and denying their own names. The cause of the children's strange behaviour is the ghostly spirit of disfigured boy-preacher Josiah. Abandoned by his unwed mother and raised by travelling evangelists, he has returned to seek revenge on the inhabitants of the small rural community who burned him alive in the cornfields. Soon the youngsters' teeth are falling out as they take on the names of children who died years earlier. When the town's adults start being slaughtered with a variety of sharp implements, only Grace can prevent Josiah from taking the soul of her secret daughter on the night of the Harvest Moon.

'The world needs another *Children of the Corn* movie like it needs a *Bio-Dome* Part 2...Director Greg Spence deserves credit for beefing up this predictable hokum with bizarre hallucinations and a handful of energetic moments, but the movie never generates much interest.'
Fangoria #159, January 1997

'The series has been unusual in starting out dismally and then getting better with each subsequent offering...The most unusual aspect of the film is its lead characters, whom we actually come to care about.'
Cinefantastique vol 28 no 10, April 1997

BASED ON THE STORY "CHILDREN OF THE CORN" BY STEPHEN KING

CHILDREN OF THE CORN IV THE GATHERING

Producer Gary DePew returned from *Children of the Corn III Urban Harvest* (1994) for this follow-up in name only in the direct-to-video franchise series.

Continuing the series' tradition — dating back to R.G. Armstrong's cameo in the first *Children of the Corn* (1984) — of featuring well known character actors in supporting roles, Karen Black's paranoid recluse is dragged to her death in a barn while William Windom's kindly town doctor (whose name is spelled 'Larsen' in the film) ends up being chopped in half by a pair of possessed twins.

Filmed in Austin, Texas, and Los Angeles, this unconnected entry (minus a title numeral) included the usual impalings, decapitations and crucifixions, courtesy of special make-up effects designer Gary Tunnicliffe and his crew. Clive Barker was amongst those thanked in the end credits.

This third sequel in the series did not appear on video in the United Kingdom until February 1999, by which time *Children of the Corn V Fields of Terror* had already been made and released domestically. ✝

Stephen King's Thinner

Be Careful What You Wish for... You Just Might Get It.

USA, 1996. Director: **Tom Holland**. Producers: **Richard P. Rubinstein** and **Mitchell Galin**. Screenplay: **Michael McDowell** and **Tom Holland**. Based on the Novel by **Stephen King**. Director of Photography: **Kees Van Oostrum**, ASC. Production Designer: **Laurence Bennett**. Editor: **Marc Laub**. Special Makeup Creator: **Greg Cannom**. Costume Designer: **Ha Nguyen**. Executive Producer: **Stephen F. Kesten**. Music Composer: **Daniel Licht**. Casting: **Leonard Finger**. Spelling Films, Inc/Paramount Pictures/Republic Pictures. Colour. 92 minutes.

Robert John Burke (Billy Halleck), **Michael Constantine** (Tadzu Lempke), **Lucinda Jenney** (Heidi Halleck), **Kari Wuhrer** (Gina Lempke), **John Horton** (Judge Cary Rossington), **Sam Freed** (Dr Mike Houston), **Daniel Von Bargen** (Chief Duncan Hopley), **Joe Mantegna** (Richie Ginelli), **Elizabeth Franz** (Leda Rossington), **Walter Bobbie** (Kirk Penschley), **Lucinda Jenney** (Heidi Halleck), **Joy Lenz** (Linda Halleck), **Time Winters** (Prosecutor), **Howard Erskine** (Judge Phillips), **Terrence Garmey** (Bailiff), **Randy Jurgensen** (Court Clerk), **Jaff Ware** (Max Duggenfield), **Antonette Schwartzberg** (Mama Ginelli), **Terrence Kava** (Gabe Lempke), **Adriana Delphine** (Gypsy Woman), **Ruth Miller** (Billy's Secretary), **Irma St Paule** (Suzanne Lempke), **Stephen King** (Pharmacist [Dr Bangor]), **Patrick Farrelly** (Henry Halliwell), **Bridget Marks** (Ginelli Bar Girl), **Mitchell Greenberg** (Male Clinic Doctor), **Angela Pietropinto** (Female Clinic Doctor), **Michael Walker** (Clinic Waiter), **Ed Wheeler** (Detective Deevers), **Peter Maloney** (Bill Quigley), **Robert Fitch Sr** (Flash Enders), **Sean Hewitt** ('DR' Fander), **Josh Holland** (Frank Spurton), **Allelon Ruggiero** (Delivery Boy).

Unpleasant and overweight attorney William F. Halleck, put on a liquid diet at home by his wife Heidi, is actually gorging himself on huge helpings of food while defending his client Richie Ginelli, who is on trial for attempted murder. After winning an acquittal for the grateful Ginelli, Billy Halleck is driving home from a celebratory dinner when he is distracted by his wife's sexual ministrations and accidentally runs down and kills an old gypsy woman. When the shady lawyer is exonerated by both the town judge and the chief of police, the woman's husband, 106 year-old gypsy king Tadzu Lempke, seeks his own justice. Touching Billy's cheek, he whispers the curse 'Thinner'. Soon Halleck discovers that he can eat as much as he wants to and still lose weight uncontrollably, while the judge and police chief are no longer able to go out in public due to their own physical deformities. Billy turns to his gangster friend Ginelli to force Lempke to lift the curse before he wastes away to nothing.

Left: Chief Hopley (Daniel Von Bargen) suffers the gypsy curse.

Based on the 1984 novel by Stephen King, his fifth written under the 'Richard Bachman' alias. The book initially sold a respectable 28,000 hardcover copies before King announced in February 1985 in *The Bangor Daily News* that he was really Bachman. The book's sales subsequently shot up to 300,000 copies.

Richard P. Rubinstein had acquired the rights to the novel in the late 1980s and commissioned novelist and screenwriter Michael McDowell to script it. For Rubinstein and director Tom Holland it was the end of a seven-year wait since they had first met while the film was being initially developed by Warner Bros.

The project had subsequently been turned down by various studios, and Holland estimated that he had rewritten the script around ten or fifteen times

over a five-and-a-half year period. 'Michael McDowell had drafted a *Thinner* screenplay, and I tightened it up,' Holland told Rodney A. Labbe in *Fangoria*. 'We didn't lose anything, though every studio was pushing for a happy ending.'

'It was a great script,' said King, who also did an uncredited polish on the screenplay himself.

Casting began in February 1995 in New York, and the author had very specific ideas about who he wanted to play the role of cursed attorney Billy Halleck. 'John Candy would be perfect,' King told Gary L. Wood in *Cinefantastique*, adding prophetically, 'He'd have to lose some weight, and maybe it'd save his life.'

In the end, actor Robert John Burke (*RoboCop 3* [1993], etc) was cast and lost twenty pounds for the role. When veteran make-up supervisor Dick Smith pulled out because of other commitments, Academy Award-winner Greg Cannom and his crew had only two and a half months of pre-production — instead of the six requested — before shooting began. It took them between one and a half and two and a half hours to apply Burke's heavy make-up, which the actor sometimes had to wear for between thirteen and fifteen hours a day on set.

Although set in the fictional town of Fairview, Connecticut, the $17 million production started filming in and around the Camden-Rockport area of Maine in mid-August 1995. 'It's like they're doing *Misery* on a *Graveyard Shift* budget,' King told Linda Marotta in *Fangoria* at the time. 'I've been down there as much as I could be, because they're in Maine just down the road apiece.'

Although King was not happy with some of the choices made in casting the principal actors, he did admit: 'I liked Joe Mantegna's performance — I thought he was great.' The author himself also turned up in a cameo as a pharmacist named after his home town. 'I think his acting is improving, actually,' quipped Holland.

Principal photography wrapped during the first week of November and Paramount had planned to release *Thinner* on 3 May, but complaints from test-screening audiences that the ending was too subtle led to extra make-up effects being added to bolster Billy's demise. In the original ending, which mirrored the author's novel, Billy ate the gypsy pie and it was left up to the viewer to assume that he and his family died.

However, at the end of April, Holland and his crew were reunited with Robert Burke in Maine for six days to shoot new sequences showing the corpses of Billy's wife and daughter (the latter not used in the final cut).

King, who admitted that it perhaps was not his favourite picture due to 'disappointed expectations', revealed to Bill Warren in *Fangoria*: 'When they finished it, it seemed like such a barker, and I don't mean Clive, I mean a dog. We all tried our hand at cutting it, but in the end they turned it over to the suits at Spelling. I don't know who finally made the creative editing decisions, except they *weren't* creative decisions — they were made by people who have no sense of humour.'

Because of the reshoots, *Thinner* did not make it to the screens until 25 October, where it quickly disappeared once audiences discovered that Holland's mean-spirited film did not have a single likeable character. 'The movie actually made a little money,' said King, 'and I don't think any of us expected that.'

It was finally released directly to video in the United Kingdom in 1997. The American video also included a twenty-minute behind-the-scenes featurette entitled *The Magic of Special Effects Make-Up* (1997). ✝

STEPHEN KING'S THE SHINING

Sometimes the Family Can Drive You a Little Crazy.

USA, 1997. Director: **Mick Garris**. Teleplay: **Stephen King**. Based Upon the Novel by **Stephen King**. Producer: **Mark Carliner**. Executive Producer: **Stephen King**. Director of Photography: **Shelly Johnson**. Production Designer: **Craig Stearns**. Editor: **Patrick McMahon**, ACE. Music: **Nicholas Pike**. Lakeside Productions, Inc/Warner Bros Television/ABC-TV. Colour. 259 minutes.

Rebecca De Mornay (Wendy Torrance), **Steven Weber** (Jack Torrance), **Melvin Van Peebles** (Dick Halloran), **Wil Horneff** (Tony), **Elliott Gould** ([Stuart] Ullman), **Pat Hingle** (Pete Watson), **Courtland Mead** (Danny Torrance), **John Durbin** ([Horace M.] Derwent), **Stanley Anderson** ([Delbert] Grady), **David Zambrano** (Mitch), **Mick Garris** (Alcoholic Hartwell), **Shawnee Smith** (Waitress), **Ron Allen** (TV Weatherman), **Richard Beall** (Airline Gate Agent), **Joyce Bulifant** (Customer), **Cynthia Garris** (217 Woman), **Micky Giacomazzi** (2nd Waiter), **Lois Hicks** (Bookstore Lady), **Wendelin Harston** (Car Rental Clerk), **Stephen King** (Gage Creed), **Billie McBride** (Principal), **Sam Raimi** (Gas Station Howie), **Lisa Thornhill** (Rita Hayworth Lookalike), **Frank Darabont** (Bald Ghost Guest*), **Christa Faust** (Gowned Ghost Guest With Seer*), **Peter James** (1st Diner Customer), **Roger Baker** (Waiter Ghost*), **Richard Christian Matheson** (Vampire Costume Ghost Guest*), **Richard Peterson** (2nd Diner Customer*), **David J. Schow** (Seer Ghost Guest*), **Preston Sturges** (Elegant Ghost Guest*). [* Uncredited in the final print.]

Recovering alcoholic and aspiring playwright Jack Torrance is the new winter caretaker of the luxurious but isolated Overlook Hotel, nestled in the heart of Colorado's Rockie Mountains. With his wife Wendy and their young son Danny, he is hoping that this time alone will give his family a chance to heal. However, as the snow falls, the family are completely cut off from the outside world in the closed-up hotel. Soon the family find themselves trapped by the Overlook's malevolent spirits, who will stop at nothing to possess the one thing they need — Danny's special psychic abilities. The hotel's similarly gifted cook, Halloran, tells Danny that his young mind holds the power to 'shine', which allows him to see the nightmarish secrets of the Overlook's gruesome past and foresee his family's terrifying future.

Left: *Young Danny Torrance (Courtland Mead) shouldn't open that door...*

Stephen King never made any secret of the fact that he was not particularly happy with Stanley Kubrick's 1980 version of his 1977 novel. 'I had a screenplay of *The Shining* that I had a contract for,' he told Linda Marotta in *Fangoria*. 'When they sold the rights to Warner Bros, my screenplay came with it. Then when Stanley Kubrick came on the scene, he wanted to do his own screenplay and the film happened. But I've always wanted to go back and do something that really reflected the book.'

Following the success of the mini-series *It* (1990) and *The Stand* (1994), and given his previous working relationship with ABC-TV, network head William Haber asked the author what he wanted to do next. 'I told them that I'd like to remake *The Shining*,' King told Joseph B. Mauceri in *Shivers*. After Warner Bros had negotiated a 'rather enormous' payment to Kubrick, who owned the sequel/remake rights, King wrote a script based on the six-hour television format. 'ABC didn't ask for a single change,' he

Greetings from the Overlook Hotel

'This adaptation is a success for each of the principals in the creative life of *The Shining*. It is a triumph for Mick Garris, and a showcase for his diverse directorial skills. It is a vindication for Stephen King, who has written his best and most frightening script to date, and who at last is able to share his vision of his novel with millions.'

Fangoria #163, June 1997

revealed proudly. 'We went from first draft script to production. I think that's amazing.'

Among the major script changes King made from Kubrick's version was to visualise Jack's inner demons through a series of flashbacks, and to allow the character's eventual descent into madness to unravel more gradually. The new script also restored the wasp-attack on the family. 'We hope to make this the scariest mini-series ever broadcast on American television,' said King.

After his success with *The Stand*, director Mick Garris was attached to two projects — an original King script entitled *Rose Red* to be produced by Steven Spielberg, and Clive Barker's much-touted remake of *The Mummy* — both of which eventually stalled. King then showed his script for *The Shining* to Garris. Although the director considered Kubrick to be 'a brilliant film-maker' and 'a genius', he also described King's work as 'certainly one of the best scripts I've ever read.'

The $23 million production was given a schedule of seventy-two days. Much of the new version of *The Shining* was filmed between February and June 1996 at The Stanley Hotel in the small town of Estes Park, Colorado, situated just outside the Rocky Mountain National Park. The historic hotel was built in 1901 by F.O. Stanley, the man who invented the Stanley Steamer automobile, and was the actual hotel that

inspired the author to write his novel during a night's stay in the summer of 1973.

King, whose original novel includes a note extolling the virtues of Colorado's resort hotels, had apparently heard stories about a caretaker who had gone mad and killed himself there, and during the shoot there were a number of reports by various cast and crew members (who lived in the hotel during filming) about strange voices and unexplained noises heard in the old building.

After considering Gary Sinise and a number of other actors who were reluctant to follow in Jack Nicholson's footsteps as Jack Torrance, Garris and King were on the verge of shutting down the project when they finally cast Steven Weber just four days before shooting began. (Tim Daly, Webber's co-star from NBC's light comedy series *Wings* [1989-97], was another one of those who had previously turned the role down.)

Rebecca De Mornay was always King's choice, and the actress received top billing as Wendy Torrance, the central character in the author's version of his story.

Veteran writer, director and actor Melvin Van Peebles (the father of actor Mario) decided to give a very different performance as cook Dick Hallorann from the late Scatman Crothers, while Courtland Mead, who was cast after several readings as the psychic Danny, had previously appeared in *Hellraiser Bloodline* (1996).

As the Torrance family were supposed to be snowed in for the winter, production was scheduled for apparently the snowiest month of the year in the Rocky Mountains. However, as Garris revealed, 'We discovered once we started shooting that the Stanley Hotel and Estes Park itself were built in a snow shadow.' Despite some success, even the services of a Native American Ute shaman was unable to produce enough flakes, and consequently it cost the production nearly $100,000 to ship in snow, ice-trucks and snow-making machines from Los Angeles. Night shoots often took place in temperatures as low as four to eighteen degrees below zero.

One sequence which was missing from Kubrick's earlier film was the hotel's topiary sculptures coming to life. Although Garris had originally scheduled half a day, he ended up shooting the topiary for three days. However, in the new adaptation the bushes shaped like various animals were eventually brought to life through computer animation after full-size mechanical puppets designed and operated live on set by Steve Johnson's XFX team were mostly dropped from the final cut.

As Garris explained to Frederick C. Szebin in *Cinefantastique*: 'The fact that we've chosen to go back to the book in another film says noth-

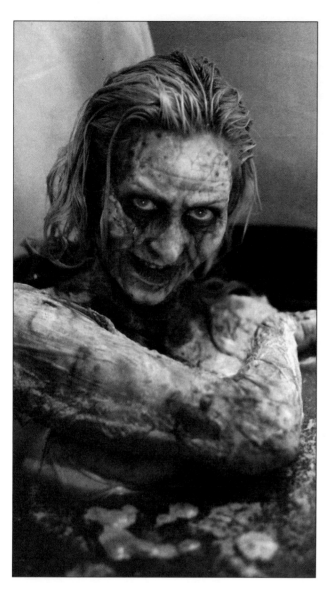

Sturges (son of the 1940s Hollywood director) and horror writers Christa Faust and Richard Christian Matheson.

Other special appearances included director Sam Raimi as a mechanic, British author Peter James (whose book became the basis of Garris' next project, *Virtual Obsession* [1996]) as a Florida diner customer and the director himself as a member of Alcoholics Anonymous.

Additional scenes were shot on a sound stage at Denver's Colorado Studios, just an hour and a half away from the Stanley Hotel.

Although ABC wanted to protect its working relationship with King, the network's Standards and Practices did request some cuts in the show's final hour. 'They asked for far more than they ended up getting,' Garris told Szebin in *Cinefantastique*. 'We would always give them reasons for what we shot.' Final editing removed around thirty-eight minutes of footage — 'I don't think I lost anything I really liked,' said Garris. The three part mini-series was first shown over six hours on ABC-TV on Sunday 27 April, Monday

ing about Kubrick and what he did, other than we wanted to make the book.'

Also reluctantly cut by the director was most of a sequence in which the faces of bandleader Gage Creed and his ghostly orchestra melted away. King obviously enjoyed himself playing the sleazy-looking bandleader (named after the author's resurrected child in *Pet Sematary* [1989]). 'What I really wanted to do was play the Cab Calloway of the dead,' the author told Bill Warren in *Fangoria*.

Despite being understaffed and paid only scale, up to 150 extras were made up over three days as the walking dead for the climactic ballroom sequence by Johnson's make-up crew, headed by Bill Corso. 'Mick made up a term for those of us who showed up to cameo in Estes Park at his invitation — 'executive extras',' explained author and screenwriter David J. Schow. The celebrity party-goers also included Frank Darabont (who agreed to do his beardless cameo so he could talk to King about adapting *The Green Mile*), scriptwriter Preston

28 and Thursday 1 May 1997. It was released directly to video in the United Kingdom the following year.

'I like *The Shining* mini-series because it seems like it follows the book pretty closely,' King told Bill Warren, 'and has a lot of the detail that mini-series can provide and theatrical films can't. You can use a lot more character and a lot more nuance and develop motivation in a more leisurely fashion. So on the whole, I'm very happy with it.'

Nominated for three Emmy Awards, the show won for Steve Johnson's special make-up effects.

'While the ratings were good, certainly better than a lot of other stuff ABC did last year,' King told *Fangoria*'s Michael Rowe, 'they did not live up to expectations. Critically, we got off a lot better than I thought we would.' †

Left: *Cynthia Garris as the woman in Room 217.*
Below: *Bernie Wrightson's cover and interior artwork for the special Collector's Edition of* TV Guide.

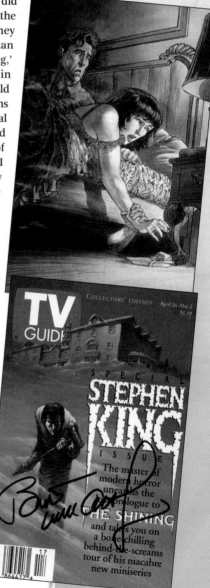

Take a Ride...Into the Dark Heart of America.

USA, 1997. Writer for Television and Director: **Mick Garris**. Based on the Short Stories 'Chattery Teeth' by **Stephen King** and 'The Body Politic' by **Clive Barker**. Producers: **Mick Garris** and **Ron Mitchell**. Co-Executive Producers: **Tarquin Gotch** and **Bob Lemchen**. Executive Producers: **John McTiernan**, **Donna Dubrow** and **Sandra Ruch**. Director of Photography: **Shelly Johnson**. Production Designer: **Craig Stearns**. Editor: **Norman Hollyn**. Music: **Mark Mothersbaugh**. Twentieth Century Fox Film Corporation/National Studios, Inc/Fox Network. 90 minutes.

Christopher Lloyd (Aaron Quicksilver), **Matt Frewer** (Charlie/Dr Charles George), **Raphael Sbarge** (Kerry [Parker]/Bill Hogan), **Missy [Melissa] Crider** (Olivia Parker), **Silas Weir Mitchell** (Hitchhiker [Brian Adams]), **Bill Nunn** (Dr Jeudwine), **Veronica Cartwright** (Myra), **Bill Bolender** (Scooter), **Amelia Heinle** (Darlene), **Clive Barker** (Anesthesiologist), **Cynthia Garris** (Ellen [George]), **Kevin Grevioux** (Police Sergeant), **Christopher Hart** (Lefty), **William Knight** (Rhinoplasty Man), **John Landis** (Surgical Assistant), **Shawn Nelson** (Driver), **Sherry O'Keefe** (Harriet DaVinci), **Dana Waters** (Hand Chaser), **Constance Zimmer** (Female Patient), **Lin Shaye*** (Woman), **Rick Overton*** (Wendell), **Kevin Grevioux*** (Police Sergeant), **Mick Garris*** (Doctor). [* Uncredited in the final print.]

Newly married couple Carey and Olivia Parker find themselves stranded in the Nevada desert with a flat tyre. While the husband sets out to find help, his young bride encounters the enigmatic Aaron Quicksilver, a collector of true stories from 'the black heart of America'. Thankful for the company, the newlywed takes refuge in his trailer, where she grows ever more apprehensive and her teeth start chattering with fear. So the stranger tells her a bizarre tale. In 'Chattery Teeth', travelling salesman Bill Hogan picks up a psychopathic hitchhiker who he previously ignored on the road, and is saved by the eponymous novelty wind-up toy bought at a roadside grocery store. Professional pickpocket Charlie is on the run from the cops at the Pacific Park carnival when he enters the tent of the Quicksilver Exposition of Delightful Horrors. There he encounters the stranger as well, who has another odd tale to tell. In 'The Body Politic', the hands of Beverly Hills cosmetic surgeon Dr Charles George suddenly take on a life of their own and lead a revolution against the tyranny of the body. Soon other disembodied limbs join the rebellion.

According to Stephen King, *Quicksilver Highway* was 'Really something different that Mick Garris is doing. It's a kind of pilot for a series he'd like to put together where there would be two episodes every week with the same cast of actors, but they'd be different stories.'

The project came about when Garris was asked to script a one hour pilot for a projected series about urban ghost stories to be directed by John McTiernan (*Die Hard* [1988], etc) and produced by his wife, Donna Dubrow. Thinking about the idea, Garris came up with a concept that 'would be a different geographic location across our country each week. Initially, what I wanted to do was put together an ensemble of actors who would be in the stories every week, playing different parts each time.'

The idea was initially pitched by New World Television to ABC-TV (for whom Garris had previously made two successful Stephen King mini-series, *The Stand* [1994] and *The Shining* [1997]) with Brandon Tartikoff attached as one of the producers.

After writing a one hour script based on King's silly story 'Chattery Teeth', originally published in the fall 1992 issue of *Cemetery Dance* magazine and reprinted in *Nightmares and Dreamscapes* (1993), Garris turned it in to ABC. When it became apparent that the network was not interested in a horror series, a couple of the more enthusiastic executives suggested making a 'back door pilot' to sell the idea.

As he admitted to Bill Warren in *Fangoria*: 'The two-hour teleplay is simply the one-hour pilot script with the next script stapled to it, with no changes whatsoever. That became our movie.'

The additional one hour script was an adaptation of Clive Barker's short story 'The Body Politic' (from the fourth volume of *Books of*

Blood [1985], aka *The Human Condition*), updating the concept to modern-day America and changing the main protagonist into a plastic surgeon.

Garris then took the concept to the Fox Network. '*Quicksilver Highway* was a movie I put together to get the crew of *The Shining* back together as soon as I could,' Garris revealed. 'It was written very quickly, with very generous options on the stories from Barker and King. Fox wanted to do it as a TV movie, so I added the Barker story.'

Once pre-production started, McTiernan became one of the show's executive producers and Garris suddenly found himself back in the director's chair. 'We basically shot the first draft of the script,' Garris explained.

Initially titled *Route 666* before the network objected, filming on the $4 million production started in February 1997 in and around Los Angeles. During a tight twenty-three day schedule, the carnival sequence was set among the rides at Santa Monica Pier (also the setting for Curtis Harrington's atmospheric *Night Tide* [1961]), while the desert scenes were shot in the Mojave Desert near Lancaster, California.

Each story is linked by Christopher Lloyd as Aaron Quicksilver, who looked like Boris Karloff in a fright wig. He travelled across the country in a 1965 Rolls-Royce Silver Cloud pulling an Airstream trailer. 'I wanted to create a character who is mysterious and interesting and fascinating and enigmatic who claims to be *only* a storyteller,' Garris told Warren, 'but who, of course, is really much more than that.'

The chattery teeth were created by Steve Johnson's XFX, Inc, while ninety per-cent of the crawling hands were digitally visualised by William and John Mesa and Flash Filmworks, Inc. Christopher Hart, whose right hand appeared as Thing in *The Addams Family* (1991) and *Addams Family Values* (1993), portrayed Frewer's rebellious left hand.

Along with his own trademark cameo in the second story, Garris also included appearances by Clive Barker as a mugging anesthesiologist and John Landis as a surgical assistant.

Televised in late May 1997, the same month as *The Shining*, *Quicksilver Highway* was released directly to video in the United Kingdom on 7 January the following year.

'It was a lot of fun,' said Garris, 'and though not many people saw it (it was run on the Fox Network — at that time not at all known for making films for television — during 'sweeps', up against the last season of *Seinfeld* and George Clooney's farewell episodes on *E.R.*), I have a very warm place in my heart for it. The best reviews were actually in Britain.'

Garris also admitted that if *Quicksilver Highway* did ever become a series, he would probably end up executive producing (as he did on the 1990-91 television series *She-Wolf of London*). 'I would probably want to write the wrap-arounds, just because I created the character of Quicksilver and Chris Lloyd was so enthusiastic about the work we did together.' †

Above top: From left to right: John Landis, Clive Barker, Mick Garris and Matt Frewer, behind-the-scenes.
Above: New bride Olivia (Missy Crider) is told a story by the enigmatic Aaron Quicksilver (Christopher Lloyd).

Evil Has a Flight Plan.

USA, 1997. Director: **Mark Pavia**. Producers: **Richard P. Rubinstein** and **Mitchell Galin**. Screenplay: **Mark Pavia** and **Jack O'Donnell**. Based on a Story by **Stephen King**. Executive Producer: **David Kappes**. Co-Producer: **Alfredo Cuomo**. Director of Photography: **David Connell**, ACS. Special Effects Make-up: **KNB EFX Group, Inc**. Editor: **Elizabeth Schwartz**. Production Designer: **Burton Rencher**. Costume Designer: **Pauline White**. Original Music: **Brian Keane**. Casting: **Leonard Finger**, CSA, and **Lyn Richmond**. New Amsterdam Entertainment Inc/Stardust International Ltd/Medusa Film SPA/Home Box Office/New Line Cinema. Colour. 97 minutes.

Miguel Ferrer (Richard Dees), **Julie Entwisle** (Katherine Blair), **Dan Monahan** (Merton Morrison), **Michael H. Moss** (Dwight Renfield), **John Bennes** (Ezra Hannon), **Beverly Skinner** (Selida McCamon), **Rob Wilds** (Buck Kendall), **Richard Olsen** (Claire Bowie), **Elizabeth McCormick** (Ellen Sarch), **J.R. Rodriguez** (Terminal Cop #1), **Bob Casey** (Terminal Cop #2), **Ashton Stewart** (Nate Wilson), **William Neely** (Ray Sarch), **Windy Wenderlich** (Henry Gates), **General Fermon Judd Jr** (Policeman), **Deann Korbutt** (Linda Ross), **Rachel Lewis** (Libby Grant), **Kristen Leigh** (Dottie Walsh), **Simon Elsworth** (Duffery Bartender), **Jim Grimshaw** (Gas Station Attendant), **Matthew Johnson** (Caretaker), **Terry Neil Edlefsen** (Drunk), **Joy Knox**, **Randal Brown**, **Laurie Wolf**, **Keith Shepard** and **Ruth Reid** (Dream Vampires), **Matt Webb**, **David Zum Brunnen**, **April Turner** and **Manya K. Rubinstein** (Reporters), **Kelley Sims** (Intern).

> 'Without question, the primary reason for the film's success is Ferrer, who makes Dees an unlikely but riveting hero. He's amoral, morbid and will go to any lengths to get his story — even if it means smearing blood on a tombstone in order to make it more photogenic.'
>
> *Fangoria* #169

Opposite top: *The true face of Dwight Renfield (Michael H. Moss) is revealed.*
Below: *Richard Dees (Miguel Ferrer) finally meets the high-flying bloodsucker.*

FACT FILE

An eighty-one piece *Night Flier* jigsaw puzzle was also available from the production company for $15.95.

Richard Dees is a cynical and ruthless senior tabloid photo-journalist for Inside View *magazine. Now he is competing with enthusiastic newcomer Katherine Blair for the story of Dwight Renfield, a classical vampire who flies into remote airfields in his private black Cessna Skymaster aeroplane and first hypnotises, then slaughters the inhabitants for their blood.*

'Sometimes a supporting character in a novel catches a writer's attention and refuses to go away, insisting he has more to say and do,' Stephen King explained in his 1993 collection *Nightmares and Dreamscapes*. 'Richard Dees, the protagonist of 'The Night Flier', is such a character.' Dees had originally appeared in King's 1979 novel *The Dead Zone*, and he turned up again in the writer's underdeveloped story, which first appeared in editor Douglas E. Winter's 1988 anthology *Prime Evil*.

Originally planned as a two-hour movie for television, a film version had been in development with Laurel's Richard P. Rubinstein since the story was first published. King had reportedly attempted to write his own script before giving up after forty pages.

Horror film fan Mark Pavia was just eight years old when he made his first film,

a two-minute version of *Dracula* using equipment borrowed from a neighbour. He continued to make films through grade school and high school before he met Jack O'Donnell in a screenwriting class at Chicago's Columbia College. They discovered that they shared a love of the old Universal horror movies of the 1930s and '40s, and over the next decade they collaborated on a number of student films, including *Drag* (1993), a forty-minute love story between George Romero-style zombies shot on a budget of just $25,000.

After sending their short film to various

Never believe what you publish... Never publish what you believe.

Stephen King's THE NIGHT FLIER

NEW AMSTERDAM ENTERTAINMENT INC.
IN ASSOCIATION WITH
STARDUST INTERNATIONAL & MEDUSA FILM SPA PRESENTS
A RICHARD P. RUBINSTEIN PRODUCTION A MARK PAVIA FILM
STEPHEN KING'S "THE NIGHT FLIER"
SCREENPLAY BY MARK PAVIA & JACK O'DONNELL BASED ON A STORY BY STEPHEN KING
CO-PRODUCER ALFREDO CUOMO EXECUTIVE PRODUCER DAVID KAPPES
PRODUCED BY RICHARD P. RUBINSTEIN AND MITCHELL GALIN
DIRECTED BY MARK PAVIA

West Coast studios as a calling-card, it was a viewing of *Drag* that prompted Rubinstein and King to offer the creative team *Night Flier*. 'Stephen and Richard were working on *The Stand* when they saw our picture,' explained Pavia to Wilson Goodson in *Cinefantastique*, 'and they gave me a call.'

Following a meeting in New York, Pavia and O'Donnell started work on a treatment, eventually breaking down every scene in the original story onto around seventy index cards. 'What we did was remain faithful to Stephen's feel of the story and the characters,' continued Pavia, 'and we then padded it out. And Stephen and Richard were involved every step of the way.'

King acted mostly as a story editor, reading the drafts and giving his suggestions. He never visited the set.

Although Dees doesn't venture inside the plane in King's tale, associate producer Neal Stevens thought it would be a good idea for audiences to see the interior of the vampire's lair. 'Stephen was like, "Oh man, I should've put that in my story!"' revealed co-producer O'Donnell. 'It was really a collaborative effort.'

The pair completed six drafts of the screenplay in six months. When Laurel Entertainment was dissolved as a result of a merger deal, Rubinstein and Mitchell Galin formed a new production company, New Amsterdam Entertainment, Inc. 'We had the final script about six months after that,' explained O'Donnell to Randy Palmer in *Fangoria*.

Filming began in Wilmington, North Carolina, without any deal with a domestic distributor in place. Production was delayed for only a day when Hurricane Bertha hit the North Carolina coast. Although the two producers and King deferred their fees, Rubinstein estimated that 'a comparable budget would be $10 million.'

Pavia storyboarded the entire movie, although once shooting started, the first-time director was allowed to deviate from the original script when new and better ideas presented themselves. Star Miguel Ferrer called him, 'the most prepared guy I have ever worked with.'

'It's very much a vampire picture,' explained Pavia, 'but the main character is Richard Dees, the character played by Miguel Ferrer, and his descent into his own personal Hell.'

'I first heard about the *Night Flier* project from Mick Garris,' revealed the actor. 'I got the script and I thought, 'This is a really, *really* ingenious adaptation.'

Newcomer Julie Entwisle made her motion picture début as Dees' fellow reporter,

Katherine Blair, a character not in King's original story. As the high-flying vampire Dwight Renfield (an inside joke for those who know their 1931 *Dracula*), actor Michael H. Moss was brought to ugly life by a KNB EFX crew supervised by Howard Berger.

'We end up with this forty-minute climax which is hellish!' King told Joseph B. Mauceri. 'It's hard to look at, but at the same time it's hard to look away...This is like *Dawn of the Dead*. It goes beyond the limits and makes discussions of good taste meaningless.'

'The people who are usually responsible for making these pictures don't give one hoot about Stephen King,' claimed Pavia, 'or if they do it's just because of the monetary reasons. They don't care about or respect the work itself. I do.'

After being shown on the HBO cable network in November 1997, the film was given a selected theatrical release in the United States the following February and quickly disappeared before resurfacing on video and DVD three months later.

'Mark Pavia did a super job,' King told Bill Warren in *Fangoria*. 'It's on a shoestring, and looks it, but it's a throwback to a lot of pictures you probably remember with real affection, like *The Flesh Eaters* and *Night of the Living Dead*. Yet it's not like any of those — Mark is his own person. It's interesting, it's really interesting.' ✝

'The always creepy effects by KNB add to the eeriness of the ending rather nicely, and nobody can play an interesting unsympathetic character like Ferrer, but *The Night Flier* simply doesn't have the wings to sustain its feature length.'
Cinefantastique vol 29 no 12, April 1998

U-Turn, U-Die!

Canada/USA, 1997. Director: **Chris Thomson**. Screenplay: **Brian Taggert**. Co-Producers: **Michael Scott**, **Bruce David Eisen** and **Jonathon Komack Martin**. Executive Producers: **Mark Amin** and **Derek Mazur**. Director of Photography: **Rob Draper**, ACS. Music Composer: **Michael Richard Plowman**. Editor: **Lara Mazur**. Production Design: **David Ferguson**. Casting: **Ellen Meyer**. Based on a Short Story by **Stephen King**. Trucks Productions/USA Pictures/Trimark Pictures/Leider-Reisberg/Credo Entertainment/USA Network. Colour. 99 minutes.

Timothy Busfield (Ray), **Brenda Bakke** (Hope), **Aidan Devine** (Trucker Bob), **Jay Brazeau** (Jack), **Brendan Fletcher** (Logan), **Amy Stewart** (Abby), **Roman Podhora** (Thad), **Victor Cowie** (George), **Sharon Bajer** (June), **Jonathan Barrett** (Brad), **Rick Skene** (Trucker Pete), **Don Granbery** (Sheriff), **Barbara-Lee Edwards** (TV Reporter), **Gene Pyrz** (Refrigerator Truck Driver), **Kirk Harper** (Lino), **Harry Nelken** (Phil).

Right: Ray (Timothy Busfield, right) leads the survivors.

'The short story is nicely fleshed-out and kept moving with a minimum of clichéd nonsense from the two redneck truckers trapped in the diner. Main characters get their dramatic 'moments' to reveal character, but not so much time that the story finds itself stalling for lack of supernatural trucking mayhem.'

Cinefantastique vol 29 no 12, April 1998

Widower Ray and his son Logan run a secluded diner and gas station in the small desert town of Lunar, Nevada, the site of a meteorite impact thousands of years earlier. When a number of driverless trucks suddenly come to life and begin menacing the locals, a group of survivors take refuge in the restaurant. However, the vengeance-seeking vehicles appear to be intent on destroying everyone trapped inside the truck stop, including a couple of redneck truckers, a group of backpackers and a bickering married couple.

A ccording to Stephen King, this television movie remake of the author's own dismal directorial début, *Maximum Overdrive* (1986), was the pilot for a series that never happened.

It was also based on the eponymous short story from the June 1973 issue of the men's magazine *Cavalier*, later reprinted in the 1978 *Night Shift* collection. 'I got $500 for it,' King told Mick Farren in *Interview*, 'the most money I had ever gotten for a short story. It was always my favourite of those early short stories.'

The beleaguered characters included all the usual stereotypes: an alienated father and daughter, a philosophical New Age tourist, a pair of redneck troublemakers, an attractive tour guide, and a father and son struggling to survive by running a roadside business along with their friendly cook.

Filmed on location in a cement

quarry in Manitoba, Canada, Brian Taggert's screenplay presented a number of possible reasons for the trucks' rebellion: a recent comet shower (also alluded to in the original film), an independent space monitoring project and even the nearby secret US Air Force base of Area 51.

Originally screened on the USA Network on 29 October 1997, the DVD release from Trimark featured some extra death sequences that were not included in the television version. †

CHILDREN OF THE CORN V
FIELDS OF TERROR

In a Deserted Town...the Terror Continues!

USA, 1998. Writer and Director: **Ethan Wiley**. Producers: **Jeff Geoffray** and **Walter Josten**. Based on the Short Story 'Children of the Corn' by **Stephen King**. Executive Producer: **Jeffrey Kurz**. Line Producer: **Jo Ann May-Pavey**. Director of Photography: **David Lewis**. Editor: **Peter Devaney Flanagan**. Music: **Paul Rabjohns**. Production Designers: **Deborah Raymond** and **Dorian Vernacchio**. Casting: **Ed Mitchell** and **Robyn Ray**, CSA. Miramax Film Corp/Dimension Films/Blue Rider Pictures/Dimension Home Video. Colour. 83 minutes.

Stacy Galina (Alison), **Alexis Arquette** (Greg), **Adam Wylie** (Ezekiel), **Greg Vaughan** (Tyrus), **Eva Mendez** (Kir), **Ahmet Zappa** (Laszlo), **Angela Jones** (Charlotte), **Fred Williamson** (Sheriff Skaggs), **David Carradine** (Luke [Enright]), **Olivia Burnette** (Lilly), **Aaron Jackson** (Zane), **David Buzzotta** (Jacob), **Matthew Tait** (Jared), **Kane Hodder** (Bartender), **Jennifer Badger** (Judith), **Hiro Koda** (Caleb), **Frank Lloyd** (Deputy Earl), **Gary Bullock** (Farmer), **Season Hubley** (Lilly's Mother), **Edward Edwards** (Lilly's Father), **Sicily** (Chloe), **Diva Zappa** (Drill Girl), **Christopher Stinson** (Evil Corn Kid), **Danny Goldring** (Mr O'Brien), **Deborah Strang** (Mrs O'Brien).

College students Alison, Greg, Kir and Tyrus are stranded in a deceptively quiet small town while attempting to spread the ashes of their recently-deceased friend. They soon discover that their other companions, Charlotte and Laszlo, have been murdered in the corn fields and that Alison's runaway brother, Jacob, is a member of a local cult of homicidal children who sacrifice themselves to 'He Who Walks Behind the Rows' when they turn eighteen.

T he fourth follow-up to the 1984 original was produced by Blue Rider Pictures, who had previously been hired to come up with sequels to such horror franchises as *Witchboard* (1986), *Night of the Demons* (1987) and *Leprechaun* (1992). The project was developed by Miramax and then handed over to the company, who did all the actual production work on a for-hire basis.

Director Ethan Wiley (*House II The Second Story* [1987], etc) decided to ignore the previous sequels and go back to the original source. He admitted that his script was based on his own personal take on Stephen King's story. He also found inspiration in a file on cults which he had been compiling over the years.

Wiley explained to *Cinefantastique*'s Michael Beeler why he felt that the basic theme was so successful: 'There's something in the contrast or conflict of having children, who are usually considered innocent, personifying evil.'

The film was shot in July 1997 in the Californian cities of Oxnard and Camarillo, sixty miles north of Los Angeles. While Wiley filmed with the main crew, second unit direc-

tor James Isaac (who went on to supervise the special effects on David Cronenberg's *eXistenZ* [1999]) was shooting footage simultaneously which would be edited later into the same scene.

This entry included celebrity cameos by Fred Williamson, who plays the town sheriff whose head is incinerated, and David Carradine as Luke, the long-dead leader of the cult which sacrifices its followers in an 'eternal flame' burning in a corn silo.

Sota FX, who worked on the previous film in the series, also did the special effects make-up for this entry. The fire effects were created by Ken Wheatly and Eric Beauchamp, under the supervision of stunt coordinator Kane Hodder (who also had a small role).

Subtitled *Field of Screams* during production, the tongue-in-cheek appellation was changed by Miramax/ Dimension a few months prior to the film's release directly to video in July 1998. 'Everyone thought that the original title was very clever,' Wiley told Beeler. 'It always got a smile from people.'

The series finally returned to its roots for the next entry, *Children of the Corn 666 Isaac's Return* (1999). †

THE NEWEST AND MOST SHOCKING CHAPTER...

CHILDREN OF THE CORN V
FIELDS OF TERROR

BASED ON THE STORY "CHILDREN OF THE CORN" BY STEPHEN KING

FACT FILE

Children of the Corn V includes two of the late rock star Frank Zappa's children, Ahmet and Diva.

Apt Pupil

If You Don't Believe in the Existence of Evil You Have a Lot to Learn.

USA, 1997. Director: **Bryan Singer**. Screenplay: **Brandon Boyce**. Based on the Novella 'Apt Pupil' by **Stephen King**. Producers: **Jane Hamsher**, **Don Murphy** and **Bryan Singer**. Executive Producer: **Tim Harbert**. Co-Producer: **Thomas DeSanto**. Director of Photography: **Newton Thomas Sigel**. Production Designer: **Richard Hoover**. Editor: **John Ottman**. Costume Designer: **Louise Mingenbach**. Music: **John Ottman**. Casting: **Francine Maisler**, CSA, and **Kathryn Eisenstein**, Associate. Phoenix Pictures/Canal+ DA/Bad Hat Harry/TriStar. Colour. 111 minutes.

Ian McKellen (Kurt Dussander/Arthur Denker), **Brad Renfro** (Todd Bowden), **Bruce Davison** (Richard Bowden), **Elias Koteas** (Archie), **Joe Morton** (Dan Richler), **Jan Triska** (Isaac Weiskopf), **Michael Byrne** (Ben Kramer), **Heather McComb** (Becky Trask), **David Schwimmer** (Edward French), **Ann Dowd** (Monica Bowden), **Joshua Jackson** (Joey), **Mickey Cottrell** (Sociology Teacher), **Michael Reid MacKay** (Nightmare Victim), **James Karen** (Victor Bowden), **Marjorie Lovett** (Agnes Bowden), **David Cooley** (Gym Teacher), **Blake Anthony Tibbetts** (Teammate), **Katherine Malone** (Student), **Grace Sinden** (Secretary), **Anthony Moore** (Umpire), **Kevin Spirtas** (Paramedic), **Danna Dennis** (Nurse), **Michael Artura** (Detective Getty), **Donna Marie Brown** (Mother), **Mark Flythe** (Darren), **Warren Wilson** (Newscaster), **Jill Harris** (Reporter), **Norbert D. Singer** (Hospital Administrator #1), **Mildred Singer** (Hospital Administrator #2), **Mary Ottman** (Doctor).

1984: Sixteen year-old Todd Bowden is one of the top students in his high school class. He is also fascinated by Nazi Germany. When he discovers that former SS war criminal Kurt Dussander is secretly living in quiet seclusion as 'Arthur Denker' in the same, small Californian suburb of Santo Donato, Todd confronts the old man. In exchange for his silence, Todd blackmails Dussander into describing the nightmarish atrocities he committed in the death camps during the Holocaust. As the manipulative all-American teenager becomes obsessed by these first-hand accounts of torture and genocide, the pair play out a game of psychological warfare that spirals out of control, resulting in the boy ending up more corrupt than his corrupter.

Director Bryan Singer made his breakthrough with the Academy Award-winning crime drama *The Usual Suspects* (1995). However, instead of following up that boxoffice hit with the offers of a Hollywood blockbuster, the then-thirty-one year-old Singer used its success to make a more personal project, a $15 million adaptation of Stephen King's psychological thriller *Apt Pupil*, written as a spec script by first-time screenwriter and the director's long-time friend Brandon Boyce.

It was the third story (following 'The Body' and 'Rita Hayworth and Shawshank Redemption') to be taken from King's 1982 collection of four novellas, *Different Seasons*. 'It was just a very lucky work,' explained the author about the collection, 'the first thing I had done that was sort of outside the horror genre. The book was real successful, and the movies have been fantastic.'

'It was a very hard movie to get people to make,' Singer revealed to Anthony C. Ferrante in *Fangoria*. 'This is by far the most cursed movie ever.' That 'curse' began nearly a decade earlier, when a previous attempt to film *Apt Pupil* was closed down with little more than a week of filming remaining.

The rights to King's story had been in litiga-

Opposite page: Brad Renfro as troubled teen Todd Bowden.
Left: Former Nazi Kurt Dussander (Ian McKellen) tells Todd about the atrocities he committed.

tion for several years when Singer discovered that they had reverted back to the author. After King was sent Singer's own personal print of the then-unreleased *The Usual Suspects* to view, he agreed to option the property for six months for just a dollar. Singer then started looking around for a production deal.

He initially set the project up in 1996 at Spelling Films and Paramount (who also produced the King adaptation *Thinner* the same year). However, despite spending $1 million on building sets and hiring the cast, internal problems between the two companies resulted in the picture being closed down. 'I think they got cold feet about the subject matter,' Singer explained to *Fangoria*. The film was subsequently revived at Phoenix Pictures, who had a distribution deal with TriStar.

Although he usually becomes involved in film adaptations of his material, in this particular instance King restricted his participation to granting the rights and reading a few drafts of the script.

'I decided the first act of the book [sic], the very beginnings of the horror, would be our entire story,' Singer explained to Alan Jones in *Shivers*. 'When I showed King the script he agreed wholeheartedly with our argument.' In the original novella, Todd became a multiple murderer, but it was decided to tone down the ending of Boyce's script. 'I think Todd has the potential to become one,' Singer told Dan Scapperotti in *Cinefantastique*. 'Stephen King put it best. He said, "If you had done the book [sic] as written it would have been a different kind of movie. The wrong kind of movie."'

But the problems did not end there. While filming at Occidental Studios in Los Angeles, several minors working on the picture as extras claimed in the press that they were forced to strip naked for a shower scene and their parents filed a lawsuit claiming sexual harassment, invasion of privacy and emotional distress. Although all the charges were subsequently dismissed by the district attorney, the very brief sequence was re-shot anyway to avoid the possibility of any further legal injunctions. 'After an investigation by the labour commission, they didn't prosecute,' Singer explained to Ferrante. 'The Screen Actor's Guild didn't either. Ultimately, it became a civil litigation trying to extort money from the studio, which didn't work.'

With an anticipated April release in America moved back to 16 October 1998, just in time for Halloween, it was always going to be difficult to market *Apt Pupil*, especially given the film's controversial subject matter and the fact that it did not fall neatly into King's horror *oeuvre*. In a year filled with teen slasher flicks such as *I Still Know What You Did Last Summer*, *Urban Legend* and Gus Van Sant's *Psycho* remake, it failed to gross even $10 million domestically.

Perhaps even more unfortunately, the film was released in the United Kingdom a month after two separate American high school shootings in April 1999, when students killed fellow classmates and teachers before turning the guns on themselves. 'Art imitating life, and life imitating art happens often and sometimes it hits the headlines,' Singer explained to Scapperotti, 'but I try not to pay too much attention to it.'

However, King did, and the author asked his publisher Penguin to withdraw from publication his 1977 novel *Rage* — actually written the summer before his freshman year and originally issued under his 'Richard Bachman' byline — with the next printing. ✝

SOMETIMES THEY COME BACK FOR MORE (AKA FROZEN)

Hell Has Finally Frozen Over.

USA, 1998. Director: **Daniel Berk**. Writers: **Adam Grossman** and **Darryl Sollerh**. Producers: **Diana Zahn** and **Daniel Berk**. Based on Characters Created by **Stephen King** from the Short Story 'Sometimes They Come Back'. Executive Producers: **Mark Amin** and **Michael Meltzer**. Co-Producers: **Phillip B. Goldfine** and **Bruce David Eisen**. Director of Photography: **Christopher Walling**. Editor: **Todd Clark**. Production Designer: **Trae King**. Music: **Brian Langsbard**. Costume Designer: **Bonnie Stauch**. Casting: **Betsy Fels**. Trimark Pictures. 89 minutes.

Clayton Rohner (Captain Sam Cage), **Faith Ford** (Dr Jennifer Wells), **Damian Chapa** (Dr Kent Schilling), **Chase Masterson** (Major Callie O'Grady), **Max Perlich** (Lieutenant Brian Shebanski), **Michael Stadvec** (Captain Robert Reynolds), **Douglas Stoup** (Lieutenant Baines), **Stephen Hart** (Major Frank Whittaker), **Jennifer O'Dell** (Mary), **Frank Ceglia** (Soldier in Bar).

Right: Dr Jennifer Wells (Faith Ford) prepares to defend herself against the walking dead.

FACT FILE

Thirty-two year-old co-writer Adam Grossman directed the previous entry, *Sometimes They Come Back...Again* (1995), and went on to both write and direct *Wes Craven Presents Carnival of Souls* (1998) for the same producers.

After a doctor goes on a murder spree at the remote Ice Station Erebus, a secret US mining outpost deep in Antarctica, military policemen Captain Sam Cage and Major Callie Wilson are sent to investigate. When Wilson is killed by a mysterious intruder, Cage and surviving medical officer Dr Jennifer Wells are attacked by the revived corpses of the killer's victims. With Wells about to be sacrificed in an ice cave in the deepest level of the gas-filled mine, Cage is forced to renounce his demonic birthright and confront his immortal half-brother Carl.

This second video sequel was nominally linked to the previous two films by a pentagram design being used by Cage's demon-worshipping brother to raise their father, Satan himself.

Clayton Rohner (*The Relic* [1997], etc) portrayed the half-devil hero, while Louisiana-born actress Faith Ford, best known for her Emmy Award-nominated role as Corky Sherwood in CBS-TV's long-running sit-com *Murphy Brown* (1988-98), made her feature film début in the non-glamorous role as the surviving medical officer.

'She's an accomplished actress known for one thing,' co-producer Phillip B. Goldfine explained to Craig Reid in *Cinefantastique*. 'But she is so much more than that...She just gives this emotional gut-wrenching performance.'

Filmed in studios situated in the California foothills of Santa Clarita, the film was released directly to video in the United Kingdom on 6 January 1999. A domestic video release followed in the spring of that year under the title *Frozen*, and it was apparently given the Alistair MacLean-like title *Ice Station Erebus* for its Australian video début.

'Essentially it is a scary thriller as opposed to a gore fest like the last one,' Goldfine told Reid. †

Stephen King's Storm of the Century

Something Terrifying is About to Begin.
And No One Knows How It Will End.

USA/Canada, 1999. Director: **Craig R. Baxley**. Writer: **Stephen King**. Producer: **Thomas H. Brodek**. Executive Producers: **Mark Carliner** and **Stephen King**. Line Producer: **Robert F. Phillips**. Director of Photography: **David Connell**, ACS. Editor: **Sonny Baskin**. Production Designer: **Craig Stearns**. Music: **Gary Chang**. Casting: **Lynn Kressel**. Greengrass Productions, Inc/Mark Carliner Productions/Walt Disney Television/ABC-TV. Colour. 254 minutes.

Tim Daly (Michael Anderson), **Colm Feore** (Andre Linoge), **Debrah Farentino** (Molly Anderson), **Casey Siemaszko** (Alton 'Hatch' Hatcher), **Jeffrey DeMunn** (Robbie Beals), **Julianne Nicholson** (Cat Withers), **Dyllan Christopher** (Ralph Anderson), **Becky Ann Baker** (Ursula Godsoe), **Spencer Breslin** (Donny Beals), **Kathleen Chalfant** (Ms Stanhope), **Nada Despotovich** (Sandra Beals), **Steve Rankin** (Jack Carver), **Adam Zolotin** (Davey Hopewell), **Myra Carter**, **Jeremy Jordan** (Billy Soames), **Ron Perkins**, **Adam LeFevre**, **Torri Higginson** (Angie Carver), **Denis Forest** (Kirk Freeman), **Peter MacNeill**, **Beth Dixon** (Tess Marchant), **Soo Garay** (Melinda Hatcher), **Christopher Marren** (Henry Bright), **Leif Anderson** (Johnny Harriman), **Marcia Laskowski** (Linda St George), **John Innes** (Reverend Riggins), **Jack Jessop** (George Kirby), **Nancy Beatty** (Octavia Godsoe), **Richard Blackburn** (Andy Robichaux), **Gaylyn Britton** (Mary Hopewell), **Michael Copeman** (Upton Bell), **Kristin Baxley** (Annie Huston), **Tyler Bannerman** (Frank Bright), **Skye McCole Bartusiak** (Pippa Hatcher), **Harley English-Dixon** (Heidi St Pierre), **Stephen Joffe** (Buster Carver), **Sam Morton** (Harry Robichaux), **Cayda Rubin** (Sally Godsoe), **Shawn Doyle** (Lucien Fournier), **Norma Edwards** (Betty Soames), **Victor Ertmanis** (Alex Harber), **Richard Fitzpatrick** (Jonas Stanhope), **Joan Gregson** (Della Bissonette), **Jennifer Griffin** (Carla Bright), **Nicky Guadagni** (Jenna Freeman), **David Hughes** (Burt Soames), **Helen Hughes** (Roberta Coign), **Joel Keller** (Cal Freese), **Hardee T. Lineham** (Bill Toomey), **Arlene Mazerolle** (Jill Robichaux), **Gerard Parkes** (Orville Boucher), **Michael Rhoades** (Stan Hopewell), **Lynne Griffin** (Mrs Kingsbury), **Kay Tremblay** (False Mother), **Rita Tuckett** (Martha Clarendon), **Stephen King*** (Lawyer on TV), **David Ferry** (Lloyd Wishman), **Martha Burns** (Counselor), **Matt Koruba** (Ralphie [14 Years Old]). [* Uncredited in the final print.]

Nine years ago: a massive blizzard is about to hit the remote community of Little Tall Island off the New England coast. But the hurricane-force winds are also bringing something else. Something unbelievably evil. A stranger carrying a walking stick topped by a living silver wolf's head arrives and ruthlessly crushes the skull of one of the region's oldest residents. He knows the townsfolk will come for him. He wants them to. For he has come to the island for one reason. When local grocery store owner and the island's level-headed constable Mike Anderson arrests the stranger, he reveals that his name is Andre Linoge and tells the inhabitants to 'Give me what I want and I'll go away'. As the ferocious snow storm hits, the island is soon cut off from all communication with the outside world. But nobody is safe from the ageless Linoge's supernatural powers, and as he seductively reveals each person's darkest secret, murder and madness overwhelm the tight-knit community. When the islanders finally discover exactly what it is Linoge wants before he will leave them alone, they are forced to choose between two impossible evils...

'I t's been fun, the mini-series thing, to learn how to write that way,' King told Bill Warren after *The Shining* (1997), 'so I'd like to take the skills I've learned and put them to work not as an adapter of my own work, but working directly in this form, making it all up for the first time.'

True to his word, the author contacted ABC-TV executive Maura Dunbar and Mark Carliner, who had produced *The Shining* for the network, and asked them if they would be interested in an original novel written exclusively for television.

When ABC responded with an immediate 'yes' to his proposal, King wrote the script between December 1996 and February 1997. The author claimed that the idea for his reworking of the Peter Pan and Pied Piper legends came to him with a single image he could not get out of his mind: 'An extremely evil man' sitting in a prison cell, eyes unblinking, heels drawn up on the bunk with his arms resting across his knees. 'Gradually,

FACT FILE

Tim Daly is the brother of actress Tyne Daly and is best known as pilot Joe Hackett in the NBC-TV series *Wings* (1989-97), in which he co-starred with Steven Weber (*The Shining* [1997], etc).

the story started to spin out from the man,' added King.

He also admitted that he wrote the script exactly as he would have written a novel: 'Keeping a list of characters but no other notes, working to a set schedule of three or four hours every day.' And when he and his wife travelled to watch the Maine women's basketball team play its away games, he took along his Mac PowerBook and worked out of hotel rooms.

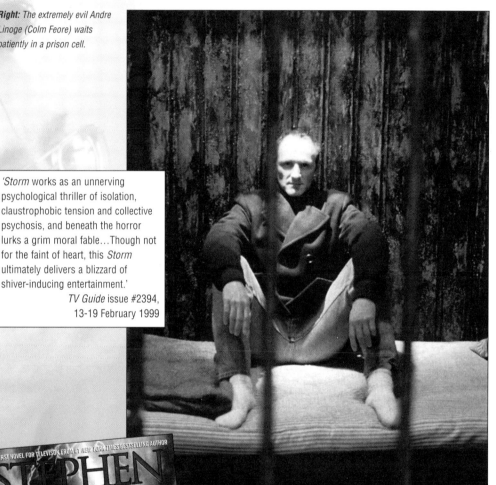

Right: The extremely evil Andre Linoge (Colm Feore) waits patiently in a prison cell.

'*Storm* works as an unnerving psychological thriller of isolation, claustrophobic tension and collective psychosis, and beneath the horror lurks a grim moral fable...Though not for the faint of heart, this *Storm* ultimately delivers a blizzard of shiver-inducing entertainment.'
TV Guide issue #2394, 13-19 February 1999

THE FIRST NOVEL FOR TELEVISON FROM #1 *NEW YORK TIMES* BESTSELLING AUTHOR

STEPHEN KING

AN ORIGINAL SCREENPLAY

STORM OF THE CENTURY

WITH AN INTRODUCTION BY THE AUTHOR

'As a writer, I like the length of television, the fact that you can expand a bit,' continued King. 'There are two kinds of writers, the taker-outers and the putter-inners. I'm a putter-inner. I like the idea of a lot of characters and a lot of story.'

Despite the project's horror pedigree, and perhaps being mindful of ABC's Standards and Practices department, Mark Carliner pointed out that, 'We were not going for blood; we weren't going for the cheap and easy. This was about real

psychological horror.'

'The thing about *Storm of the Century* that amazes me is that nobody asked for any changes at ABC,' King added. 'No one said, "Let's make it four hours instead of six." No one said it cost too much. They just said, "Make it".'

Having previously worked with him on the ABC-TV mini-series *The Stand* (1994) and *The Shining*, Mick Garris was King's logical first choice to direct *Storm of the Century*. 'I sometimes joke that we're in danger of becoming the Billy Wilder and I.A.L. Diamond of the horror genre,' revealed the author. However, when Garris was unable to commit because of other projects, King and Carliner had to look for another director.

They eventually chose former California surfer and ex-stuntman Craig R. Baxley. When they discovered that Baxley was available, King sent him a copy of the 300-page script and followed it up with a meeting over dinner at his daughter Naomi's restaurant in Portland, Maine. 'What I liked most of all was that the sheer size of the project didn't seem to faze him,' explained King.

The author insisted early on that he did not want to cast someone well-known in the role of the demonic Andre Linoge. 'He didn't want someone who everyone knew,' Carliner told *Fangoria*. 'He wanted someone who was a terrific actor but not very well known.' The producers eventually convinced ABC executives that stage actor Colm Feore would be perfect for the part, and the Canadian performer decided to play Linoge as, 'Just a regular guy, who is chockablock with information. He's wired into the deepest thoughts and feelings and secrets of the town. So all he has to do is slowly reveal these secrets.'

Filming began in late February 1998 in Southwest Harbor, on Mount Desert Island, Maine, and finished around eighty days later in San Francisco.

Exteriors were also filmed in Canada, where

King, who has a cameo as a lawyer on a television ad, described it as, 'The harrowing tale of a remote community under siege from both nature's full fury and the supernatural forces of evil.'

Billed as 'An ABC Television Event!' and originally shown in three two-hour segments over 14, 15 and 18 February 1999, the network made the mistake of scheduling the final episode of this 'original novel for television' against George Clooney's farewell episode of *E.R.* 'I don't actually love starting against *The X Files* and finishing against *E.R.*,' King told *The New York Times* television section. 'If I do my job the first two nights, and people want to see how things turn out the third night, maybe they'll hang in with me and tape *E.R.*' Unfortunately, despite receiving mostly good reviews, in the end American audiences apparently preferred Clooney's easy charm over King's be-sieged inhabitants of Little Tall Island (also the setting for *Dolores Claiborne*).

Although the first two instalments delivered viewer demographics which would be considered good under normal circumstances, numbers were lower than for any previous King adaptation on television. According to industry analysts, this was particularly disappointing after ABC's promotional blizzard had enveloped the nation for five months and was extensively highlighted during the final weeks with the slogan 'ABC is Taking February by Storm'. The network also managed to upset some of its affiliate stations and the emergency services when it ran a crawl along the bottom of the screen during its evening comedy shows on 17 February which began: 'ABC Storm Alert'.

When asked why the miniseries wasn't the ratings success everyone had expected, Larry Hyams, vice-president of research for ABC, simply replied, 'Who knows?'

King's script, with an introduction by the author, was published by Pocket Books in 1999. ✝

Left: Andre Linoge arrives on the island carrying a walking stick topped by a living wolf's head.

> 'As chilling and gripping as any Stephen King film since Stanley Kubrick's classic movie of *The Shining*…It comes with a terrific kicker about the aftereffects of the storm. Stephen King may be our master of horror; no one ever called him the master of the happy ending.'
> *The New York Times*,
> 12 February 1999

Little Tall Island's snow-bound Main Street was recreated exactly to scale inside an abandoned sugar-refining silo, situated about twenty miles north of Toronto in Oshawa, Ontario. The $1 million reconstruction, used for only six days of shooting, was reportedly one of the largest indoor sets ever constructed. Miniatures were shot in Tempe, Arizona, and another $5 million was spent on digital effects.

With 260 special effects shots, supervisor Michael Kavanagh and his crew of up to two dozen technicians used truckloads of synthetic snow made from bleached potato flakes, foam, shredded plastic and 300 pound blocks of chipped ice blown through snow-making machines to enhance a late February 1998 snow fall on the Maine set. 'They'd yell "Cut!" and we'd be picking this crap out of our eyes and every orifice and spitting it,' forty-two year-old star Tim Daly complained. 'And then you'd look behind the camera and see sixty people wearing goggles and respirators.'

Stephen King's Storm of the Century included sixty-five speaking roles and had a budget of $35 million, making it the network's most expensive mini-series to that date.

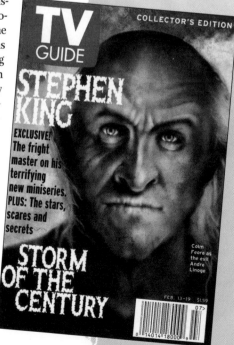

TV GUIDE COLLECTOR'S EDITION

STEPHEN KING

EXCLUSIVE! The fright master on his terrifying new miniseries. PLUS: The stars, scares and secrets

STORM OF THE CENTURY

Colm Feore as the evil Andre Linoge

FEB. 13-19 $1.59

Every Teen Thinks Terrible Thoughts... Hers Are Deadly.

USA, 1999. Director: **Katt Shea**. Screenplay: **Rafael Moreau**. Based on the Characters Created by **Stephen King**. Producer: **Paul Monash**. Executive Producer: **Patrick Palmer**. Director of Photography: **Donald M. Morgan**, ASC. Production Designer: **Peter Jamison**. Editor: **Richard Nord**. Costume Designer: **Theoni V. Aldredge**. Music: **Danny B. Harvey**. Casting: **Gretchen Rennell Court**. United Artists Pictures/Red Bank Films. Colour. 104 minutes.

Emily Bergl (Rachel Lang), **Jason London** (Jesse Ryan), **Dylan Bruno** (Mark), **J. Smith-Cameron** (Barbara Lang), **Amy Irving** (Sue Snell), **Zachary Ty Bryan** (Eric Stark), **John Doe** (Boyd), **Gordon Clapp** (Eric's Father), **Rachel Blanchard** (Monica), **Charlotte Ayanna** (Tracy), **Justin Urich** (Brad), **Mena Suvari** (Lisa), **Elijah Craig** (Chuck), **Eddie Kaye Thomas** (Arnie), **Clint Jordan** (Sheriff Kelton), **Steven Ford** (Coach Walsh), **Kate Skinner** (Emilyn), **Rus Blackwell** (Sheriff), **Harold Surratt** (School Principal), **David Lenthall** (English Teacher), **Kayla Campbell** (Little Rachel), **Robert D. Raiford** (Senior D.A.), **Katt Shea** (Deputy D.A.), **Deborah Meschan** (Party Girl), **Robert Treveiler** (Smiling Patient), **Gina Stewart** (Female Vet), **Claire Hurst** (Night Nurse), **Albert E. Hayes** (Head-Banging Patient), **Colin Fickes** (Tuba Player), **Rhoda Griffis** (Saleswoman), **Eric Hill** (Jesse's Spotter), **Jennifer Nicole Parillo** (Fleeing Party Girl), **Jessica Cowart** (Gardening Girl), **Tiffany LeShai McMinn** (Girl), **Steven Culbertson** (The Ref).

THE **RAGE**
CARRIE 2

LOOKS CAN KILL

'This second — and let's hope last — instalment to Brian De Palma's benchmark 1970s classic may be more remake than sequel, but is — predictably enough — inferior on every count.'

Empire, June 2000

Seventeen year-old Rachel Lang is not like other kids at Bates High School. She does not belong to the right crowd, wear the right clothes or go to the right parties. With her mother locked away in Arkham asylum, she lives in a private world which she shares only with her beloved dog, Walter, and her best friend Lisa. But when Lisa jumps to her death from the school roof, Rachel's insulated existence is shattered and she is sent to former pupil-turned-guidance counsellor Sue Snell. Sue soon notices that the black-clad teen outcast has the secret gift of telekinesis, which enables her to move things with her mind — just like Carrie White — and she attempts to help the girl before her powers become unmanageable. Meanwhile, when Rachel falls for handsome football player Jesse Ryan, the shell she has built around herself begins to crack. But as she slowly learns to trust, the leader of the popular football team plans a cruel trick at a party that will humiliate her in front of everybody. However, making Rachel angry could prove fatal for everyone...

More than two decades after director Brian De Palma helped turn Stephen King into a household name, *Carrie* (1976) finally got a sequel.

Originally announced as *The Curse*, British-born newcomer Emily Bergl was cast back in 1996 while still in college. However, the production became stalled for nearly two years before a title change put it back on the fast-track again. The film marked the talented young stage actress' motion picture début. 'It's not really a remake, and it's not a sequel,' she revealed in an interview with Randy Palmer. 'It's the same kind of story, but a very different take on it.'

Amy Irving, who made her feature début in *Carrie*, recreated her role of Sue Snell, the lone survivor from the earlier film, now grown-up but still seeking redemption. Working as a high school counsellor, in one particularly unlikely scene, she takes Rachel to the burned-out site of the original school prom, which nobody has bothered to clean up during the intervening twenty-three years! 'Initially, I kind of laughed at the idea,' recalled the actress about making a sequel. 'The original *Carrie* was such an extraordinary film, I just couldn't imagine anybody except Brian De Palma making a second.

'Sue Snell was my first film role, and I thought if a decent film was going to be made, it would have been very strange to have someone else playing the character I originated!

'I talked to Brian De Palma about it,' continued Irving, 'to get his blessing, and he thought it was a great idea and I should go for it.'

Mena Suvari, who portrayed the doomed Lisa, changed the colour of her hair and made a much bigger impression the same year as the teenage object of Kevin Spacey's obsession in Sam Mendes' *American Beauty*.

Filming commenced in April 1998 on location in Charlotte, North Carolina, under the direction of Robert Mandel (*FX Murder By Illusion* [1986], etc). However, he soon left the project over the ubiquitous 'creative differences' and was replaced by low budget Roger Corman protégé Katt Shea [Ruben], whose credits include *Stripped to Kill* (1986) and *Poison Ivy* (1992) starring Drew Barrymore. As a result, the project lost nearly a week of production and Mandel's footage was scrapped. Director of photography Lauro Escorel was also subsequently replaced by Donald M. Morgan.

After appearing in such films as De Palma's *Scarface* (1983) and *Psycho III* (1986), Shea's cameo role in *The Rage Carrie 2* as the sympathetic Deputy District Attorney marked the first time she had acted in one of her own films. 'Carrie was a modern-day classic,' the director explained to *Fangoria*, 'and I wasn't sure we could make one as good as the first... But I just do the best I can and see what happens.'

Somewhat confusingly, despite the title, there is no character actually named Carrie in the film. 'My character is named Rachel, not Carrie,' Bergl helpfully told *Fangoria*, 'but she does have a genetic link...The way it ties in to the original plot makes sense; it's not like some unbelievable bullshit sequel. It's very clever and plausible.' In the sequel, it is intimated that the girl's powers come from a genetic recessive trait in Carrie's father, Ralph White, who ran away with another woman — Rachel's schizophrenic mother. The film also includes scenes of Sue Snell being haunted by flashbacks to the first film of Sissy Spacek covered in blood.

After a brief title change to *Carrie: Say You're Sorry*, United Artists noticed the success of *Halloween H20* (1998) and decided they had another potential summer boxoffice hit on their hands. Consequently, an original distribution date of 15 January 1999 was pushed back to the Fourth of July weekend.

However, when Walter Hill's troubled *Supernova* (1999) was removed from the spring release schedule, *Carrie 2* was hurriedly pushed out on 12 March.

Producer Paul Monash, whose previous credits included the first *Carrie* and the 1979 mini-series of Stephen King's *'Salem's Lot*, decided against including another prom scene because of possible negative comparisons with the original. So this time Rachel unleashes her telekinetic powers at an after-hours party. 'We needed to do something as powerful as having pig's blood thrown on you,' Shea told *Fangoria*, 'and I believe we accomplished it.'

'What happens is pretty shocking,' revealed Bergl. 'It's very different and very disturbing at the same time.' ✝

Left: *Like her half-sister before her, Rachel Lang (Emily Bergl) uses her paranormal powers.*
Below: *Amy Irving returns as Sue Snell, now a school guidance counsellor.*

CHILDREN OF THE CORN 666
ISAAC'S RETURN

The Latest & Most Horrifying Chapter...

USA, 1999. Director: **Kari Skogland**. Writers: **Tim Sulka** and **John Franklin**. Producers: **Bill Barry** and **Jeff Geoffray** and **Walter Josten**. Based on the Short Story 'Children of the Corn' by **Stephen King**. Director of Photography: **Richard Clabaugh**. Editor: **Troy T. Takaki**. Music: **Terry Michael Huud**. Production Designer: **Stuart Blatt**. Costume Designer: **Niklas J. Palm**. Casting: **Ed Mitchell** and **Robyn Ray**, CSA. Executive Producers: **Jenni Sherwood** and **Louis Spiegler**. Miramax Film Corp/Dimension Films/Blue Rider Pictures/Dimension Home Video. Colour. 82 minutes.

Nancy Allen (Rachel [Colby]), **Natalie Ramsey** (Hannah Martin), **Paul Popowich** (Gabriel), **Alix Koromzay** (Cora), **John Patrick White** (Matt), **Nathan Bexton** (Jesse), **John Franklin** (Isaac), **Stacy Keach** (Doc Michaels), **William Prael** (Jake), **Sydney Bennett** (Morgan), **Gary Bullock** (Zachariah).

The Latest & Most Horrifying Chapter...

CHILDREN OF THE CORN 666 ISAAC'S RETURN

Right: *Issac (John Franklin) menaces Rachel Colby (Nancy Allen), the mother of a supernatural offspring.*

FACT FILE

Stacey Keach's father, Stacy Keach Sr, was a member of the Loop Group who dubbed the Stephen King adaptation *Pet Sematary* (1989).

Nineteen years after the events in the first film, the original children of the corn have grown up. Rachel Colby sent her daughter Hannah away for adoption when she was an infant to protect her. Now, guided by her visions, the girl has returned on the eve of her birthday to the town of Gatlin, Nebraska. There she discovers that, according to Isaac's prophecy, her supernatural offspring will become the leader of a new generation of those who worship 'He Who Walks Behind the Rows'.

Back in 1984, the then-eighteen year-old John Franklin was cast as the androgynous-looking preacher, Isaac, in New World Pictures' Stephen King adaptation *Children of the Corn*. Fifteen years and four video sequels later, Franklin returned to the franchise as both star and co-writer. 'Hollywood casting directors don't exhibit much imagination when it comes to an actor who is five feet tall,' Franklin revealed to David Hughes in *Empire* magazine, 'so it looks like I'll just have to write my own movies.'

According to the diminutive actor, he went to the Dimension office and pitched the idea of Isaac coming back: 'We lucked out by getting to them just as the project was beginning. We worked our butts off with the writing — it is just so difficult to write and try to please six or seven producers and Bob Weinstein.'

Dimension chose Keri Skogland to direct because the studio was apparently looking for a different type of sequel in the wake of its successful *Scream* (1995) franchise. 'This is a sequel to that first one,' the director explained to Dan Scapperotti in *Cinefantastique*. 'All the other ones which kind of have their own life, own look, were not relevant to this story. This story was really Isaac.'

This time the cult leader wakes from a nineteen-year coma and picks up where he

left off. Nancy Allen played the mother whose daughter returns seeking her heritage and Stacy Keach was cast as the drunken town doctor who is electrocuted for betraying Isaac.

Filmed in and around Los Angeles in November 1998 by sequel specialists Blue Rider Pictures, the production discovered two small cornfields in the area which stood in for Nebraska. Described as 'a reality-driven movie' by Skogland, most of the film's special effects were created in-camera.

Children of the Corn 666 Isaac's Return was released domestically directly to video on 19 October 1999, and in the United Kingdom eighteen months later. 'The mandate was to make a horror film that was smarter and cooler and more happening,' Skogland told Scapperotti. 'Given all the constraints — only so many locations and speaking parts, and just about zero special effects — plus, trying to write for too many cooks, I think it turned out better than I would have thought possible,' added Franklin.

Despite the demise of its title character, Dimension followed it with *Children of the Corn 7 Resurrection* (2001), filmed in Canada by director Guy Magar. ✝

THE GREEN MILE

Paul Edgecomb Didn't Believe in Miracles.
Until the Day He Met One.

USA, 1999. Writer for the Screen and Director: **Frank Darabont**. Producers: **David Valdes** and **Frank Darabont**. Based on the Novel by **Stephen King**. Director of Photography: **David Tattersall**, BSC. Production Designer: **Terence Marsh**. Editor: **Richard Francis-Bruce**, ACE. Music: **Thomas Newman**. Costume Designer: **Karyn Wagner**. Casting: **Mali Finn**, CSA. CR Films, LLC/Castle Rock Entertainment/Darkwoods/Warner Bros. Colour. 188 minutes.

Tom Hanks (Paul Edgecomb), **David Morse** (Brutus 'Brutal' Howell), **Bonnie Hunt** (Jan Edgecomb), **Michael Clarke Duncan** (John Coffey), **James Cromwell** (Warden Hal Moores), **Michael Jeter** (Eduard Delacroix), **Graham Greene** (Arlen Bitterbuck), **Doug Hutchison** (Percy Wetmore), **Sam Rockwell** ('Wild Bill' Wharton), **Barry Pepper** (Harry Dean Stanton), **Jeffrey DeMunn** (Harry Terwilliger), **Patricia Clarkson** (Melinda Moores), **Harry Dean Stanton** (Toot-Toot), **Dabbs Greer** (Old Paul Edgecomb), **Eve Brent** (Elaine Connelly), **William Sadler** (Klaus Detterick), **Mack C. Miles** (Orderly Hector), **Rai Tasco** (Man in Nursing Home), **Edrie Warner** (Lady in Nursing Home), **Paula Malcomson** (Marjorie Detterick), **Christopher Ives** (Howie Detterick), **Evanne Drucker** (Kathe Detterick), **Bailey Drucker** (Cora Detterick), **Brian Libby** (Sheriff McGee), **Brent Briscoe** (Bill Dodge), **Bill McKinney** (Jack Van Hay), **Gary Sinise** (Burt Hammersmith), **Rachel Singer** (Cynthia Hammersmith), **Scotty Leavenworth** (Hammersmith's Son), **Katelyn Leavenworth** (Hammersmith's Daughter), **Bill Gratton** (Earl the Plumber), **Dee Croxton** (Woman at Del's Execution), **Rebecca Klingler** (Wife at Del's Execution), **Gary Imhoff** (Husband at Del's Execution), **Van Epperson** (Police Officer), **Reverend David E. Browning** (Reverend at Funeral).

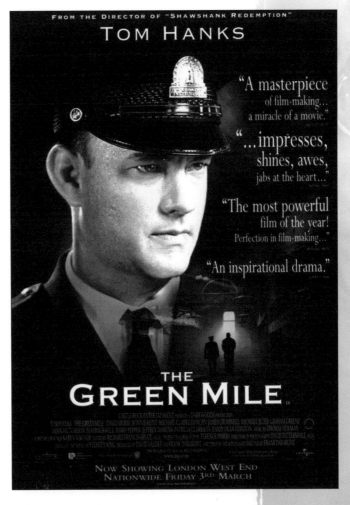

Told in flashback from the Georgia Pines Nursing Home by the elderly Paul Edgecomb, who recalls his Depression-era job as the head guard on Death Row at Louisiana's Cold Mountain Penitentiary. Shortly after the arrival of convicted child-killer John Coffey to the lime-green corridor of the condemned cells (known as the 'Mile'), Edgecomb discovers that his new inmate has secret healing powers. He may also be divine. By touching the sick, the mountainous black man can absorb their malady and then exhale it as a cloud of tiny black insects. After curing Edgecomb's painful urinary infection, Coffey restores to life Mr Jingles, the intelligent pet mouse of fellow prisoner Eduard Delacroix, which was stamped to death by the Row's bullying guard Percy Wetmore. The more that Edgecomb observes the gentle giant and comes to understand his philosophy, the more he believes that Coffey is innocent of the rape and slaughter of two young twin girls. Despite his own investigations into Coffey's case, Edgecomb discovers that he cannot prevent Coffey's final appointment with 'Old Sparky'. Back in the present, there is still one more magical revelation to come involving a storage shack in the woods...

'The Green Mile began with an image of a huge black man standing in his jail cell and watching the approach of a trusty selling candy and cigarettes from an old metal cart with a squeaky wheel,' recalled Stephen King.

At the initial suggestion of HarperCollins' former fiction publishing director Malcolm

Edwards and King's agent Ralph Vicinanza, the author agreed to write a new novel to be published serially. 'The idea was brought to me because it's the way [Charles] Dickens issued some of his books,' King told Linda Marotta in *Fangoria*, 'and I just thought what a hoot it

Above: Gentle giant John Coffey (Michael Clarke Duncan) is escorted by Paul Edgecomb (Tom Hanks, left) and Brutus Howell (David Morse).
Below: From left to right: Tom Hanks, Jeffrey DeMunn and David Morse.

would be, because nobody can look ahead and see the end.'

The Green Mile was released in six monthly paperback instalments between April and September 1996 by Penguin Books. At one point, all six volumes were on both *The New York Times*' and *Publishers Weekly*'s bestseller lists.

'I always loved stories told in episodes,' said King. 'It is a format I first encountered in the *Saturday Evening Post*.

'When the first episode, 'The Two Dead Girls', was about to go on sale, I thought to myself, "I've made the biggest mistake of my life". Nobody had any idea that it would succeed to the level it did, least of all me.'

King always had Frank Darabont in mind for *The Green Mile*, and before the first part was even published or any studio had committed to the project he explained to the writer/director his idea for the story. 'I was still working on it,' King told Joseph B. Mauceri in *World of Fantasy*. 'He was really excited by it, and I

told him I'd send him the parts.'

'I told him that if he liked it, he could do it,' King said. 'He now says that he is carving out the world's smallest film niche — making Stephen King prison stories set in the '50s.'

However, the author made Darabont wait for each instalment, just like everybody else.

'Steve was sort of devilish about that,' the director recalled for London's *Evening Standard* newspaper, 'which at the end of the day, I think was pretty smart. And anyway, when that first book was published he hadn't written the last one. Talk about balls. Talk about guts. It's truly a high-wire act.'

'Steve, to me, is like Dickens,' Darabont told *Film Review*. 'He is a storyteller, an old-fashioned storyteller in the best sense of the word. Both Stephen and Dickens were accused by the literary snobs of their day of being horribly populist, pandering writers because, God forbid, there should be a plot. It's not just about plot with Steve.'

Darabont travelled to Colorado, where director Mick Garris was filming *The Shining* (1997), to confirm with King that he wanted to go ahead with the project. It then took him around eight weeks to condense the serial novel into a workable screenplay — approximately the same amount of time it had taken him to adapt *The Shawshank Redemption* (1994). King termed the script, 'the best film adaptation I've ever read.'

When the screenplay was completed, Darabont sent it to Academy Award-winner Tom Hanks, who he had always envisioned for the role of the sympathetic Death Row guard, Paul Edgecomb. The actor committed to the project within forty-eight hours, receiving his now-customary fee of $20 million. 'I was afraid to read the original novels,' Hanks told *Film Review*, 'thinking that Frank would have cut corners and made changes just to make it fit into the confines of a movie. But I found that to be the opposite case. Frank distilled it down perfectly.

'With Stephen King you think you're going to get this very particular brand of horror story,' Hanks continued, 'and this is really not that.'

King couldn't believe his luck when he learned that Hanks would be playing the lead. 'Edgecomb is a Stephen King narrator if there ever was one,' said the author. 'Tom fits like an old shoe. The minute that Frank mentioned his

Left: Frank Darabont rehearses with
Tom Hanks, while Harry Dean Stanton
(centre) looks on.

name to me, I thought, "This can't be, it's too good to be true".'

Filmed on a budget of $65 million, Darabont meticulously directed every scene, which was shot primarily on a single soundstage. 'There are things about how Frank works that drive me absolutely nuts,' King told David Hochman in *Entertainment Weekly*. 'I think he's a total anal retentive, but unlike Stanley Kubrick, he's an anal retentive you can talk to.'

'You must understand this about Frank,' Hanks told *Premiere*. 'It's all about the details. He went well into the double digits on a lot of set-ups, because he was making a kind of textured look to this movie, right down to the glistening wetness of the brick, the jangling of our equipment, and the sound of the leather belts we wore.'

But Darabont saw directing a different way: 'You just have to show up and keep putting one foot in front of the other,' he explained. 'It really does become a forced march after a while.'

King celebrated his birthday on set at the Warner Hollywood Studios. Darabont had a birthday cake prepared for the author with a replica of the cover of the fourth volume of *The Green Mile* in icing. Observing Terence Marsh's meticulously detailed set design, King told *Cinefantastique*'s Patrick Hobby, 'It's like being inside the country of my own imagination.'

Weather problems at the few Nashville, Tennessee, locations used eventually pushed the production behind schedule and a reported $10 million over budget. Because of questions about whether Hanks should play the part in make-up, the film's modern-day bookend sequences featuring then-eighty-two year-old character actor Dabbs Greer were finally shot in Blowing Rock, North Carolina, in July 1999, some eight months after the production was scheduled to finish.

Even though some critics on both sides of the Atlantic complained about the film's running time of more than three hours, *The Green Mile* opened on 10 December 1999, and in less than two months had passed the $120 million mark at the North American boxoffice.

The film earned Darabont both Writers Guild and Director's Guild of America award nominations, and it was awarded the Humanitas Award and the Scriptor Award from the University of Southern California. *The Green Mile* was also nominated for four Academy Awards: Best Picture, Best Screenplay Based on Material Previously Produced or Published, Sound and Best Supporting Actor — for six foot, five inch former Chicago bouncer Michael Clarke Duncan (*Armageddon* [1998], etc), who weighed 315 pounds for his role as the simple-minded giant convicted of the rape and murder of two young white children.

'Like *Shawshank*, this story is uplifting,' Darabont said, 'but this has a much more complex tone. It's also got a sort of lovely melancholy thing going on. I'm looking for something that is hopeful, and that's what I find attractive in these stories. I want something my heart can believe in.'

'I don't think I'd want to do another serial novel,' King said afterwards, 'but I wouldn't have missed the experience for the world.'

Darabont's script was published by Scribner in the United Kingdom, and included a foreword by King. Constantine Nasr's ten minute behind-the-scenes documentary *Walking the Mile* (2000) featured interviews with the author and major cast and crew members. †

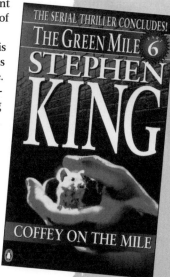

Hearts in Atlantis

What if One of Life's Great Mysteries Moved in Upstairs?

USA/Australia, 2001. Director: **Scott Hicks**. Screenplay: **William Goldman**. Based on the Book by **Stephen King**. Executive Producers: **Bruce Berman** and **Michael Flynn**. Producer: **Kerry Heysen**. Director of Photography: **Piotr Sobocinski**. Production Designer: **Barbara Ling**. Film Editor: **Pip Karmel**. Music: **Mychael Danna**. Castle Rock Entertainment/Warner Bros/Village Roadshow Pictures/NPV Entertainment. Colour.

Anthony Hopkins (Ted Brautigan), **Anton Yelchin** (Bobby Garfield), **Hope Davis** (Liz Garfield), **Mika Boorem** (Carol Gerber), **David Morse** (Adult Bobby Garfield), **Alan Tudyk** (McQuown), **Tom Bower** (Len Files), **Celia Weston** (Alana Files), **Adam Lefevre** (Donald Biderman), **Will Rothhaar** (Sully), **Dierdre O'Connell** (Mrs Gerber), **Timothy Reifsnyder** (Harry Doolin), **Eric Eggen** (Coast Guardsman at Carnival), **Kathie France** (Rider at Carnival), **Steve Little** (Lowman), **Kristina Lash** (Carousel Rider at Carnival), **Jim Hild** (Lowman), **Bourke Floyd** (Lowman), **Sara Hamilton** (Hot Dog Vendor at Carnival), **Wes Johnson** (Sports Announcer), **David Rivitz**.

Above: *Publicity image: Anthony Hopkins as the enigmatic Ted Brautigan.*

FACT FILE

Cinematographer Piotr Sobocinski was found dead in a Vancouver hotel room on 26 March 2001, soon after completing *Hearts in Atlantis*.

A look at America of the early 1960s, before the impact of the Vietnam War tore an entire generation apart. When the adult Bobby Garfield solemnly returns home to Harwich, Connecticut, for the first time in forty years to attend the funeral of one of his best childhood friends, the aftermath of those years is made starkly real with remembered horrors. For eleven year-old Bobby his childhood is a disturbing time, as life seems more complicated than it should be. His father died six years earlier, and the young boy's closest friends are 'cool bastard' Sully-John and Carol Gerber, the girl who will become the love of his life. Then his working mother, Liz, takes in a mysterious border: the well-read Ted Brautigan reveals to the boy that he is being hunted by men in yellow coats because of his supernatural ability to see through a 'window' into the future, where he can uncover people's hidden secrets. When Bobby learns that he may share a similar 'gift', his life is forever changed as the enigmatic stranger with a troubled past becomes a paternal figure to the fatherless boy. With Bobby's return to his hometown, one final secret, the hope of redemption and his heart's desire may finally await him...

Based on Stephen King's 1999 novel of five parts, which used interweaving storylines and characters to tell its story of a generation. As with the author's 1982 novella, 'The Body' (in *Different Seasons*), it charts a young boy's loss of innocence and his coming of age against a very specific period in American history. About the book, King said: 'Although it is difficult to believe, the sixties are not fictional: they actually happened...I have tried to remain true to the spirit of the age.'

Castle Rock Entertainment purchased the rights in November 2000, just two months after the book was published. Scriptwriter William Goldman (*Misery* [1990], etc) was briefly touted as director before the job went to Scott Hicks (*Shine* [1996], etc).

Goldman's 117-page second draft only adapted the first and last sections of King's book, 'Low Men in Yellow Coats' and 'Heavenly Shades of Night Are Falling', with the latter used as the framing story. Although the script reportedly paid homage to the 1960 film *Village of the Damned* (starring George Sanders and based on John Wyndham's 1957 science fiction novel *The Midwich Cuckoos*), King's original references to William Golding's *Lord of the Flies* and *Roland the Gunslinger* from the author's own *The Dark Tower* series were cut.

Filming began on 2 October 2000 in the Richmond, Virginia Beach and Staunton areas of Virginia. Earlier in the year, Sir Anthony Hopkins had also filmed *Hannibal* (2001), the much-anticipated sequel to *The Silence of the Lambs* (1991), in the same central Richmond location. The film was released on 28 September 2001, in the United States. †

Stephen King's Rose Red

USA, 2002. Director: **Craig R. Baxley**. Teleplay: **Stephen King**. Producer: **Tom Brodek**. Executive Producers: **Stephen King** and **Mark Carliner**. Director of Photography: **David Connell**, ACS. Production Designer: **Craig Sterns**. Greengrass Productions/Victor Television Productions/Mark Carliner Productions/ABC-TV. Colour.

Nancy Travis (Joyce Reardon), **Robert Blanche** (George Wheaton), **Judith Ivey**, **Kimberly J. Brown**, **Julian Sands**, **Matt Keeslar**, **Kevin Tighe**, **Emily Deschanel**, **Yvonne Sciò**, **Matt Ross**, **Tsidii LeLoca**, **Julia Campbell** (Ellen Rimbauer), **David Dukes**, **Melanie Lynskey**, **Paul Brewster** (Harry Corbin), **Stephen King** (Pizza Delivery Man).

The eponymous haunted house, built in 1907 by a Seattle oil magnate, has lain dormant for years and is set for demolition. Now attempts to awaken its ghosts by obsessed psychology professor Joyce Reardon, accompanied by a fifteen year-old autistic girl with telekinetic powers and a team of psychic investigators, unleash myriad spirits and bring to light the horrifying secrets of the generations that have lived and died in the malevolent mansion.

Rose Red was originally set to be a $40 million collaboration between Stephen King and Steven Spielberg in the mid-1990s. As King revealed to *Fangoria* in 1996: 'It went into turnaround. Steven and I have tried to work together on a couple of occasions, starting with *Poltergeist*, and we've just never been able to do it...What happened with *Rose Red* was that he stayed in touch and asked if I still wanted to do a haunted house story.'

However, on receiving a script, Spielberg began suggesting additional ideas to be incorporated into the story. After three drafts, King felt the original idea was getting away from him. 'Steven also wanted a bigger, more positive kind of feeling than I wanted to go for,' explained King. 'He wanted that *whoooosh* thing and I wanted to scare the shit out of people. We finally got to a point where it seemed like the best thing for me was to step away.'

King finally returned to the project almost half a decade later, describing it as 'an expansion of a screenplay I wrote some years ago'.

After a frustrated effort to develop the idea with director Mick Garris, on Friday 18 June 2000, he pitched the concept to executive producer Mark Carliner during a long phone conversation. Carliner reportedly loved the story idea, and King was supposed to start writing the script on the Monday.

However, the following day King was hit by a mini-van while out walking and he spent a month in the hospital. When he returned home, he resumed work on *Rose Red* and adapted the idea as a mini-series for television while convalescing.

'The accident did not take away even a bit of Stephen's edge,' said Carliner, whose Mark Carliner Productions also produced King's 1999 mini-series *Storm of the Century*. 'This is some of his best writing ever.'

'We're delighted to have Stephen King back at ABC,' executive vice president of movies and mini-series Susan Lyne said. 'I can't wait to see these characters brought to life.'

Although the script was originally set in Los Angeles, King rewrote it for Seattle after the producers found Thornewood Castle, a Gothic Tudor mansion in Lakewood, near Tacoma, Washington State. Pre-production began in July 2000, and filming lasted from 22 August until mid-December. The $3 million interior sets were built inside three airplane hangers at the former Sand Point Naval Base in Seattle.

According to producer Tom Brodek, the story concerned 'a very wealthy banker and railroad executive who decides to build a home for a bride he hasn't met yet. The couple honeymoons in Europe for three years, only to return to a grand home where the executive and their child die mysteriously. His wife learns that she won't die if she continues adding on to the house...'

Post-production was scheduled to take six months, with Carliner Productions planning to deliver the six-hour, three-part mini-series to ABC-TV by Labor Day 2001. Promotion was set to begin in November, and the show aired over the 27th, 28th, and 29th of January 2002.

A tie-in book, *The Diary of Ellen Rimbauer: My Life at Rose Red*, purportedly edited by research psychologist Joyce Reardon, PhD, was published by Hyperion in 2002 and backed by a $200,000 marketing campaign. †

THE DIARY OF ELLEN RIMBAUER

MY LIFE AT ROSE RED

EDITED BY JOYCE REARDON, PH. D.

FACT FILE

55 year-old actor David Dukes (*Gods and Monsters* [1998], etc), died suddenly while playing tennis on 9 October 2000 after suffering what doctors believed was a massive heart attack. The actor had already finished filming the majority of his sequences for *Rose Red*, and only had his death scene left to shoot.

Above: Fledgling director Frank Darabont with Dee Croxton, behind-the-scenes on Stephen King's The Woman in the Room.

THE BOOGEYMAN

USA, 1982. Director/Editor/Screenplay: **Jeffrey C. Schiro**. Based on the Short Story by **Stephen King**. Music: **John Coté**. Director of Photography: **Douglas Meltzer**. Jeffrey C. Schiro/New York University School of Undergraduate Film/Tantalus Pictures/Granite Entertainment Group. Colour. 28 minutes.

With: **Michael Reid** (Lester Billings), **Bert Linder** (Dr Harper), **Terence Brady** (Sgt Garland), **Mindy Silverman** (Rita Billings), **Jerome Bynder** (Coroner), **Bobby Persichtti** (Denny), **Michael Dagostino** (Andy), **Nancy Lindeberg** (The Neighbor), **James Holmes** (Husband), **John Macdonald** (Cop 1), **Dave Burr** (Cop 2), **Rich West** (Attendent 1), **John Cote** (Attendent 2), **Brooke Trivas** (Dispatch Voice).

STEPHEN KING'S THE WOMAN IN THE ROOM

USA, 1983. Director: **Frank Darabont**. Producer: **Gregory Melton**. Executive Producer: **Douglas Venturelli**. Associate Producer: **Mark Vance**. Production Manager: **Michael Sloane**. Cinematographer: **Juan Ruiz Anchia**. Screenplay: **Frank Darabont**. Based on the Story by **Stephen King**. Darkwoods/Granite Entertainment Group. Colour. 30 minutes.

With: **Michael Cornelison** (John [Elliott]), **Dee Croxton** (Mother [Donna Elliott]), **Brian Libby** (Prisoner), **Bob Brunson** (Guard #1), **George Russell** (Guard #2).

DISCIPLES OF THE CROW

USA, 1983. Director: **John Woodward**. Producers: **Johnny Stevens** and **John Woodward**. Screenplay: **John Woodward**. Based on a Story by **Stephen King**. Simitar Entertainment, Inc. Colour.

With: **Ellese Lester** (Vickey), **Gabriel Folse** (Burt).

THE LAST RUNG ON THE LADDER

USA, 1987. Directors: **James Cole** and **Dan Thron**. Producer: **James Cole**. Screenplay: **James Cole** and **Dan Thron**. Based on a Story by **Stephen King**. Director of Photography: **Dan Thron**. Editor: **James Cole**. Music: **Anne Livermore**. Colour. 12 minutes.

THE LAWNMOWER MAN

USA, 1987. Director/Producer: **Jim Gonis**. Screenplay: **Mike De Luca**. Based on a Story by **Stephen King**. Director of Photography: **Ethan Reiff**. Editor: **Andy Huelsebusch**. Music: **Charles Nieland**. Colour. 12 minutes.

With: **E.D. Phillips** (Howard Parkette), **Andy Clark** (Karras), **Helen Hanft** (Mrs Parkette), **Tony Di Sante** (Cop), **Robert Tossberg** (Cop 'Bannerman'), **Neil Schimmel** (Neighbour 'Castonmeyer'), **Becky Taub** (Girl), **Fayth Schlossberg** (Sheila).

GHOSTS

(aka **MICHAEL JACKSON'S GHOSTS**)

USA, 1997. Director/Screenplay: **Stan Winston**. Based on a Story by **Stephen King**. Colour. 38 minutes.

With: **Michael Jackson** (Maestro/Mayor/Ghoul Mayor/Super Ghoul/Skeleton), **Pat Dade**, **Amy Smallman**.

CAIN ROSE UP

USA, 1999. Director/Screenplay: **David Britten Prior**. Based on a Story by **Stephen King**. Colour.

With: **Deborah Offner** (Birdette Cain).

PARANOID

USA, 2000. Director: **Jay Holben**. Adapted from the Poem 'Paranoid: A Chant' by **Stephen King**. Editor: **Eric Tozzi**. Art Director: **Jennine Dwyer**. Director of Photography: **Jay Holben**. Original Score: **Buck Sanders**. Sound Design: **Alek Vila**. Producer: **Jay Holben**. Adakin Productions. Black and White/Colour. 8 minutes.

With: **Tonya Ivey** (Woman), **Mark Reynolds**, **Tamara Balyan**, **Patrick Gealogo** and **Jeff Gabe** (Faceless Men).

'**I** love movies,' Stephen King revealed in his introduction to *The Shawshank Redemption: The Shooting Script*. 'When people ask how come so many films have been made from my work (twenty-five or so, including half a dozen pretty good ones), I say it's simple: I love the movies.'

The author had always been a fan of what he liked to call 'outlaw pictures' made by independents. Which was why, around 1977 when his books were just starting to become successful, that he 'saw a way to give back a little of the joy the movies had given me.'

Ignoring the objections of his accountant, King established a policy that he would allow any student film-maker the right to create a movie out of any short story — not novel — he had written, so long as he still owned the film rights. He charged a one-time rights fee of $1, and all he asked in return was that the film-maker should send him a video tape of the completed work and sign an agreement promising not to exhibit the film commercially without his approval. 'I'd look at the films (usually alone and usually just once; in many cases one viewing was all a person could bear), then put them up on a shelf I had marked 'Dollar Babies',' explained the author.

In 1980, a twenty year-old film-maker named Frank Darabont wrote to King and asked if he could make a film out of 'The Woman in the Room' from the author's 1978 *Night Shift* collection.

Darabont also loved the movies, ever since his older brother Andy had taken his five year-old sibling to see *Robinson Crusoe on Mars* (1964). 'From there, I embarked on a childhood watching everything I could clap my eyeballs on,' Darabont recalled in his introduction to the *Shawshank* script book. 'I revelled in the Universal monster flicks. I rejoiced at the George Pal movies. I wallowed in Ray Harryhausen effects spectaculars. I fell on the detonator plunger with Alec Guinness, blowing up the bridge that spanned the River Kwai. I went on a journey beyond time and space with a computer named Hal. I went back and saw *The Ωmega Man* a dozen times. I soaked up every potboiler and grade Z melodrama I could stay up late enough to watch...'

Which perhaps made his choice of 'The Woman in the Room' all the more unusual. The story happened to be a particularly personal one for the author — a 'cry from the heart' after his mother's long, painful death from cervical cancer at the relatively young age of sixty-two. 'We could hear the pause after each rasping breath she drew growing long and longer,' recalled the author in his memoir *On Writing*. 'Finally there were no more breaths and it was all pause.'

'He found it very odd I wanted to make it because usually film-makers go for something more obviously horrific,' Darabont later told *Empire* magazine.

However, King granted the request and received his dollar. Three years after giving his permission, the author received a video cassette of Darabont's half-hour movie.

After having negotiated for the rights with King's then-publisher Doubleday, the film was completed in 1983 for $35,000, shortly after director/writer/co-editor Darabont and producer/art director Greg Melton graduated from film school.

Beautifully photographed by Juan Ruiz Anchia (*Maria's Lovers* [1984], etc), the slow but intense drama involves attorney John Elliott (Michael Cornelison) who, in-between defending a professional killer, contemplates euthanasia while waiting at the hospital bedside of his terminally-ill mother. A short nightmare sequence involving the mother's

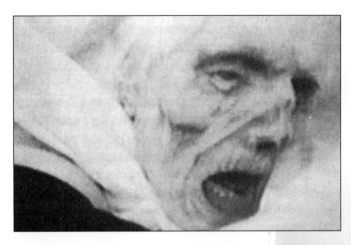

corpse in a wheelchair was added to the story to appease King fans.

'There's a real running thread of humanity in his work that I find very compelling,' Darabont later told *Film Review*. 'I may be the only person who's ever compared him to Frank Capra, but if you really follow the paths of the characters in his stories — which many of the adaptations have not, though the good, I think, have — you find a real humanist at work. Steve's work, more often than not, really has something to say.'

'I watched it in slack-jawed amazement,' King admitted. 'I also felt a little sting of tears. *The Woman in the Room* remains, twelve years later, on my short list of favourite film adaptations.'

'Steve is simply a nice guy,' explained Darabont. 'You can believe him when he says he wants to give something back. The man walks it like he talks it. I'm living proof of that.'

In January 1985, *Stephen King's The Woman in the Room* was announced for release by Gerard Ravels' Native Son International as part of a video compilation that also included James Greco's original horror short *Stranglehold* and Jeffrey C. Schiro's own Stephen King adaptation, *The Boogeyman*.

In Schiro's film, Canadian actor Michael Reid portrayed Lester Billings, who is suspected by the police of murdering two of his young children. However, in an interview with psychiatrist Dr Harper he claims that he did not commit the crime and that the killer is actually the 'Boogey-man' hiding in the closet. When Billings returns unexpectedly to the doctor's office, he uncovers a secret that results in him becoming the next victim.

King's story was originally published in the March 1973 issue of *Cavalier* and later reprinted in the *Night Shift* collection. Maine-born Schiro was a Hitchcock fan and still in the graduate film programme at New York University

Above: *The rotting corpse seen briefly in* Stephen King's The Woman in the Room.

Below: *Dee Croxton as the dead mother in the nightmare sequence from* Stephen King's The Woman in the Room.

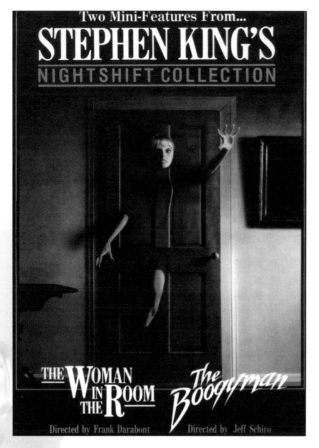

effectively than the 1984 feature adaptation.

It was double-billed with Jack Garrett's non-King related student film *The Night Waiter* (1987), about a ghost haunting an old hotel, on Simitar Entertainment's forty-minute video *Two Mini-Features from Stephen King's Night Shift Collection* (1991). *Disciples of the Crow* won a Gold Hugo Award at the Chicago Film Festival and a National Merit Award.

The Last Rung on the Ladder was another student film, shot in 1987 on Super-8mm for $1,500 by James Cole and Dan Thron. Based on a ten-page story from *Night Shift* about a childhood game played by brother and sister Larry and Katrina, the tale was optioned again by Maine-based independent production company Edge Productions in 1998.

King gave writer Frank Welch and director Lucas Knight permission to film his story as long as they did not use his name above the title. The planned ambitious thirty or forty minute short had a proposed budget of around $60,000. 'It is not a traditional Stephen King horror story,' Knight told Steve LeCroix in *Cinefantastique*. 'It is a drama, about how things can take a turn for the worse for a young girl who was blessed with the miracle of life after a tragic fall.'

The 1987 version of *The Lawnmower Man* was apparently much more faithful to King's original story (first published in the May 1975 *Cavalier* and reprinted in *Night Shift*) than the infamous 1992 feature version.

For the low budget production, Ethan Reiff, Barry Sherman and Jim Gonis taped a smoke bomb inside the mysterious mower produced by the grossly overweight Karras to create an 'exhaust' effect. The same team was also responsible for using a guinea pig as a stand-in for a live mole, plus boiled liver, food colouring and a rabbit pelt as a substitute for a dead mole shredded by the mower.

Scripted by future screenwriter and New Line production executive Michael De Luca (John Carpenter's *In the Mouth of Madness* [1994], etc), the twelve minute short was shown at the Horrorfest '98 film festival.

Written and directed by Oscar-winning special effects supervisor Stan Winston (*The Terminator* [1984], etc), *Ghosts* (1997) was a short film based on a story by King. It served as a showcase for singer Michael Jackson, who appeared in several roles, including a strange hermit living in a haunted house and the town's mayor who tries to get him to leave.

David Britten Prior's *Cain Rose Up* (1999) was based on one of Stephen King's earliest published stories, which originally appeared in the spring 1968 issue of the University of Maine's college literary magazine *Ubris* and was later reprinted in the 1985 collection *Skeleton Crew*. Inspired by real-life Texas

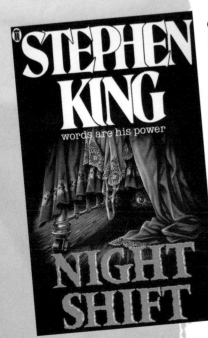

Film School when he made *The Boogeyman* in 1982 for just $20,000 after negotiating the rights with Doubleday.

When Frank Darabont discovered that Native Son had failed to obtain the rights to both the King stories and had been distributing copies of the video compilation prior to signing any agreement, the release was cancelled.

Darabont subsequently learned that Gerard Ravel had also arranged a theatrical screening of *The Woman in the Room* in Los Angeles without first consulting him.

Almost a year later, Granite Entertainment Group bought the licence to distribute the two King adaptations on video as *Stephen King's Night Shift Collection* (1985).

Stephen King's The Woman in the Room also eventually aired on a local PBS television channel and made the semi-final Academy Awards ballot for best dramatic short film of 1983. Meanwhile, Schiro's *The Boogeyman* won an award at the New York University Film Festival.

John Woodward's 1983 short *Disciples of the Crow* was based on the King story 'Children of the Corn' (originally published in the March 1977 issue of *Penthouse* and reprinted the following year in *Night Shift*). This student short was relocated to Oklahoma in 1971 and apparently told the story much more sniper Charles Whitman, it involved a college student who opens fire with a hunting rifle on a shopping mall.

Paranoid (2000) was an eight-minute short from director and cinematographer Jay Holben based on the 100-line poem 'Paranoid: A Chant' in *Skeleton Crew*.

As his unbalanced protagonist, Holben hired Tonya Ivey, an actress and friend he had worked with back in his hometown of Scottsdale, Arizona. 'Tonya and I worked pretty closely for about two weeks to really get inside the mind of the woman and hone Tonya's performance,' he explained to Ray Garraty. 'We recorded her voice-over a few days prior to actually shooting with the intention of using her own voice as playback on the set — but I found that it worked much better if we just ran off of single moments and raw emotions for each shot rather than specifically tie a reaction to a particular line of dialogue.

'It was absolutely crucial to me, however, to maintain one hundred per-cent integrity to King's words. I very carefully studied the structure of how the text was printed on the page. Where lines were broken — where new paragraphs were made — taking note of each punctuation mark and trying to really understand the cadence that King had created. His words were the backbone to the whole film and I took my cues from the imagery that he created in the poem.'

All the scenes taking place inside a motel room were shot in a single day, in May 1999 in Los Angeles, while the woman's monochrome delusions were filmed over three evenings during the previous week. *Paranoid* was shot on 35mm colour stock with Panavision cameras and lenses. All of the black and white sequences were also shot in colour but were desaturated in post-production. King granted his permission and his blessing for the film in September 2000.

'I liked it,' the author is quoted as saying, while *Rolling Stone* writer David Wild described it as 'a stunning and artful rendering of madness, turning a poem by Stephen King into a vivid and compelling nightmare vision.'

Plans to release the film on DVD the following March (as a giveaway with the magazine *Total Movie*, which folded beforehand) were postponed after problems with music clearances, but the short was still set to début on the internet in the summer of 2001.

Among the other projects filmed under King's 'dollar-deal' were Guy Maddin's *Here There Be Tygers* (1988), adapted from the early short story written for his son Owen and published in the spring 1968 issue of *Ubris* and later reprinted in *Skeleton Crew*. It was about a young boy in the third grade who encounters something hungry and terrible in the school bathroom.

'My first-grade teacher in Stratford, Connecticut, was Mrs Van Buren,' King recalled in *Skeleton Crew*. 'She was pretty scary. I guess if a tiger had come along and eaten her up, I could have gotten behind that. You know how kids are.'

A precursor to *The Stand* (1978) and 'Children of the Corn', *Night Surf* was based on an early short story first published in the spring 1969 issue of *Ubris* and later revised for publication in the August 1974 *Cavalier* and the *Night Shift* collection. It was about a group of wild teenagers waiting for their inevitable death from an apocalyptic super-flu nicknamed 'Captain Trips'.

More recently, a new adaptation of King's 1983 novel *Pet Sematary* was announced for video distribution in 2001, starring John Sharian and Briony Glassco.

'What I've found is that I usually come out better for the movie experience when I just sell the rights and don't get involved,' King explained to Marc Shapiro in *Fangoria*. 'That way it becomes a no-lose situation: if the movie is good, I can say it's based on my work, and if it stinks, I can say I had nothing to do with it.' ✝

listen

listen

do listen

you must listen

STEPHEN KING'S

PARANOID

a film by JAY HOLBEN

ADAKIN PRODUCTIONS presents a film by JAY HOLBEN TONYA IVEY is PARANOID
adapted from the poem by STEPHEN KING art direction by JENNINE DWYER edited by ERIC TOZZI
sound design by ALEK VILA original score by BUCK SANDERS photographed and directed by JAY HOLBEN

STEREO NR Not Rated

www.paranoidthemovie.com

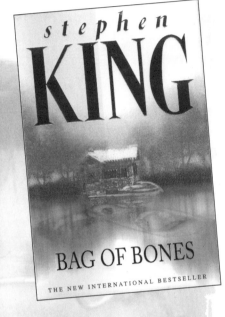

Not since the mid-1980s have so many Stephen King projects been in active development. The following titles have all been announced, but that is of course no guarantee that they will actually make it to the screen:

ASYLUM

USA (forthcoming). Director: **Jonathan Demme**. Screenplay: **Stephen King**. Based on the Novel by **Patrick McGrath**. Paramount Pictures. Colour. With: **Liam Neeson**, **Natasha Richardson**.

It was announced in 2001 that Stephen King had done a re-write on an adaptation of the 1996 novel by Patrick McGrath, about an insane asylum superintendent's wife who falls in love with a murderous patient. It was the first time that King had adapted someone else's work.

BAG OF BONES

USA (forthcoming). Based on the novel by **Stephen King**. Producers: **Bruce Willis** and **Arnold Rifkin**. Cheyenne Productions. Colour.

It was reported in 2001 that Stephen King sold the rights to his 1998 supernatural novel — about a best-selling author with writer's block who tries to protect a young girl and her mother from the clutches of a tyrannical millionaire — to the actress Deborah Raffin (*Scanners II The New Order* [1991], etc) and her movie producer husband Michael Viner.

DOLAN'S CADILLAC

USA/Mexico, 2002 [tbc]. Director: **Stacy Title**. Screenplay: **Stacy Title**. Based on the Novella by **Stephen King**. Producer: **Paula Wagner**. C/W Productions/Franchise Pictures. Colour. With: **Sylvester Stallone** (Jim Dolan), **Kevin Bacon** (Robinson).

Based on Stephen King's 1989 novella, originally published in a limited edition of around 500 copies and revised for the collection *Nightmares and Dreamscapes* (1993), about a female school teacher who is murdered after witnessing a Mafia hit and her husband's bizarre revenge

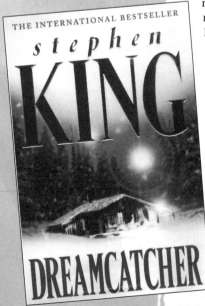

on Dolan, the Las Vegas mob boss responsible.

'If nothing else,' explained King, 'it's a kind of archetypal horror story, with its mad narrator and its account of a premature burial in the desert.'

Filming was due to begin in late April 2001 from writer/director Stacy Title (*The Last Supper* [1995]) through the Tom Cruise-Paula Wagner production partnership.

DREAMCATCHER

USA, 2002 [tbc]. Director: **Lawrence Kasdan**. Producer: **Lawrence Kasdan**. Screenplay: **William Goldman**. Based on the Novel by **Stephen King**. Castle Rock Entertainment. Colour. With **Morgan Freeman** (Colonel Kurtz), **Thomas Jane** (Rr. Henry Devlin), **Tom Sizenore** (Owen Underhill).

With filming due to begin in January 2002, Castle Rock favorite William Goldman adapted Stephen King's science fiction novel, published in 2001 and set in Derry, Maine (also the local of *It* and *Insomnia*). A quarter of a century earlier, four friends stood together to rescue a young autistic boy. Reunited as adults on an annual hunting trip in the north woods, the quartet encounter a disoriented stranger who mutters about weird lights in the sky before 'giving birth' to something with very sharp teeth. The survivors' only chance of defeating an invasion from another world is found in the telepathic powers they were rewarded with all those years ago.

THE EYES OF THE DRAGON

USA, 2001 [tbc]. Based on the Novel by **Stephen King**. WAMC Entertainment. Colour.

'The one time in my life I ever went against writers wanting to write what they couldn't find on library shelves was when I wrote a fantasy for my daughter,' Stephen King revealed to Jo Fletcher in *Knave*. 'She doesn't like horror stories and she had never read very much of my stuff, so I thought Godamnit, if the mountain won't come to Mohammed...I knew she liked fantasy and in the end I really got into it and I did her the courtesy of writing *Eyes of the Dragon* for myself too, because if you're writing just for someone else, you write down.'

King's 1984 (revised in 1987) fantasy novel

was originally titled *The Napkins* and is loosely connected to his other novels *The Talisman*, *The Stand* and *The Dark Tower* series. It was optioned in 2000 as a $45 million animated feature film and tells the story of young Prince Peter, falsely imprisoned for the murder of his father, who must defeat the evil magician Flagg to gain control of the magical kingdom of Delain, which is inhabited by dragons, wizards and brave knights.

'It would make such a *great* cartoon,' King had said back in 1989.

THE GIRL WHO LOVED TOM GORDON

USA, 2002 [tbc]. Director: **George A. Romero**. Screenplay: **George A. Romero**. Based on the Novel by **Stephen King**. Castle Rock Entertainment. Colour.

Based on Stephen King's slim 1999 novel, published worldwide to coincide with the start of the American baseball season.

Nine year-old Trisha McFarland is lost in the New England woods and creates an imaginary friendship with her hero, the eponymous real-life Boston Red Sox and later Chicago Cubs baseball relief pitcher (set to play himself).

Romero began writing the script in 2000. However, because the film was almost all exteriors and shooting would have to be completed by early summer, it was unlikely that it would go into production before an impending writers' and actors' strike in Hollywood.

THE KINGDOM

USA, 2002-2003 [tbc]. Writer: **Stephen King**. Executive Producer: **Stephen King**. Columbia TriStar Television/Touchstone Television/ABC-TV. Colour.

In July 2001, the ABC Network announced that it had ordered fifteen episodes of this remake of Danish director Lars von Trier's creepy 1994 mini-series, about the strange events which plague the eponymous high-tech hospital built over an ancient graveyard. According to the press release: 'The doctors have put their faith into science and technology, and are dismissive of any suggestion of mysticism or unseen powers...at their own peril.'

Columbia TriStar had been developing the project as a feature film until King — who had discovered von Trier's original in a video store in Colorado while working on *The Shining* in 1997 — signalled his willingness to become involved. 'Stephen has been after this for years,' said Stu Blomberg, co-chairman of ABC Entertainment Television Group. 'He is writing the first two hours. He loves the project. He is going to make it very much his own.'

The show will première with a two-hour installment and then be followed by thirteen one-hour episodes, some or all of which may be scripted by King. If successful, additional seasons may follow.

RIDING THE BULLET

USA (forthcoming). Director: **Mick Garris**. Screenplay: **Mick Garris**. Based on the Story by **Stephen King**. Colour.

Mick Garris personally optioned King's 16,000 word novella, which was released exclusively on the Internet in 1999.

'When I first read 'Riding the Bullet' on a downloaded file, something about it resonated within me,' revealed Garris. 'I couldn't get that simple little ghost parable out of my head. It has all of King's trademarks, and straddles the two worlds that don't normally collide: one, it was a ghost story, a creepshow — the boogie-boogie that King's work is perhaps best known for; but two, it also straddled the nostalgic drama of 'The Body' and 'Rita Hayworth and Shawshank Redemption' and the non-supernatural tales. I loved the combination of horror and sentiment, and asked if I could pursue it as a film.'

When King agreed, the writer/director wrote his first spec script in years. 'I changed the setting to 1969 (the short story takes place today) and added material to flesh it out into a movie,' continued Garris, 'but all of the story is there. The combination of fear and heart is unique to his work, and with luck, it will make its way to the screen that way.'

STUD CITY

USA, 2001 [tbc]. Director: **Sean Parlaman**. Screenplay: **Sean Parlaman**. Based on the Story by **Stephen King**. Sound of Thunder Productions. Colour.

Independent semi-sequel to *Stand by Me* (1986), based on a story in a 1970 issue of *Greenspun Quarterly* and later revised and incorporated into the novella 'The Body' from the 1982 collection *Different Seasons*.

The story of the self-despairing Edward May, known as 'Chico' to his friends, it would include characters and scenes to tie-in with Rob Reiner's film and be shot in Browsnsville, Oregon, on many of the same locations.

Amongst the 'ideal cast list' chosen (but not confirmed) for the production were Anette O'Toole as Virginia May, Patrick Duffy as Sam May and veteran Jack Elam as

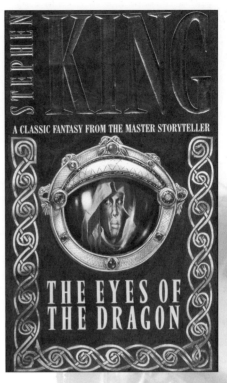

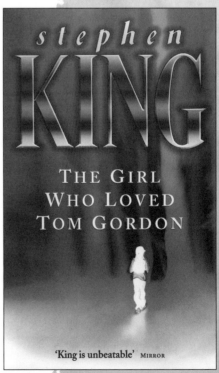

Brownie Quidacioluo. King approved the project and script in 1999 and production was originally set for fall 2000 with a release in early 2001.

THE SUN DOG

USA (forthcoming). Screenplay: **Lawrence D. Cohen**. Based on the Story by **Stephen King**. Producer: **Lawrence D. Cohen**. I-Max. Colour. 18 minutes.

'Castle Rock is really just the town of Jerusalem's Lot without the vampires,' explained Stephen King. ''The Sun Dog' is a story about cameras and photographs.'

This 3-D I-Max short is based on Stephen King's Castle Rock novella (a prologue to his 1991 novel *Needful Things*) from the collection *Four Past Midnight* (1990). It involves a supernatural Polaroid photograph and the eponymous creature that should not exist at all. Production was supposed to begin in 2000 for a 2001 release. However, the project is currently on hold.

THE TALISMAN

USA, 2002 [tbc]. Director: **Mick Garris**. Producers: **Steven Spielberg** and **Kathleen Kennedy**. Screenplay: **Mick Garris**. Based on the Novel by **Stephen King** and **Peter Straub**. DreamWorks SKG/Kennedy-Marshall Production Company/ABC-TV. Colour.

According to a report in *Variety*, Steven Spielberg (who originally had Universal purchase the project for his Amblin Entertainment in 1984) and Stephen King will be producing a four hour TV mini-series, based on the 1984 novel co-written by King and Peter Straub, which will run during a 'sweeps' week.

The fantasy involves twelve year-old Jack Sawyer's quest for the eponymous magical object to save his dying mother and his epic trek across the United States using the ability to jump between parallel worlds known as the Territories.

A screenplay was apparently written by Richard LaGravenese (*The Fisher King* [1991], etc) in the mid-1990s, although director and regular King col-

laborator Mick Garris has rewritten the script. King and Spielberg nearly worked together in 1982 when the author was approached by Amblin to script *Poltergeist*.

Although Straub has said he still thinks Spielberg would be the best person to make the show, he explained: 'Without ever having had an actual life, the ABC *Talisman* mini-series has the half-life of a relic of Chernobyl. Once every four or five years, someone pops up out of nowhere to say that Steven Spielberg is finally getting around to doing it, or that Spielberg and Kathleen Kennedy have decided to produce it, and then the thing goes back into hibernation. By this point, I don't believe any of these rumours any more. It would be lovely to see it get made, of course.'

More recent productions based on concepts created by Stephen King include Guy Magar's Children of the Corn 7 Resurrection *(see page 126) and Robert Iscove's four-hour mini-series* Firestarter: Rekindled *(see page 39). Meanwhile, amongst those projects currently being developed or in pre-production are a television series of Stephen King's* The Dead Zone *(see page 31),* The Mangler 2 *(see page 95),* The Mist *(see page 140),* The Monkey *(see page 142), and both a theatrical remake and a four-hour mini-series of* Salem's Lot *(see page 18).* ✝

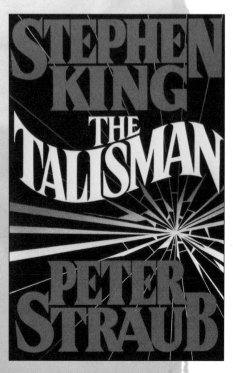

STEPHEN KING:
UNPRODUCED PROJECTS

The following Stephen King projects were announced but never made:

DAYLIGHT DEAD
(aka **NIGHT SHIFT**)

USA, circa 1978. Producers: **Michael Wise** and **Frank Leavy**. Screenplay: **Stephen King**. The Production Company/Twentieth Century-Fox/NBC-TV.

This is an unproduced Stephen King screenplay, based on three stories reprinted in his 1978 *Night Shift* collection, which the author sold in the late 1970s.

'I Know What You Need' (which first appeared in the September 1976 *Cosmopolitan*) involves a strange boy with extrasensory powers. 'Battleground' (originally published in the September 1972 issue of *Cavalier*) features a mob hitman battling for his life against an army of tiny toy soldiers. Originally written in an hour and a half on college napkins, 'Strawberry Spring' (from the fall 1968 issue of *Ubris* and later revised for the November 1975 *Cavalier*) is about a knife-wielding campus killer named 'Springheel Jack' who turns out to be the unreliable narrator.

As King explained to Peter S. Perakos in *Cinefantastique*, the latter story 'is of course violent. NBC Standards and Practices called me and said, "We can't have this lunatic running around stabbing people to death." And I said, "Well, that kind of shoots the story down, doesn't it?" And NBC replied, "Oh, no! Stabbing is out, but he can *strangle* them."'

Despite later attempts by Aaron Spelling and others to turn the concept into a *Night Shift* series which King would write and host, the idea was eventually scrapped in the early 1980s because NBC's Standards and Practices office decided that it would be too intense and gruesome for television.

'My own feeling is that television ate up Rod Serling and spit him out,' King told Paul R. Gagne, 'and I don't want to get into something like that.'

DESPERATION
USA, circa 1999. Director: **Mick Garris**. Screenplay: **Stephen King**. Based on the Novel by **Stephen King**. New Line Cinema.

Based on Stephen King's hefty 1996 novel (a twisted version of his 'Richard Bachman' novel *The Regulators*), in which a group of travellers find themselves trapped in the eponymous small Nevada ghost town by an evil force. A 135-page draft screenplay, written in early 1998, was put into turnaround by New Line Cinema the following year because of concerns over the budget.

'*Desperation* is the most on-again, off-again project I've ever been involved in,' revealed Mick Garris. 'It was originally set up at New Line, but Bob Shaye, who runs the company, decided he didn't want to spend $30 million on a horror movie...especially one not about teenagers and punch lines.'

'Basically, I've said to whoever comes around that I want Mick Garris to direct this for theatrical,' King told Bill Warren in *Fangoria*. 'Mick is worried, and rightly so, about having this sort of dark-half career where his only real job is to interpret me for film...so what I'm saying is that if you want to make a deal on *Desperation*, first you have to do a *Mick Garris* picture...That's the deal — take both, or take neither.'

The story is set in the eponymous Nevada town, where a group of disparate strangers are attacked and imprisoned by an insane, demonic cop who has murdered all the locals and speaks the language of the dead.

'It's a real return to the classic supernatural horror novels that I did earlier on,' King explained. 'It's a pretty hard-hitting script by King,' added Garris, 'very faithful to his book, and with the religious aspects coupled with the visceral nature of the horror, it's not exactly what the studios have been looking for.'

INSOMNIA
USA, circa 1997. Based on the Novel by **Stephen King**. Producer: **Mark Carliner**. Co-executive Producer: **Stephen King**. Mark Carliner Productions

Based on Stephen King's 1994 novel (the first draft was actually written in four months in

#1 NEW YORK TIMES BESTSELLER
STEPHEN KING
DESPERATION
SIGNET

Based on the 1979 novel written under Stephen King's 'Richard Bachman' byline (a name inspired by a Richard Stark book and the rock group Bachman-Turner Overdrive), this was the pseudonymous author's most successful title, remaining in print for six years and developing a cult following of its own.

It was actually King's first novel, completed in 1967 when the author was a twenty year-old college freshman, and involves a near-future 450-mile marathon across an ultra-conservative America where death awaits those whose pace drops below four miles per hour for more than two minutes.

George A. Romero was approached about directing a film version.

THE MACHINES

UK, circa 1981. Producer: **Milton Subotsky**. Screenplay: **Edward** and **Valerie Abraham**. Based on the Stories by **Stephen King**. Sword & Sorcery Productions.

The first of two episodic trilogies developed by British-based producer Milton Subotsky, who bought the rights to the 'machine' stories, 'Lawnmower Man', 'The Mangler' and 'Trucks', from Stephen King's 1978 *Night Shift* collection outright from publisher Doubleday.

This anthology movie, for which he tried to get backing from MGM, would allegedly contain only five minutes of dialogue. After optioning all three stories in the mid-1980s to Dino De Laurentiis, Subotsky eventually sold him only 'Trucks'. 'We finally agreed on a price,' he told Alan Jones in *Cinefantastique*, 'because I desperately needed the money.'

All three stories were subsequently adapted into separate movies.

THE MIST

USA, circa 1979. Screenplay: **Dennis Etchison**. Based on the Story by **Stephen King**.

'A story like 'The Mist' is my homage to the B-pictures of my childhood,' Stephen King told Michael Rowe in *Fangoria*. 'It was my *Godzilla*. I always thought that as a film it would be great in black and white, widescreen.'

King's short novel — originally published in the 1980 anthology *Dark Forces*, edited by the author's then-agent Kirby McCauley and reprinted in the 1985 collection *Skeleton Crew* — was written with a film treatment in mind. 'I thought it was wildly funny,' said King, 'what *The Alamo* would have been like if directed by Bert I. Gordon.'

It is about a strange mist which acts as a gateway for giant monsters from another dimension to lay siege to a small New England town and trap a number of people in the Federal Foods Supermarket.

Californian writer and fellow McCauley

1990) about a widower who sees coloured auras around the people he meets and is apparently the only person to notice the bald-headed doctors who gather at every death.

As the author told Michael Rowe in *Fangoria*: 'Before Mark [Carliner] and I got [*Storm of the Century*] going, we talked about *Insomnia* and he actually had a screenplay done of that which was okay, but it didn't have any real pop to it.'

THE LONG WALK

USA, circa 1988. Director: **George A. Romero**. Based on the Novel by **Richard Bachman**.

client Dennis Etchison was brought in to write a film script in late 1978. After a series of meetings with King and McCauley in Maine, Etchison recalled: 'King saw it as fairly short and modestly budgeted, with most of the terror and suspense arising from what is not shown but only suggested by unearthly sounds and shapes moving just out of sight in the mist. The commercial realities of filmmaking meant that it would have to be shot in colour, but perhaps the image could be desaturated and made slightly grainy, in the style of Roger Corman's low-budget science fiction films of the 1950s, which King and I both remembered fondly.'

Among the actors discussed during these preliminary meetings were Roy Scheider as the hero, Blythe Danner as his wife and Randy Quaid as the best friend. 'Before long we had the film cast in our minds and were discussing favourite directors,' continued Etchison, who also admitted that he found King's original conclusion unsatisfying. As an alternative, he offered an additional scene to show the survivors pulling up to a roadside diner where other frightened travellers have taken refuge, ending with an aerial shot of still more prehistoric bugs swarming out of the sky to settle ominously over the roof. 'This was probably my homage to Hitchcock's The Birds,' explained Etchison, 'or at least to an even bleaker ending contemplated for that film but never shot, in which Rod Taylor and company cross back into San Francisco, only to find the entire Golden Gate Bridge blackened by millions of waiting crows.'

After Etchison wrote three or four drafts of the script, which King eventually approved, McCauley hired an artist to illustrate key sequences. 'The main special effects set-pieces would be the tentacles grabbing the boxboy in the loading bay, the attack of the flying bugs in the market and the passing of the 'walker' in the woods,' revealed Etchison, 'a creature so tall that only one foot and part of a leg appear onscreen.'

However, after the illustrations were submitted to Disney Studios and Carlo Rambaldi for estimates on the cost of the special effects, the film never progressed any further. 'I have always thought that was a shame because it is such a visual story,' said Etchison, 'and King's millions of fans would have loved to see it brought to life on the big screen.'

Etchison's script was eventually adapted for radio in 1984 by Tom Lopez of Boston's ZBS Foundation, and later issued as an eighty minute audio tape production with binaural stereo effects. Etchison's preferred ending was not used.

The rights to The Mist have been owned since the mid-1990s by director Frank Darabont, who at one time wanted Bernie Wrightson to work as a designer on the project. 'My hope is to still make it and my hope is to scare the crap out of people,' Darabont told Gary L. Wood in Cinefantastique.

'Frank Darabont and I have talked a lot about it,' King revealed to Joe Mauceri in Shivers. 'We need to find an ending that works in terms of the story, and that will please people in Hollywood, who are uncomfortable with the way the story ends. It just tails off into the mist. No one is looking for a sugary ending, but they need a sense of closure.'

'Years later,' Etchison revealed, 'when I heard that Frank Darabont was preparing a film version of The Mist, I offered to show him my notes of those meetings for free, no strings attached, so that he would at least know how King had imagined the film as well as our solutions to what we thought were story problems, but he wasn't interested. I'm sure he has his

Opposite top: Robert Englund in The Mangler *(1994), originally part of Milton Subotsky's* The Machines.
Below: *Robert Hays in 'The Ledge' episode from* Cat's Eye *(1984), originally part of Subotsky's* Night Shift.

own approach and I hope that it is even more effective than ours would have been.'

'Stephen King's *The Mist* is a project currently on my back-burner,' Darabont explained. 'I intend to move it off the back-burner and write the screenplay adaptation sometime in 2002. The same goes for King's story 'The Monkey', which I will most likely produce for a cable venue.'

NIGHT SHIFT

UK, circa 1981. Producer: **Milton Subotsky**. Screenplay: **Edward** and **Valerie Abraham**. Based on the Stories by **Stephen King**. Sword & Sorcery Productions.

Producer Milton Subotsky had the Abrahams script this second anthology movie based on the Stephen King 'revenge' stories 'Quitters, Inc.', 'The Ledge' and 'Sometimes They Come Back' from the 1978 *Night Shift* collection. He later sold the rights to Dino De Laurentiis, who subsequently adapted the three stories into two movies.

NIGHTSHIFT

USA, circa 1981. Screenplay: **Lee Reynolds** and **George P. Erengis**. Based on the Stories by **Stephen King**. Martin Poll Productions/The Production Company.

In 1981, Martin Poll Productions and The Production Company attempted to develop some of Stephen King's *Night Shift* stories for theatrical release. Lee Reynolds and George P. Erengis were reportedly among those who reworked King's original NBC-TV scripts for *Daylight Dead* and would have shared the writing credit.

Erengis' script for 'Strawberry Spring' apparently added a lame comedy reporter, black magic and an unnecessary reference to the town of Jerusalem's Lot. In *Fear Itself*, Bill Warren describes the screenplay as 'reprehensible' and went on to say that 'we can all feel relieved that it wasn't filmed.'

ROSE MADDER

USA, circa 1998. Based on the Novel by **Stephen King**. Home Box Office.

Based on Stephen King's 1995 novel about a battered wife who builds a new life for herself with the aid of a mysterious painting, this was reportedly in development for cable TV network HBO.

THE SHOTGUNNERS

USA, circa 1985. Director: **Sam Peckinpah**. Screenplay: **Stephen King**.

Stephen King's 1996 'Richard Bachman' novel *The Regulators*, itself a twisted companion piece to King's *Desperation*, actually began life as an original spec screenplay which the author had 'written in about a week' in the early 1980s.

King showed it to Sam Peckinpah during a meeting with the legendary director, who was still recovering from a heart attack, at the UN Plaza in 1985. 'Sam read it, liked it a lot and suggested some things for the script that were really interesting,' King told Joe Mauceri. Unfortunately, Peckinpah died of a heart attack before a second draft could be completed, and some ideas from the discarded script found their way into the novel.

King's script synopsis involved a suburban Western community, cut off from the rest of the world, which was being menaced by gunfire from a fleet of long, ghostly black Cadillacs. 'Nobody in Hollywood wanted to have anything to do with it,' the author explained to W.C. Stroby in *Fangoria*. 'because it didn't make rational sense at the end...What I wanted to talk about in the screenplay were the things that come out of nowhere and drive you nuts, and there's no real answer to them.'

'I would still like to see *The Shotgunners* made,' King revealed in *Fangoria*. 'That would be a classy movie.'

THE STEPHEN KING PLAYHOUSE

USA, circa 1990. Based on the Stories by **Stephen King**. Producer: **Richard P. Rubinstein**. Laurel Entertainment/CBS-TV.

Laurel producer Richard P. Rubinstein received an offer from CBS-TV to produce sixteen episodes of this proposed television series, sight unseen. Stephen King would chose the stories, script them if he wanted to and introduce each episode. He turned down the idea because 'That's more time than I'm willing to take right now.'

TRAINING EXERCISE

USA, circa 1987. Screenplay: **Stephen King**.

Apparently this was an early script about Marines.

Following his directorial début with *Maximum Overdrive* (1986), this was supposed to have been Stephen King's next film with Dino De Laurentiis. However, it was cancelled when De Laurentiis' North Carolina Film Corporation Film Studios in Wilmington shut down.

'Everything went bankrupt in North Carolina,' King told *Cinefantastique*, 'Dino walked away.' ✝

Stephen King contributed in some capacity to the following productions:

KNIGHTRIDERS

USA, 1981. Writer and Director: **George A. Romero**. Producer: **Richard P. Rubinstein**. Executive Producer: **Salah M. Hassanein**. Director of Photography: **Michael Gornick**. Associate Producer: **David E. Vogel**. Music: **Donald Rubinstein**. Stunt Coordinator: **Gary Davis**. Production Manager: **Zilla Clinton**. Editors: **George A. Romero** and **Pasquale Buba**. Production Designer: **Cletus Anderson**. United Film Distribution Co/United Artists Corporation/Laurel. Colour. 145 minutes. 141 minutes [in the UK].
With: **Ed Harris** (Billy), **Gary Lahti** (Alan), **Tom Savini** (Morgan), **Amy Ingersoll** (Linet), **Patricia Tallman** (Julie), **Christine Forrest** (Angie), **Warner Shook** (Pippin), **Brother Blue** (Merlin).

Made by many of the same team who worked on *Creepshow* (1982), George Romero's $4 million reworking of the Arthurian legend has the proud knights swapping their steeds for motorbikes in modern-day America. As a vagabond group, the Knightriders tour the country, entertaining the public with medieval jousting tournaments. But as their fame grows, they are forced to uphold the principles laid down by King Arthur himself so many centuries before. This includes Romero regulars John Amplas, Ken Foree, John Harrison and Bingo O'Malley, while Stephen King turns up in a couple of brief cameo appearances (along with his wife Tabitha) as a country redneck eating a hoagie.

The film had distribution problems in America and was initially pulled from release by UFD after grosses proved disappointing. Shortened by thirty minutes and with a new advertising campaign, it flopped again at the boxoffice. It was finally released directly to video in the United Kingdom in 1987.

Romero admitted to Tony Crawley of *Starburst* that he was shellshocked from the experience: 'Not about the film. It has more to do with the politics and the sales. That's the shit that gets to me.'

THE SIMPSONS: INSANE CLOWN POPPY

USA/South Korea, 2000. Director: **Bob Anderson**. Writers: **John Frink** and **Don Payne**. Producers: **Richard Sakai** and **Denise Sirkot**. Twentieth Century Fox Film Corporation/Gracie Films/Fox Network. Colour. 22 minutes.
Voices: **Dan Castellaneta** (Homer J. Simpson/Krusty the Clown), **Julie Kavner** (Marge Simpson), **Nancy Cartwright** (Bart Simpson), **Yeardley Smith** (Lisa Simpson), **Hank Azaria** (Apu/Moe/Dr Nick Riviera/Professor Frink), **Harry Shearer** (Ned Flanders/Reverend Tim Lovejoy), **Drew Barrymore** (Sophie), **Stephen King** (Himself), **Joe Mantegna** (Fat Tony), **Jay Mohr** (Christopher Walken), **Amy Tan**, **John Updike** (Himself), **Pamela Hayden** (Milhouse), **Tress MacNeille**, **Karl Wiedergott**.

Popular half-hour cartoon TV series (1990-), created by Matt Groening, about the titular yellow-skinned family.

In this episode from season twelve, first broadcast on 12 November 2000, Lisa decides to celebrate her birthday by attending Springfield's Festival of Books, where Marge meets Stephen King and hears about his latest volume. Meanwhile, Krusty the Clown is finally reunited with his long-lost daughter, Sophie. After getting some tips on fatherhood from Homer, he loses her violin in a poker game with mob boss Fat Tony. Theme by Danny Elfman.

FRASIER: MARY CHRISTMAS

USA, 2000. Director: **Pamela Fryman**. Teleplay: **Eric Zicklin**. Producer: **Maggie Blanc**. Co-Producer: **Bob Daily**. Producers: **Gayle Abrams** and **Eric Zicklin**. Supervising Producer: **Lori Kirkland**. Co-Executive Producers: **Rob Hanning**, **Sam Johnson**, **Chris Marcil** and **Jon Sherman**. Executive Producers: **Mark Reisman** and **Dan O'Shannon**. Colour. Paramount Pictures/Grub Street Productions/NBC-TV. 22 minutes.
With: **Kelsey Grammer** (Dr Frasier Crane), **Jane Leeves** (Daphne Moon), **David Hyde Pierce** (Dr Niles Crane), **Peri Gilpin** (Rozalind 'Roz' Doyle), **John Mahoney** (Martin Crane), **Kim Coles** (Dr Mary), **Bess Armstrong** (Kelly Kirkland), **Peter Haskell** (Bob Vernon), **Donovan Scott** (Santa), **Karl T. Wright** (Producer), **Pam Levin**

(Woman at Parade), **Stephen King** (Voice of Brian), **Wolfgang Puck** (Voice of Tom).

Popular half-hour sitcom, a spin-off from NBC's *Cheers* (1982-93) created by executive producers David Angell, Peter Casey and David Lee, about pompous Boston psychiatrist Frasier Crane (executive producer Grammer), who becomes a Seattle radio talk show host.

In this eighth season episode, first telecast on 12 December 2000, a scheming Frasier finally works his way into hosting Seattle's annual televised Christmas parade. However, he is horrified to discover that his highly successful protégé and radio rival, Dr Mary, will be his substitute co-host. Stephen King guested as the voice of 'Brian'.

MONKEYBONE

USA, 2001. Director: **Henry Selick**. Writer: **Sam Hamm**. Based on the Graphic Novel 'Dark Town' Created by **Kaja Blackley**. Producers: **Michael Barnathan** and **Mark Radcliffe**. Executive Producers: **Lata Ryan**, **Henry Selick**, **Sam Hamm** and **Chris Columbus**. Director of Photography: **Andrew Dunn**, BSC. Production Designer: **Bill Boes**. Editors: **Mark Warner**, **Jon Poll** and **Nicholas C. Smith**, ACE. Music Supervisor: **Dawn Solér**. Music: **Anne Dudley**. Costume Designer: **Beatrix Aruna Pasztor**. Twentieth Century Fox/1492. Colour. 92 minutes.
With: **Brendan Fraser** (Stu Miley), **Bridget Fonda** (Dr Julie McElroy), **Chris Kattan** (Organ Donor Stu),

Below: Brendan Fraser with the eponymous animated star of Monkeybone.

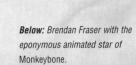

Giancarlo Esposito (Hypnos), **Rose McGowan** (Kitty), **Whoopi Goldberg** (Death), **Dave Foley** (Herb), **Megan Mullally** (Kimmy), **Lisa Zane** (Medusa), **John Turturro** (Voice of Monkeybone).

Troubled comedy feature based on Kaja Blackley's comic book *Dark Town* (the film's working title), published by Canada's Mad Monkey Press. This combination of live action and stop-motion animation from director Henry Selick (*The Nightmare Before Christmas* [1993], etc) had its planned November 2000 release postponed until February 2001 for further post-production tinkering after a number of test screenings.

Brendan Fraser starred (after Nicolas Cage and Ben Stiller turned the role down) as underground comic book artist Stu Miley, who is involved in a car crash and falls into a coma. He finds himself in Dark Town, a bizarre, hallucinatory netherworld where strange creatures thrive by watching human nightmares on television. When his manic monkey character Monkeybone leaves his mind and returns to the real world in Stu's body, the cartoonist follows in the dead body of an organ donor (Chris Kattan in special make-up effects created by Greg Cannom) to prevent his evil creation from spreading 'nightmare juice' through farting Monkeybone dolls.

While still trapped in Dark Town, Stu is thrown into a dungeon where he meets such other nightmare-makers as Edgar Allan Poe, Jack the Ripper and Stephen King (portrayed by an actor), who have also had their bodies stolen by figments of their imagination. 'King planned to play himself,' revealed director Henry Selick, 'but then he had that near-fatal accident.'

Characters, ideas and concepts either based on or inspired by Stephen King's work have also turned up in the following movies and television shows, and as such these titles are of associational interest to any King filmography:

THE SPELL

USA, 1977. Director: **Lee Philips**. Producer: **David Manson**. Teleplay: **Brian Taggert**. Charles Fries Production. Colour. 86 minutes.
With: **Lee Grant** (Marion Matchett), **James Olson** (Glenn Matchett), **Susan Myers** (Rita Matchett), **Helen Hunt** (Kristina Matchett), **Barbara Bostock** (Jill), **Leila Goldini** (Jo Standish), **Jack Colvin** (Dale Boyce), **Richard Carlyle** (Hugh), **James Green** (Stan Restin), **Kathleen Hughes** (Fenetia), **Wright King** (Rian Bellamy), **Doney Oatman** (Jackie Segal), **Arthur Peterson** (Ross), **Robert Gibbons** (Waiter).

Made the year after *Carrie*, this blatant TV movie rip-off featured Susan Myers as Rita

Matchett, an overweight fifteen year-old who uses her telekinetic powers to avenge herself on those fellow students who constantly tease her. A woman neighbour is incinerated from within, and Rita uses her mental abilities to attack her mother (who also possesses powers) with flying kitchen knives!

Former actor-turned-director Lee Philips was apparently more interested in showing how paranormal forces can fracture the average American family than he was in trying to scare his viewers.

JENNIFER
(aka **JENNIFER [THE SNAKE GODDESS]**)
USA, 1978. Director: **Brice Mack**. Producer: **Steve Krantz**. Screenplay: **Kay Cousins**. Based on a Story by **Steve Krantz**. American International Pictures. Colour. 90 minutes. With: **Lisa Pelikan** (Jennifer Baylor), **Bert Convy** (Jeff Reed), **Nina Foch** (Mrs Calley), **Amy Johnston** (Sandra Tremayne), **John Gavin** (Senator Tremayne), **Jeff Corey** (Luke Baylor), **Louise Haven** (Jane Delano), **Ray Underwood** (Dayton Powell), **Wesley Eure** (Pit Lassiter), **Florida Friebus** (Miss Tooker), **Georganne La Piere** (DeeDee Martin).

A surprisingly good cast featured in this low budget rip-off of *Carrie* (1976), in which the eponymous school outcast unleashed her hillbilly power to control snakes (hence the TV retitling) by conjuring up a large serpent to avenge herself on the taunting students of the exclusive Green View School for Girls.

DEADLINE
(USA: aka **ANATOMY OF A HORROR**)
Canada, 1981. Director: **Mario Azzopardi**. Producer: **Henry Less**. Screenplay: **Mario Azzopardi** and **Richard Oleksiak**. Story: **Mario Azzopardi**. Horror Picture Films/ACFC. Colour. 85 minutes. With: **Stephen Young** (Steven Lessey), **Sharon Masters** (Elizabeth Lessey), **Marvin Goldhar** (Burt Horowitz), **Jeannie Elias** (Darlene Winters), **Cindy Hinds** (Sharon Lessey), **Phillip Leonard** (Philip Lessey), **Tod Woodcroft** (David Lessey), **Bev Marsh** (Martha Lessey), **Carole Pope**, **Kevan Staples** and **Rough Trade** (Punk Rock Band Members), **Mary Risk** (Professor), **Ken Camroux** (Moderator), **Philip Akin** (Student #1), **Bill Yak** (Student #2).

In this neglected psychological horror film, Stephen Young portrayed horror novelist and screenwriter Steven Lessey (based on you-know-who), who is driven insane by his success

and family problems

His life begins to spin out of control when the pressure to come up with new ideas becomes too much and his two sons hang his daughter after watching one of his movies. He eventually writes this film and then kills himself!

Co-writer/director Mario Azzopardi visualised a number of extracts of Lessey's work, including a mutant baby, a mad Nazi scientist using the sound of a punk band (Carole Pope and Rough Trade) to make people explode and, best of all, vampire nuns. This was released directly to video in the United Kingdom.

Enter a startling world beyond the limits of your wildest imagination.

DREAMSCAPE

BRUCE COHN CURTIS presents
DENNIS QUAID MAX VON SYDOW CHRISTOPHER PLUMMER
EDDIE ALBERT and KATE CAPSHAW in DREAMSCAPE
Music by MAURICE JARRE Director of Photography BRIAN TUFANO Edited by RICHARD HALSEY
Executive Producers STANLEY R. ZUPNIK and TOM CURTIS Co-Produced by JERRY TOKOFSKY
Screenplay by DAVID LOUGHERY, CHUCK RUSSELL, JOSEPH RUBEN Story by DAVID LOUGHERY
Produced by BRUCE COHN CURTIS Directed by JOSEPH RUBEN

DREAMSCAPE

USA, 1983. Director: **Joseph Ruben**. Producer: **Bruce Cohn Curtis**. Screenplay: **David Loughery**, **Chuck Russell** and **Joseph Ruben**. Story: **David Loughery**. Music: **Maurice Jarre**. Co-Producer: **Jerry Tokofsky**. Executive Producers: **Stanley R. Zupnik** and **Tom Curtis**. Special Makeup: **Craig Reardon**. Visual Effects: **Peter Kuran**. Editor: **Richard Halsey**, ACE. Director of Photography: **Brian Tufano**. Bella Productions/Zupnik-Curtis Enterprises. Colour. 99 minutes.
With: **Dennis Quaid** (Alex Gardner), **Max von Sydow** (Paul Novotny), **Christopher Plummer** (Bob Blair), **Eddie Albert** (The President), **Kate Capshaw** (Jane DeVries), **David Patrick Kelly** (Tommy Ray Glatman), **George Wendt** (Charlie Prince), **Larry Gelman** (Mr Webber), **Cory 'Bumper' Yothers** (Buddy), **Redmond Gleeson** (Snead), **Peter Jason** (Babcock), **Chris Mulkey** (Finch).

Inventive $8 million fantasy/adventure, co-scripted by associate producer Chuck Russell and directed with style by Joseph Ruben, that surprisingly failed at the boxoffice when released in 1984.

When scientist Dr Paul Novotny invents a machine that can project someone's consciousness into other people's dreams, creepy spy boss Bob Blair decides to use it for his own ends. Likeable psychic Alex Gardner has to enter the nuclear nightmares of the President of the United States, which include some post-Apocalyptic zombies, to stop hired assassin Tommy Ray Glatman, who is also in the dreamscape and has the power to transform into a murderous Snakeman (Larry Cedar). This featured great make-up effects created by Craig Reardon, Greg Cannom and others, stop-motion effects by James R. Aupperle and visual effects by Peter Kuran's VCE, Inc. With George Wendt (NBC's *Cheers* [1982-93], etc) as horror writer 'Charlie Prince' (get it?).

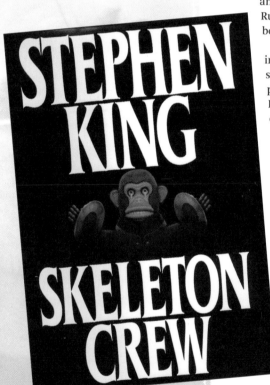

THE DEVIL'S GIFT

USA, 1984. Director: **Kenneth J. Berton**. Screenplay: **Kenneth J. Berton**, **José Vergelin** and **Hayden O'Hara**. Based on a Story by **Kenneth J. Berton** and **José Vergelin**. Producers: **Kenneth J. Berton** and **José Vergelin**. Directors of Photography: **K. Daniels** and **C. Palm**. Music: **Todd Hayden**. Zenith International/ Windridge/AEI/Live Home Video/Vestron Video. Colour. 112 minutes.
With: **Bob Mendelsohn** (Michael Andrews), **Vicki Saputo** (Susan), **Struan Robertson** (Michael Andrews), **Bruce Parry** (Pete), **Madelon Phillips** (Adrianne), **J. Renee Gilbert** (Gramma), **Ángeles Olazábal** (Girl on Bike).

Apparently an uncredited adaptation of Stephen King's story 'The Monkey' (from the November 1980 issue of *Gallery* and the author's 1985 collection *Skeleton Crew*), this low budget release is about an evil demon that inhabits a young boy's monkey doll and takes over the mind of his suburban mother.

'I saw a guy selling wind-up monkeys on the street,' King recalled in *Skeleton Crew*. 'They looked really scary to me, and I spent the rest of my walk back to the hotel wondering why.'

Frank Darabont is currently planning an official adaptation of King's story, probably for cable TV.

HOUSE

USA, 1985. Director: **Steve Miner**. Producer: **Sean S. Cunningham**. Screenplay: **Ethan Wiley**. Story: **Fred Dekker**. Editor: **Michael N. Knue**. Director of Photography: **Mac Ahlberg**. Production Designer: **Gregg Fonseca**. Associate Producer: **Patrick Markey**. Casting: **Melissa Skoff**. Music: **Harry Manfredini**. Sean S. Cunningham/New World Pictures. Colour. 93 minutes.
With: **William Katt** (Roger Cobb), **George Wendt** (Harold Gorton), **Richard Moll** (Big Ben), **Kay Lenz** (Sandy), **Mary Stavin** (Tanya), **Michael Ensign** (Chet Parker), **Susan French** (Aunt Elizabeth).

First and best in an unrelated series of four *House* movies.

When Stephen King-like horror author Roger Cobb moves into his aunt's old mansion after she hangs herself, he is soon seeing her ghost and other strange creatures that populate a bedroom closet. He finally discovers a doorway to Hell through the bathroom cabinet and rescues his missing son Jimmy (Erik and Mark Silver) from the rotting zombie corpse of Big Ben (the excellent Moll), a Vietnam war buddy he left behind to die.

This starts off as an effective haunted house chiller, but the film-makers got cold feet halfway through, adding a couple of pointless songs, some unnecessary comedy relief and not a lot of plot sense.

Despite this, Katt and Wendt (as a nosey neighbour) are likeable, and the various monsters are quite effective. With Felix Silla as one of the Little Critters and a clip from S.F. Brownrigg's *Don't Look in the Basement* (1973) on TV.

PERRY MASON: THE CASE OF THE SINISTER SPIRIT

USA, 1987. Director: **Richard Lang**. Teleplay: **Anne Collins**. Story: **Dean Hargrove** & **Joel Steiger** and **Glenn Benest** & **Timothy Wurtz**. Based on Characters Created by **Erle Stanley Gardner**. Producer: **Barry Steinberg**. Supervising Producer: **Joel Steiger**. Editor: **David Solomon**. Art Director: **Paul Staheli**. Director of Photography: **Arch Bryant**. Music: **Dick DeBenedictis**.

Original Perry Mason Theme by **Fred Steiner**. Viacom Productions/Strathmore/The Fred Silverman Company/NBC-TV. Colour. 97 minutes.
With: **Raymond Burr** (Perry Mason), **Barbara Hale** (Della Street), **William Katt** (Paul Drake Jr), **Robert Stack** (Jordan White), **Dwight Schultz** (Andrew Lloyd), **Kim Delaney** (Susan Warrenfield), **Dennis Lipscomb** (Michael Light), **Jack Bannon** (Donald Sayer), **Leigh Taylor-Young** (Maura McGuire), **Matthew Faison** (David Hall), **David Ogden Stiers** (Michael Reston), **Percy Rodrigues**, **Ed O'Brien**, **Burt Douglas**, **Richard Jury**, **Michael K. Osborn**, **Kathryn Christopher**.

The fifth in a series of two-hour made-for-TV movies (1986-93) which revived the old *Perry Mason* CBS-TV show (1957-66), based on the character created by novelist Erle Stanley Gardner in 1933.

First broadcast on **24 May 1987**, this time the eponymous attorney finds himself defending his old friend, publisher Jordan White, who is accused of murdering best-selling horror author David Hall in an Overlook-type hotel in Colorado. Mason has a premonition about a falling chandelier and there is a supposed haunting when a painting apparently comes to life. However, despite the supernatural trappings, everything is revealed as a clever case involving a secret room and swapped identities.

Series regulars Burr, Hale and her real-life son Katt (*House* [1985], etc) are obviously having fun with the spooky material, and Stephen King even gets a name-check.

QUANTUM LEAP: THE BOOGIEMAN

USA, 1990. Director: **Joe Napolitano**. Writer: **Chris Ruppenthal**. Producer: **Chris Ruppenthal**. Co-Producers: **Paul Brown** and **Jeff Gourson**. Supervising Producers: **Harker Wade** and **Robert Wolterstorff**. Co-Executive Producers: **Michael Zinberg** and **Deborah Pratt**. Theme: **Mike Post**. Music: **Velton Ray Bunch**. Universal City Studios/Belisarius Productions/NBC-TV. Colour. 45 minutes.
With: **Scott Bakula** (Dr Sam Beckett), **Dean Stockwell** (Al Calavicci), **Valerie Mahaffey** (Mary [Greeley]), **Paul Linke** (Sheriff [Ben Masters]), **Fran Ryan** (Dorothy [Yeager]), **David Kriegel** (Stevie [King]), **Donald Hotton** (Tully [Maltin]), **Jan Stratton*** (Nurse), **Chris Ruppenthal*** (Joshua Rey). [* Uncredited in the final print.]

Popular hour-long TV series (1989-93), created by executive producer Donald P. Bellisario, about research scientist Dr Sam Beckett who, during an experiment in time travel in 1999, finds himself forced to leap into the bodies of different people to solve their problems. Sam is aided by Al, a hologram only he can see, and the computer Ziggy.

In this genuinely creepy episode, originally

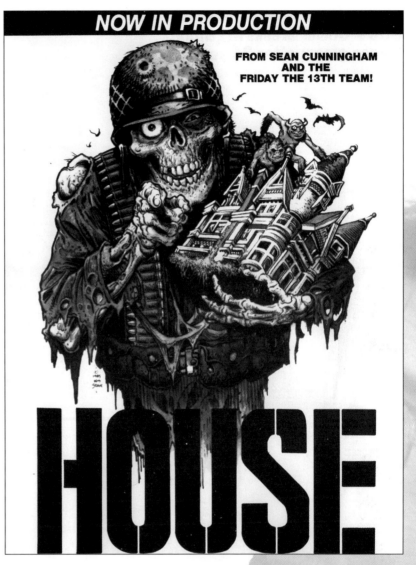

broadcast on 26 October 1990, Sam leaps back to 31 October 1964 and into the body of famous Maine horror novelist Joshua Rey ('a second-rate H.P. Lovecraft'). However, as those around him begin to die in various mysterious ways, Sam suspects that the supernatural may be involved.

Despite an enigmatic 'it-was-all-a-dream' ending, Sam gets to confront the Devil himself (also played by Stockwell) and gives a teenage Stevie King a few good ideas for such future books as *Christine*, *Cujo* and *Carrie*.

THE SIMPSONS: THE SIMPSONS HALLOWEEN SPECIAL V

USA/South Korea, 1994. Director: **Jaundiced Jim Reardon**. Writers: **Count Greg Danula**, **Dearly Departed Dan McGrath**, **David Cohen's Severed Hand** and **Blob Kushell**. Producer: **Redrum Richard Sakai**. Twentieth Century Fox Film Corporation/Gracie Films/Fox Network. Colour. 22 minutes.
Voices: **Ro-Dan Castellaneta [Dan Castellaneta]**

FACT FILE

The 1999 *Simpsons* episode 'Maximum Homerdrive' has nothing to do with Stephen King except for the titular pun.

(Homer J. Simpson/Grampa Simpson/Groundskeeper Willie/Kodos), **Jooooolie [Julie] Kavner** (Marge Simpson), **Nancy Heart-Fright [Nancy Cartwright]** (Bart Simpson), **Grave-Yeardley [Yeardley] Smith** (Lisa Simpson), **The Shaws-Hank Azaria [Hank Azaria]** (Moe/Chief Wiggum), **Harry (O.J.) Shearer** (C. Montgomery Burns/Smithers/Ned Flanders/Principal Skinner/Kang), **James Earl Boggins Jones**, **Macabre Marcia Wallace** (Edna Krabappel), **Demonic Doris Grau** (Lunchlady Doris), **Pamela Poltergeist Hayden** (Milhouse), **Rancid Russi Taylor** (Uter).

Halloween episode of the popular half-hour cartoon TV series (1990-), created by Morbid Matt Groening, about the eponymous dysfunctional family.

After an opening in the style of *The Outer Limits*, the Simpsons become the caretakers of an old lodge (complete with an elevator full of blood and a hedge maze) where Bart learns he has the power of 'The Shinning' ('You want to get sued?') and Homer goes crazy when he discovers that there is no cable TV or beer.

Then, a reworking of a classic Ray Bradbury story, 'Time and Punishment' has Homer sucked into a vortex and transported back in time to a prehistoric jungle while fixing a toaster. After killing a mosquito, he returns to the present to find that Ned Flanders is the Unquestioned Lord and Master of the World. Finally, in 'Nightmare Cafeteria', Bart and Lisa discover that the cannibalistic staff of Springfield School are eating the students.

Theme by Danny Skellingelfman.

SUPERSTAR

Canada/USA, 1999. Director: **Bruce McCulloch**. Writer: **Steven Wayne Koren**. Based on a Character Created by **Molly Shannon**. Producer: **Lorne Michaels**. Executive Producers: **Robert K. Weiss** and **Susan Cavan**. Director of Photography: **Walt Lloyd**. Production Designer: **Gregory Keen**. Editor: **Malcolm Campbell**. Co-Producers: **Erin Fraser** and **Steven Wayne Koren**. Costume Designer: **Eydi Caines-Floyd**. Music Supervisor: **Elliot Lurie**. Music: **Michael Gore**. Casting: **Phyllis Huffman**. Superstar Productions/NBC Studios/Paramount Pictures/SNL Studios. Colour. 78 minutes.

With: **Molly Shannon** (Mary Katherine Gallagher), **Will Ferrell** (Sky Corrigan/Jesus), **Elaine Hendrix**

(Evian), **Harland Williams** (Slater), **Mark McKinney** (Father Ritley), **Glynis Johns** (Grandma), **Jason Blicker** (Howard), **Gerry Bamman** (Father John), **Emmy Laybourne** (Helen), **Jennifer Irwin** (Maria), **Rob Stefaniuk** (Thomas).

Molly Shannon recreates her accident-prone character from the NBC-TV series *Saturday Night Live* (1975-) in this high school comedy.

Movie-obsessed teenager Mary Katherine Gallagher just wants a Hollywood-type kiss from fellow student Sky Corrigan. When *Catholic Teen Magazine* sponsors a talent contest at her school, Mary Katherine decides to become a superstar.

This includes Mary suffering a *Carrie*-style revenge during the talent show audition, plus a clip from Brian De Palma's 1976 movie on TV. Drew Barrymore's future husband, comedian Tom Green, also turns up.

It was released directly to video in the United Kingdom in 2000.

NASSE SCHLÜPPER

Germany/USA, circa 2000. Erotic-Entertainment/XXL-Video. Colour. 86 minutes.

With: **Mandy Mystery** (Girl on Rooftop*), **Chris Charming** (Janitor*), **Rick Masters** (Father*), **Little Romeo** (Boy*), **Kate Frost** (1st Little Girl*), **Dyna-Mite** (2nd Little Girl*), **Trevor** (Teacher*), **Cloey Adams** (Pupil*), **Fawna** (Girl in Truck*), **Giuseppe** (Man in Truck*). [* Uncredited in the final print.]

Hardcore anthology movie filmed in Los Angeles and starring blonde German porno actress Mandy Mystery.

The second of four unconnected episodes is apparently an uncredited version of Stephen King's *The Shining*, in which dwarf actor Little Romeo (in the Danny Torrance role) talks to his finger and rides down a corridor on a tricycle, where he has a scary vision of two schoolgirl ghosts (Frost and Dyna-Mite). When he tells his caretaker father (bondage regular Masters), the latter is soon prowling the building, axe in hand... †

Right: This is all we can show you from Nasse Schlüpper.

STEPHEN KING:
CAMEOS

Stephen King, who describes himself as a 'frustrated actor', has made Alfred Hitchcock-style cameos in the following movies and television mini-series:

1981	*Knightriders* (as Hoagie Man)
1982	*Creepshow* (as Jordy Verrill)
1986	*Maximum Overdrive* (as Man at Cashpoint*)
1987	*Creepshow 2* (as Truck Driver)
1989	*Pet Sematary* (as Minister)
1991	*Golden Years* (as Bus Driver)
1992	*Sleepwalkers* (as Cemetery Caretaker)
1994	*Stephen King's The Stand* (as Teddy Weizak)
1995	*The Langoliers* (as Tom Holby)
1996	*Thinner* (as Pharmacist)
1997	*Stephen King's The Shining* (as Gage Creed)
1999	*Stephen King's Storm of the Century* (as Lawyer on TV*)
2000	*The Simpsons*: 'Insane Clown Poppy' (as Himself)
2000	*Frasier*: 'Mary Christmas' (as Voice of Brian)
2002	*Stephen King's Rose Red* (as Pizza Delivery Man)

[* Uncredited in the final print.]

Below: Richard Hagstrom (Bruce Davison) discovers a word processor that can change his life in Tales from the Darkside: 'The Word Processor of the Gods'.

Along with the following adaptations and countless interviews about his work, some of Stephen King's other notable television appearances have included commercials for American Express, Comedy Central and Barnes & Noble, being a celebrity contestant on the ABC-TV quiz show Jeopardy!, *appearing on Laurens C. Postma's* Channel 4 *documentary* David Cronenberg Long Live the New Flesh *(1986) and as a contributor on* Baseball *(1994), a major television documentary mini-series about the history of the author's favourite sport, as well as profiles on the A&E Network's* Biography *(1999),* Omnibus: Stephen King Shining in the Dark *(1999) for BBC/ The Learning Channel and the MSNBC-TV series* Headliners and Legends *(2001).*

TALES FROM THE DARKSIDE: THE WORD PROCESSOR OF THE GODS

USA, 1984. Director: **Michael Gornick**. Teleplay: **Michael McDowell**. Based on a Story by **Stephen King**. Producer: **William Teitler**. Laurel-TV/JayGee Productions. Colour. 22 minutes.
With: **Bruce Davison** (Richard Hagstrom), **Karen Shallo** (Lina Hagstrom), **Patrick Piccininni** (Seth Hagstrom), **William Cain** (Mr Nordhoff), **Jon Mathews** (Jonathan), **Miranda Beeson** (Belinda), **Paul Sparer** (Narrator).

Episode of the half-hour, shot-on-video syndicated anthology series (1983-88), executive produced by Richard P. Rubinstein, George A. Romero and Jerry Golod. First broadcast in November 1984, it is based on Stephen King's story 'The Word Processor' from the January 1983 issue of *Playboy*, which was reprinted under the new title in the 1990 collection *Skeleton Crew*.

Henpecked husband Richard Hagstrom inherits a word processor constructed by his late nephew, Jonathan, which makes anything typed on it come true when the 'execute' and 'delete' keys are pressed. He decides to use

it to transform his life by 'deleting' his obnoxious wife and son and replacing them with his dead sister-in-law and nephew.

King himself began using a Wang computer as his principal writing tool in 1982 and this tale (inspired by W.W. Jacobs' classic 1902 story 'The Monkey's Paw'), for which he was initially paid $2,000, was one of the first pieces of fiction he composed on the machine while suffering from a nasty cold that kept him awake.

'Not the best story I ever wrote,' King confessed in his Introduction to *Skeleton Crew*, 'not one that's ever going to win any prizes. But it's not too bad, either. Sort of fun.'

This episode was available on video as part of Worldvision's first *Tales from the Darkside* compilation.

THE TWILIGHT ZONE: GRAMMA

USA, 1986. Directors: **Bradford May** and **Harlan Ellison***. Teleplay: **Harlan Ellison**. Based on the Short Story by **Stephen King**. Executive Producer: **Philip DeGuere**. CBS Inc/CBS Entertainment Productions/ Persistence of Vision/MGM-UA/CBS-TV. Colour. 21 minutes.
With: **Barret Oliver** (George), **Darlanne Fluegel** (Mother), **Frederick Long** (Gramma), **Piper Laurie*** and **Harlan Ellison*** (Voice of Gramma), **Charles Aidman*** (Narrator). [* Uncredited in the final print.]

This episode of the half-hour revival (1985-89) of the classic 1960s anthology show created by Rod Serling was first broadcast on CBS-TV on 14 February 1986. Based on Stephen King's story in the spring 1984 issue of *Weirdbook* no 19 and reprinted in his collection *Skeleton Crew*, it was inspired by the time, in 1961, when the young King discovered that his invalid grandmother had died in her sleep in the family house in Durham, North Carolina.

Left alone in the house by his mother, eleven year-old Georgie is reluctant to enter the room of his dying 'gramma', a hideous old witch who owns a copy of the legendary *Necronomicon* and is plotting to possess her grandson's soul.

'When I came on board *The Twilight Zone*, at the outset of the pre-production process,' recalled scriptwriter Harlan Ellison, 'one of the

spring 1986   STEPHEN KING ** RICHARD L. TIERNEY ** GERALD W. PAGE
ARDATH MAYHAR ** DARRELL SCHWEITZER ** J. N. WILLIAMSON
STEVE RASNIC TEM ** JESSICA AMANDA SALMONSON ** JANET FOX $5

WEIRDBOOK 19

first problems set before me as creative consultant was the purchase by CBS of a couple of stories that seemingly were unadaptable. The network had paid a stiff price for them, but no one had been able to 'break' them in terms of finding a way to convert them to the visual medium. One of those stories was Stephen King's 'Gramma'.

'Phil DeGuere and producer Jim Crocker had me read the stories, and asked me to bring my evaluation of how to proceed with them to a story conference soon thereafter.

'When I read the story, it was clear to me why no one had been able to beat the problem: 'Gramma' was an internal monologue by an eleven year-old child, in which virtually nothing happened. At least, nothing that could produce a visual sequence.

'So when we all gathered for the daily story-conference, and 'Gramma' reared its head yet again, I launched into a long and detailed exposition of how many ways the story was static and what a chowderhead was the guy who'd bought it in the first place. And, not knowing when to leave well enough alone, I went on and on about what ways were feasible to adapt the yarn...if they could find a writer clever enough to do the job.

'And when I finished ranting, I realised that all four of them were staring at me the way a buzzard leers at a lame rabbit.

'So I was the one who got the assignment.'

'Harlan did what I consider to be one of his most brilliant scripts,' executive story consultant Alan Brennert told Ben Herndon in *Cinefantastique*. 'And it is terrifying. Even though I had read King's original story, as I read Harlan's script I kept right on the edge of my seat wondering what was gonna happen next. There are some moments in there which will just scare the shit outta people...'

Originally set to be helmed by William Friedkin (who pulled out due to family commitments), credited director Bradford May was also the cinematographer for many first season episodes, including this one.

'It fell to me to design the 'sound portrait' that enhanced the visuals,' continued Ellison. 'In the scene where Georgie opens the false floorboard and finds the *Necronomicon*, to get

Above left: George (Barret Oliver) visits his hideous 'Gramma' in the Twilight Zone *episode of the same name.*
Above: The issue of Weirdbook *that first published 'Gramma'.*

Above: Horror novelist William Weiderman (Arthur Taxier, left) should enjoy his family while he can in Tales from the Darkside: 'Sorry, Right Number'.

the sense of a stygian pit that looked down into the nether regions of Hell, I used the sound of sizzling bacon. When Gramma reaches out suddenly to grab Georgie's hand, I combined the crack of a bullwhip with the sound made by a striking puff adder.

'But even though the great Piper Laurie was superlative at creating the sepulchral, demonic voice of Gramma when she called to Georgie, or she demanded tea, or she intoned the name of the Lovecraftian elder god Cthulhu, Ms Laurie wasn't able to give me the rasping, hissing, monstrous catarrh sounds I needed when Gramma turns violent. So I did them myself. But to get that phlegmy, ghastly sound, I had to go up the block to a market, had to buy a pint of heavy cream and a block of brie, had to eat them all at once, and then make the gurgling, depraved sounds I needed.'

Some time after this episode, Ellison quit the show in a much-publicised dispute over creative freedom.

TALES FROM THE DARKSIDE: SORRY, RIGHT NUMBER

USA, 1986. Director: **John Sutherland**. Writer: **Stephen King**. Producer: **Anthony Santa Croce**. Supervising Producer: **T.J. Castronova**. Associate Producer: **Erica Fox**. Laurel-TV/JayGee Productions. Colour. 21 minutes.
With: **Deborah Harmon** (Katie Weiderman), **Arthur Taxier** (William Weiderman), **Rhonda Dotson** (Dawn), **Katherine Britton** (Polly), **Brandon Stewart** (Jeff), **Nicole Huntington** (Connie), **Catherine Battistone** (Voice on Phone), **Paul Sparer** (Narrator).

'Steve was regarded as a novelist,' coexecutive producer Richard P. Rubinstein told *Fear* magazine, 'and Laurel helped Steve turn a corner as a screenwriter. As part of the *Tales from the Darkside* television series, Steve wrote his first original teleplay, called 'Sorry, Right Number'.'

In fact, the story had first been submitted to executive producer Steven Spielberg's disap-

pointing half-hour anthology series *Amazing Stories* (1985-87), but had been rejected by Spielberg because, according to King, 'they were looking for *Amazing Stories* that were a little more upbeat.'

Katie Weiderman is talking on the telephone with her sister Lois when the other line rings. All Katie can hear is a woman's voice she recognises crying incoherently. Later that same night her husband, successful horror novelist Bill Weiderman, dies unexpectedly from a heart attack. Five years later, Katie realises that *she* was the woman on the phone that night, trying to warn her younger self that her husband was seriously ill.

King's first draft script was eventually published in his 1993 collection, *Nightmares and Dreamscapes*. Originally broadcast in November 1987, this episode includes clips from coexecutive producer George A. Romero's *Dawn of the Dead* (1978) on TV. It was available on video as part of Worldvision's compilation *Tales from the Darkside Vol.4*.

THIS IS HORROR

(aka **STEPHEN KING'S WORLD OF HORROR**)
USA, 1989. Directors: **John Simmons** and **Rick Marchesano**. Producer: **John Simmons**. John Simmons/Simmons-Fortune/DSL Entertainment/DD Distribution/Leisure View Video. Colour. 22 minutes [per episode]. 42 minutes [per video].
With: **Stephen King** (Himself), **Henry Strozier** (Narrator).

Subtitled *From the Archives of Stephen King's World of Horror*, this series was originally released in 1990 on four sell-through video compilations in the United Kingdom before a late-night television screening the following year on the ITV network. This 'Video Encyclopedia of Horror', created by John Simmons, includes excerpts from a long interview with Stephen King, obviously shot some years earlier in and around his home in Maine.

Also featured are numerous extended clips, behind-the-scenes footage, plus interviews with such film-makers and writers as Dario Argento, Charles Band, Clive Barker, Robert Bloch, John Carpenter, Joel and Ethan Cohen, Wes Craven, Alfred Hitchcock, Steve Johnson, Fred Olen Rey, Brian Yuzna and others.

According to a review in *Fear* no 15 (March 1990): 'There is nothing of substance on the tapes; most of the interviews are shallow and the visuals tell you less than the static pictures in an ordinary film magazine.'

MONSTERS: THE MOVING FINGER

USA, 1990. Director: **Ken Meyers**. Teleplay: **Haskell Barkin**. Story by **Stephen King**. Producer: **Michael**

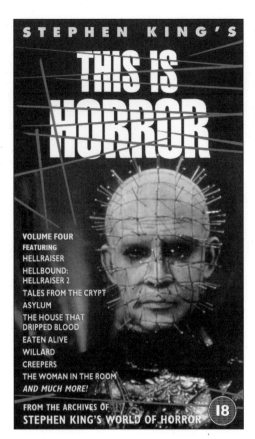

STEPHEN KING'S

THIS IS HORROR

VOLUME FOUR
FEATURING
HELLRAISER
HELLBOUND:
HELLRAISER 2
TALES FROM THE CRYPT
ASYLUM
THE HOUSE THAT
DRIPPED BLOOD
EATEN ALIVE
WILLARD
CREEPERS
THE WOMAN IN THE ROOM
AND MUCH MORE!

FROM THE ARCHIVES OF
STEPHEN KING'S WORLD OF HORROR **18**

Gornick. Supervising Producer: **Jan Saunders**. Series Special Effects Make-up Consultant: **Dick Smith**. Laurel EFX Inc/Tribune Entertainment. Colour. 21 minutes. With: **Tom Noonan** (Howard Mitla), **Alice Playten** (Violet Mitla), **Sharon Cornell** (Policewoman), **Richard B. Shull** (Announcer), **Anne Byrne** (Game Contestant), **Robert E. Weil** (Neighbor).

Final episode of the half-hour, syndicated shot-on-video anthology series (1988-91) created by executive in charge of production Mitchell Galin and executive producer Richard P. Rubinstein. First telecast on 26 April 1992 after being delayed until re-runs, it is based on Stephen King's short story (originally published in the December 1990 issue of *The Magazine of Fantasy & Science Fiction* and reprinted in his 1993 collection *Nightmares and Dreamscapes*).

While watching his favourite game shows on TV, Howard Mitla is haunted by an elongated human finger that emerges from the plug-hole of his bathroom washbasin. King described his comedic story as 'a perfectly valid metaphor for how we cope with the nasty surprises life holds in store for all of us.'

THE OUTER LIMITS: THE REVELATIONS OF 'BECKA PAULSON

Canada/USA, 1997. Dir: **Steven Weber**. Writer: **Brad Wright**. Based on the Short Story 'The Revelations of 'Becka Paulson' by **Stephen King**. Producer: **Brent Karl**

Clackson. Executive Producer: **Jonathan Glassner**. Co-Executive Producers: **Brad Wright** and **Sam Egan**. Outer III Productions/Trilogy Entertainment Group/Atlantis Films/Metro Goldwyn Mayer/CanWest Global System/TMN The Movie Network/CFCF Television/Superchannel/Showtime. Colour. 43 minutes.
With: **Catherine O'Hara** ('Becka Paulson), **John Diehl** (Joe Paulson), **Bill Dow** (Dr Fink), **Marilyn Norry** (Flo), **Steven Weber** (8x10 Guy), **Barry Mickelson** (Doctor), **Jon Chardiet** (Moss), **Preston Maybank** (Hank), **Russell B. Porter** (Actor), **Carla White** (Actress), **Jo-Ann MacDonald** (Cashier), **David Glyn-Jones** (Poker Pal), **Kevin Conway*** (Control Voice). [* Uncredited in the final print.]

Stephen King's comedy Christmas story (originally published in *Rolling Stone*, 19 July-2 August 1984, and later incorporated into the 1987 novel *The Tommyknockers*) was adapted for this surprisingly successful cable television revival (1995-) of the original 1963-65 science fiction anthology series.

'It's one of the most atypical, if not *the* most atypical *Outer Limits* that's ever been done,' story consultant Naren Shanker told *Cinefantastique*. 'it was quirky, odd and funny in a *Twin Peaks* kind of way. A lot of people gravitated toward it.'

Scripted by co-executive producer Brad Wright (*Stargate SG-1* [1997-]) and originally telecast on 9 May 1997, Catherine O'Hara portrayed the eponymous soap opera fan who lives with her mailman husband Joe in a Derry trailer park. When she accidentally discharges a pistol she finds in a closet, the bullet lodges in her forehead and she begins to see and hear strange things. Especially when a man in a 8x10 inch photograph comes to life and begins talking to her...

'That show was fresh and different from mainstream styling,' explained co-executive producer Pen Densham. 'It broke some of the original rules a little bit.'

Steven Weber (from the ABC-TV mini-series of *The Shining* [1994], etc) both directed and played the man in the picture frame. Original series producer Joseph Stefano was executive consultant, and creator Leslie Stevens the programme consultant.

THE X FILES: CHINGA

(UK: **THE X FILES: BUNGHONEY**)
USA/Canada, 1998. Director: **Kim Manners**. Writers: **Stephen King** and **Chris Carter**. Executive Producer:

Below: The issue of The Magazine of Fantasy & Science Fiction *that first published 'The Moving Finger'.*

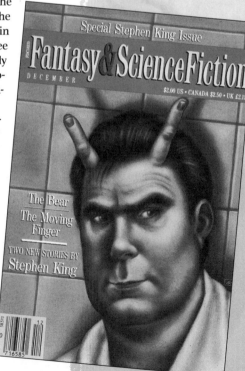

Special Stephen King Issue

Fantasy & ScienceFiction

DECEMBER

$2.00 US • CANADA $2.50 • UK £2.15

The Bear
The Moving Finger

TWO NEW STORIES BY
Stephen King

Right: FBI agent Dana Scully (Gillian Anderson) encounters a young girl (Jenny-Lynn Hutcheson) and her diabolical doll in the naughtily-titled The X Files *episode 'Chinga'.*

R.W. Goodwin. Co-Executive Producer: **Frank Spotnitz**. Supervising Producer: **Vince Gilligan**. Producers: **Kim Manners**, **Joseph Patrick Finn** and **Paul Rabwin**. Co-Producers: **John Shiban** and **Lori Jo Nemhauser**. Consulting Producer: **Ken Horton**. Director of Photography: **Joel Ransom**. Production Designer: **Graeme Murray**. Editor: **Casey O Rohrs**. Music: **Mark Snow**. Twentieth Century Fox Film Corporation/Ten Thirteen Productions/Fox Network. Colour. 42 minutes.

With: **David Duchovny** (Fox Mulder), **Gillian Anderson** (Dana Scully), **Susannah Hoffmann** (Melissa Turner), **Larry Musser** (Captain Jack Bonsaint), **William MacDonald** (Buddy), **Jenny-Lynn Hutcheson** (Polly Turner), **Harry Beckman** (Fisherman), **Carolyn Tweedle** (Jane Frolich), **Dean Wray** (Rich Turner), **Gordon Tipple** (Assistant Manager), **Harrison R. Coe** (Dave the Butcher), **Ian Robison** (Ranger), **Elizabeth McCarthy** (Shopper), **Tracy Lively** (Clerk), **Sean Benbow** (Customer).

'I'd love to write an *X Files* some time,' Stephen King told Frank Barron in a 1997 edition of *Cinefantastique*. 'That would be a kick.'

Although he originally contacted series creator Chris Carter to talk about scripting an episode of the companion show *Millennium* (1996-99), King finally ended up writing this fifth season episode of the popular hour long paranormal series. 'In *The X Files*, Scully and Mulder are real people,' the author told Bill Warren. 'Audiences root for them and think they're cool and groovy. That's the ideal situation — you come to the show to see your friends. And the scares and creeps you get on top of that, which are exceptionally well done, are like icing on the cake — it's so beautiful.'

However, King eventually insisted on sharing the scripting credit with executive producer Carter, who substantially re-wrote the author's original draft. First broadcast on 8 February 1998, this disappointing episode involves FBI agent Dana Scully weekend vacationing in Maine, where she encounters rumours of witchcraft and the autistic Polly Turner, a young girl in the power of her malevolent, murderous talking doll ('I want to play').

'There are some familiar King touches,' revealed *Cinefantastique* (October 1998), 'seemingly innocent lines of dialogue and song lyrics turn menacing when repeated in conjunction with the horrific events. But there is none of the specificity of Maine's small town life that make King's books so vivid.'

'There are high expectations of an *X Files* episode co-written by the prolific novelist Stephen King,' said *Shivers* (April 1998). 'That this is a grisly horror-themed episode comes as no surprise, but that King's particular style of terror adheres to the *X Files* formula so convincingly almost confounds belief.'

The word 'Chinga' is the name of a meteorite which crashed into Siberia in 1913 and is also supposed to be the name of the girl's deadly doll. Apparently, it can also mean 'fuck' in Mexico, depending on the type of Spanish spoken. When Fox executives discovered this, it was too late for the American and Canadian airings, but they made Carter change the title for overseas markets. †

STEPHEN KING:
SELECTED OTHER MEDIA

Along with film and television, Stephen King's fiction has also been adapted in the following media:

STAGE

CARRIE THE MUSICAL

USA/UK, 1988. Director: **Terry Hands**. Choreography: **Debbie Allen**. Musical Director: **Paul Schwartz**. Music Supervisor: **Harold Wheeler**. Orchestrations: **Anders Eljas**, **Harold Wheeler** and **Michael Starobin**. General Manager: **Waissman and Buckley Associates**. Casting: **Lyons/Isaacson**. Production Stage Manager: **Joe Lorden**. Assistant Director: **Louis W. Scheeder**. Sound Design: **Martin Levan**. Lighting Design: **Terry Hands**. Costume Design: **Alexander Reid**. Set Design: **Ralph Koltai**. Book: **Lawrence D. Cohen**. Lyrics: **Dean Pitchford**. Music: **Michael Gore**. Based on the Novel by **Stephen King**. Friedrich Kurz/RSC/Whitecap Productions, Inc/Martin Barandes.
With: **Barbara Cook/Betty Buckley** (Margaret White), **Darlene Love** (Miss Gardner), **Gene Anthony Ray** (Billy Nolan), **Charlotte d'Amboise** (Chris Hargenson), **Paul Gyngell** (Tommy Ross), **Sally Ann Triplett** (Sue Snell), **Linzi Hateley** (Carrie White), **Jamie Beth Chandler** (Jamie), **Catherine Coffey** (Cath), **Michéle Du Verney** (Michéle), **Michelle Hodgson** (Shelley), **Rosemarie Jackson** (Rose), **Kelly Littlefield** (Kelly), **Madeleine Loftin** (Maddy), **Michelle Nelson** (Michelle), **Mary Ann Oedy** (Mary Ann), **Suzanne Maria Thomas** (Squeezie), **Gary Co-Burn** (Gary), **Kevin Coyne** (Kevin), **David Danns** (David), **Matthew Dickens** (Matthew), **Eric Gilliom** (Eric), **Kenny Linden** (Kenny), **Joey McKneely** (Joey), **Mark Santoro** (Mark), **Christopher Solari** (Chris), **Scott Wise** (Scott), **Darryl Eric Tribble** (Swing).

Two-act, thirteen-scene musical adaptation of Stephen King's first novel, written by Lawrence D. Cohen (who also scripted the 1976 movie version) and performed by the Royal Shakespeare Company at England's Stratford-on-Avon for four weeks of previews prior to a disastrous opening on 12 May 1988 on Broadway at the Virginia Theatre, where it ran for just five shows. In the United States, Betty Buckley (who played gym teacher Miss Collins in the film) replaced Barbara Cook as Margaret White. Seventeen year-old newcomer Linzi Hateley was cast as Carrie, and Phil Spector vocalist Darlene Love (whose hit songs include 'He's a Rebel' and 'Da Do Ron Ron') played teacher Miss Gardner. Music and lyrics were by

Academy Award-winners Michael Gore and Dean Pitchford (*Fame* [1980], etc), and Debbie Allen was the choreographer.

'I don't think I've ever witnessed a more pointless musical effort where every wrong decision in practically every conceivable area was taken... *Carrie* is a monumental failure in adapting King's book,' said Alan Jones in *Starburst* no 116 (April 1988), while Wayne Drew decided in *Fear* no 24 (December 1990) that: 'The show stank from first to last. It was a drab, dreary and misconceived, sleazy production.'

Francis X. Clines in *The New York Times* (2 March 1988) revealed: 'The teen-age heroine, beset by gland and glamour in Mr. King's carmine variation on Cinderella, is evolving on

Below: Betty Buckley and Linzi Hateley star in the 1988 Broadway flop Carrie The Musical.

the boards here at the Royal Shakespeare Theater as full-throated as Annie. She even hoofs a bit with her empty white prom dress in one of the ghostly special effects being rushed daily into the production as the musical is frantically basted and audience-tested eight times a week in the truly frightening occurrence that is the Broadway preview process.'

The show's $630,000 production costs and a minimum profit of $360,000 were apparently guaranteed by West German businessman/producer Friedrich Kurz, whose first Broadway production this was. With a loss of $8 million, it still stands as one of the biggest flops in stage history.

A featurette entitled *Carrie the Musical*, with commentary by Betty Buckley, was included on the film's Special 25th Anniversary Edition DVD (2001).

RAGE
USA, 1990. Based on the Novel by **Richard Bachman**.

This Los Angeles stage production was based on Stephen King's 1977 'Richard Bachman' book (originally titled *Getting it On*), which was the author's first attempt at a serious novel, written the summer before his freshman year. It involved psychopath Charlie Decker holding a Maine classroom of fellow students hostage. Following the Columbine and Littleton high school shootings in April 1999, when students killed fellow classmates and teachers before turning the guns on themselves, King asked his publisher, Penguin, to withdraw the book from publication with the next printing.

MISERY
UK, 1992. Director: **Simon Moore**. Writer: **Simon Moore**. Based on **Stephen King**'s *Misery*. Design: **Patrick Connellan**. Lighting: **Tim Mitchell**. Music: **Gavin Greenaway**. Sound Design: **Matt McKenzie**. Associate Director: **Ali Hodge**. Brian Eastman/Andrew Welch/ Carnival Theatre.
With: **Sharon Gless** (Annie Wilkes), **Bill Paterson** (Paul Sheldon).

The first dramatic adaptation of Stephen King's best-selling novel and the 1990 Oscar-winning film, which opened at London's Criterion Theatre, Piccadilly Circus, on 17

Brian Eastman & Andrew Welch for Carnival Theatre present
Sharon Gless Bill Paterson
Misery
Based on **Stephen King's** *Misery*
Written and Directed by **Simon Moore**
Designed by **Patrick Connellan**
Lighting by **Tim Mitchell**
Music by **Gavin Greenaway**
Opening performance at the Criterion Theatre 17 December 1992

December 1992. Written and directed by film and TV director Simon Moore (*Under Suspicion* [1992], etc), American actress Sharon Gless (who had put on weight since co-starring in TV's *Cagney and Lacey* [1982-88], making her better suited to the role as depicted in King's novel) was cast as the psychotic Annie, while Scottish actor Bill Paterson (*The Witches* [1989], etc) portrayed crippled romantic novelist Paul Sheldon.

'It is gripping stuff if you can take it,' said John Gross in *The Sunday Telegraph* (20 December 1992), 'Sharon Gless is excellent as Annie, especially in her sudden swings of mood and moments of girlishness; Bill Paterson, more Caledonian than Coloradan, wisely declines to enlist easy sympathy as her victim.'

While criticising the second act's botched climax, Paul Taylor in *The Independent* (19 December 1992) explained that 'Moore's two-handed play puts the frighteners on you in a broad, giggly sort of way, but it doesn't have the sly, purposeful humour of the book or movie,' while Michael Billington complained in *The Guardian* (19 December 1992): 'As a metaphor, it may be revealing; as a play, however, it's ugly, depressing and predictable.'

MISERY
USA, 2000. Director: **Ken Stack**. Writer: **Simon Moore**. Based on **Stephen King**'s *Misery*.
With: **Robert Libby** (Paul Sheldon), **Catherine LeClair** (Annie Wilkes).

Simon Moore's West End stage adaptation of Stephen King's novel and movie was revived at the Acadia Repertory Theatre in Somesville, Maine, in July 2000.

Alicia Anstead in the *Bangor Daily News* (3 July 2000) revealed that director Ken Stack was 'having an unadulterated blast' with the show, allowing 'shadows, sweet music, a rustic set and episodic escalation to build a potboiler.' Having described the overall production as 'an entertaining and amusing grabber,' she also pointed out that 'more than one audience member squirmed at the realism of the action', going on to add: 'it's a hit, so to speak, and the stage phrase "break a leg" has some real depth here.'

MISERY
USA, 2001. Director: **Ron Peierls**. By **Stephen King**. Adapted for the Stage by **Simon Moore**. Scenic Design: **Randall A. Parsons**. Lighting Design: **Russ Behrens**. Costumes: **Brent Erlanson** and **Bonnie Vidal**. Technical Direction: **Full Stage Production**. Properties: **Julie Hoffman**. Stage Manager: **Tricia Panasci**. Theatre Three Productions Inc.
With: **Edward Kassar** (Paul [Sheldon]), **Sheila Sheffield** (Annie [Wilkes]).

Simon Moore's two-act stage adaptation of Stephen King's novel was presented over 13 January-10 February 2001 by Theatre Three at Athena Hall, Port Jefferson, New York.

'Theatre Three director Ron Peierls — with a strong assist from Randall Parsons' cabin-fever set and Russ Behrens' flickering-candle lighting — has created a claustrophobic thriller that focuses on the interior of an author's worst nightmare' said Steve Parks in the Weekend Section of *Newsday* (19 January 2001), concluding that the production was 'almost a match for a Stephen King page-turner'. However, local reviewer Caryn Moller-Pietrzak thought that 'the plot left much to be desired' and added 'Stephen King fans may enjoy seeing the stage version of *Misery*, but it didn't suit this reviewer's tastes.'

THE MAN IN THE BLACK SUIT

USA, 2001 [tbc]. Libretto: **Eve Beglarian** and **Grethe Barrett Holby**. Music: **Eve Beglarian**. American Opera Projects.

This short story, which appeared in the 1995 Halloween issue of *The New Yorker* and won both the O. Henry Award and the World Fantasy Award, is in the planning stages to be made into a musical production by American Opera Projects.

'I think a lot of the people who read the story don't recognize it as being typical of my work because they haven't read much of my work,' Stephen King explained to Linda Marotta in *Fangoria*.

UNTITLED GHOST STORY MUSICAL

USA, 2001 [tbc]. Writers: **Stephen King** and **John Mellencamp**.

In October 2000, it was announced that part-time musician Stephen King (in The Rock Bottom Remainders with Mitch Albom, Amy Tan, Dave Berry and others) and rock singer John Mellencamp were teaming up to write a ghost story musical which they hoped would eventually play on Broadway in fall 2001. Following a meeting in February, King wrote the story and Mellencamp composed the score. Set in a cabin in the woods, it is about the connection between two brothers who hate each other and two deceased uncles who shared a similar antipathy.

'I was in Florida,' revealed King, 'so John came down and told me the plot. It was kind of a ghostly thing, which is why he thought of me, I guess.'

The Midwest singer admitted that they were bound to make mistakes along the way, but added: 'That's part of the fun of it. See, that's the great thing about this for Steve and I; we really don't have to do this.'

RADIO

STEPHEN KING'S SALEM LOT

UK, 1994-95. Director: **Adrian Bean**. Writer: **Gregory Evans**. Based on the Novel by **Stephen King**. Music: **Elizabeth Parker/BBC Radiophonic Workshop**. BBC Radio 4.
With: **Stuart Milligan** (Ben Mears), **Danny Kanaber** (Mark Petrie), **Peter Yapp** (Father Gordon), **Teresa Gallagher** (Susan Norton), **Doug Bradley** (Barlow), **John Moffatt** (Straker), **Gavin Muir** (Matt Burke), **Matt Zimmerman** (Larry Crocket), **Shelley Thompson** (Ann Norton), **Harry Towb** (Bill Norton), **Peter Whitman** (Weasel Craig/Radio DJ), **Frances Jeater** (Eva Miller/Nurse), **Don Fellows** (Parkins Gillespie), **Ronald Fernee** (Mike Ryerson/McDougall), **David Jarvis** (Tony Glick), **David Fried** (Danny Glick), **Nigel Anthony** (Father Callahan), **Kerry Shale** (Jimmy Cody), **Shelley Thompson** (Ann Norton), **Susannah Corbett** (Check-out girl/Florist), **Vincent Marzello** (Henry Petrie), **Lorelei King** (June Petrie).

THEATRE THREE
at Athena Hall
Live Theatre At Its Very Best!

Misery

• The 2000-2001 Main Stage Season •

Below: Annie Wilkes (Sheila Sheffield) menaces her favourite author (Edward Kassar) in the Theatre Three production of Misery.

'What I wanted to do was take familiar elements and put them together in an entirely new way,' Stephen King explained, going on to reveal that he had restructured and updated 'the basic elements of Bram Stoker's *Dracula* to create *'Salem's Lot.'*

This dramatisation of the classic 1975 vampire novel was personally authorised by King himself and originally broadcast on BBC Radio 4 in seven weekly parts on Thursdays, from 15 December-26 January 1995. Producer/director Adrian Bean said he was aiming for, 'Terrifying psychological realism with no-holds-barred action and horror.'

The sinister voice behind the urbane vampire Barlow was none other than actor Doug Bradley, better known to horror film fans as Pinhead in the *Hellraiser*

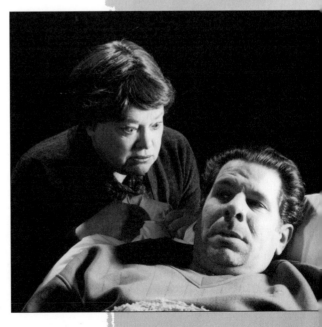

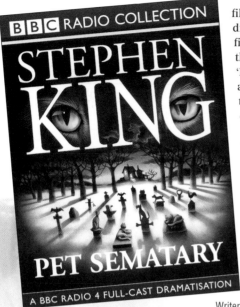

films. 'Barlow is driven by a very direct hunger — a direct need to find humans and drain them of their blood,' explained the actor. 'He's also thousands of years old and I was moved by that aspect of the character, this terribly lonely existence he has...'

The serial apparently marked the first time that one of King's novels had been dramatised on radio and, as Bean pointed out: 'I don't think he had any worries about it not translating. He is a fan of radio horror...he knows the kind of terrifying intimacy that radio can create.'

PET SEMATARY

UK, 1997. Director: **Gordon House**. Writer: **Gregory Evans**. Based on the Novel by **Stephen King**. Music: **David Chilton** and **Nicholas Russell-Pavier**. BBC Radio 4.

With: **John Sharian** (Louis Creed), **Briony Glassco** (Rachel Creed), **Lee Montague** (Jud Crandall), **Sarah Benichou** (Ellie Creed), **William Roberts** (Irwin Goldman), **Liza Ross** (Dory Goldman), **Stuart Milligan** (Steve Masterton), **Mark Bonnar**, **Helen Horton**, **Alice Arnold**, **Garrick Hagon**, **Ioan Meredith**, **Percy Helm**, **Kerry Shale**, **Alan Tilvern**, **Gordon Sterne**, **Colleen Prendergast**, **Hugh Dickson**, **William Roberts**, **Erin Williams**, **Sean Baker**.

Having already successfully dramatised King's *'Salem's Lot* for radio back in 1994, Gregory Evans took a shot at the author's darker 1983 novel, originally broadcast on BBC Radio 4 in six weekly parts on Thursdays, from 20 February-27 March 1997. It was released later the same year as a 180-minute audio compilation on the BBC Radio Collection.

SECRET WINDOW, SECRET GARDEN

UK, 1999. Director: **Gordon House**. Writer: **Gregory Evans**. Based on the Novella by **Stephen King**. Music: **David Chilton**. BBC Radio 4.

With: **Henry Goodman** (Morton Rainey), **William Roberts** (John Shooter), **Barbara Barnes**, **Lee Montague**, **Kerry Shale**, **Helen Horton**, **Ryan McCluskey**, **Bob Sherman**, **Stephen Critchlow**.

'Writing, it seems to me,' said Stephen King, 'is a secret act — as secret as dreaming — and that was one aspect of this strange and dangerous craft I had never thought much about.'

After previously dramatising

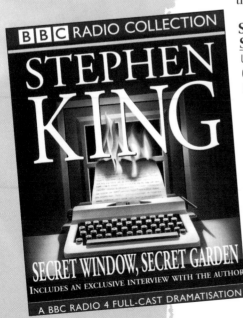

King's *Pet Sematary* in 1997, director Gordon House and scriptwriter Gregory Evans reunited for this adaptation of the author's novella from the 1990 collection *Four Past Midnight*. Written between drafts of *The Dark Half* (1989), the author described it as his 'last story about writers and writing, and the strange no man's land which exists between what's real and what's make-believe.'

Originally broadcast on BBC Radio 4 in three weekly parts on Mondays, from 17-27 May 1999, novelist Morton Rainey is astounded to be unjustly accused of plagiarism by the fanatical John Shooter, who begins a violent vendetta against him.

'Stephen King's gripping story starts out as a mystery but heads into dark corners', promised the *Radio Times* (15-21 May 1999).

Secret Window, Secret Garden was subsequently released by the BBC Radio Collection as a 115-minute 'Full Cast Dramatisation' which also included a 1998 interview with King which was recorded for *Front Row*.

COMPUTER GAMES

THE DARK HALF

Orion Interactive. Produced interactive game, scripted and designed by authors **F. Paul Wilson** and **Matt Costello**, based on the novel by **Stephen King**.

'We worked up this intricate, multi-level structure that would have been a truly kick-ass game with some very over-the-top gameplay,' explained Wilson. 'We even managed to gross-out one of the producers with a creature called 'Birthing woman'. He told us: "No way! Now you've gone too far!" But just as the script and design were completed, MGM bought Orion and the project was instantly and permanently orphaned.'

STEPHEN KING'S F13

Blue Byte Software.

Titled after the non-existent thirteenth function key on a computer keyboard, this CD-ROM compilation, originally announced as *The Stephen King Desktop Companion*, included a previously unpublished novella, 'Everything's Eventual', horror-themed screensavers and audio files, a trivia quiz about the author, a bibliography and interactive mini-games which involved splatting cockroaches, feeding piranha and whacking zombies.

Billed as 'an interactive time-killer', it was released by the then-independent software developer (now owned by Ubi Soft) in January 2000, and was available on Hybrid PC or Mac CD at a recommended price of $29.95. †

Stephen King:
Recurring Talent

In *many Stephen King adaptations, the same names crop up more than once both in front of and behind the camera. Here are brief biographical sketches of some of the key talent to have worked on multiple King projects...*

BROOKE ADAMS

Former American child actress, born in 1949 in New York City. After studying at the famed High School for the Performing Arts and School of the American Ballet, she worked in summer stock and on television until she was

eighteen. After turning down an offer to be one of TV's original *Charlie's Angels*, she returned to her acting career in such films as *Shock Waves* (1976) and the first remake of *Invasion of the Body Snatchers* (1978). However, despite co-starring roles in Terence Malick's *Days of Heaven* (1978) and Richard Lester's *Cuba* (1979), her career has never really taken off and she has ended up in such direct-to-video dross as Larry Cohen's *The Stuff* (1985) and *The Unborn* (1991).
qv: *The Dead Zone* (1983); *Sometimes Come Back* (1991).

NANCY ALLEN

American actress born in 1953, and the former wife of director Brian De Palma, with whom she made several films. Best known for her recurring role as Officer Anne Lewis in the first three *RoboCop* films, she has also co-starred in *Strange Invaders* (1983), *The Philadelphia Experiment* (1984), *Poltergeist III* (1988) and *Limit Up* (1989).
qv: *Carrie* (1976); *Children of the Corn 666 Isaac's Return* (1999).

ALEXIS ARQUETTE

Born in Los Angeles into the family that also includes his actor siblings Rosanna, Patricia and David, he made his film début at the age of seventeen in *Last Exit to Brooklyn* (1989). Since then he has appeared in more than thirty films, including *Jack Be Nimble* (1993) and a memorable cameo as Damien, the doomed Goth boyfriend of Jennifer Tilly, in *Bride of Chucky* (1998).
qv: *Sometimes They Come Back...Again* (1995); *Children of the Corn V Fields of Terror* (1998).

CLIVE BARKER

British-born author, artist, screenwriter, producer and director. Born in Liverpool in 1952, Stephen King famously described him as 'the future of horror'. Six volumes of his ground-breaking horror stories were published as *Books of Blood* in 1984-85 and a string of best-selling novels followed. Founder of the Liverpool theatre group The Dog Company, he made his directorial début with the influential *Hellraiser* (1987), but had less success with *Nightbreed* (1990) and *Lord of Illusions* (1995). Barker moved to Los Angeles in 1991, where he has executive produced the *Candyman* series (based on his short story) and *Gods and Monsters* (1998).
qv: *This is Horror* (1989); *Sleepwalkers* (1992); *Quicksilver Highway* (1997).

Above: Nancy Allen.
Left: Brooke Adams.

Above: Alexis Arquette (right) in
Sometimes They Come Back...Again.

Above: Clancy Brown as psycho sheriff Gus Gilbert in Pet Sematary II.

Above: From left to right: Mark Carliner, Courtland Mead, Mick Garris, Stephen King and Steven Weber, behind-the-scenes on The Shining.

DREW BARRYMORE
(aka BLYTHE BARRYMORE)

Born in 1975 in Los Angeles, the only daughter of Ildiko Jaid and Hollywood hellraiser John Drew Barrymore Jr, she is descended from one of America's greatest theatrical families. Her grandfather John, great uncle Lionel and great aunt Ethel were the 'Royal Family' of the American stage and screen during the first few decades of the twentieth century. Her first professional performance was at the age of eleven months in a dog food commercial. She made her movie début at the age of four in *Altered States* (1979), but it was her role as Gertie, the little sister in her godfather Steven Spielberg's *E.T. The Extra-Terrestial* (1982), that got her noticed. After successfully battling against drug abuse, alcoholism and a suicide attempt, her later screen credits include *Poison Ivy* (1992), *Doppelganger* (1992), *Batman Forever* (1995) and *Scream* (1995). More recently she starred in and co-produced the big screen revival of *Charlie's Angels* (2000).
qv: *Firestarter* (1984); *Cat's Eye* (1984).

KATHY BATES

Large American character actress born in 1948 in Memphis, Tennessee. Primarily a stage performer, after appearing in supporting roles in such films as *Arthur 2 On the Rocks* (1988) and *Dick Tracy* (1990) she finally won an Oscar and a Golden Globe award for her portrayal of the crazed fan, Annie Wilkes, in Rob Reiner's *Misery*. She also read the abridged audio book of Stephen King's 1996 novel *Desperation*.
qv: *Misery* (1990); *Stephen King's The Stand* (1994); *Dolores Claiborne* (1995).

CRAIG R. BAXLEY

American director and former second unit/stunt director on such TV shows as *The A-Team* (1983-86), whose feature credits include *Action Jackson* (1988), *I Come in Peace* (aka *Dark Angel*, 1989), *Deep Red* (1994) and the cable network movies *Sudden Fury* (1993) and *Deconstructing Sarah* (1994).
qv: *Stephen King's Storm of the Century* (1999); *Stephen King's Rose Red* (2000).

BONNIE BEDELIA

American actress and former Broadway dancer, born in 1946 in New York, whose career has shifted between interesting independent features and big-budget Hollywood blockbusters. A Hunter College graduate whose early career included six major plays on Broadway, she has appeared in *They Shoot Horses, Don't They?* (1969), *The Strange Vengeance of Rosalie* (1972), *Heart Like a Wheel* (1983), *Presumed Innocent* (1990) and the first two *Die Hard* films.
qv: *Salem's Lot* (1979); *Needful Things* (1993).

CLANCY BROWN

Tough-looking, six-foot three-inch American character actor, born in 1959 in Urbana, Ohio, who attended Chicago's Northwestern University on a track scholarship. After some local stage experience, he made his film début in Rick Rosenthal's *Bad Boys* (1983). Following a move to Los Angeles, he has appeared in *The Adventures of Buckaroo Banzai Across the 8th Dimension* (1984), *The Bride* (1985; as Frankenstein's sympathetic creature), *Highlander* (1986) and the Lovecraftian TV movie *Cast a Deadly Spell* (1991). He was a regular on the Amblin Studios produced NBC-TV series *Earth 2* (1994-95).
qv: *Pet Sematary II* (1992); *The Shawshank Redemption* (1994).

MARK CARLINER

Producer and executive producer of a number of Stephen King mini-series through his Mark Carliner Productions. His other credits include *The President's Plane is Missing* (1971), Walter Hill's *Crossroads* (1986) and the Emmy Award-winning *Stalin* (1992), scripted by Paul Monash.
qv: *Stephen King's The Shining* (1997); *Stephen King's Storm of the Century* (1999); *Stephen King's Rose Red* (2002).

RUSSELL CARPENTER

American cinematographer.
qv: *The Lawnmower Man* (1992); *Pet Sematary II* (1992).

RICHARD CLABAUGH

American director of photography.
qv: *Children of the Corn The Gathering* (1996); *Children of the Corn 666 Isaac's Return* (1999).

LAWRENCE D. COHEN

American screenwriter, born in 1947, who began his career as a production executive on Martin Scorsese's *Alice Doesn't Live Here Anymore* (1974). He scripted the disappointing 1981 film adaptation of Peter Straub's *Ghost Story* and the disastrous stage musical of *Carrie*, while his screenplay for *Needful Things* (1993) was not used.
qv: *Carrie* (1976); *Carrie The Musical* (1988); *It* (1990); *The Tommyknockers* (1993).

DAVID CONNELL

American cinematographer.
qv: *Stephen King's Storm of the Century* (1999); *Stephen King's Rose Red* (2002).

DEE CROXTON

American character actress sometimes associated with Frank Darabont's films.
qv: *Stephen King's The Woman in the Room* (1983); *The Green Mile* (1999).

FRANK DARABONT

Screenwriter and director, born in 1959 in Montebeliard, France, in a Hungarian refugee camp. He began his career as a production assistant on such low budget films as *Hell Night* (1981) and *The Seduction* (1982), before working for six years in the art department as a set dresser and in set construction. He co-scripted *A Nightmare on Elm Street Part 3 Dream Warriors* (1987), *The Blob* (1988), *The Fly II* (1989) and *Mary Shelley's Frankenstein* (1994; 'Which still stands as my single worst experience in this business as a result of Branagh's breathtakingly ham-fisted direction'). Darabont also worked as an uncredited script doctor, with varying degrees of creative success, on such films as *Eraser* (1996), *The Rocketeer* (1991) and *Saving Private Ryan* (1998; 'my best experience by far'). As well as scripting two 1994 episodes of the TV series *Tales from the Crypt* (1989-96) and eight episodes of *The Young Indiana Jones Chronicles* (1992-93), he also directed the made-for-cable TV movie *Buried Alive* (1989). More recently, he scripted and co-executive produced the HBO movie *Black Cat Run* (1997), co-produced *The Salton Sea* (2001) for Castle Rock Entertainment and directed *The Majestic* (2001) starring Jim Carrey and Martin Landau.
qv: *Stephen King's The Woman in the Room* (1983); *The Shawshank Redemption* (1994); *Stephen King's The Shining* (1997); *The Green Mile* (1999).

WILLIAM B. DAVIS

Canadian character actor, now better known as the menacing Cigarette-Smoking Man on TV's *The X Files* (1993-). A former artistic director of the National Theatre School and of the Vancouver Playhouse Acting School, he founded The William Davis Centre for Actors' Study in Vancouver.
qv: *The Dead Zone* (1983); *It* (1990).

BRUCE DAVISON

American character actor, born in 1948, who made an early impact as the twitchy psychopath in *Willard* (1971) and went on to carve a solid career in films such as *Crimes of Passion* (1984), *Longtime Companion* (1990), *Steel and Lace* (1990) and *X-Men* (2000). He also starred in the Fox TV sitcom *Harry and the Hendersons* (1989-92) and is married to actress Lisa Pelikan (*Jennifer* [1978], etc).
qv: *Tales from the Darkside*: 'The Word Processor of the Gods' (1984); *Apt Pupil* (1987).

DINO DE LAURENTIIS

Born in Torre Annunciata, Italy, in 1918, the son of a Naples pasta manufacturer, De Laurentiis was raised and educated in Italy. At the age of seventeen he enrolled in Rome's Centro Sperimentale di Cinematografia, working as an actor, extra, prop man, unit manager and as an assistant director to gain practical experience in film production. He produced his first film at the age of twenty, eventually winning Best Foreign Film Oscars for Federico Fellini's *La Strada* (1954) and *Nights of Cabiria* (1956). He relocated to Hollywood in 1973, since when he has been responsible for such titles as *King Kong* (1976), *Orca Killer Whale* (1977), *Flash Gordon* (1980), *Amityville II The Possession* (1982), *Conan the Barbarian* (1982), *Amityville 3-D* (1983), *Dune* (1984), *Red Sonja* (1985) and *Hannibal* (2001) amongst his more than 500 credits. He was awarded the prestigious Irving Thalberg Memorial Award in 2001. Stephen King once likened De Laurentiis to Captain Ahab with himself as the Great White Whale.

qv: *The Dead Zone* (1983); *Firestarter* (1984); *Cat's Eye* (1984); *Silver Bullet* (1985);

Above: *Darlanne Fluegel in* Pet Sematary II.

Right: *Matt Frewer in* The Stand.

Maximum Overdrive (1986); *Sometimes They Come Back* (1991).

JEFFREY DeMUNN

Dependable American character actor, born in 1947 in Buffalo, New York. He studied in Britain at the Bristol Old Vic Theatre School, and subsequently returned to America as a member of the National Shakespeare Company. A Tony Award-winner for his role in the Broadway production of *K2*, he was also nominated for an Emmy Award for his portrayal of a Russian serial killer in the cable TV movie *Citizen X* (1995). His other film credits include the 1988 remake of *The Blob*, co-scripted by Frank Darabont.
qv: *The Shawshank Redemption* (1994); *Stephen King's Storm of the Century* (1999); *The Green Mile* (1999).

ROBERT EASTON

Occasional character performer and respected acting and dialogue coach.
qv: *Pet Sematary II* (1992); *Needful Things* (1993).

MIGUEL FERRER

Born in 1954 in Santa Monica, California, the son of American actor and director José Ferrer and singer Rosemary Clooney, he started his career as a professional drummer at the age of seventeen. After forming a band with his childhood friend Billy Mumy, he studied acting at the Beverly Hills Playhouse. Ferrer has given interesting performances in often uninteresting films, and his credits include *The Last Horror Film* (1982), *Star Trek III The Search for Spock* (1984), *RoboCop* (1987), *Deepstar Six* (1989), *The Guardian* (1990), *Twin Peaks Fire Walk With Me* (1992) and *Traffic* (2000). His cousin is George Clooney.
qv: *Stephen King's The Stand* (1994); *The Night Flier* (1997).

DARLANNE FLUEGEL

American film actress whose career has never really taken off. Her various movie credits include *Eyes of Laura Mars* (1978), *Battle Beyond the Stars* (1980), *Project: Alien* (1989) and *Scanner Cop* (1993).
qv: *The Twilight Zone*: 'Gramma' (1986); *Pet Sematary II* (1992).

JOHN FRANKLIN

Born in 1967, the four-foot eleven-inch actor weighed less than ninety pounds when he made his major film début as Isaac, the sub-teen preacher who masterminded the slaughter of all the adults

Above: *John Franklin in* Children of the Corn.

in the first *Children of the Corn*. From Blue Island, Illinois, Franklin is a fine arts graduate from the University of Illinois who appeared in many stage productions in Chicago before moving to Los Angeles, where his movie credits include *Child's Play* (1988), Cousin Itt in both *The Addams Family* (1991) and *Addams Family Values* (1993), *Tammy and the T-Rex* (1993), *Tower of Terror* (1997) and *Python* (2000). He returned to the *Corn* franchise as writer and star of the fifth direct-to-video sequel.
qv: *Children of the Corn* (1984); *Children of the Corn 666 Isaac's Return* (1999).

MATT FREWER

Excitable Canadian character actor, born in Washington DC, in 1958, whose big break came when he was cast as the eponymous computer-generated TV presenter in the British-made pilot film *Max Headroom* (1985) and the subsequent American TV series (1987). As well as starring in two seasons of the Canadian series *Psi Factor Chronicles of the Paranormal* (1996-), he has also appeared in such films as *Supergirl* (1984) and *Honey, I Shrunk the Kids* (1989).
qv: *Stephen King's The Stand* (1994); *Lawnmower Man 2 Beyond Cyberspace* (1995); *Quicksilver Highway* (1997).

MITCHELL GALIN

American producer and executive in charge of production with Richard P. Rubinstein at Laurel Entertainment. They subsequently formed New Amsterdam Entertainment together in the mid-1990s.
qv: *Tales from the Darkside*: 'Sorry, Right Number' (1986); *Creepshow 2* (1987); *Pet Sematary* (1989); *Tales from the Darkside The Movie* (1990); *Monsters*: 'The Moving Finger' (1990); *Golden Years* (1991); *Stephen King's The Stand* (1994); *The Langoliers* (1995); *Thinner* (1996); *The Night Flier* (1997).

CYNTHIA GARRIS

The actress wife of writer/director Mick Garris, whose characters invariably end up dead in her husband's productions. 'Killing her periodically has kept us happy for sixteen blissful years,' Garris joked with Bill Warren during the making of *Quicksilver Highway*.

qv: *Sleepwalkers* (1992); *Stephen King's The Stand* (1994); *Stephen King's The Shining* (1997); *Quicksilver Highway* (1997).

MICK GARRIS

American writer and director, born in 1951. A former Universal publicist, his movies and TV mini-series include Walt Disney's *Fuzzbucket* (1986), *Critters 2* (1988), *Psycho IV The Beginning* (1990) and the Peter James adaptation *Virtual Obsession* (1998). As the supervising producer, he also directed several episodes (including the pilot) of the supernatural TV series *The Others* (1999-2000), plus one episode each of *Freddy's Nightmares* (1988) and Steven Spielberg's *Amazing Stories* (1985-87). His scriptwriting credits include *Coming Soon!* (1982, with John Landis), **Batteries Not Included* (1987, story only), *The Fly II* (1989, with Frank Darabont, and Jim and Ken Wheat), Disney's *Hocus Pocus* (1993, with Neil Cuthbert), ten episodes of *Amazing Stories*, an episode of *Tales from the Crypt*, and with Tom McLoughlin he created and co-wrote the pilot for the series *She-Wolf of London* (1990-91). His short stories have appeared in several anthologies and magazines and have been collected in *A Life in the Cinema* (2000), which includes a foreword by Stephen King and cover art by Clive Barker.

qv: *Sleepwalkers* (1992); *Stephen King's The Stand* (1994); *Stephen King's The Shining* (1997); *Quicksilver Highway* (1997).

JEFF GEOFFRAY

American film producer.

qv: *Children of the Corn V Fields of Terror* (1998); *Children of the Corn 666 Isaac's Return* (1999).

WILLIAM GOLDMAN

Outspoken American screenwriter and novelist, born in 1931 in Highland Park, Illinois, who is famous for his opinion that 'nobody knows anything' in the film business. Beginning his career as a novelist in 1957, he won Oscars for his screenplays for *Butch Cassidy and the Sundance Kid* (1969) and *All the President's Men* (1976), and in 1985 received the Laurel Award for lifetime achievement in screenwriting. Goldman has also received Lifetime Achievement Awards from the New York Film Board of Review, the Writers Guild of America and the Writers Guild of Great Britain. His books include *Adventures in the Screen Trade* (1985), *Hype and Glory* (1990) and *The Big Picture: Who*

Killed Hollywood? and Other Essays (2000).

qv: *Misery* (1990); *Dolores Claiborne* (1995); *Hearts in Atlantis* (2001).

MICHAEL GORNICK

A Penn State graduate in film-making, associate producer Gornick developed his filmmaking skills during his service in the US Air Force, where he worked as a photographer, film editor and sound editor. He began his long association with George A. Romero as a sound editor on *The Crazies* (aka *Code Name: Trixie*, 1973) before becoming director of photography on *Martin* (1976), *Dawn of the Dead* (1978), *Day of the Dead* (1985) and other Laurel productions. He directed several episodes of the syndicated TV series *Tales from the Darkside* (1983-88) before making his feature début as director of *Creepshow 2*.

qv: *Knightriders* (1981); *Creepshow* (1982); *Tales from the Darkside*: 'The Word Processor of the Gods' (1984); *Creepshow 2* (1987); *Monsters*: 'The Moving Finger' (1990); *Golden Years* (1991); *Stephen King's The Stand* (1994); *The Langoliers* (1995).

BRAD GREENQUIST

American actor who also appeared in the *Monsters* TV episode 'The Gift' (1990).

qv: *Pet Sematary* (1989); *Golden Years* (1991).

MOSES GUNN

Born in 1929 in St. Louis, Missouri, the eldest of seven children, Gunn began doing dramatic readings in local churches and community centres at the age of nine. His studies in speech and drama at Tennessee State University were interrupted in 1954 by a stint in the service, after which he moved to New York, where he began appearing in stage productions and was one of the founding members of the Negor Ensemble Company. A guest star on numerous episodic TV shows, his films include *Shaft* (1972), *Shaft's Big Score!* (1972), *Rollerball* (1975), *The Ninth Configuration* (aka *Twinkle, Twinkle, Killer Kane*, 1979), *Amityville II The Possession* (1982) and the TV movie *Haunts of the Very Rich* (1972). Gunn was originally set to play Judge Ferris in *Stephen King's The Stand* (1994), but he was replaced by Ossie Davis after shooting for one day and suffering a flu-induced asthma attack on the set. After being hospitalised in Salt Lake City, he died in December 1993.

qv: *Firestarter* (1984).

BOB GUNTON

American character actor, usually cast in authority roles. A former seminary student and Vietnam veteran with the US Army, California-born Gunton made his profession-

Above: *Cynthia Garris and Mick Garris, behind-the-scenes on* Stephen King's The Stand.

Above: *Bob Gunton in* The Shawshank Redemption.

Above: John Harrison on the set of Tales from the Darkside The Movie.

al stage début at the age of twenty, since when he has appeared in such films as *Rollover* (1981), *Born on the Fourth of July* (1989), *Jennifer Eight* (1992), *Demolition Man* (1993) and the TV mini-series *Wild Palms* (1993).
qv: *The Shawshank Redemption* (1994); *Dolores Claiborne* (1995).

ED HARRIS

Born in 1950 in Tenafly, New Jersey, Harris made his acting début in Sam Shepard's off-Broadway production of *Fool for Love*. After graduating from the California Institute of the Arts in 1975 with a Bachelor of Fine Arts degree, his first feature film appearance was in *Coma* (1978), since when he has appeared in such titles as *The Right Stuff* (1983), *The Abyss* (1989), *The Truman Show* (1998) and the Oscar-nominated *Pollock* (2000).
qv: *Knightriders* (1981); *Creepshow* (1982); *Needful Things* (1993); *Stephen King's The Stand* (1994).

JOHN HARRISON
(aka JOHN SUTHERLAND)
After graduating in 1973, Pittsburgh-born Harrison teamed up with friends to create independent production company The Image Works. He began his career as the star, composer and executive producer of the 16mm feature *Effects* (1979), which also involved Tom Savini as actor and effects technician. After appearing in George A. Romero's *Knightriders* and *Dawn of the Dead* (1978), he took over as assistant director and created the music score on *Creepshow*. He also wrote and directed several episodes of the syndicated Laurel TV series *Tales from the Darkside* (1983-88) and *Monsters* (1988-91). Harrison made his directorial début on the feature version of the former and went on to script Disney's *Dinosaur* (2000), and wrote and

Above: Tom Holland (left) with Stephen King, behind-the-scenes on The Langoliers.
Right: Tobe Hooper (left) with Richard Kobritz, behind-the-scenes on Salem's Lot.

directed the Sci-Fi Channel's six-hour mini-series of Frank Herbert's *Dune* (2000).
qv: *Knightriders* (1981); *Creepshow* (1982); *Tales from the Darkside The Movie* (1990).

DOUGLAS HIGGINS
Vancouver-born production designer, whose credits include working as an assistant art director on *The Exorcist* (1973).
qv: *It* (1990), *Needful Things* (1993).

PAT HINGLE
(aka MARTIN PATTERSON HINGLE)
Stout American character actor, born in 1924 in Denver, Colorado. After his parents divorced while he was still an infant, Hingle travelled around the country with his school teacher mother, eventually entering the University of Texas in 1941. He served with the US Navy during World War II and joined the Actor's Studio in 1952. He made his film début in *On the Waterfront* (1954), and his numerous credits include several movies with Clint Eastwood, the sci-fi spoof *Not of This World* (1991) and the recurring role of Commissioner Gordon in the 1989-97 series of *Batman* films.
qv: *Maximum Overdrive* (1986); *Stephen King's The Shining* (1997).

TOM HOLLAND
(aka THOMAS HOLLAND)
American director and screenwriter, born in 1943 in Poughkeepsie, New York, who began his career by scripting *The Beast Within* (1982), before going on to work on *Psycho II* (1983), *Class of 1984* (1984) and *Scream for Help* (1984), and directing *Fright Night* (1985), *Child's Play* (1988) and *The Temp* (1993).
qv: *Stephen King's The Stand* (1994); *The Langoliers* (1995); *Thinner* (1996).

TOBE HOOPER
Born in 1943 in Austin, Hooper studied cinematography and music in his native Texas. He made two films — a PBS documentary on singing group Peter, Paul and Mary, and a

psychedelic art film called *Eggshells* — before his breakthrough independent feature *The Texas Chain Saw Massacre* (1974) became a cult hit. Aside from the notable exception of *Poltergeist* (1982), he has followed his horror début up with such disappointing credits as *Eaten Alive* (aka *Death Trap*, 1976), *The Funhouse* (1981), *Lifeforce* (1985), *Invaders from Mars* (1985), *The Texas Chainsaw Massacre 2* (1986), *Spontaneous Combustion* (1990), *I'm Dangerous Tonight* (1990), *Tobe Hooper's Night Terrors* (1993) and *Body Bags* (1993, with John Carpenter).
qv: *Salem's Lot* (1979); *Sleepwalkers* (1992); *The Mangler* (1994).

AMY IRVING

American stage and screen actress, born in 1953 in Palo Alto, California, to actress Priscilla Pointer and drama teacher Jules Irving. She trained at the American Conservatory Theater and the London Academy of Music and Dramatic Art. After appearing in Brian De Palma's *Carrie* and *The Fury* (1978), she was married to director Steven Spielberg from 1985-89. Her other credits include an Oscar-nominated performance in *Yentl* (1983), *Rumpelstiltskin* (1987; directed by her brother, David), *Crossing Delancey* (1988) and providing the singing voice of Jessica Rabbit in *Who Framed Roger Rabbit* (1988). More recently she appeared in the TV movie *Twilight Zone Rod Serling's Lost Classics* (1994) and has been involved in various independent film productions.
qv: *Carrie* (1976); *The Rage Carrie 2* (1999).

SHELLY JOHNSON

American director of photography who has subsequently worked with Mick Garris on such TV series as *The Others* (1999-2000).
qv: *Stephen King's The Shining* (1997); *Quicksilver Highway* (1997).

STEVE JOHNSON

American special effects make-up artist, born in 1960. An assistant on *An American Werewolf in London* (1981) and other movies in the early 1980s, he has since graduated to creating his own monsters, most notably with more werewolves in *Bad Moon* (1996) and the direct-to-video *Howling* series through his Steve Johnson's XFX, Inc.
qv: *This is Horror* (1989); *Pet Sematary II* (1992); *Stephen King's The Stand* (1994); *The Langoliers* (1995); *Stephen King's The Shining* (1997); *Quicksilver Highway* (1997); *Stephen King's Storm of the Century* (1999).

WALTER JOSTEN

American film producer.
qv: *Children of the Corn V Fields of Terror*

Above: *Steve Johnson (right) with Ruby Dee, behind-the-scenes on* The Stand.

(1998); *Children of the Corn 666 Isaac's Return* (1999).

RICHARD KOBRITZ

Born in 1941 in San Francisco, Kobritz is a former vice-president for production at Warner Bros Television who entered the film industry in 1964. He worked as an assistant director on a number of Doris Day comedies before becoming a production manager on three Gene Kelly-directed movies: *A Guide for the Married Man* (1967), *Hello Dolly!* (1969) and *The Cheyenne Social Club* (1970). After working as an associate producer for director Martin Ritt, he produced John Carpenter's NBC-TV movie *Someone's Watching Me!* (1978).
qv: *Salem's Lot* (1979); *Christine* (1983); *Apt Pupil* (1988).

MARY LAMBERT

(aka LOUISE LAMBERT)
Arkansas-born Lambert received her Bachelor of Fine Arts in painting from the Rhode Island School of Design. After co-producing the award-winning short film *Rapid Eye Movements*, she became a music video director working with such notable artists as Madonna, Sting, Janet Jackson and Mick Jagger. Following her controversial drama *Siesta* (1987) and the two *Pet Sematary* films, she made the historical cable TV movie *Grand Isle* (1992) and directed a 1989 episode of TV's *Tales from the Crypt*.
qv: *Pet Sematary* (1989); *Pet Sematary II* (1992).

JOHN LANDIS

Enthusiastic American writer, producer and director, born in 1950 in Chicago, Illinois. He

Above: *Ed Lauter.*

ED LAUTER

Gaunt American character actor, born in 1940 in Long Island, New York. His numerous credits include Alfred Hitchcock's *Family Plot* (1976), *King Kong* (1976), *Magic* (1978), *Timerider* (1983), *The Rocketeer* (1991) and *Python* (2000).

qv: *Cujo* (1983); *Golden Years* (1991).

GEOFFREY LEWIS

Weaselly American character actor, a natural successor to Elisha Cook Jr. Born in 1935 in San Diego, California, his many credits include a number of films with Clint Eastwood, the TV movie *The Return of the Man from U.N.C.L.E. 'The Fifteen Years Later Affair'* (1983), *Night of the Comet* (1984), *Out of the Dark* (1989), *Disturbed* (1990), *Wishman* (1993) and *Maverick* (1994). His daughter Juliette is also an actress.

qv: *Salem's Lot* (1979); *The Lawnmower Man* (1992).

BRIAN LIBBY

American character actor who played the resurrected killer zombie battling Chuck Norris' Texas sheriff in *Silent Rage* (1982). A regular in Frank Darabont's films, he also turned up in the director's TV movie *Buried Alive* (1990).

qv: *Stephen King's The Woman in the Room* (1983); *The Shawshank Redemption* (1994); *The Green Mile* (1999).

TERENCE MARSH

British-born production designer, whose work was Oscar-nominated for *Scrooge* (1970) and *Mary, Queen of Scots* (1971). His other films include *The Adventures of Sherlock Holmes' Smarter Brother* (1975), *Magic* (1978), *Haunted Honeymoon* (1986), *Spaceballs* (1987) and *The Hunt for Red October* (1990).

qv: *The Shawshank Redemption* (1994); *The Green Mile* (1999).

E.G. MARSHALL

(aka EDDA GUNNAR MARSHALL)

Respected American stage and screen actor, born in 1910. His many film appearances included *The Caine Mutiny* (1954), *Twelve Angry Men* (1957), the TV movie *Vampire* (1979), *Superman II* (1980) and George Romero and Dario Argento's *Two Evil Eyes* (1989). He had more than 500 television credits, winning two Emmy Awards for his role as attorney Lawrence Preston in *The Defenders* (1961-65), and he also hosted the CBS *Radio Mystery Theatre*. In 1988 the liberal Marshall formed the environmentalist Preservation Party to support anti-development candidates in New York. He died after a

started out working in the mail room at Twentieth Century-Fox and played an ape in his first feature, *Schlock* (1972), before finding success with the comedies *National Lampoon's Animal House* (1978) and *The Blues Brothers* (1980). A true fan of the genre, his credits include *An American Werewolf in London* (1981), Michael Jackson's *Thriller* (1983), the ill-fated *Twilight Zone The Movie* (1983), *Innocent Blood* (1993) and *Beverly Hills Cop III* (1994). His movies usually include numerous guest appearances, and he often turns up in cameo roles in other directors' films.

qv: *Sleepwalkers* (1992); *Stephen King's The Stand* (1994); *Quicksilver Highway* (1997).

PIPER LAURIE

(aka ROSETTA JACOBS)

A leading actress in the 1950s, she appeared in *Francis Goes to the Races* (1951), *Son of Ali Barber* (1952) and *The Golden Blade* (1953) before her career hit a peak with an Oscar nomination for her role in *The Hustler* in 1961. The following year she married film critic Joseph Morgernstern and they moved to Woodstock, outside New York City, to raise a daughter. *Carrie* marked her first film appearance in fifteen years, since when her credits have included *Ruby* (1978), *Return to Oz* (1985), *Appointment With Death* (1988), Dario Argento's *Trauma* (1993) and the cult TV series *Twin Peaks* (1990-91).

qv: *Carrie* (1976); *The Twilight Zone*: 'Gramma' (1986).

short illness on 24 August 1998, aged 88.
qv: *Creepshow* (1982); *The Tommyknockers* (1993).

RICHARD MASUR

American character actor born in 1948. His many film credits include *Heaven's Gate* (1980), John Carpenter's *The Thing* (1982), *My Science Project* (1985), *The Believers* (1987), *Encino Man* (aka *California Man*, 1992) and the TV movies *When the Bough Breaks* (1986) and *The Big One: The Great Los Angeles Earthquake* (1990).
qv: *Apt Pupil* (1987); *It* (1990).

MICHAEL McDOWELL
(aka McEACHERN McDOWELL)

American author and screenwriter, born in 1950, who entered the horror field in the late 1970s with a string of superior novels, including *The Amulet* (1979), *Cold Moon Over Babylon* (1980), *The Elementals* (1981), *Toplin* (1985) and the six-part *Blackwater* series (1983). Under the pseudonym 'Nathan Aldyne', he teamed up with Dennis Schuetz to write four gay detective novels, and as 'Axel Young' the pair wrote the dark fantasies *Blood Rubies* (1982) and *Wicked Stepmother* (1983). Following scripts for such TV series as *Tales from the Darkside* (1983-88), *Amazing Stories* (1985-87) and *Monsters* (1988-91), he scripted the movies *Beetle Juice* (1988, with Warren Skaaren), *High Spirits* (1988) and *The Nightmare Before Christmas* (1993). McDowell was diagnosed with the AIDS virus in 1994, and he died of complications from the disease in December 1999 in Boston. He was working on a *Beetle Juice* sequel and a new version of *The Nutcracker* at the time of his death.
qv: *Tales from the Darkside*: 'The Word Processor of the Gods' (1984); *Tales from the Darkside The Movie* (1990); *Thinner* (1996).

PATRICK McMAHON
(aka PAT McMAHON)
American film editor.

qv: *Stephen King's The Stand* (1994); *Stephen King's The Shining* (1997).

KENNETH McMILLAN

Portly American character actor, born in 1932 in Brooklyn, New York. His film credits included *Heartbeeps* (1981) and Dino De Laurentiis' production of *Dune* (1984), while on TV he portrayed Valerie Harper's boss during the last two seasons of *Rhoda* (1974-78). He died of liver disease in January 1989.
qv: *Salem's Lot* (1979); *Cat's Eye* (1984).

GREGORY MELTON

Production designer and producer, the son of Frank Darabont's drama teacher at Hollywood High.
qv: *Stephen King's The Woman in the Room* (1983); *Children of the Corn II The Final Sacrifice* (1992).

MICHAEL MELTZER

American producer of *The Hidden* (1987) and *The Hidden II* (1993) who, with former entomologist Phillip B. Goldfine, produced *Wes Craven Presents Carnival of Souls* (1998) and the *Sometimes They Come Back* sequels.
qv: *Sometimes They Come Back...Again* (1995); *Sometimes They Come Back For More* (1998).

PAUL MONASH

American Emmy Award-winning producer and screenwriter, born in 1917 in New York, who created the popular TV series *Peyton Place* (1964-69). His other credits include *Butch Cassidy and the Sundance Kid* (1969), *Slaughterhouse-Five* (1972), *The Friends of Eddie Coyle* (1974) and *Big Trouble in Little China* (1986). His draft scripts for *The Dead Zone* (1983) were not used.
qv: *Carrie* (1976); *Salem's Lot* (1979); *The Rage Carrie 2* (1999).

RANDY MOORE

American art director, who often works with Craig Stearns.
qv: *Stephen King's The Shining* (1997); *Quicksilver Highway* (1997); *Stephen King's Storm of the Century* (1999); *Stephen King's Rose Red* (2002).

DAVID MORSE

Baby-faced American leading man, born in 1953 in Hamilton, Massachusetts. After making his feature film début in 1980 in Richard Donner's *Inside Moves*, his subsequent credits include the updated Frankenstein TV movie *Prototype* (1983), the remake of *The Getaway* (1994), *Contact* (1997) and *Proof of Life* (2000). As Dr Jack 'Boomer', he was a regular on the Emmy Award-winning TV

Left: *E.G. Marshall in* Creepshow.

Above: Carlo Rambaldi in a publicity shot from Cat's Eye.

series *St. Elsewhere* (1982-88).

qv: *The Langoliers* (1995); *The Green Mile* (1999); *Hearts in Atlantis* (2001).

GIORGIO POSTIGLIONE

African-born production designer who moved with his family at the age of five to Italy. After studying in Rome and London, he started to buy and sell antiques, developing the business into the largest prop house in Italy. He has worked with such directors as Federico Fellini, Bernardo Bertolucci and Ingmar Bergman, and his more than 350 credits include such Dino De Laurentiis productions as *Flash Gordon* (1980), *Conan the Barbarian* (1982) and *Amityville 3-D* (1983).

qv: *Firestarter* (1984); *Cat's Eye* (1984).

SAM RAIMI

American director, writer and actor, born in 1959 in Royal Oak, Michigan, who made his name with a trilogy of post-modern horror films: *The Evil Dead* (1982), *Evil Dead II* (1987) and *Army of Darkness* (1992). His other films include *Darkman* (1990), *The Quick and the Dead* (1995), *A Simple Plan* (1998) and *The Gift* (2000). Raimi has also become a successful TV producer, with such series as *M.A.N.T.I.S.* (1994-95), *American Gothic* (1995-96), *Hercules: The Legendary Journeys* (1995-99), *Xena Warrior Princess* (1995-2000) and *Spy Game* (1997) to his credit.

qv: *Stephen King's The Stand* (1994); *Stephen King's The Shining* (1997).

CARLO RAMBALDI

An Oscar-winner for his work on *King Kong* (1976), *Alien* (1979) and *E.T. The Extra-Terrestrial* (1982), special effects creator Rambaldi was born in 1925 in northern Italy, where he won numerous regional prizes for his engraving and sculpting work. His many other credits include *Barbarella* (1967), *Flesh for Frankenstein* (1973), *Blood for Dracula* (1974), *Close Encounters of the Third Kind* (1977), *The Hand* (1981), *Dune* (1984) and *Conan the Destroyer* (1984).

qv: *Cat's Eye* (1984); *Silver Bullet* (1985).

Above: George A. Romero.

ROB REINER

Born in 1947 in New York City, the son of director Carl Reiner, this former Emmy Award-winning comic actor quit the hit American sitcom *All in the Family* (1971-78) to try his hand at directing. Formerly married to actress and director Penny Marshall from 1971-79, his credits include *This is Spinal Tap* (1985), *The Princess Bride* (1987), *When Harry Met Sally...* (1989) and *North* (1994). He runs his own production company, Castle Rock Entertainment (named after Stephen King's fictional town), and still acts in other people's films.

qv: *Stand by Me* (1986); *Misery* (1990).

GEORGE A. ROMERO

American writer and director, born in 1940 in New York City, who began his career in television commercials and industrial films in Pittsburgh and who transformed the entire zombie genre with his début feature, *Night of the Living Dead* (1968). He followed it with two sequels, *Dawn of the Dead* (aka *Zombies*, 1978) and *Day of the Dead* (1985), plus *Martin* (1976), *Monkey Shines* (1988) and *Two Evil Eyes* (1989, with Dario Argento). Through his connection with Laurel, his name has probably been linked with more Stephen King projects than any other director.

qv: *Creepshow* (1982); *Tales from the Darkside*: 'The Word Processor of the Gods' (1984); *Tales from the Darkside*: 'Sorry, Right Number' (1986); *Creepshow 2* (1987); *Tales from the Darkside The Movie* (1990); *The Dark Half* (1992).

RICHARD P. RUBINSTEIN

Born in Brooklyn in 1947, producer Rubinstein began his film career in the early 1970s, working for sales agent Irwin Shapiro before receiving a Masters of Business Administration degree from Columbia University in 1971. After two years as a consultant to a Wall Street brokerage firm, he met and became friends with George A. Romero while interviewing him for the *Filmakers' Newsletter*. This led directly to the formation of independent film production company Laurel Entertainment, Inc, with Rubinstein as President and Chairman. He was also one of the executive producers of Laurel's syndicated television series *Tales from the Darkside* (1983-88) and *Monsters* (1988-91). After Laurel was dissolved in the mid-1990s, he formed New Amsterdam Entertainment with Mitchell Galin. He recently produced the six-hour mini-series of *Dune* (2000) for the Sci-Fi Channel.

qv: *Creepshow* (1982); *Tales from the Darkside*: 'The Word Processor of the Gods' (1984); *Tales from the Darkside*: 'Sorry, Right Number' (1986); *Creepshow 2* (1987); *Pet Sematary* (1989); *Tales from the Darkside The Movie* (1990); *Monsters*: 'The Moving Finger' (1990); *Golden Years* (1991); *Stephen King's The Stand* (1994); *The Langoliers* (1995); *Thinner* (1996); *The Night Flier* (1997).

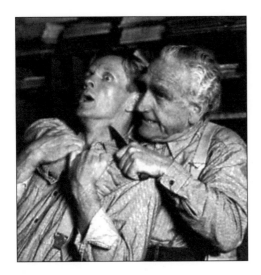

WILLIAM SADLER

(aka BILL SADLER)
Gaunt-looking American character actor, born in Buffalo, New York, in 1950, whose film credits include *Hard to Kill* (1990), *Bill & Ted's Bogus Journey* (1991; as the Grim Reaper), *Freaked* (1993), *Tales from the Crypt Presents Demon Knight* (1995) and *Tales from the Crypt Presents Bordello of Blood* (1996). As Sheriff Jim Valenti, he is a regular on the Warner Bros teen TV series *Roswell* (1999-).
qv: *The Shawshank Redemption* (1994); *The Green Mile* (1999).

TOM SAVINI

American special effects make-up designer, actor and director, born in 1947. Dubbed 'The Godfather of Gore' for his inventive stalk 'n' slash deaths in such films as *Friday the 13th* (1980) and *Maniac* (1980), his long collaboration with George A. Romero — *Martin* (1976), *Dawn of the Dead* (aka *Zombies*, 1978), *Day of the Dead* (1985), *Monkey Shines* (1988), *Two Evil Eyes* (1989), etc — led to him directing the 1990 colour remake of *Night of the Living Dead*. He was forced to drop out of the TV mini-series *Stephen King's The Stand* because of a scheduling conflict.
qv: *Knightriders* (1981); *Creepshow* (1982); *Creepshow 2* (1987).

MARTHA J. SCHUMACHER

Born in Piqua, Ohio, Schumacher enrolled at Ball State University in Indiana when she was eighteen, where she studied business education. After working as a New York model and in junior fashion photography, she began her career in the entertainment industry as the assistant auditor on the CBS-TV mini-series *The Dain Curse* (1978), becoming a much in-demand location auditor on a number of TV shows before switching to movies. She

worked with director/producer Walter Hill on *The Warriors* (1979), as assistant casting director of *Wolfen* (1981), and with Dino De Laurentiis on *Amityville II The Possession* (1982) and *Amityville 3-D* (1983) before being asked to associate produce *Firestarter*. She made her producing début with *Cat's Eye*. Schumacher was president of De Laurentiis' North Carolina Film Corporation Film Studios in Wilmington, Delaware, and married the Italian-born producer in 1990, becoming president of his new company, Paradise Films.
qv: *Firestarter* (1984); *Cat's Eye* (1984); *Silver Bullet* (1985); *Maximum Overdrive* (1986).

MARTIN SHEEN

(aka RAMON ESTEVEZ)
Born to an Irish mother and Spanish father in Dayton, Ohio, in 1940, Sheen adopted his stage name from Roman Catholic Bishop Fulton J. Sheen when he began his professional acting career in his early twenties. After being nominated for a Tony Award for his performance opposite Jack Albertson in the 1964 Broadway production of *The Subject Was Roses*, the young actor made his movie début three years later in *The Incident*. He moved to Los Angeles in 1969, where he guest-starred in various television series, including *My Three Sons* (1960-72), *Mod*

Above: *Richard P. Rubinstein (left) and Stephen King, behind-the-scenes on* The Langoliers.
Left: *William Sadler (left) and James Whitmore in* The Shawshank Redemption.

Above: *Tom Savini, behind-the-scenes on* Creepshow.

Squad (1968-73) and *Cannon* (1971-76), before his film career took off with *Catch-22* (1970), *Badlands* (1973) and *Apocalypse Now* (1979). His many other credits include *The Final Countdown* (1980), *The Believers* (1987) and *Spawn* (1997), although such TV movies as *Roswell* (1994), *Storm* (1999) and *Thrill Seekers* (1999) are a waste of his talent. He is currently playing President Josiah Bartlet in the NBC-TV series *The West Wing* (1999-).
qv: *The Dead Zone* (1983); *Firestarter* (1984).

W. MORGAN SHEPPARD

Grizzled British-born character actor who began his career on a scholarship at the Royal Academy of Dramatic Arts. He

Above: *Frances Sternhagen.*

both *Forrest Gump* (1994) and *Apollo 13* (1995) before appearing in a cameo in *The Green Mile*.

qv: *Stephen King's The Stand* (1994); *The Green Mile* (1999).

SHAWNEE SMITH

American character actress, whose credits include the 1988 remake of *The Blob*, co-scripted by Frank Darabont. She replaced Diane Lane in *The Stand* TV mini-series when the latter actress became pregnant.

qv: *Stephen King's The Stand* (1994); *Stephen King's The Shining* (1997).

MICHAEL STADVEC

American character actor.

qv: *Sometimes They Come Back...Again* (1995); *Sometimes They Come Back For More* (1998).

HARRY DEAN STANTON

Lanky American character actor, born in 1926 in West Irvine, Kentucky. After serving in the US Navy during World War II, he studied drama at the Pasadena Playhouse before settling in Los Angeles in 1958. He made his motion picture début a year earlier in *Dragoon Wells Massacre*, and his subsequent credits have included *Cool Hand Luke* (1967), *Farewell, My Lovely* (1975), *Alien* (1979), *Wise Blood* (1979), *Repo Man* (1984), *Paris, Texas* (1984), *Wild at Heart* (1990) and *Twin Peaks Fire Walk With Me* (1992), along with guest-appearances in numerous TV series. He also sings and plays guitar with The Harry Dean Stanton Band.

qv: *Christine* (1983); *The Green Mile* (1999).

CRAIG STEARNS

American production designer.

qv: *Stephen King's The Shining* (1997); *Quicksilver Highway* (1997); *Stephen King's Storm of the Century* (1999); *Stephen King's Rose Red* (2002).

FRANCES STERNHAGEN

Distinguished American stage and screen actress, born in Washington DC in 1930, With classic and contemporary roles both on and off Broadway, her film credits include *The Hospital* (1971), *Fedora* (1978), *Outland* (1981), *Communion* (1988) and Brian De Palma's *Raising Cain* (1992). She has a recurring role on the NBC-TV series *E.R.* (1994-).

qv: *Misery* (1990); *Golden Years* (1991).

MILTON SUBOTSKY

Born in 1921, this American-born producer and screenwriter lived and worked in Britain from the late 1950s onwards. He teamed up with financier Max J. Rosenberg

appeared in repertory theatre and London's West End before joining the Royal Shakespeare Company in 1963, remaining with them for twelve years. On Broadway he played the lead in *Marat/Sade* as well as the role of Craigin in *Sherlock Holmes*. Sheppard has guest-starred in countless TV shows on both sides of the Atlantic, and he was a regular on *Max Headroom* (1987-88) and as a hologram in Steven Spielberg's *SeaQuest DSV* (1993-95). His many film credits include *Hawk the Slayer* (1980), *The Elephant Man* (1980), *The Keep* (1983), *The Doctor and the Devils* (1985), *Elvira Mistress of the Dark* (1988) and *Wild at Heart* (1990).

qv: *Needful Things* (1993); *Sometimes They Come Back...Again* (1995).

RALPH S. SINGLETON

Born in 1940 in Fall River, Massachusetts, Singleton was the Emmy Award-winning producer on the popular CBS-TV series *Cagney & Lacey* (1982-88) who made his directorial début with *Graveyard Shift*. His other production credits include *Harlem Nights* (1989) and *Another 48 Hours* (1990).

qv: *Pet Sematary* (1989); *Graveyard Shift* (1990); *Pet Sematary II* (1992).

GARY SINISE

American leading man, born in 1955 in Blue Island, Illinois. A co-founder of Chicago's Steppenwolf Theatre Company in 1974, he began his Hollywood career by directing two episodes of the NBC-TV series *Crime Story* (1986-88). He made his motion picture acting début in *A Midnight Clear* (1992) and went on to both direct and appear in the 1992 remake of *Of Mice and Men* alongside fellow Steppenwolf member John Malkovich. Sinise previously co-starred with Tom Hanks in and, following *City of the Dead* (1960), they created Amicus Productions, which along with American International Pictures became the only serious rival to the House of Hammer. He successfully revived the anthology format with *Dr. Terror's House of Horrors* (1965), and Amicus followed it up with a string of low-budget horror, fantasy and science fiction releases, including *Dr. Who and the Daleks* (1965), *The Skull* (1965), *Torture Garden* (1967), *The House That Dripped Blood* (1970), *Asylum* (1972), *Tales from the Crypt* (1972), *Vault of Horror* (1973) and *The Land That Time Forgot* (1974). The partnership broke up acrimoniously in the mid-1970s, and Subotsky's subsequent genre projects were variable at best. Subotsky died in June 1991, aged 70, and is posthumously credited on a number of Stephen King adaptations.

qv: *Cat's Eye* (1984); *Maximum Overdrive* (1986); *Sometimes They Come Back* (1991); *The Lawnmower Man* (1992); *Sometimes They Come Back...Again* (1995).

LEWIS TEAGUE

Born in Brooklyn in 1941, Teague joined the US Army at the age of seventeen and was stationed in Germany for three years before returning to America and earning a degree in theatre arts. He became an English major and as an elective took a film course. His prize-winning short *It's About the Carpenter* brought him to the attention of Universal, and he directed such TV series as *Barnaby Jones* (1973-80), *A Man Called Sloane* (1979-80) and *Vega$* (1978-81) for the studio. After working as an editor and second unit director for Roger Corman, he made his feature début as a director with *The Lady in Red* (1979). His subsequent credits include the inventive *Alligator* (1980), *The Jewel of the Nile* (1985), *Navy SEALS* (1990) and *Deadlock* (1991).

qv: *Cujo* (1983); *Cat's Eye* (1984).

J.T. WALSH

Born in San Francisco and raised in Europe, former salesman Walsh began his acting career on the stage. After appearing in a large number of off-Broadway plays, he began to be noticed in such mainstream productions as *Glengarry Glen Ross*, *Macbeth* and *Rose*. His prolific film credits include *Good Morning, Vietnam* (1987), *Backdraft* (1991), *Red Rock West* (1993), *Miracle on 34th Street* (1994) and *Pleasantville* (1998), and he starred as Colonel Frank Bach in the NBC-TV series *Dark Skies* (1996-97). He died of a heart attack, aged fifty-four, while on vacation in February 1998.

qv: *Misery* (1990); *Needful Things* (1993).

STEVEN WEBER

American leading man of stage, screen and TV, best known for his co-starring role as Brian Hackett opposite Tim Daly in the successful NBC-TV sit-com *Wings* (1989-97). He has also appeared in such films as *Single White Female* (1992), *The Temp* (1993) and *Dracula Dead and Loving It* (1995). A title change to *The Weber Show* could not save his troubled NBC fantasy series *Cursed* (2000-2001).

qv: *Stephen King's The Shining* (1997); *The Outer Limits*: 'The Revelations of 'Becka Paulson' (1997). †

Above: Lewis Teague (right) with Drew Barrymore, behind-the-scenes on Cat's Eye.
Left: Milton Subotsky.
Below: J.T. Walsh prepares to blow himself up in Needful Things.

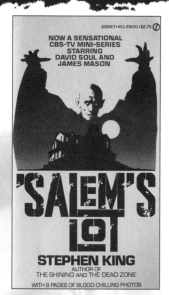

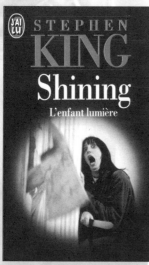

The following is a selected list of primary American/British first editions by Stephen King. Most of the author's books have, of course, gone through multiple printings and editions since their initial publication.

NOVELS OR SEPARATE BOOK PUBLICATION

The Pit and the Pendulum [chapbook] (VIB, 1961)

The Invasion of the Star-Creatures [chapbook] (VIB, 1961)

Carrie (Doubleday, 1974/New English Library, 1975)

'Salem's Lot (Doubleday, 1975/New English Library, 1975)

Rage [as Richard Bachman] (New American Library/Signet, 1977/New English Library, 1977)

The Shining (Doubleday, 1977/New English Library, 1977)

The Stand (Doubleday, 1978/New English Library, 1979)

The Long Walk [as Richard Bachman] (New American Library/Signet, 1979/New English Library, 1979)

The Dead Zone (Viking, 1979/Raven, 1979)

Firestarter (Viking, 1980/Viking, 1980)

Roadwork [as Richard Bachman] (New American Library/Signet, 1981/New English Library, 1981)

Stephen King [omnibus] (William Heinemann/Octopus Books, 1981)

Cujo (The Mysterious Press, 1981/Macdonald, 1981)

Creepshow [graphic novel] (New American Library/Plume, 1982)

The Dark Tower: The Gunslinger (Donald M. Grant, 1982/Sphere, 1988)

The Running Man [as Richard Bachman] (New American Library/Signet, 1982/New English Library, 1983)

Christine (Viking, 1983/Hodder and Stoughton, 1983)

Cycle of the Werewolf (Land of Enchantment, 1983/New English Library, 1985)

Pet Sematary (Doubleday, 1983/Hodder and Stoughton, 1983)

Thinner [as Richard Bachman] (New American Library, 1984/New English Library, 1985)

The Eyes of the Dragon (Philtrum Press, 1984/Macdonald, 1987)

The Talisman [with Peter Straub] (Viking/Putnam, 1984/Viking, 1984)

The Bachman Books: Four Early Novels by Stephen King [omnibus] (New American Library, 1985/New English Library, 1986)

Silver Bullet (New American Library/Signet, 1985)

The Plant (Philtrum Press, 1982, 1983, 1985)

It (Viking, 1986/Hodder & Stoughton, 1986)

Misery (Viking, 1987/Hodder & Stoughton, 1987)

The Dark Tower II: The Drawing of the Three (Donald M. Grant, 1987/Sphere, 1989)

The Tommyknockers (Putnam, 1987/Hodder & Stoughton, 1988)

My Pretty Pony [with Barbara Kruegar] (Library Fellows of the Whitney Museum of American Art, 1988)

Dolan's Cadillac (Lord John Press, 1989)

The Dark Half (Viking, 1989/Hodder & Stoughton, 1989)

The Stand: The Complete and Uncut Edition (Doubleday, 1990/Hodder & Stoughton, 1990)

The Dark Tower III: The Waste Lands (Donald M. Grant, 1991/Sphere, 1992)

Twice the Power: Needful Things & Four Past Midnight [presentation proof] (Hodder & Stoughton, 1991)

Needful Things (Viking, 1991/Hodder & Stoughton, 1991)

Gerald's Game (Viking, 1992/Hodder & Stoughton, 1992)

Dolores Claiborne (Viking, 1992/Hodder & Stoughton, 1992)

Carrie/The Tommyknockers [omnibus] (Hodder & Stoughton, 1994)

Insomnia (Mark V. Ziesing, 1994/Hodder & Stoughton, 1994)

Rose Madder (Viking, 1995/Hodder & Stoughton, 1995)

Umney's Last Case (Penguin, 1995)

The Green Mile [six volumes] (Penguin/Signet, 1996/Penguin, 1996)

Desperation (Donald M. Grant, 1996/Hodder & Stoughton, 1996)

Desperation & The Regulators [as Richard Bachman] [boxed set] (Hodder & Stoughton, 1996)

The Regulators [as Richard Bachman] (Penguin/Dutton, 1996/Hodder & Stoughton, 1996)

The Green Mile [single volume] (Penguin/Plume, 1997/Orion, 1998)

The Dark Tower IV: Wizard and Glass (Donald M. Grant, 1997/Hodder & Stoughton, 1997)

Bag of Bones (Simon & Schuster/Scribner, 1998/Hodder & Stoughton, 1998)

Storm of the Century (Pocket, 1999)

The Dark Tower [boxed set] (Donald M. Grant, 1999)

The Girl Who Loved Tom Gordon (Simon & Schuster/Scribner, 1999/Hodder & Stoughton, 1999)

The New Lieutenant's Rap [chapbook] (Philtrum Press, 1999)

Zenith Rising: Book One of the Plant [chapbook]

(Philtrum Press, 2000)

Dreamcatcher (Simon & Schuster/Scribner, 2001/
Hodder & Stoughton, 2001)

Black House [with Peter Straub] (Random House,
2001)

From a Buick Eight (forthcoming)

The Dark Tower V: The Crawling Shadow (forthcoming)

COLLECTIONS

Night Shift (Doubleday, 1978/New English Library,
1978)

Different Seasons (Viking, 1982/Macdonald, 1982)

Skeleton Crew (Putnam, 1985/Macdonald, 1985)

Four Past Midnight (Viking, 1990/Hodder & Stoughton,
1990)

Nightmares and Dreamscapes (Viking, 1993/Hodder
& Stoughton, 1993)

King etc (Books etc, 1998)

Hearts in Atlantis (Simon & Schuster/Scribner,
1999/Hodder & Stoughton, 1999)

*Secret Windows: Essays and Fiction on the Craft of
Writing* (Book-of-the-Month Club, 2000)

NON-FICTION

Danse Macabre (Everest House, 1981/Macdonald,
1981)

Nightmares in the Sky: Gargoyles and Grotesques
[with f-stop Fitzgerald] (Viking, 1988)

On Writing: A Memoir of the Craft (Simon & Schuster/
Scribner, 2000/Hodder & Stoughton, 2000)

ORIGINAL AUDIOBOOKS

Blood and Smoke (Simon & Schuster Audio, 1999)

LT'S Theory of Pets (Hodder Headline Audiobooks,
2001/Simon & Schuster Audio, 2001)

E-BOOKS

Riding the Bullet (Scribner, 1999)

The Plant: Book One: The Rise of Zenith (Philtrum
Press, 2000)

SCRIPTS

Daylight Dead (unproduced, circa 1978)

The Shining (unproduced, circa 1978)

Children of the Corn (unproduced, circa 1978)

The Dead Zone (unproduced, circa 1981)

Cujo (unproduced, circa 1981)

Creepshow (Laurel Show, Inc, 1982)

Cat's Eye (Famous Films Productions B.V., 1984)

The Shotgunners (unproduced, circa 1985)

Silver Bullet (Famous Films Productions B.V., 1985)

Maximum Overdrive (Dino De Laurentiis Productions
Inc, 1986)

Tales from the Darkside: 'Sorry, Right Number'
(Laurel-TV, 1986)

Pet Sematary (Paramount Pictures, 1989)

Golden Years (Laurel-King Inc, 1991)

Sleepwalkers (Columbia Pictures, 1992)

Stephen King's The Stand (Greengrass Productions,
1994)

Stephen King's The Shining (Lakeside Productions,
1997)

The X Files: 'Chinga' [with Chris Carter] (Twentieth
Century Fox Film Corporation, 1998)

Desperation (unproduced, circa 1999)

Stephen King's Storm of the Century (Greengrass
Productions, 1999)

Stephen King's Rose Red (Greengrass Productions,
2002)

The Kingdom (Columbia TriStar Television, 2002)

Asylum (Paramount Pictures, [forthcoming])

According to Douglas E. Winter, the first script written by
King was based on Ray Bradbury's 1960 novel
Something Wicked This Way Comes, 'for his personal
amusement and education.' This was to help him learn
how to write screenplays, and had nothing to do with the
1983 Walt Disney film. 'I loved the book,' King told David
Chute in *Take One*, 'and I think that of all the screenplays
I've done, that was the best.'

As well as an untitled screenplay about a haunted
radio station that King never finished, the author also
reportedly wrote an unproduced script for Dan Simmons'
1989 novel *Carrion Comfort*, while an untitled eighty-one
page screenplay and *They Bite*, a 115-page screenplay
about giant insects, are stored at The Special Collections
Archive of The Raymond Folger Library at the University
of Maine at Orono. ✝

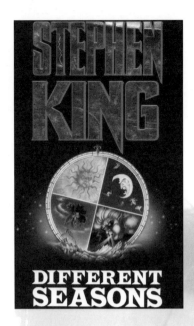

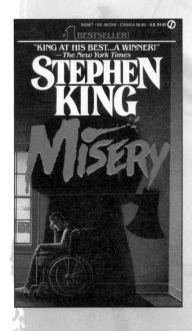

An Interview with Stephen King

Stephen Edwin King was born in Portland, Maine, on 21 September 1947. One of the millions of baby-boomers born after the Second World War, he grew up with his mother and older brother after his father walked out on the family when he was two years old. Surrounded by the popular culture of the day — rock 'n' roll music, television, paperback books and the omnipresent threat of the atomic bomb — he found his own entertainment in the cosmic horror stories of H.P. Lovecraft and EC comic books' lurid tales of revenge and redemption.

After sending examples of his early fiction to Forrest J Ackerman's legendary *Famous Monsters of Filmland* and other magazines, his first professional sale was to Robert A.W. Lowndes' *Startling Mystery Stories* in 1967, for which he earned the princely sum of $35. He continued to sell short stories to such men's magazines as *Adam* and *Cavalier*, but it was not until the publication in 1974 of his first novel, *Carrie*, and Brian De Palma's movie version released two years later, that he began his stratospheric climb to the top of the bestseller lists.

Today he is the world's best selling novelist, the author of more than thirty books, including *Carrie*, *The Shining*, *It*, *Misery*, *The Stand*, *Dolores Claiborne* and *Desperation*. He lives near Bangor, Maine, with his wife, novelist Tabitha King. The couple have three children: Naomi Rachel, Joe Hill and Owen Philip. Two of his recent novels are *Bag of Bones* and *The Girl Who Loved Tom Gordon*, the latter about a young girl lost in the woods who creates an imaginary friendship with her hero, the real-life Red Sox baseball relief pitcher of the title. The book had a 1.25 million copy first hardcover printing in America.

Bag of Bones is set in King's beloved Maine. It tells the story of forty year-old best-selling novelist Mike Noonan who, still unable to stop grieving after the sudden death of his wife four years earlier, has suffered from acute writer's block ever since.

Plagued by vivid nightmares that appear to centre around his summerhouse on the lake, 'Sara Laughs', Mike is inexorably drawn back to the town, where he becomes embroiled in a struggle between ruthless millionaire Max Devore and his daughter-in-law Mattie over the custody of Mattie's three year-old daughter Kyra. As Mike begins to fall in love with the young widow and her child, he also becomes involved in the mystery of Sara Laughs, and the ghostly visitations and escalating nightmares that surround the lakeside retreat.

It is quintessential King and, as the author himself has said, he wanted to write at least one more really good scary story before turning fifty. He has described the book as 'A haunted love story', and has gone on to say that he 'wanted to tell a story which would please my old friends and perhaps make a few new ones as well. *Bag of Bones* is the result — a summation of all I know about lust, secrets and the unquiet dead.'

So did he think that he had succeeded in achieving what he set out to accomplish?

'I like the book. Sometimes when you finish them and you've gone through them three or four times, you never want to see them again. I

Below: *Stephen King as good-guy Teddy Weizak in* The Stand.

Above and opposite page: Stephen King signed for three hours at London's Forbidden Planet bookstore on 14 May 1983, to mark the UK publication of Christine.

His latest book is *Dreamcatcher*, a science fiction novel about the insidious invasion of Earth by a fungus-like alien growth. The first draft was written by hand, which the author revealed, 'put me in touch with the language as I haven't been for years.'

He also explained that his wife, Tabitha, convinced him to change the novel's original title, which was *Cancer*. 'She considered it both ugly and an invitation to bad luck and trouble,' he said. 'Eventually I came around to her way of thinking, and she no longer refers to it as "that book" or "the one about the shit-weasels".'

Looking back over more than a quarter of a century, how does King now view his early success as a writer?

'I think the success part was a fluke,' he replies. 'I like to think that if the writing is something that appeals to people and people are getting the sense of seeing a reflection of their own lives, then it's going to happen for you. But the way I think it happened to me was a fluke — the fact that the Brian De Palma movie was a success propelled me at that time. On my office wall I have a cartoon by Garry Larson that shows this mob of people approaching this hapless, balding man's house, and the caption underneath says, "The world needed a scapegoat — they found Wayne".

'In the case of my generation, they needed a pop-novelist and they found me.'

So is it true that he had both *Carrie* and *'Salem's Lot* written before he sold his first book?

'I'll tell you what happened. *Carrie* sold while I was about half way through the first draft of *'Salem's Lot*, and the day after I finished *'Salem's Lot* I found out that *Carrie* had sold in paperback for enough money so I could just write. So the two of them were actually written before I knew that I was going to make any more than $2,500 advance for *Carrie* — with which we planned to buy a car.'

Yet, despite being a multi-millionaire and one of the biggest selling writers of all time, over the years King has had mixed success with the many film adaptations of his work. For every acclaimed and successful title such as *Stand by Me* and *The Shawshank Redemption*, there have also been such boxoffice bombs as *Sleepwalkers* or *Thinner*.

However, King remains very much a movie fan at heart, so I wondered what his opinion was of his own film career?

'If you asked me what I'm proud of,' he told me, 'I guess I would say *Carrie* and *The Shawshank Redemption* — both got nominated for Best Picture of the year. Neither of them won it, but that was a real kick. Particularly with *Carrie*, because I was new to the business,

feel that way about *Rose Madder*. I felt that way about *'Salem's Lot* when I was done with it, even though I know it's a favourite of a lot of people. *The Dark Half* the same way. But I like this book. I can pick it up and look at it, and have pleasant memories of writing it. I think I succeeded pretty well.

'I wanted to catch a little bit of the flavour that's in Daphne Du Maurier's *Rebecca*. I wanted to do something that felt romantic, lush, Gothic, but at the same time retain something of that edge of horror. It's a step back to my earlier books in terms of the setting, which is an isolated area in Maine and, other than *The Shining*, I had never really tried to write a ghost story. The reason why is that, to me, ghosts are not very frightening. There's something Cosmo Topper about them. Even the movie *The Uninvited* has a kind of hokey feeling. I always wondered "How much can ghosts hurt you if you can reach right through them? They can't really hurt you." And the more I thought about it, the more it seemed like a challenge to write a scary ghost story.'

I had just started out. To have Kathy Bates win the Best Actress Oscar for *Misery*, that was tremendous.

'I guess what I am trying to say is that I've been treated well by a lot of the people who have done the adaptations, and even when I didn't think that the adaptations were successful, they were interesting. There are some things, like *Cujo* and *Cat's Eye*, that are really pretty good pictures. As far as my own screenwriting career is concerned, I've written a lot of TV mini-series, I've written two or three different movies, I've directed a picture, and like anybody else in the film business, I didn't set out to do that. I just kind of stumbled into it.'

So how long was it after the publication of his first book that Hollywood became interested in buying *Carrie*?

'Well, there was interest in *Carrie* right away. It just wasn't strong in terms of money. So they decided to hold it back until publication, gambling that the book would be a hardcover bestseller and the interest in the movie rights would go up again. So they released the book in hardcover — it didn't exactly die, but it didn't do wonders in hardcover, either. It was published in April 1974 and the movie rights were sold in August. We didn't do wonderfully well out of it, but I got a piece of the action, so the money end of it was all right.'

Looking back, did he feel fortunate as a first time author that Brian De Palma did such a good job?

'Yeah. It's a comparative thing. There are so many guys that write books, and the movie will come out and they get butchered. My favourite example is *The Day of the Dolphin*. So, comparatively speaking, I was pleased because, for one thing, there hadn't been that many good horror novels that were turned into good movies.'

Soon after King's first collection, *Night Shift*, was published in 1978, British-based producer Milton Subotsky bought six of the stories to use in two omnibus movies.

'He said, "Would you like to direct? You're welcome to",' recalls King. 'It was, I think, kind of a carrot, but it was scary to me. The thing is, you write a book and a book is something you do by yourself — in your office or wherever. You talk about directing a movie and you're talking about this "team sport" where a lot of money is at stake, particularly in Subotsky's case where he ran on a shoe-string to begin with. He was very conscious of the dollar and that's how he made money. And in a way I admired him, because there was no self-indulgence there. Granted, he made a lot of movies that weren't very good, but he also made movies that made money.

'However, the idea of directing, to me, was frightening! I was afraid I would get into it and

I wouldn't have time to do anything else and that I might fail. I didn't like the idea of failing.'

I asked him how he felt about the ongoing sequels and spin-off series, such as *Sometimes They Come Back*, *Children of the Corn*, *The Lawnmower Man* and even the recent *The Rage Carrie 2*, which often bear no resemblance to his books or even to the original movies based upon them. I was not prepared for the intensity of his response.

'They suck!' he shouted. 'All of them, they suck. *Carrie 2*? What's the point of it? Get a life, you guys. There are thousands of good scripts, there are thousands of good screenwriters out there, but their work is going begging because these people are so intellectually bankrupt that they have to do *Carrie 2* or *Children of the Corn VI*. I mean, come on! It makes me crazy!'

I pointed out that there have also been recent remakes of two of his films. *Trucks* was a made-for-television movie based on the same short story that the author himself directed back in 1986 as *Maximum Overdrive*.

'I looked at it with some trepidation,' he admitted. 'When I directed *Maximum Overdrive*, I did it for Dino De Laurentiis and I did it with an Italian film crew that were basically loyal to him. I'd never directed before, so I was really a lamb to the slaughter. So I looked at the TV movie, which was a pilot for a series that never happened, and I thought, "What if this is better than what I did?" But it wasn't. It was worse, actually. And that's hard to do.'

While we were on the subject of flawed adaptations of his work, was he surprised that Warner Bros chose a director of Stanley Kubrick's stature to make *The Shining*?

'They didn't pick him, *he* picked the book. Somebody else had it. An outfit called The Producer Circle Co, which was bankrolled by Johnson & Johnson's Band Aid money! A woman named Mary Lou Johnson, the Band Aid heiress, formed a group of people and  they bought it and were going to do it. It would probably have ended up being a Producer Circle/Lew Grade production, like *The Boys from Brazil* or *Raise the Titanic!*.

'Kubrick read the book and wanted it, and he had a three-picture contract with Warner Bros. *Barry Lyndon* was one of those pictures, and I think maybe *A Clockwork Orange* was the other one. And *The Shining* would be the third one. So he said he wanted it and The Producer Circle Co sold it back to Warner Bros for him. He was totally in charge of it.

'He had nice things to say about the book. Apparently he had read a lot of books and just sort of thrown them away. I heard this from somebody else, from somebody that he had collaborated with in the past: Kubrick came raving in and shaking the book and saying, "This is the one. This is it! Make the deal. Make the deal!"'

I wondered when he had first heard that Kubrick was going to be involved?

'Jesus, let's see. The book was published in January or February of 1976, I think. I must have heard about it in March or April of 1977. Shortly after that he called on the telephone to talk about some of the plans that he had for it. To me it sounded very much like an ending that I had tried on and then rejected. He said, "You think audiences will buy this?" and I said, "Frankly, no. If you get them interested in these people and you're plumping for some of them to escape from this terrible place, and then at the end they all die, I don't think audiences are going to like that."

'And I kept telling him that it was his movie and, I mean, Christ Almighty, he bought it and supposedly he knew what he was doing. So I told him I thought that he should do what

Opposite page: Another purr-fect publicity shot for Cat's Eye.
Below: Stephen King is about to suffer 'The Lonesome Death of Jordy Verrill' in Creepshow.

seemed right for him. Of course, I didn't have to tell him that — he'd do it anyway.'

So was his script for the 1997 four-and-a-half-hour mini-series of The Shining an attempt to erase the memory of Kubrick's 1980 version?

'I always wanted to do the book. Kubrick didn't really do the book, he did a Stanley Kubrick film. It expressed a number of his ideas. I wanted to do the hedge animals. I wanted to do Jack as a younger man. I wanted to do Wendy as a beautiful, desirable woman. And as far as wiping out the Kubrick version, that's not what happened. It's as if our version doesn't exist. In America there's no video tape version of it. There's no DVD version. Because Warner Bros' deal with Kubrick apparently is that those things would not be released. So it only existed as a TV show.'

King's involvement in television actually dates back to the late 1970s, when he wrote an unproduced screenplay for NBC-TV entitled Daylight Dead, based on three stories from his Night Shift collection.

'Twentieth Century-Fox liked it. They bought it. But back then the atmosphere in American TV when it came to violence was terrible. You couldn't show somebody getting punched in the face. They'd cut it.'

Given the atmosphere of self-censorship back then, had his first TV adaptation, the mini-series of 'Salem's Lot, encountered any problems with the network?

'CBS-TV, who were the people who did that, originally brought up their standards of practise and they threw out fifty or sixty objections to the book on the basis of violence and children in moral danger of their lives, and all that sort of thing. Movie people can be very childish in terms of their business dealings, which is why so much money goes down the toilet in movies. Something will come along and the old project gets dropped in favour of the new. Warner Bros bought the book outright on the last day of the option. They pumped $1 million into Salem's Lot without having shot a frame of film or ever assembling a production crew.'

In early 1998 King co-wrote an episode of The X Files entitled 'Chinga', about a young girl whose favourite doll asserts a supernatural hold over everyone around her. I asked him how that came about, and how rewarding was the experience of writing for a network television show?

'You really can't do that for money,' he replied, 'the money is chump change. But I worked hard, I worked real hard on that episode because I had to work with Chris Carter. The subject came up because I was on a celebrity episode of the game show Jeopardy! with David Duchovny. And he said, "You should write for The X Files sometime." And I said that would be great, because I like the show and my kids love it. So basically, what happened is that I had an idea for a story, and it was wildly different from what you saw. I did

Above: Stephen King's cameo as a Minister in Pet Sematary.

Below right: Summing up his one and only experience as a director, Stephen King's T-shirt says it all, behind-the-scenes on Maximum Overdrive.

a treatment and they said okay. It was a lot more like *Firestarter* than it was like Chucky. The evil doll thing — that was mostly Chris Carter's contribution. In fact, I'd say that was entirely his contribution. So, I did a treatment, I did two or three drafts of a script and he rewrote me entirely. He puts his trademark, his stamp, on the show. It's his show and you know it's his show when you're finished.

'They wanted it to go out with "Written by Stephen King", and I really wanted that sole credit because I'd worked hard for it. But in the end I told them I couldn't allow my name on it unless Chris Carter took credit. So we got the co-writing credit.

'However, Chris is a good person to work with. He's smart, and at least we were able to collaborate. I've tried on three different occasions to collaborate with Steven Spielberg and I can't. Because, basically, Steven wants all the marbles at the end of the day. And I'm not willing to do that. If there were a dozen marbles, he could have eight and I'd have four, but that's not enough. With Chris Carter that's the way it turned out. Eight marbles for Chris and four for Steve King. But Steven Spielberg wants twelve marbles at the end of the day and you have none. You get your credit, but that's it.

'I had another idea and I talked with Chris about it. I said that I would like to do an *X Files* with George Romero directing and I'd like to call it 'Night of the Living Dead'. I'd like it to open with this couple going up to a graveyard, and basically replay the whole first scene of the movie. She's really afraid of the place and says, "Oh, Johnny...sometimes they come back. Look, there's one now." And there's this guy walking towards them through the graveyard — who in the movie is a zombie who kills the guy and goes after the girl — and here he turns out to be Fox Mulder. And, as she runs away, this hand reaches up through the ground and grabs her and she dies of fright. I wanted to combine

Night of the Living Dead with another movie called *I Bury the Living.*'

More recently, he was closely involved with *Stephen King's Storm of the Century*, an original six-hour mini-series he created especially for ABC-TV in America.

'It's the best of all of them,' he enthuses. It's set on the same island where *Dolores Claiborne* and a couple of the short stories are set. There's a huge storm that comes and cuts the island off from the mainland, and there's a stranger on the island who murders an old woman and then allows himself to be taken captive so that, basically, he can attract the town's attention. He says to these people, "If you give me what I want, I'll go away. And if you don't, I'll kill you all." And there's no way for them to get help because they are cut off. It's a small town and the sheriff is also the town butcher, so the cell they have him locked up in is really no cell at all, it's just a little room in the back of the supermarket.

'I like it because the acting is good and because we got a gigantic effects budget. The budget of the show is $35 million, and most of that is below the line. We recreated a whole town on a soundstage in Canada. I love the way it turned out.'

So I asked King if it was true that all of his television work has his name in the title because of contract deals with the networks and production companies.

'I don't care,' he laughs, 'if they want to stick it in the title, if they think that's what sells. It's the networks' way of brand-naming. They want you to know exactly what you are going to get. But what they get from me is not necessarily

what they think they are going to get.

'In a way, that's my stock in trade. I'm not supposed to give you exactly what you think you're going to get...'

So when did he first realise that he was a best-selling author?

'*The Shining* was the first hardback bestseller that I ever had,' he recalls. 'It was a bestseller in terms of whatever that means. When *Carrie* came out in paperback nobody knew me from anything. I was nobody — and it did about a million copies, and then when the movie came out it went right through the roof!'

A few years ago the author admitted, 'I looked down the calendar and saw fifty staring me in the face. Fifty is a dangerous age, a time when a writer may have to find a few new pitches if he's going to continue to be successful.' Obviously, given his phenomenal success, Stephen King need never publish another word. So what is it about getting older that worries him so much and why does he continue to write?

'Once you're fifty you can't kid yourself that you're a kid any more. I was talking about the film version of *Needful Things* over dinner at the Bel Air hotel with an executive from Castle Rock Entertainment when I had this epiphany. It qualifies as a real epiphany. I looked at this guy and I thought to myself, "Holy shit, he's younger than I am. He's at least five years younger than I am." And that was the first time that I realised that the balance of power was shifting and I was starting to be "an older guy".

'Until then, I had always been a sort of *enfant terrible*, and you get used to that. In the

Above: *Stephen King's cameo as ghostly bandleader Gage Creed in* Stephen King's The Shining.
Below: *Stephen King's cameo as the Chairman of the Board in* The Langoliers.

sense I was a young guy when I started, twenty-five or twenty-six years old, and for a while I would go to the conventions and Fritz Leiber would be there, Robert Bloch, Frank Belknap Long, Richard Matheson, and all these writers were another generation. So I felt like a kid, then all at once I realised that time had gone by and I really wasn't a kid any more.

'So when you get to fifty you stop being able to fool yourself and, I think especially at the point in my career that I had reached, I was forced to sit down and look back and say, here's what you have done, is it possible to do anything new with these old materials that you've dealt with time and time again? And as you know, you can take ghost stories, you can take horror stories, and it is literally endless

Above: Stephen King's uncredited cameo as an 'asshole' in Maximum Overdrive.
Opposite page: Stephen King keeps his hat on as director of Maximum Overdrive.

the number of things you could do. But a person is finite, and you get to a point where you have to say to yourself, I'm really not able to do anything original with this material any more. And I think if you get to that point, you ought to hang it up, you ought to be done.

'I'm not saying that I'm done, but I am saying that I'm a lot closer to the end than I am to the beginning and that I hope that I'll have the sense, when I get to that point, to avoid self-parody. I don't want to be the Harold Robbins of horror. There's no excuse.

'I go on because it's fun and because I'm buzzing myself. I'm having a great time because I love what I do. I love it if it moves people — if people have a hot-button reaction to it — and because it is what I was built to do. It isn't for the money any more, it isn't for the recognition, it isn't for the fame.

'I don't know how close I am to the end, but

I can almost guarantee you that I'll never be in England doing promotion again because I'll never be in the States doing promotion again. That stuff's pretty much done.'

So what does the future hold for Stephen King?

'I don't have any immediate plans to write another non-*Dark Tower* novel in my life. Maybe I will, I'm not saying that I won't, but this is the first time that I've ever got to a point where I've thought I really don't have anything that I feel like I need to say. I need to finish the *Dark Tower* books, there are three more to write. I've got a book of four stories out — a *Different Seasons* kind of thing called *Hearts in Atlantis* — they are different lengths but they are all fairly long, and then there's a book called *On Writing: A Memoir of the Craft* and then the three *Dark Tower* books. And at that point if there's something else to write, that's fine. And if there isn't, that's fine too.'

So what, exactly, is it like these days to *be* Stephen King?

'It's about the same it was in the 1980s, except a little bit slower,' he replies with an easy grin. 'It's great. It's great and I'm enjoying myself. The kids are growing up — my older son is married — I still enjoy writing books, I don't enjoy flying any more than I used to, but life has settled down a little bit. At some point, I would say in the last ten or twelve years, I developed into, not an elder statesmen, but certainly I'm not a young turk any more. So life's a little more settled.'

However, on 19 June 1999, Stephen King's life was changed dramatically when he was seriously injured while taking his daily four-mile walk along a rural highway near his lake-side summer home in western Maine. He was struck from behind by a 1985 blue Dodge Caravan after forty-two year-old driver Bryan Edwin Smith lost control when he was distracted by his Rottweiler dog attempting to get into a beer cooler. At first the driver thought he had hit 'a small deer'. King was thrown fourteen feet and suffered multiple fractures to his right leg and hip, a chipped spine, broken ribs, a punctured lung, a lacerated scalp and various facial injuries. 'I was surprised he was even alive,' revealed a local man, who witnessed the accident from his pick-up truck. 'He was in a tangled-up mess, lying crooked, and had a heck of a gash in his head. He kept asking what had happened.'

The author was taken to the Central Maine Medical Center in Lewiston where, after surgery, he was described as being in a serious but stable condition. He was released on 9 July after four more operations on his injuries and faced several months of physical therapy.

While the driver faced charges of aggravated assault and driving to endanger (his driver's

license had already been suspended four times previously), King bought the mini-van which hit him for $1,500 and revealed to a local newspaper that he was 'Going to take a sledgehammer and beat it.' To avoid jail, Smith later pleaded guilty to the lesser charge of driving to endanger after a charge of aggravated assault was dropped. He received a suspended jail sentence of six months and was banned from driving for a year. King described the plea deal as 'irresponsible'.

Weeks after the near-fatal accident, confined to a wheelchair or walking with the aid of a cane, the author wondered if he would ever write again. However, despite injuries to his pelvic bones which prevented him from sitting for long periods at the word processor, it was not long before he was back at his work station, with the blessing of his wife. 'As my leg begins to heal and my mind reaccustoms itself to its old routine, I feel that old buzz of happiness,' he revealed, 'that sense of having found the right words and put them in a line.'

In a bizarre footnote, nine months later, on 22 September, Bryan Smith was found dead in his trailer home in Fryeburg, Maine, by his deputy sheriff brother (who had coincidentally been the first officer at the scene of the accident). The former construction worker had suffered from a number of health problems, including arthritis brought on by an old back injury, carpel tunnel syndrome and depression. An empty bottle of painkillers was found near the body and, according to the medical

Below: Stephen King and his son Joe relax behind-the-scenes on Creepshow.

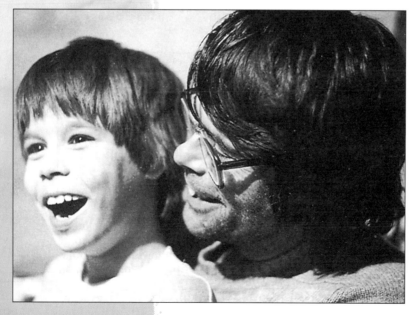

examiner, toxicology reports indicated that Smith died of an accidental overdose of the painkiller Fentanyl. 'I was very sorry to hear of the passing of Bryan Smith,' King told the media. 'The death of a forty-three year-old man can only be termed untimely. I would wish bet-

ter for anyone.

'Our lives came together in a strange way. I'm grateful I didn't die. I'm sorry he's gone.'

While he was convalescing from his injuries, King released his new 16,000 word novella, 'Riding the Bullet', exclusively on the Internet. 'I'm curious to see what sort of response there is and whether this is the future,' he said. The initial demand was phenomenal, with 400,000 downloads in the first twenty-four hours. The author estimated that he would make as much as $450,000 for the story (he would have received around $10,000 if he had sold it to *The New Yorker* or a similar magazine).

More recently, King stirred up plenty of publicity by offering an episodic horror novel at $1 per download through his Philtrum Press website. 'In the 1980s, I started an epistolary novel called *The Plant*,' he explained. 'I published limited editions of the first three short volumes, giving them out to friends and relatives (folks who are usually, but not always, the same) as funky Christmas cards. I gave *The Plant* up not because I thought it was bad, but because other projects intervened.

'I was intrigued by the success of 'Riding the Bullet' (stunned would probably be a more accurate word), and since then have been anxious to try something similar.'

However, commentators on both sides of the Atlantic were quick to accuse King of attempting, single-handedly, to overturn the entire publishing industry. It was a charge which the author vehemently denied: 'I suspect that the growth of the Internet has been something of a boom when it comes to reading,' King told *Time* magazine. 'People with more Beanie Babies than books on their shelves spend more time reading than they used to as they surf from site to site. But it's not a book, damnit, that perfect object that speaks without speaking, needs no batteries and never crashes unless you throw it in the corner. So, yes, there'll be books. Speaking personally, you can have my gun, but you'll take my book when you pry my cold, dead fingers off the binding.'

There were more than 152,000 downloads of the first 5,000-word instalment of *The Plant* during the first week, with over 76% paying the fee under an honour system. 'We've proved that the guy who shops for entertainment on the Net can be as honest as the one in a retail bricks-and-mortar store,' said King. 'These numbers aren't equal to 'Riding the Bullet' — at least not yet — but our publicity campaign was almost non-existent. News travels fast on the web, however; it's the 21st century version of the jungle telegraph, and the number of downloads seems to be staying hot.'

However, after King increased the price to $2 and the number of downloads dropped below 46%, the author announced in

November 2000 that *The Plant* was 'Going back into hibernation' after Chapter 6 and continuation of the story would be postponed indefinitely. He also said that he needed to write more novels and the break would allow foreign translations of the story to catch up with the US version. In early 2001, the author announced that the story had netted more than $463,000 after expenses.

Around the same time, it was reported that King and his wife Tabitha were suing his insurance company over medical bills and lost income from the van accident of two years earlier. The couple alleged that The Commercial Union York Insurance Co improperly paid them after the incident, and that they should have received the full amount of the $10 million policy.

Throughout most of the previous decade, horror had been heading into a terminal slump, and it had almost become a pejorative term amongst publishers and booksellers. Yet King received an estimated $48 million advance for the American and British rights to two new novels, *Dreamcatcher* and *From a Buick Eight*, plus a new collection. As one of the authors who was responsible for creating the horror boom of the 1970s and '80s, how does he view the current state of the horror market and what does he think is the secret of his continuing success?

'Well, I don't think that, comparatively, I am the success I was ten years ago. I don't think that the books are as easy to sell as they were. Horror is something that appeals to young people. I've said this before. Because young people feel healthy, they view it the way they view amusement park rides: it's a thrill, it's a kick, it's a gas, but you don't really think it's going to happen to you.

'But now my generation is reaching an age where we don't really need the hidden cancer metaphors of a movie like *Alien*. When we have friends who are coming down with the disease or we are worried about the disease ourselves. A lot of the fears, a lot of the terrors and a lot of interest that drive a movie like *Scream* or *Scream 2* or *I Know What You Did Last Summer* is closer to the sensibility of such juvenile novels as the *Goosebumps* books, the R.L. Stine phenomena. In fact, I think that, in America, the *Scream* movies are driven by people who cut their teeth on R.L. Stine rather than Stephen King and are now old enough to get into 'R' rated films.

'I'm very grateful that I continue to sell. But I do think that the bottom line is that if people are getting a story that they really like and that they will get involved in — if it's going to do for them what the novel is supposed to do, which is to entertain and take you away — then they will continue to come back. Because the genre isn't as important, I don't think, as the feeling that they are getting a story. The horror thing has always been secondary to me. I never did consider myself a horror writer, but you can call me whatever you want.

'I write what comes to me to write. In the time it took *Carrie* to be published I wrote two mainstream novels, which I put away because I wasn't sure how they'd be taken. You know, one of the things that's going to happen is someday I'm going to wake up and just don't want to write about horror any more, or more trips of fantasy, or anything else. Then probably I'll write *The Man in the Grey Flannel Suit* and I'll go down the tubes and nobody will ever hear of me again!' †

I would like to thank the following for all their help and support in producing this book: Kim Newman, Mandy Slater, David J. Schow, Randy and Sara Broecker, Jo Fletcher, Bernie Wrightson, Seamus Ryan, Dennis Etchison, Harlan Ellison, Alan Jones, Jay Holben, Douglas E. Winter, Frank Darabont, Les and Val Edwards, Nicolas Barbano, Peter Atkins, Ashley Laurence, Peter Straub, Michael Marshall Smith, Barry Forshaw, Lucy Ramsey, F. Paul Wilson, Doug Bradley, Caroline Grimshaw, Neil Gaiman, Henry Selick, Gillian Christie, Lucy Dixon (Hodder & Stoughton), Martin Eden, Theatre Museum (London), Marsha DeFilippo (Assistant to Stephen King), Marci Bing (Theatre Three Productions Inc), Russell Leven (Nobles Gate Film & Television Production), Simon Gosden, Helen McAleer, Lisa Morton and, of course, Mick Garris, who could not have been nicer or more helpful to work with, even though he was shooting the NBC-TV mini-series *Steve Martini's The Judge* in Toronto at the time.

Very special thanks to Simon Bacal, Frank Barron, David Bassom, Michael Beeler, Pat Cadigan, Mike Childs, Michel Ciment, Tony Crawley, Thomas Crow, Mark Dawidziak, Phil Edwards, David Everitt, Mick Farren, Arnie Fenner, Anthony C. Ferrante, Jo Fletcher, Nigel Floyd, Todd French, Charlie Frick, Paul R. Gagne, Ray Garraty, John Gilbert, William Goldman, Wilson Goodson, Edward Gross, Ben Herndon, Tim Hewitt, Patrick Hobby, David Hochman, Janet Huck, David Hughes, Allan Hunter, Alan Jones, Bill Kelley, Marty Ketchum, Bruce Kirkland, Jack Kroll, David Kuehls, Rodney A. Labbe, Charles Leayman, Steve LeCroix, Randy Lofficier, Tim Lucas, J.B. Macabre, Linda Marotta, Bob Martin, Joseph B. Mauceri, Alan McKenzie, Edward Murphy, Kim Newman, Steve Newton, Gregory Nicoll, Thomas Nilsson, Eric Norden, Philip Nutman, Randy Palmer, Abe Peck, Peter S. Perakos, Adam Pirani, Craig Reid, Patricia Ross, Michael Rowe, Mark Salisbury, Dan Scapperotti, Marc Shapiro, W.C. Stroby, Steve Swires, Frederick C. Szebin, Paul Taylor, Bill Warren, Harry Wasserman, David Wild, Gary L. Wood, and everyone else from whose work quotes are used throughout the text. Finally, my sincere appreciation to Stephen King for the interviews over the years, and without whom...

As always, my gratitude and respect goes out to my 'constant editors' at Titan Books — David 'Baz' Barraclough, Jo Boylett, Adam Newell and Katy Wild — for putting up with me on this project for almost a year. ✝

Left: Stephen King is transformed by an alien fungus in 'The Lonesome Death of Jordy Verrill' episode of Creepshow.

SOURCES

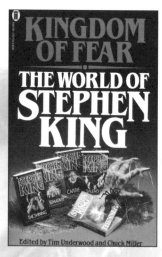

The following primary sources were consulted in the compilation of this book:

Bare Bones: Conversations on Terror With Stephen King (Warner Books, 1989) edited by Tim Underwood and Chuck Miller

Best New Horror Volumes 1-5 (Robinson Publishing/Carroll & Graf, 1990-94) edited by Stephen Jones and Ramsey Campbell

Best New Horror Volumes 6-12 (Robinson Publishing/Carroll & Graf, 1995-2001) edited by Stephen Jones

The BFI Companion to Horror (Cassell/British Film Institute, 1996) edited by Kim Newman

The Big Picture: Who Killed Hollywood? and Other Essays (Applause Books, 2000) by William Goldman

The Boxtree Encyclopedia of TV Detectives (Boxtree, 1992) by Geoff Tibballs

Cinefantastique

Creative Screenwriting

Creature Features: The Science Fiction, Fantasy, and Horror Movie Guide, Updated Edition (Berkley Boulevard, 2000) by John Stanley

Danse Macabre (Macdonald, 1981) by Stephen King

The Dark Side

Empire

Encyclopedia of TV Science Fiction (TV Times/Boxtree, 2000) by Roger Fulton

Entertainment Weekly

Entertainment Weekly Online (http://www.ew.com)

The Essential Monster Movie Guide (Titan Books, 1999) by Stephen Jones

Evening Standard

Fangoria

Fear

Fear Itself: The Horror Fiction of Stephen King (Pan Books, 1990) edited by Tim Underwood and Chuck Miller

Feast of Fear: Conversations with Stephen King (Underwood-Miller, 1989) edited by Tim Underwood and Chuck Miller

Film Review

Films and Filming

The Films of Stephen King (Brown Books, 1993) by Ann Lloyd

Halliwell's Filmgoer's Companion (HarperCollins) edite by John Walker

Kingdom of Fear: The World of Stephen King (New English Library, 1987) edited by Tim Underwood and Chuck Miller

Knave

Kubrick (William Collins Sons & Co, 1983) by Michel Ciment

Leonard Maltin's Movie and Video Guide (Signet/Penguin) edited by Leonard Maltin

Locus

A Life in the Cinema (Gauntlet Publications, 2000) by Mick Garris

Monthly Film Bulletin

National Enquirer

Newsweek

The New York Times

On Writing: A Memoir of the Craft (Hodder & Stoughton, 2000) by Stephen King

Playbill: The National Theatre Magazine

Playboy

Premiere

Psychotronic

The Psychotronic Video Guide (St Martin's Griffin, 1996) by Michael J. Weldon

Radio Times

Reign of Fear: Fiction and Film of Stephen King (Underwood-Miller, 1988) edited by Don Herron

The Shawshank Redemption: The Shooting Script (Newmarket Press, 1995) by Frank Darabont

Shivers

Shock Xpress

Sight and Sound

Slippage: Previously Uncollected, Precariously Poised Stories (Houghton Mifflin Company/Mariner Books, 1997) by Harlan Ellison

Starburst

Starmont Reader's Guide 16: Stephen King (Starmont House, 1982) by Douglas E. Winter

Stephen King Goes to Hollywood (New American Library, 1987) by Jeff Conner

stephenkingnews.com

The Stephen King Story (Little, Brown and Company, 1993) by George Beahm

Stephen King: The Art of Darkness (New American Library, 1984) by Douglas E. Winter

Terror on Tape: A Complete Guide to Over 2,000 Horror Movies on Video (Billboard Books, 1994) by James O'Neill

Triad Style

TV Guide

utopianweb.com

VideoHound's Golden Movie Retriever (Visible Ink Press)

Which Lie Did I Tell? More Adventures in the Screen Trade (Pantheon Books, 2000) by William Goldman

World of Fandom.

Title page illustration by Bernie Wrightson; p4 photograph by Seamus A. Ryan; p5 (top) Spelling Films, Inc; p5 (bottom) Paradise Films; p6 Columbia Pictures Industries, Inc; p7 photograph by Mark Holzberg; p8 (top) Greengrass Productions; p8 (bottom) Lakeside Productions, Inc; p9 (top) Greengrass Productions; p9 (bottom) Lakeside Productions, Inc; pp10-14 United Artists Corporation, except p14 (bottom) New English Library; pp15-23 Warner Bros Inc, except p18 (bottom) New English Library; p22 (bottom) New English Library; pp24-25 Laurel Show, Inc; p26 (top left) Laurel Show, Inc; p26 (top right) illustration by Tom Savini; p26 (bottom) New American Library; pp27-28 Sunn Classic Pictures, Inc; pp29-31 Dino De Laurentiis Corporation; pp32-33 Columbia Pictures Industries, Inc; pp34-36 New World Pictures; pp37-39 Universal City Studios, Inc, except p38 (top left) The Viking Press; pp40-41 Famous Films Productions NV; pp42-43 Famous Films BV, except p43 (bottom) illustration by Bernie Wrightson; pp44-46 Dino De Laurentiis Productions Inc; pp47-49 Columbia Pictures Industries, Inc; pp50-51 New World Pictures; p52 Granat Entertainment; pp53-54 Taft Entertainment Pictures, except p54 (bottom) New English Library; pp55-56 Warner Bros Inc; pp57-59 Paramount Pictures Corporation, except p59 (bottom) Doubleday & Company Inc; pp60-61 Laurel Darkside Movie, Inc; pp62-63 Graveyard, Inc; pp64-65 Lorimar Television, except p65 (bottom) New English Library; pp66-68 Castle Rock Entertainment, except p67 (bottom) Penguin Books USA Inc/Signet; pp69-70 Paradise Films; pp71-72 Laurel-King Inc; pp73-75 Allied Vision Ltd, except p75 (bottom) Pan Books Ltd; pp76-77 Columbia Pictures Industries, Inc; pp78-79 Paramount Pictures Corporation; pp80-81 Fifth Avenue Entertainment; pp82-83 Orion Pictures Corporation, except p83 (bottom) Hodder and Stoughton; pp84-85 Konigsberg-Sanitsky Productions, except p85 (bottom) Hodder and Stoughton; pp86-89 Greengrass Productions, except p87 (bottom) TV Guide Magazine Group, Inc, p89 (bottom) illustration by Bernie Wrightson; pp90-94 Castle Rock Entertainment (p93 storyboards by Peter von Sholly); p95 Investec Bank Ltd; pp96-97 Castle Rock Entertainment, except p97 (bottom right) Hodder and Stoughton; pp98-99 Park Avenue Productions; pp100-101 Laurel-King Inc, except p101 (bottom) New English Library; pp102-103 Allied Film Productions; pp104-105 Trimark Pictures; p106 Miramax Film Corp; pp107-108 Spelling Films, Inc, except p108 (bottom) New English Library; pp109-111 Lakeside Productions, Inc, except p111 (bottom) TV Guide Magazine Group, Inc/illustrations by Bernie Wrightson; pp112-113 Twentieth Century Fox Film Corporation (p113 [top] photograph by Larry Watson); pp114-115 New Amsterdam Entertainment Inc, except p115 (bottom) Transworld Publishers Ltd/Bantam Press; p116 Trucks Productions; p117 Miramax Film Corp; pp118-119 Phoenix Pictures; p120 Trimark Pictures; pp121-123 Greengrass Productions, Inc, except p122 (bottom) Pocket Books/Simon & Schuster Inc; p123 (bottom) TV Guide Magazine Group, Inc; pp124-125 United Artists Corporation; p126 Miramax Film Corp; pp127-129 CR Films, LLC, except p129 Penguin Books Ltd; p130 Castle Rock Entertainment; p131 Hyperion; pp132-133 Darkwoods; p134 (top) Granite Entertainment Group; p134 (bottom) New English Library; p135 Adakin Productions; pp136 Hodder and Stoughton; p137 (top) Macdonald; p137 (bottom) Hodder and Stoughton; p138 (top) Hodder and Stoughton; p138 (right) Barnholtz Entertainment; p138 (bottom) Penguin Books Ltd/Viking Penguin Inc; p139 Penguin Books USA Inc/Signet; p140 (top) Investec Bank Ltd; p140 (bottom) Simon & Schuster Audio; p141 Famous Films Productions NV; p142 (top) New English Library; p142 (bottom) Hodder and Stoughton; p143 United Film Distribution Co; p144 Twentieth Century Fox Film Corporation; p145 Bella Productions; p146 G. W. Putnam's Sons/Putnam Publishing Group Inc; p147 Sean S. Cunningham/New World Pictures; p148 (top) Superstar Productions; p148 (bottom) Erotic Entertainment; p149 Lakeside Productions, Inc; p150 Laurel-TV; p151 (top) Laurel-TV; p151 (right) W. Paul Ganley; p152 Laurel-TV; p153 (top) DD Distribution; p153 (bottom) Mercury Press, Inc; p154 Twentieth Century Fox Film Corporation; p155 Whitecap Productions, Inc; p156 Carnival Theatre; p157 Theatre Three Productions Inc; p158 BBC Worldwide Ltd; p153 BBC Spoken Word; p159 (left) United Artists Corporation; p159 (top) Orion Pictures; p159 (bottom) Trimark Pictures; p160 (top) Paramount Pictures Corporation; p160 (bottom) Lakeside Productions, Inc; p161 (top) Dino De Laurentiis Corporation; p161 (right) CR Films, LLC; p161 (bottom) Paramount Pictures Corporation; p162 (top) New World Pictures; p162 (left) Paramount Pictures Corporation; p162 (right) Greengrass Productions; p163 (top) Greengrass Productions; p163 (bottom) Castle Rock Entertainment; p164 (top) Laurel Darkside Movie, Inc; p164 (left) Laurel-King Inc; p164 (bottom) Warner Bros Inc; p165 Greengrass Productions; p166 Twentieth Century Fox Film Corporation; p167 Laurel Show, Inc; p168 (top) Famous Films Productions NV; p168 (bottom) Dawn Associates/United Film Distributors Co; p169 (top left) Castle Rock Entertainment; p169 (top right) Laurel-King Inc; p169 (bottom) Laurel Show, Inc; p170 (top) Warner Bros Inc; p170 (bottom) Greengrass Productions; p171 (top) Famous Films Productions NV; p171 (right) Castle Rock Entertainment; p172 (top) New American Library, Inc/Signet; p172 (middle) Éditions J'ai Lu; p172 (bottom) New English Library; p173 (bottom row) New English Library; p173 (right top) Macdonald; p173 (right middle) Penguin Books USA Inc/Signet; p173 (right bottom) Hodder and Stoughton; p174 Greengrass Productions; p175 photograph by Seamus A. Ryan; pp176-177 photographs by Gamma, courtesy of Forbidden Planet; p178 Laurel Show, Inc; p179 Famous Films Productions NV; p180 (top) Paramount Pictures Corporation; p180 (bottom) Dino De Laurentiis Productions Inc; p181 (top) Lakeside Productions, Inc; p181 (bottom) Laurel-King Inc; pp182-183 Dino De Laurentiis Productions Inc; p184 Laurel Show, Inc; p185 Graveyard, Inc; p186 New World Pictures; p187 Laurel Show, Inc; p188 (top and bottom) New English Library; p188 (middle) Hodder and Stoughton; p189 New World Pictures; p190 (top) New World Pictures; p190 (middle) Taft Entertainment Pictures; p190 (bottom) Laurel Darkside Movie, Inc; p191 (top and bottom) Castle Rock Entertainment; p191 (middle) New Amsterdam Entertainment Inc; p192 photograph by Seamus A. Ryan.

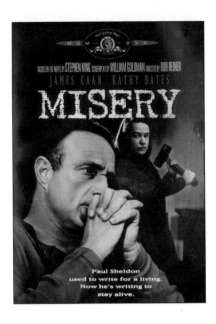

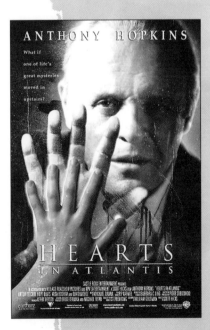

Above: *The two Steves of horror: Stephen Jones and Stephen King, London, 22 August 1998.*

STEPHEN JONES first met Stephen King at the Fourth World Fantasy Convention, being held just outside Fort Worth, Texas, in 1978. Over grits and coffee he had breakfast with the already best-selling author. They would meet up again at various conventions, until King stopped attending them in the early 1980s because of the huge crowds his presence attracted. Since then, Jones has worked as a genre movie publicist, as well as becoming one of Britain's most acclaimed anthologists of dark fantasy and horror. He has had more than sixty books published and is the winner of two World Fantasy Awards, three Horror Writers Association Bram Stoker Awards and two International Horror Guild Awards, as well as being a thirteen-time recipient of the British Fantasy Award and a Hugo Award nominee. He still lives in Wembley, England. Stephen King has become a multi-millionaire, selling more than 350 million copies of his books in more than thirty languages around the world, and is one of the biggest selling writers of all time. He still lives in Bangor, Maine. ✝